上海市人民政府发展研究中心系列报告 | 面向未来30年的上海发展战略研究

COLLABORATIVE GOVERNANCE & SHARED DEVELOPMENT

上海2050
协同治理与共享发展

联合国第三届世界城市日
全球城市论坛实录

The Record of Global Cities Forum
on the Third UN World Cities Day

周国平 主编　Chief Editor　Zhou Guoping

格致出版社　上海人民出版社

PREFACE I

序一

　　随着全球城市化进程的不断推进，人类在享受现代城市日益丰富文明成果的同时，也面临着诸如交通拥堵、环境污染等"城市病"。要应对这些挑战，仅靠一国之力难以为继，集聚多方智慧、汇聚各种力量，协同推进现代城市治理，方是治本之策。放眼全球，虽各国国情不同，发展道路和制度各异，但在城市治理领域却有诸多共性和规律，可相互借鉴、协同努力，共同构建人类命运共同体，共同推动全球城市分享发展机会、共享发展成果。

　　2016 年 10 月 30 日，以"协同治理，共享发展"为主题的 2016 全球城市论坛在上海交通大学举行。本次论坛作为 2016"世界城市日"系列主题活动之一，由上海市人民政府发展研究中心、上海市住房和城乡建设管理委员会、上海交通大学、联合国人居署和世界银行共同主办。时任上海市市长杨雄在开幕式上致辞并为上海交通大学中国城市治理研究院揭牌。来自世界各地的专家学者结合当今世界城市发展的趋势和实践，重点围绕城市政府治理创新、城市经济转型发展、城市交通治理创新、城市生态治理创新、城市文化保护与传承等方面，共商城市发展面临的问题和解决之策，为全球城市治理与发展提供新洞见。

　　为了永续本次论坛留下的真知灼见，再现论坛上专家学者的卓越风采，我们编写了这本《协同治理，共享发展——联合国第三届世界城市日全球城市论坛实录》，真实还原了论坛上专家学者演讲发言的精彩内容，是一座城市治理研究的"富矿"，对中国乃至世界的城市治理与发展均具有重要的指导意义。

　　本书在编写过程中，得到了 2016 全球城市论坛与会专家学者的大力支持，编委会成员也为之付出了辛勤的劳动，在此一并表示感谢。

上海市人大常委会副主任
上海交通大学党委书记

With the furthering of the global urbanization progress, human beings have been enjoying the increasingly civilized and prospered society in modern cities while still faced with challenges such as traffic congestion, environmental pollution and other 'urban diseases'. The above mentioned urban challenges cannot be solved by merely one country or one person's endeavor. Instead, promoting the modern urban governance through garnering wisdom and strengths from various sources is the true solution. Think globally, urban governance shares similarities and mutual rules among countries of varied conditions, development paths and systems. Therefore, by learning from each other and by working together, we become capable to build a human community of fate, to jointly promote global cities with shared opportunities, and to enjoy development outcomes.

On October 30th, 2016, the 2016 Global Cities Forum, entitled 'Collaborative Governance, Shared Development', was held at Shanghai Jiao Tong University. This forum was one of the themed activities of '2016 World Cities Day', co-sponsored by the Development Research Center of Shanghai Municipal People's Government, Shanghai Municipal Commission of Housing Urban-Rural Development and Management, Shanghai Jiao Tong University, United Nations Human Settlements Programme and the World Bank. Mr. Yang Xiong, who worked as Mayor of Shanghai, delivered the opening speech and inaugurated the China Institute of Urban Governance of Shanghai Jiao Tong University. Experts and scholars from around the world brought their latest research of the emerging trends and practices of urban development to the forum, discussing on solutions to urban problems, as well as providing new insights for global urban governance and development. Focuses were placed on the innovation of urban government, the upgrade of urban economic development, the smart management of urban transport, the improvement of urban ecological conditions, and the preservation of urban culture and heritage.

To extend the insights from this forum, and to reappear excellent presentations of experts and scholars on the forum, we have compiled this 'Collaborative Governance, Shared Development—The Record of Global Cities Forum on the Third UN World Cities Day'. This book truly represents the wonderful speeches by experts and scholars on the forum, and is indeed a 'rich mine' for urban governance researchers to dig. It contributes as guidance for urban governance and development in China and for the rest of the world.

This book received important supports from experts and scholars of 2016 Global Cities Forum. The editorial board members also made great efforts. I would like to extend my sincere thanks to them.

Jiang Sixian

Deputy Director of Standing Committee of the

Shanghai Municipal People's Congress,

Party Secretary of Shanghai Jiao Tong University

PREFACE II

序二

    随着城市化、信息化和全球化的快速推进，城市治理正在成为国家治理的重要内容和全球治理的重要实践。建立和完善城市治理体系，不断提高城市治理能力，是国家治理体系和治理能力现代化的基本条件，也是全球治理体系和治理能力现代化的核心议题。联合国《2030可持续发展议程》明确提出建设具有包容性、安全、有复原力和可持续的城市和人类住区。第三届联合国住房和城市可持续发展大会通过的《新城市议程》也提出将城市作为经济包容性和可持续增长、社会和文化发展以及环境保护的引擎，实现转型发展和可持续发展。在人类可持续发展的重大挑战面前，迫切需要全球城市联合行动起来，在全球治理与发展方面建立更为紧密的战略协作和伙伴关系。

    2016年10月30日，以"协同治理，共享发展"为主题的2016全球城市论坛在上海交通大学徐汇校区隆重举行。本届全球城市论坛是"世界城市日"的四大主题活动之一，是自2014年联合国首届"世界城市日"活动举办以来的第三届，由上海市人民政府发展研究中心、上海市住房和城乡建设管理委员会、上海交通大学、联合国人居署、世界银行共同主办，上海交通大学中国城市治理研究院、上海交通大学国际和公共事务学院、上海世界城市日事务协调中心联合承办。本届论坛举办期间，恰逢中国城市治理研究院成立，时任上海市市长杨雄亲临大会致辞，并与上海市人大常委会副主任、上海交通大学党委书记姜斯宪共同为中国城市治理研究院揭牌。上海市人民政府秘书长肖贵玉主持开幕式。本届论坛邀请了国务院发展研究中心、联合国人居署、世界银行、美国哈佛大学、英国剑桥大学、加拿大多伦多大学等国内外城市治理相关领域的著名专家学者，聚焦上海建设卓越的全球城市的愿景目标，围绕城市政府管理、经济转型升级、交通规划管理、生态环境保护以及文化传承保护等领域，全方位、多角度探讨城市治理和发展面临的重大问题，以及全球城市协同治理和共享发展的最新议题，对探讨中国及全球城市治理和共享发展的解决方案具有重要参考意义。

展现在读者面前的《上海2050：协同治理与共享发展——联合国第三届世界城市日全球城市论坛实录》，生动再现了论坛现场的交流盛况，翔实记录了与会嘉宾的真知灼见，详细总结了全球城市治理和发展的先进经验，尤其记载了中外嘉宾对上海目前的城市治理状况以及今后的规划与发展提出的非常有建设性的意见和建议。

建设卓越的全球城市，造就美好的城市生活，需要卓越的城市治理；而卓越的城市治理需要全社会的共同参与，是各利益相关方采取联合行动的制度集群、方法集成和过程集合。上海要建设成为一座卓越的全球城市，必须全面贯彻创新、协调、绿色、开放、共享的发展理念，不断汲取全球城市治理的成功经验，大力实施制度创新、模式创新、政策创新和方法创新。让我们共同期待上海在未来30年创建成为全球城市治理的典范城市，成为向世界展示中国城市治理体系和治理能力现代化的重要窗口。

是为序。

周国平

上海市人民政府发展研究中心副主任
2017 年 9 月

With the rapid development of urbanization, informatization and globalization, urban governance is becoming a significant part of national governance and an important platform for global governance. To establish and perfect the urban governance system and improve the level of urban governance is the foundation for national governance modernization. It is also the core issue for global governance system and modernization of governance capability. *The UN 2030 Agenda for Sustainable Development* clearly stipulates to "make cities and human settlements inclusive, safe, resilient and sustainable". New Urban Agenda adopted on the third

UN Conference on Housing and Urban Sustainable Development also requires city to serve as an engine of inclusive and sustainable economic growth, social and cultural development and environmental protection, so as to realize transitional and sustainable development. Faced with the great challenge of sustainable development, it is imperative that global cities make joint efforts to establish a closer strategic partnership of coordination and cooperation in the field of global governance and development to deal with future challenges.

Themed as "Collaborative Governance, Shared Development", 2016 Global Cities Forum was solemnly held in Shanghai Jiao Tong University on October 30th, 2016. As one of the four major theme activities of 2016 World Cities Day and the third Global Cities Forum since the first UN World Cities Day in 2014, the forum is hosted by the Development Research Center of Shanghai Municipal People's Government, Shanghai Municipal Commission of Housing, Urban-Rural Development and Management, Shanghai Jiao Tong University, United Nations Human Settlements Programme and World Bank, and organized by China Institute for Urban Governance, School of International and Public Affairs of Shanghai Jiao Tong University, Shanghai World Cities Day Coordination Center. Yang Xiong, who worked as Mayor of Shanghai, has addressed the opening ceremony of the Forum and inaugurated China Institute for Urban Governance with Jiang Sixian, Deputy Director of Standing Committee of Shanghai NPC and Party Secretary of Shanghai Jiao Tong University. Xiao Guiyu, Secretary General of Shanghai Municipal People's Government, presided over the opening ceremony. Top experts and honored guests from Development Research Center of the State Council, United Nations Human Settlements Programme, World Bank, Harvard University, University of Cambridge, University of Toronto and related fields at home and abroad, focusing on Shanghai's vision of building an excellent global city, shared their in-depth views over the issues of urban governance and development, from the perspectives of urban government management, economic transformation and upgrading, transportation planning and management, ecological and environmental protection, and cultural inheritance preservation etc.. In addition, a host of valuable ideas were discussed towards the latest issues about collaborative governance and shared development of global cities, which is of great importance for China as well as the world.

Shanghai 2050 Collaborative Governance and Shared Development—The Record of Global City Forum On the Third UN World Cities Day, which vividly presents and faithfully records the highlights and valuable ideas of this forum, provides abundant first-hand information for relevant researchers and it sums up the advanced experience of global city governance and development, especially those instructive thoughts and recommendations about the current governance of Shanghai and future planning from guests at home and abroad.

Outstanding global city and fabulous city life calls for excellent urban governance. Modern urban governance calls for the active participation and joint efforts of systematic, modal and process cluster. On the way to building an excellent global city, Shanghai must fully implement the vision of innovative, coordinated, green, open and shared development, draw successful experiences from global urban governance and carry out innovation in the aspects of institution, model, strategy and method. Shanghai is expected to become an exemplary city in global city governance in the next 30 years and be an important window to show the whole world modernization of Chinese city governance system and ability.

Above is the preface.

Zhou Guoping

Deputy Director General of the Development Research

Center of Shanghai Municipal People's Government

Sept., 2017

出席联合国第三届世界城市日全球城市论坛的中外嘉宾合影

The Group Photo of domestic and foreign guests attending 2016 Global Cities Forum on the Third UN World Cities Day

联合国第三届世界城市日全球城市论坛在上海交通大学隆重举行，本次论坛由上海市人民政府发展研究中心、上海市住房和城乡建设管理委员会、上海交通大学、联合国人居署、世界银行主办，上海交通大学中国城市治理研究院、国际和公共事务学院、上海世界城市日事务协调中心承办

2016 Global Cities Forum on the Third UN World Cities Day is solemnly held in Shanghai Jiao Tong University, which is hosted by the Development Research Center of Shanghai Municipal Government, Shanghai Municipal Commission of Housing, Urban-Rural Development and Management, Shanghai Jiao Tong University, United Nations Human Settlements Programme and World Bank, and organized by China Institute for Urban Governance, School of International and Public Affairs of Shanghai Jiao Tong University, and Shanghai World Cities Day Coordination Center

时任上海市市长杨雄与出席联合国第三届世界城市日全球城市论坛的外国嘉宾亲切交谈

Yang Xiong, who worked as mayor of Shanghai, is talking with the foreign guests attending 2016 Global Cities Forum on the Third UN World Cities Day

时任上海市市长杨雄和上海交通大学党委书记姜斯宪共同为上海交通大学中国城市治理研究院揭牌

Yang Xiong and Jiang Sixian, inaugurate the China Institute for Urban Governance of Shanghai Jiao Tong University

上海市人民政府秘书长肖贵玉主持 2016 全球城市论坛开幕式

Xiao Guiyu, Secretary General of Shanghai Municipal People's Government, hosts the Opening Ceremony of 2016 Global Cities Forum

上海市城乡建设和交通工作党委书记崔明华介绍《上海手册——21世纪城市可持续发展指南·2016》

Cui Minghua, Secretary of the Party Committee of Shanghai Urban-Rural Development and Transportation Working Committee of the CPC Shanghai Municipal Committee, introduces *Shanghai Manual—A Guide for Sustainable Urban Development in the 21st Century · 2016*

时任上海交通大学党委常委副书记郭新立主持闭幕式

Guo Xinli, who worked as Executive Deputy Secretary of the Party committee of Shanghai Jiao Tong University, hosts the Closing Ceremony of 2016 Global Cities Forum

参加《上海手册——21 世纪城市可持续发展指南·2016》赠书仪式的领导和青年学生代表合影

The Group Photo of Leaders and Youth Delegates at the presenting ceremony of Shanghai Manual–A Guide for Sustainable Urban Development in the 21st Century · 2016

与会嘉宾认真聆
听会议演讲

Participants
are listening to
the speeches
carefully

CONTENTS

目 录

OPENING ADDRESSES

KEYNOTE SPEECHES

PARALLEL FORUMS

Forum I Innovation of Urban Governance

Forum II Urban Economic Transformation and Development

Forum III   Innovations in Urban Transportation Governance and Management

Forum IV   Urban Eco-Governance & Innovation

OPENING ADDRESSES

开幕致辞

时任上海市市长杨雄在 2016 全球城市论坛开幕式上致辞

Yang Xiong，who worked as Mayor of Shanghai Municipal People's Government，addresses at the Opening Ceremony of 2016 Global Cities Forum

世界银行交通和通信技术全球发展实践局副局长任斌
在 2016 全球城市论坛开幕式上致辞

Binyam Reja, Deputy Director of Transport & ICT Global
Practice Bureau of World Bank, addresses at the Opening
Ceremony of 2016 Global Cities Forum

联合国人居署中国办公室主任张振山在 2016 全球城市论坛开幕式上致辞

Zhang Zhenshan，Representative of United Nations Human
Settlements Programme in China，addresses at the Opening
Ceremony of 2016 Global Cities Forum

上海市人大常委会副主任、上海交通大学党委书记姜斯宪
在 2016 全球城市论坛开幕式上致辞

Jiang Sixian，Deputy Director of Standing Committee of Shanghai
Municipal People's Congress and Secretary of the Party Committee
of Shanghai Jiao Tong University，addresses at the Opening
Ceremony of 2016 Global Cities Forum

致辞——

杨 雄
时任上海市市长

　　"世界城市日"是首个以城市为主题的国际日,是上海世博会的重要精神遗产。全球城市论坛是"世界城市日"的重要主题活动之一,是汇集全球智慧、探讨城市治理问题的开放平台。本次论坛以"协同治理,共享发展"为主题,聚焦城市经济转型发展、生态治理、文化保护与传承等方面,全方位、多角度探讨城市治理面临的重大问题,具有十分重要的现实意义。

　　当前,我们正在编制新一轮上海城市总体规划,描绘上海未来发展蓝图。我们提出,面向 2040 年上海城市发展的愿景是"卓越的全球城市",令人向往的"创新之城、人文之城、生态之城"。我们将把握新一轮科技革命和产业变革迅猛发展的新机遇,大力实施创新驱动发展战略,加快建设国际经济、金融、贸易、航运中心,加快向具有全球影响力的科技创新中心迈进。我们将更加注重保护和传承物质文化遗产和非物质文化遗产,加强国际文化交流,在扩大开放中推进文化创新,努力建设国际文化大都市。我们将牢固树立"绿水青山就是金山银山"的理念,严格控制建设用地规模,加强水、大气等重点领域的环境治理,增加更多的绿色空间,努力建设生态宜居城市。

　　本次论坛为加强城市治理的交流合作提供了很好的平台。希望各位嘉宾围绕"协同治理,共享发展"这一主题,畅所欲言,贡献智慧。同时,希望大家对上海的城市发展,多提宝贵意见。

致辞二

任 斌
世界银行交通和通信技术全球发展实践局副局长

多年来，世界银行和中国一直在开展合作伙伴关系的建设，特别是和上海建立了很好的合作关系。上海是我们在中国的第一个基础设施开发项目所在城市，我们以此为开端开启了在中国的合作进程。我们不仅提供基础设施开发，而且还建立了以知识为基础的一些合作伙伴关系。上海市人民政府发展研究中心推进的关于面向未来30年的上海发展战略研究项目，我们也参与其中，并撰写了一些较高水平的研究报告。

目前，上海已经成为全球领先城市之一。在城市规划和经济发展领域，上海发挥了非常好的示范作用，能够成为中国很多城市乃至全球很多城市的一个样板。世界银行也非常关注上海的经济社会发展，期待上海进一步为中国的繁荣做出贡献。上海拥有非常好的基础设施，和全世界实现了良好的互联互通，这为上海成为世界领先城市奠定了非常好的基础。上海创造了非常有利的教育环境，营造了成人终身学习的氛围，在教育领域也获得了非常好的进展。此外，上海也具有非常好的环境，积极提供社会服务并帮助外来人员融入城市。当前，上海正进一步依托其强大的制造业基础和优势，发展更缜密的高端服务业，从而创造更高的附加价值。

展望未来，政府所扮演的角色将进一步优化。上海希望打造更有创新性的产业，这就要求对"人"做出进一步的投资，加快促进不同层次研究水平的提高，实现科学研究、企业孵化、产业发展的良性循环。上海的发展很快也很有前景，不仅建立了新型人才培养机制，而且在土地使用效率方面也有进一步提高。同时，上海具有非常便捷的交通网络，一些交通枢纽也在进一步完善，这将成为城市发展的重要驱动力，将为不断吸引外来人才集聚上海、推动经济进一步转型升级创造非常有利的条件。

尽管目前上海各项条件及趋势都很好，但我们还是希望上海通过本次全球城市论坛汲取更多的国际经验，从而为进一步推动上海快速、可持续发展提供助益。

世界银行能成为本次论坛的联合主办方之一，成为这个高端论坛的一部分，我们深感荣幸。我们今后不仅将继续推动与上海市政府发展研究中心及其他研究机构的合作，而且也非常期待能与中国城市治理研究院开展合作。

致辞三

张振山
联合国人居署中国办公室主任

  联合国人居署是本次论坛的主办合作者之一，我作为人居署的代表，应邀参加此次论坛倍感荣幸。在联合国人居署、中国政府和上海市的共同努力下，2013 年联合国大会通过决议，将每年 10 月 31 日设定为"世界城市日"，并将 2014 年 10 月 31 日定为首届"世界城市日"。目前，全球 50% 以上的人口已经居住在城市，这个日子也成为世界上过半数人口自己的节日。联合国人居署已将每年 10 月定性为"城市 10 月"，并在此期间开展一系列活动，已逐渐广为人知。

  近年来，城市化进程受到越来越多的关注。在过去一年多的时间里，国内外发生了一系列与城市相关的重大事件。中国时隔 37 年后召开了中央城市工作会议，专门下发了《中共中央国务院关于进一步加强城市规划建设管理工作的若干意见》。2015 年 9 月，联合国第 70 届大会通过了《2030 年可持续发展议程》，将 17 项可持续发展目标作为人类的共同愿景。2015 年底召开的巴黎气候变化大会上，相关国家签署了具有约束性的协议，确定了城市气候和减排的工作重点。

  最值得一提的是，20 年召开一次的第三届联合国住房和城市可持续发展大会刚刚（2016 年 10 月 20 日）在厄瓜多尔首都基多市结束，并通过了《新城市议程》。《新城市议程》涉及各个方面，特别强调了包容共享的发展理念，使每个城市居民都能享受到城市发展的成果。该议程为世界未来 20 年城市发展确立了框架，要求各个国家必须从立法的角度来制定城市发展政策，以此来发展经济、保护环境以及规划设计等，从而推动城市均衡、全面和可持续发展。

  今天，中国的城市化进程已从单纯的数量规模向质量效益转变，本次论坛不仅将进一步落实《新城市议程》的精神，而且将会在讨论分享各国城市治理发展的理念经验等方面起到积极的推动作用。

致辞四

姜斯宪

上海市人大常委会副主任、上海交通大学党委书记

2016 全球城市论坛，由刚刚成立不久的上海交通大学中国城市治理研究院负责承办。上海交通大学是我国历史最悠久的世界知名学府之一。建校 120 年来，为国家和社会培养了 30 余万优秀毕业生，包括一批杰出的治国英才、科学大师、商业巨子和文化精英。近年来，上海交通大学的整体实力快速上升，正朝着全面建成"综合性、研究型、国际化的世界一流大学"目标奋进。

上海交通大学得天独厚的发展优势之一，就是我们这所学校地处上海。作为中国改革开放排头兵和创新发展先行者，上海在国内外享有良好的声誉。目前，上海制定了到 2040 年建成"卓越的全球城市"的宏伟规划，而"全球城市"与"一流大学"的共生、互动，无疑让各方面充满期待。

放眼当今世界，全球的城市化进程使得更多的人获得了更美好的生活。但是，高密度的城市生活方式，也引发了不同程度的空间冲突、文化摩擦、交通拥堵、安全隐患、环境污染以及贫富分化等问题。可以说，"城市，让生活更美好"这一 2010 年中国上海世博会的主题，依然需要集聚人类的智慧和力量去求索奋斗、实践创新。

美好的城市生活，需要卓越的城市治理；而卓越的城市治理，特别是超大城市的治理，亟需跨学科、跨领域以及跨国界的各类专家深度协同参与。这实质上也是共同治理体系的重要支撑。

现代的城市治理，需要政府、社会、企业和民众等方方面面的广泛参与和协同努力。而高等院校在这一过程中所能够发挥的作用，也随着知识的爆炸显得格外突出。城市治理的实践，不仅为理论研究提供了丰富的素材，也对理论研究以及理论与实践的结合提出了更高的要求。

正是基于这样一种考虑，在杨雄市长以及上海市政府相关领导和部门的关心、支持之下，上海交通大学决定联合校内十余所学院上百位教授，组成以提供城市治理的思路、对策和解决方案，构建国际交流合作的高端平台以及培养城市治理的优秀人才为主要目的的中国城市治理研究院。这个研究院，也是上海交通大学与上海市人民政府发展研究中心共同建设的研究院。

我们衷心希望各位嘉宾关心、支持我们研究院的发展，把这个平台建设好、使用好。真诚期待通过大家的共同努力，能把城市治理的全球经验带给中国、带给上海，也把上海和中国的生动实践传递给世界其他国家。

Address I

Yang Xiong

The then Mayor of Shanghai

"World Cities Day", the first international day of its kind with city as its theme, is part of the spiritual legacy of EXPO 2010. As one of the key events of "World Cities Day", the Global Cities Forum is an open platform that attracts talents from all over the world to discuss issues on urban governance. Focusing on "Collaborative Governance, Shared Development", and adopting an all-round and multi-angle perspective, this forum intends to address important issues such as urban economic transformation and development, eco-governance, cultural inheritance and preservation , which is of great significance.

At present, we are drawing up Shanghai's new overall plan of the city, a blueprint for the city's development in the future. We envision Shanghai, in the year 2040, will become an excellent global city, an eco-friendly one of innovation and humanity which is attractive and appealing to all. Grasping the opportunity offered by the new round of science-technology revolution and industrial transformation, we will implement the strategy of innovation-motivated development, and speed up the transformation of Shanghai into a center of international economy, trade, finance and shipping, and most importantly, a center of science-technology innovation with tremendous international influence. We will do what lies in our power to protect and inherit tangible and intangible cultural heritages, enhance international communication, and push forward cultural creation in an effort to build an international cultural metropolis. By advocating the concept "Green mountains and clear waters are as precious as gold and silver mountains", we are going to strictly control the use of construction land and strengthen the environmental governance of the key areas (such as water and air). In addition, we will reserve more land for green vegetation and endeavor to construct an eco-friendly city characterized by fresh water, clean air and green environment.

This forum provides us with an excellent opportunity for exchange of ideas and for cooperation in the field of city governance. Hope all guests can voice freely your wisdom and insight revolving around the theme "collaborative governance, shared development". In the meantime, we sincerely hope that every one of us could share our opinions and suggestions concerning Shanghai's development.

Address II

Binyam Reja

Deputy Director of the Bureau of Transport，Information and Communications Technologies，Global Development Practice of the World Bank

The World Bank has been working closely with China for partnership in the past few years, especially the established sound partnership with Shanghai. As Shanghai is the city where our first infrastructure development project in China lies in, we initiated cooperation in China as a start. We've not only provided opportunities for infrastructure development, but also have established some knowledge-based partnerships. In addition, we are also involved in the research project for Shanghai's development strategy in the next 30 years initiated by the Development Research Center of Shanghai Municipal People's Government, and have presented some research reports of comparatively high quality.

As far as city planning and urban economy development are concerned, Shanghai has indeed taken the lead in the world, setting an excellent example for many Chinese cities and even those in other parts of the world. The World Bank has consistently been concerned with Shanghai's economic and social development, and expect Shanghai to make further contributions to China's prosperity. Shanghai's remarkable infrastructure and great connection with the whole world has laid a solid foundation for its status as one of the leading cities in the world. What's more, Shanghai is also blessed with its very favorable educational environment. Great strides have been made in the field of education, which is providing a good environment for life-long learning and adult education. In addition, great social environment enables Shanghai to provide active social services and help migrants to integrate with others and feel at home in the city. I am fully convinced that Shanghai will take advantage of its strength in manufacturing industry to develop sounder high-end service industries with greater additional value.

Looking forward, the role played by the government will be further optimized. In order to develop more innovative industries, Shanghai needs to invest more on human beings and enhance the research quality of different levels so as to form a virtuous cycle of scientific research, business incubation and industrial development. Shanghai is now developing very fast with great potential prospects. It has not only established new talents-cultivation mechanism, but also boasted further improvements in the efficiency of the use of land. Besides, Shanghai enjoys a very convenient transportation network. The perfection of some transportation junctions has become an important driving force of urban development and created a favorable condition for attracting outside talents to Shanghai as well as promoting further economic transformation.

Although the current conditions and development trends of Shanghai are satisfactory, we still cherish the hope that this forum will facilitate Shanghai to draw more international experiences, which will accordingly further contribute to Shanghai's quick and sustainable development.

It is a great honor for the World Bank to be one of the joint hosts of this high-end forum. Thank you for having us. We will not only continue to promote cooperation with The Development Research Center of Shanghai Municipal People's Government and other research institutions, but also look forward to the cooperation with China Institute for Urban Governance.

Address III

Zhang Zhenshan

Representative of United Nations Human Settlements Programme in China

The United Nations Human Settlements Programme is one of the hosts of this forum. I am greatly honored to be invited to this forum on its behalf. In 2013, the United Nations General Assembly adopted the resolution of setting Oct.31 as the World Cities Day, owing to the joint efforts of Shanghai, the Chinese government and the United Nations Human Settlements Programme. It designated Oct. 31, 2014 as the first "World Cities Day". At present, over 50% of the world's population are residing in urban areas, which helps to make the day a festival celebrated by over half of the world's people. Up to now, this has been the third anniversary. Since the 68th United Nations Convention, when October 31 of every year was designated as "World Cities Day", October has been called "City October" by the United Nations Human Settlements Programme, with a series of activities every year, making it more and more well-known.

The recent years have witnessed growing concern over urbanization. In the past year, great events have taken place related with cities both at home and abroad. In China, 37 years after it was first held, the central government convened a working conference on urban governance, and issued "Opinions on Urban Governance". In September 2015, the 70th convention of the United Nations passed the "Sustainable Development Agenda until 2030", listing 17 sustainable development objectives as the shared vision of human kind. And during the Paris Climate Change Conference convened at the end of 2015, a binding agreement was signed, with special emphasis on global climate and carbon emission reduction.

What is most note-worthy is that the Third United Nations Conference on housing and urban sustainable development which is held every 20 years, just ended in Quito, the capital of Ecuador, and passed "The New Cities Agendas". "The New Cities Agendas" is all-embracing, with special emphasis on the concept of "inclusiveness and sharing", which means that every city inhabitant, without exception, can enjoy the fruits of urban development. The agenda has established the framework of urban development in the future 20 years, requiring that every country make urban development policies from the perspective of legislation so that cities can expect to enjoy balanced, overall and sustainable development, with its economy developed, its environment protected and the planning properly designed.

Today, China's cities are undergoing a thorough transformation from quantitative urbanization to qualitative urbanization. This forum will not only implement the main spirits of "The New Cities Agendas", but also play an active role in promoting the excellent experiences and ideals summarized on the basis of the forum discussions.

Address IV

Jiang Sixian

Deputy Director of Standing Committee of Shanghai
Municipal People's Congress, Party Secretary of
Shanghai Jiao Tong University

The 2016 Global Cities Forum is hosted by the newly founded China Institute for Urban Governance affiliated to Shanghai Jiao Tong University, one of the most time-honored world famous universities in China, which in the past 120 years since its inception has cultivated over 300 000 outstanding graduates, including prominent government leaders, scientists, entrepreneurs and cultural elites. In recent years, the university, like a rising star, is making its way towards a "comprehensive, research-oriented and globalized" top-ranking university in the world.

One of the unique advantages of Shanghai Jiao Tong University is its location in Shanghai, the pioneering city in China's reform and opening up and creative development. As a city enjoying excellent prestige both at home and abroad, Shanghai has set out the plan to accomplish the great mission of becoming an excellent global city by 2040. There is no doubt that the co-existence and interaction of "global city" and "top university" is highly anticipated from all round.

Take a broad view of the world, and we will find that urbanization has helped more people enjoy a better life. However, the high density of urban lifestyle has also brought about problems such as space conflicts of different degrees, cultural friction, traffic jams, security risks, environmental pollution and polarization between the rich and the poor. So to speak, the dream of "better city, better life", the theme of EXPO 2010, still calls for the gathering of human's intelligence and strength to make efforts and implement innovation.

Better city life requires excellent urban governance. And the excellent urban governance, especially of a megacity, desiderates intensive and collaborative participation of various international experts endowed with cross-discipline, cross-field knowledge, which, as a matter of fact, underpins the system of co-governance.

Modern urban governance needs the active participation and joint efforts by the government, the society, the enterprises and the masses as a whole. In an era of knowledge explosion, the role played by institutions of higher education is becoming more and more prominent. The practice of urban governance not only provides rich materials for theoretical research, but also sets higher demands for the nourishment of theoretical study as well as the combination of theory and practice.

With this in mind, and under the endorsement of Mayor Yang Xiong and leaders of other relevant government sections, Shanghai Jiao Tong University determines to set up this China Institute for Urban Governance with joint efforts of nearly one hundred professors from over 10 colleges. The institute is aimed at offering ideas, strategies and solutions for urban governance, building a high-end platform for international communication and cooperation as well as cultivating talents in urban governance. It is also a research institute jointly built by Shanghai Jiao Tong University and The Development Research Center of Shanghai Municipal People's Government.

We sincerely hope that all distinguished guests present in today's forum can give us your support in making our institute a good platform that can be made full use of. We also hope that our joint efforts will bring to China, and to Shanghai in particular, the global experiences of urban governance, and at the same time, share with the rest of the world our lively practice of urban governance.

KEYNOTE SPEECHES

主旨演讲

中国科学院院士、时任上海交通大学校长张杰主持 2016 全球城市论坛主旨演讲

Zhang Jie，Academician of Chinese Academy of Sciences and then President of Shanghai Jiao Tong University，hosts the keynote speeches at 2016 Global Cities Forum

国务院发展研究中心副主任张军扩在 2016 全球城市论坛上作主旨演讲

Zhang Junkuo，Deputy Director-General of the Development
Research Center of the State Council，delivers a keynote speech
at 2016 Global Cities Forum

世界银行交通和通信技术全球发展实践局副局长任斌
在 2016 全球城市论坛上作主旨演讲

Binyam Reja，Deputy Director of
Transport & ICT Global Practice Bureau of World Bank，
makes keynote speech at 2016 Global Cities Forum

加拿大多伦多大学校长、中国城市治理研究院学术委员会主任梅瑞克·格特勒
在 2016 全球城市论坛上作主旨演讲

Meric Gertler，President of University of Toronto，and Director of
Academic Committee of the China Institute for Urban Governance of
Shanghai Jiao Tong University，delivers a keynote speech at 2016
Global Cities Forum

时任上海市人民政府发展研究中心主任、中国城市治理研究院第一副院长肖林
在 2016 全球城市论坛上作主旨演讲

Xiao Lin，then Director-General of the Development Research Center
of Shanghai Municipal People's Government，Chief Vice President
of the China Institute for Urban Governance of Shanghai Jiao Tong
University，delivers a keynote speech at 2016 Global Cities Forum

全球城市论坛主旨演讲嘉宾互动对话

The Dialogue of the Keynote Speakers at 2016 Global Cities Forum

上海建设卓越全球城市的战略思考与建议

张军扩

国务院发展研究中心副主任

1. 未来全球城市发展的两大趋势值得高度重视

人类文明发展的历史经验表明，交流与合作是推动人类不断进步的根本动力。城市作为人类生产、生活的主要聚集之所，对人们更好地分工合作、交流经验、分享知识、创造财富发挥着巨大作用。因此，有学者把城市称为人类最伟大的发明。从全球范围看，人类社会正处于城镇化发展的中期阶段，可以有把握地说，21 世纪人类社会仍将继续呈现出波澜壮阔的城市化图景。

第一，巨型城市或者超大城市的数量在不断增加。1950 年全球范围内人口超过 1 000 万的城市仅有纽约、东京，而目前人口逾 1 000 万的超大城市已经有 20 多个。根据联合国的预测，到 2020 年，人口超过千万的城市将达到 30 多个。

第二，新出现的巨型城市主要来自发展中国家，特别是新兴经济体。这些新的巨型都市不仅人口规模快速增长，城市功能也在不断完善，在全球城市体系中的地位和作用也在快速上升，比如中国的北京、上海、深圳，巴西圣保罗，印度孟买和新德里等城市。不同机构发布的全球城市榜单中，以上城市的排名都在不断攀升。

2. 发展中国家特大城市发展和治理同等重要

对发展中国家的特大城市发展而言，一方面，要通过规模效应、集聚效应，帮助越来越多的农村人口进入城市社会，参与分享现代化发展成果。另一方面，也不可避免会带来一系列城市治理问题，例如城市贫困、社会矛盾、环境污染、交通拥堵、文化冲突等等。这些城市治理问题，既包含发展阶段性因素，也包含时代性因素。比如，在生态环境治理方面，发展中国家城市发展面临的压力和可借鉴的技术手段，都与处在同样历史阶段的工业化国家城市有所不同。

未来一段时间，发展中国家的超大城市如何完善城市功能、优化城市治理、提升城市能级，实现更具效率、更富有包容性、更可持续的发展，这些都将是全球城市发展领域的重大课题，也是关系到广大发展中国家人民福祉的具有现实意义的政策课题。

对中国而言，特大城市发展和治理同样是非常重要、十分紧迫的课题。作为中国最重要的经济中心城市，上海无疑是观察、讨论特大城市发展和治理问题的最典型代表。

众所周知，自 1978 年以来，中国的改革开放取得了一系列举世瞩目的成就，而在城市层面，中国的发展成就也同样巨大。作为中国对外开放的窗口，上海经过 40 年的快速发展，从一个传统的工业城市发展成为一个现代开放的国际化大都市，在人民生活、社会文化、城市面貌等各方面都发生了翻天覆地的变化。上海作为国际经济中心、国际金融中心、国际航运中心、国际贸易中心，城市辐射能级和全球影响力也有巨大提升。按照目前的发展态势，特别是随着中国经济总量的继续增长，未来上海非常有希望进入全球城市体系的第一梯队，这就需要上海进一步提升城市能级和竞争力，并在全球分工体系中发挥更重要的组织协调和资源配置作用。

最新一轮《上海城市总体规划》提出，到 2040 年，上海要建成"卓越的全球城市"，以及"创新之城、人文之城、生态之城"的远景目标。要实现建设全球城市的战略目标，上海仍有不少发展短板需要拉长，更有许多挑战需要克服。所以，必须借鉴全球领先城市的发展经验，制定相应战略和应对政策。

3. 上海建设卓越的全球城市的五个方面建议

一是要推动产业结构和就业结构的进一步优化升级，努力向高端迈进。在全球化背景之下，一个国家的中心城市要代表国家参与全球城市竞争和全球治理，必须依托金融、商务、科技服务、信息等现代化产业，在全球经济分工体系中发挥组织协调和资源配置作用。战后，伦敦在制造业、港口运输等传统产业优势丧失的情况下，先后通过两次重大金融改革，建立了以金融、商业、房地产等为主导的现代服务业，重塑了伦敦作为全球金融中心的地位。进入 20 世纪 90 年代，伦敦充分发挥人才和金融优势，通过政府推动，实现了创意产业的大发展，使伦敦获得了"世界创意之都"的美誉。与伦敦等城市相比，上海在产业规模、经济结构和技术内涵方面，还有进一步提升的空间。未来上海要以提升全球资源配置能力和全球城市竞争力为导向，在优化结构的基础上，做大产业规模，疏解一般性制造业和服务业，大力发展高新技术制造业和高端生产性服务业，大力提升制造业的技术水平和质量档次。

二是要加快创新能力和创新体系的建设。随着人类社会迈入知识经济时代，创新能力正在逐步替代资本，成为全球城市发展的新动力。近年来，全球城市的发展越来越关注城市创新功能。纽约正在曼哈顿建设与加州硅谷相媲美的硅巷，吸引越来越多的高科技企业集聚。伦敦在建设东伦敦科技城，力争将伦敦打造成世界上最好的科技企业孵化基地。上海是中国创新资源最富集的城市，但是与建设"具有全球影响力的科技创新中心"这一目标相比，还存在着不少差距。比如高水准的科研机构、高新技术企业数量偏少，投向基础研究、应用研究的研发投入不够多，创新资源统筹和创新协同不足等等。未来上海要利用技术革新、技术革命新旧交替的机遇，实现对老牌全球城市的弯道超车，必须依靠创建良好的创新生态环境，统筹利用好自身的创新要素，构建合作创新网络，形成创新合力。

三是要着力构建绿色、宜居城市环境。注重可持续发展能力，探索资源瓶颈突破路径，实现从粗放发展模式向集约发展模式转变的绿色发展，已经成为全球城市新的文明标杆。纽约在面向 2050 年的发展规划中，将可持续发展列为四大核心目标之一，提出要将纽约发展成为世界上最大的可持续发展城市以及应对气候变化的全球领导者。伦敦未来发展规划也提出，要成为改善环境的世界领导者，要在应对气候变化、减少环境污染、发展低碳经济和高效利用资源等方面都处于领先地位。上海未来要建设绿色生态宜居城市，要以产业结构和能源结构的优化为基础，推动高质量的工业化和城镇化发展，打造更紧凑合理的城市空间格局。要增加城市绿地和开放空间，加快建立和完善生态修复、保护和治理的区域合作机制，推动长三角区域和长江经济带的协同治理。

四是要大力繁荣城市文化，提升城市文化魅力。文化发展是人类文明发展的重要内容。文化的交流融合，能够促进不同人群之间的认同、信任，是城市凝聚社会向心力的纽带。文化能够赋予城市品位和灵魂，是城市汇聚全球目光的名片。当前许多全球城市都将文化发展作为城市繁荣的基础，通过制定相关战略和政策引导，提升城市文化软实力。上海要建设全球城市，也必须把文化繁荣作为一项重大战略，加快城市文化基础设施和公共产品建设，加强对城市历史文化遗产的挖掘、保护，大力发展文化创意产业集群，积极推动文化国际传播和对外交流，打造具有中华文化特质的魅力城市。

五是要实现良性的城市治理，打造安全、稳定、和谐的城市社会。当前，不平等问题已经成为一个突出的全球性问题。不同群体的利益诉求出现巨大分化，导致公共政策制定和利益协调面临巨大挑战。近年来，纽约、伦敦、巴黎等城市，屡屡发生恐怖袭击安全事件，其深层次原因，都在于不同利益群体之间的矛盾没有被协调好。上海未来要借鉴这些方面的经验教训，积极探索城市治理制度创新、模式创新，努力保持就业稳定，进一步扩大和优化公共服务供给，加快城市法制体系建设，提升城市管理能力、管理水平，充分利用现代信息技术手段，增强城市管理的科学性、有效性和公众参与度。同时，加快构建城市精细化管理的社会协同基础，加快推进城市治理现代化。

城市是现代社会创造物质文明和精神文明的重要场所，是众多家庭栖息之所和精神家园，也是年轻人追逐梦想、成就人生的地方。建设充满活力、和谐安定、绿色宜居的现代城市，是世界各国人民的向往。要实现这样的目标，需要我们在发展理念、发展思路上不断创新，在制度和政策方面积极探索。更重要的是，要按照本届论坛"协同、共享"两大主题倡议的那样，彼此携手，以持之以恒的努力，一起推动全球城市的可持续发展。

新型城镇化背景下中国基础设施融资的改革与创新

任 斌

世界银行交通和通信技术全球发展实践局副局长

本次大会的主题是"协同治理，共享发展"。对此，我们确实可以找到很多城市治理和城市发展方面的最佳城市案例。但是，人们往往忽略了实现这些目标所需要获得的融资支持。在美国，一些经济学家经常会对规划师和工程师泼冷水，因为从经济学而言，要实现好的想法必须确保财务的可行性。

今天我演讲的主题是如何给中国的新型组织融资，包括如何应用到像上海这样的大都市和都市集群。

1. 中国财政收支框架与基础设施建设的资金来源及影响

首先，有必要了解一下有关中国财政的基本框架。中国政府的财政收支安排是依据 1994 年颁布的《预算法》及其修正案。与此同时，中央政府也在推行一系列改革，旨在增加中央政府的财政收入，而将支出责任留给地方政府。地方政府大约有 40% 的区域税收需要上缴给中央政府，结果就使得地方政府的财政收入和支出责任出现了不平衡。1994 年《预算法》明确规定，地方政府及其所属部门不得以任何方式举借债务。在这样的财政框架下，地方政府还需要发展经济和加强基础设施投资，那么地方政府应如何去做呢？像上海这样的巨型城市如何在缺少资金的情况下建设这样有吸引力的基础设施呢？

据我们观察，一些地方政府有非常好的创新来创造额外营收。我们可以通过分析中国城市基础设施投资的来源来了解这些项目是如何融资的。绝大多数基础设施投资来源于预算外资金。通常来说，这些预算外资金来源于不同的事业费收入，如水费等。土地出让金是比较大的一块，是地方

图1
1978—2008 年中国
地方政府财政收入支
出百分比

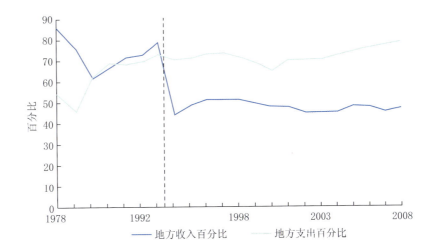

政府通过土地竞拍而获得的资金收入。这是中国地方政府的一种收入资金流。相对应地，我们来看看别的国家是如何运作的，美国的地方政府占据资本支出主要部分，但是，联邦政府也参与资本性的支出，甚至包括运营和维护（图2）。这方面和中国不一样。

美国联邦、州、当地政府在交通和水利基础设施方面的支出结构，投资分类 2014

图2
美国联邦政府和地方
政府基础设施建设和
维护的支出比例
资料来源：国会预
算办公室以行政管
理、预算局和美国
人口普查局为基础
得出的数据。

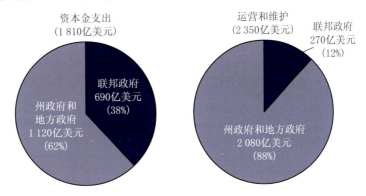

接下来，我们看传统融资模式有什么影响。

首先是地方政府大量的债务累积。2008 年全球金融危机之后，中国很多地方政府不得不通过借款来维系经济发展。从基础设施资金来源的角度去分析可以看到，一些商业银行发放了大量贷款。从 2008 年开始，中国地方政府积累了大量的债务，这给地方政府财税结构的可持续性带来了非常大的影响。

其次，就是传统融资模式对城市"摊大饼"的影响。很多地方政府依靠土地作为融资基础，甚至作为政府财政收入的主要来源。大多数地方政府会对未出让的土地进行竞拍，通过土地转让获得费用和收入，以此给城市提供供水等服务。但是，从城市可持续发展和管理的角度来说，这样的城市扩张其实未必完全是好事。

2. 中国新型城镇化的投资需求及地方政府融资模式创新

根据模型测算，在以后的数年里，中国新型城镇化的支出大概占到GDP的6%—7%。地方政府将在城市基础设施方面进行持续融资。一系列改革将会接踵而至，包括政府管理、城市公共服务、基础设施和社会保障领域等。从2015年开始，中央政府对1994年《预算法》进行了一些修正。总体来说，这次修订是对地方政府债务管理和交易采取更加宽容的态度。允许地方政府通过地方发债形式去募集资金，允许地方政府与地方融资平台或城投公司合作，从而切断预算外资金来源。通过PPP模式来设立一个资金流，或通过收入资金流授信去银行借款，推动基础设施投资。这和之前的借贷模式完全不一样，原来地方政府完全是通过银行拿贷款。现在，地方政府通过PPP融资是基于现金流和财政收入的情况，能借多少钱是和财务状况挂钩的。在过去30年里，中国的PPP模式尽管遭受了一些波折，但人们对于道路和供水的基础设施项目融资确实有一些创新，其中也不乏一些国际化企业参与到这一进程中来。

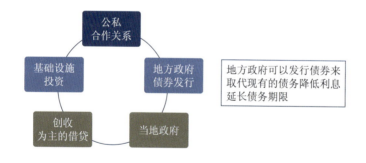

图3
新型政府财政改革和基础设施建设融资创新

1997年亚洲金融危机之后，PPP模式曾一度销声匿迹，但之后逐渐恢复了元气。2008年金融危机爆发，中央政府出台了一系列刺激经济的政策，使得PPP没有以前那么有活力。地方政府似乎更容易获得资金，可以通过本地的银行获得相当多的信贷来支持基础设施的发展。此时，它们有"一揽子"的计划，不想折腾PPP了，因为PPP有一定的难度和挑战性。但是，现在又重新推动PPP模式，它涵盖了范围更广的概念框架，不仅仅局限于基础设施融资的单一目标，而是一项重要的政策转变。2013年，中共十八届三中全会所通过的全面深化改革决定提出，要让市场在资源配置中扮演决定性作用并更好地发挥政府作用，推动基础设施开发模式和运营维护的改革。习近平总书记提出要进一步提高经济效率，大力推进供给侧结构性改革。作为地方政府，一方面要考虑如何打造这些基础设施，另一方面必须考虑如何运营和维护这些设施。像上海市政府这样的地方政府非常成功地开发了基础设施项目，但其他一些地方政府还不是很清楚，特别是能力比较弱的政府，不知如何高效地建设和维护城市基础设施。我们观察到很多地方政府比较擅长搞建设，但事后的运营和维护确实需要一些民营企业参与来提高效率。PPP 模式就是引入私营部门参与基础设施运营和维护的最佳选择。

图 4
中国城市化建设的支出结构

此外，地方政府还可以通过推进 PPP 模式来降低债务水平。从吸引私营领域投资者来看，这些部门希望通过用户的使用收入或地方政府转让的本地资源作为回报。很多地方政府之前总是希望通过私营部门直接获得资金，而不是展开相关领域的合作。

图 5
中国基础设施建设的
PPP 融资状况

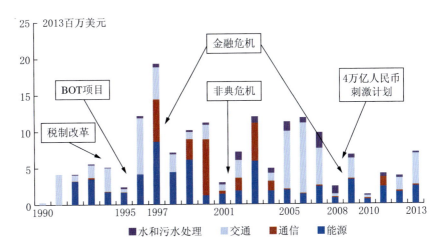

下面通过分享一些数据来看中国 PPP 项目的情况。当然你可以看到现在它真的有点过热了。从官方的统计数据来看，中国有很多 PPP 项目，大概已经有上万个，投资规模达到 3 万亿元人民币。这些数据并不让人觉得吃惊，因为涉及大多数城市的各个领域，包括交通、水供应、城市环境修复等等。当然还有一些其他领域的投资，比如养老、健康、教育等。因此，很多地方政府正把发展 PPP 项目作为融资的一种方式。通过竞标拍卖形式所达成的 PPP 交易占到项目总数的 10%。在大多数情况下，这些 PPP 项目都是通过市场机制实施的，在越来越多领域也变得更为普遍。

下面来分享一些中国的 PPP 项目案例。比如安庆城市道路建设的 PPP 项目，我们也称之为"可用性支付方式"，即通过项目可行性分析，地方政府鼓励民营资本共同参与公路建设和项目融资，也可以称其为"政府支付的 PPP 项目"或"用户支付的 PPP 项目"。再一个例子是北京市政工程有限公司与当地政府合作建设的项目，通过可用性支付方式帮助地方政府平摊其项目支出。尽管地方政府需要给私营企业支付一定费用，但引入私营企业能够有效地分散地方政府的财政责任。这种 PPP 模式不仅成本效益较高，而且能带来经济收益。理论上来讲，政府应负担道路建设的责任，但政府缺乏充裕的资金，也不能通过收税的方式来实现。因此，我们需要明确，尽管由私营企业承担可能会费用较高，但是通过私营部门的参与可以取得更大的效益。作为改革的一部分，地方政府可以通过 PPP 项目，使原本发放成本昂贵的地方政府债券转化为额外补贴。

另外一个例子是世界银行在乌鲁木齐的项目，其融资是通过世界银行、中国国家开发银行和地方政府的资源共同合作。相较之前的项目，国家开发银行在结构操作上有所不同。根据《预算法》规定，城市可以作为融资平台进行借贷。项目收入就可以用来偿还国家开发银行的贷款。具体流程如下：地方政府有自己的税收并可以向世界银行贷款；与此同时，公交运营公司不仅能通过提供服务获利，而且地方政府在项目开始前，就会给予公交公司一定补贴。只要地方政府保证其预算的公开透明，公交公司还可以去国家开发银行借额外的贷款。这种模式在全球许多城市已较为普遍，但在中国却很少见。其原因是，过去银行仅允许通过资产来贷款，而非项目本身。这种项目融资却能通过特定的方式来偿还贷款。新《预算法》对于其借贷方式和偿还贷款的收益都有明确规定。然而，我们的方法却是全新的概念。在这样的概念框架中，项目的潜在收益、贷款目标和资金分配之间是紧密相关的。地方政府必须在项目启动前给予补贴并与公交公司达成协议。根据我们的财务分析，在快速公交系统（BRT）工程实施之后，地方政府对公交公司的补贴将会持续增长，比没有实施该项目的补贴变化更加平稳。

3. 中国建立城市群区域融资体系的若干建议

再回到城市群这个问题，我们所说的城市群是指包括珠江三角洲、京津冀地区（北京—天津—河北）等类似地区。如何在这些大型城市群区域进行融资，中国目前还没有形成系统性的融资体系。由于缺乏中央政府的财政转移，我们所面临的挑战是如何更好融资建设区域交通网络，使其所获得的效益大于由各个城市单独提供。相比北京或天津单独的项目，从北京到天津的交通运输项目将会有更大的效益，所获得的资金也是针对京津冀区域层面的特定项目。

一是要有一个区域层面的规划。在美国，都市区规划机构（MPO）的主要职责就是改善区域层面的交通体系。因此，不同的城市或国家可以汇集到同一个规划组织，从而形成整体的交通规划并由美国联邦政府资助。20 世纪 70 年代，都市区规划机构在美国各个区域都建立了分支机构。它们的职责就是帮助城市建立交通规划。由于联邦政府有一笔补贴，各城市在制定规划时也必须符合所处区域的总体规划。联邦政府的资金来源于包括高速公路在内的一系列渠道。地方政府的主要职责在于提供与联邦政府相一致的资金。相较于美国，中国的财政体制更为分散，这是由于中国各级政府间存在太多规定。而对于美国的地方政府而言，它们的资金来源与政府绩效直接挂钩，因为美国州政府的收入主要来源于税收。但在中国，像税收和财产转让等传统融资所得收入已无法支持城市建设所需费用。

二是要建立城市群区域融资计划。从城市群融资框架来看，中国传统的融资来源，即通过地方政府的土地租赁和小型税费所得，已不能满足城市群项目的资金需求。因此，我们不得不借助区域有关部门的力量来融资，比如说通过征收区域交通建设税。在中国，我们很少看到中央政府财政转移的实例，短期内也很难得到改变。我建议中国采取自上而下的方式进行城市群项目的融资，建立像美国 MPO 这样的机构，通过形成合作建设计划使多方获益。

三是要保障民营经济的合法权益。从推进 PPP 项目来看，中国中央政府已提供了良好的政策环境和机制。但各地政府在对这些政策进行解读时，有些已符合标准，而有些却相差较远。因此，中国的 PPP 项目确实需要一个长期筹备的过程，而不能像有些地方政府那样冒进，因为私营企业比较倾向于参与小型资本、密度较低的项目。因此，监管的信心不足会直接导致地方政府对 PPP 项目的开展缺乏热情。PPP 项目的进展至少需要 15 年以上的时间，但各地市长的任期通常是五年，私营企业不免会担心政策的一致性是否会受到官员变动的影响。如果产生争议或分歧，由于没有区域保护机制或第三方仲裁机制，中国私营企业的利益将无法得到保障。

四是保证 PPP 项目资金来源结构的平衡。在过去 20 年中，国有企业在中国基础设施建设中占据主导地位。我们也看到国有企业的参与使得 PPP 项目中权力比重失衡。相较私企而言，国有企业资本充裕因而更易获得贷款。现今中国的国有企业代表了政策许可下 PPP 在中国运行的主要方式，比如，上海的国有企业通过 PPP 项目，可以参与湖南供水项目的竞争，但它们不能在上海操作。这是一种不同模式的 PPP 项目。此外，一些跨国企业也对中国 PPP 项目表现出了浓厚的兴趣，但它们和国内私营企业一样，对监管信心、与国企之间的竞争等问题抱有疑虑。但我认为，中国将逐步启动基础设施建设领域的快速发展，我们也期待中国在该领域的融资体系不断健全。

全球"尖顶"城市区域成功的五大要素

梅瑞克·格特勒

多伦多大学校长

毫无疑问，上海是全球最有活力的城市之一。今天，我想跟大家分享，像上海这样成功城市的背后需要具备哪些要素。我相信，对于这个问题会有很多不同的答案。托马斯·弗里德曼在他几年前的畅销书《世界是平的》里提出了"世界是平的"这样一个概念后认为，随着互联网的普及和国际合作的深化，国际边界和地理学意义上的边界越来越被弱化。我的同事，同样来自多伦多大学的理查德教授认为，全球的经济其实不是平的，而是有不同的"尖顶"。他描述了一些新兴的区域，指出这些城市区域在经济发展方面发挥的重要性依然在增长。越来越多的决策者、学者开始认识到城市区域可以为当地以及国家繁荣做出重要贡献，它们是创造力和革新力的源泉，也是促进当地经济复苏和增长的驱动力。在这一点上，上海可能比世界上其他任何城市都更为典型。上海多次成功实现了自我再造，并对中国转型做出了巨大贡献。其他很多成功的城市区域也有着相似的经历，包括伦敦、旧金山、柏林、多伦多等。这些成功的城市区域都是创新和企业家的热土、新想法和机遇的摇篮，它们的成功不是偶然的。我今天演讲的目的之一，就是剖析一下这些"尖顶"城市成功背后的共性因素，并做一些展望，探讨如何进一步运用好这些要素。

1. 这些地方可以吸引并留住一大批顶尖人才

在这些城市，人们很容易就能聚在一起分享知识。世界各地的人们可能会用不同的方法、从不同的视角做相同或相似的事情，一些文献将这一特性称为集聚效应。在人才济济的城市区域，大量资源也汇聚起来，从而推动了实业发展和新产品的开发，包括我们最宝贵的资源——人力资本和一系列专门服务。另外，城市还可以促进创新，因为城市为技术供需双方提供了展开创造性对话所需的环境，而创新就是在双方之间这种紧密、持续的互动中出现的。

这里我向大家介绍一名城市社会学家珍妮·雅各布。她起初住在纽约，后来搬到了多伦多。作为一位著名的城市学者，她指出城市为那些相同、相关或不相关行业内的企业提供了知识循环系统。这些城市区域有能力通过加速知识溢出和本土化学习，为创新提供肥沃的土壤。与此同时，信息技术也使得远距离的即时信息共享变得易如反掌。

如何培养、吸引并保留高素质人才应该是公共政策的优先任务之一，也是促进城市区域创新能力的当务之急。城市转型是许多因素共同作用下的产物，地理和物质资本固然重要，但人力资源，有创造力、有革新力、受过良好教育的人，才是根本。纽约前市长迈克尔·布隆伯格曾说，他坚信人才对资本的吸引，其效果和连贯性远远高于资本对人才的吸引。人力资本是生产力的主要要素，塑造了不同行业的企业竞争力。更重要的是，由于人才越来越紧俏，如果城市有志于增强经济活力，那么就要提高培养大量人才的能力，或者从国内外其他地方吸引人才，一定要能把人才留住。

每一年我们多伦多大学可以为社会培养 1.6 万名毕业生。像多伦多大学和上海交大这样的高校非常擅长培养人才，这也是它们对本地区域成功所做出的最重要贡献之一。通过国内以及全球的招生和师资力量的募集，它们在吸引人才方面也发挥了重要作用。多伦多大学超过 25% 的生源、一半的师资来自加拿大以外的国家和地区，因此我们是给加拿大带来大量人才的中坚力量。

2. 与外部世界有很好的互联互通性

成功的城市区域是互联互通的人才高度集聚地，同时还是通向全球网络的网关和门户，其中包括知识生成网络、商业网络和政治文化网络。当我们面临不同的挑战时，可以利用这些网络资源展开交流，通过智慧的碰撞，推出一些有创造力的产品、服务和想法。

主要城市区域在全球知识网络互通方面所发挥着重要作用。这样的互联互通性就好比我们地球的动脉和血管，在领军性的城市和区域之间进行理念和机遇的运输，不断促进各地创新能力和革新能力的发展。

对塑造成功城市区域力量的观察，可以提出一些想法和建议，帮助我们建设成功的城市区域和创新型城市集群。除了今天讨论的案例之外，还有大量类似的例子，可供我们学习和汲取经验。

3. 与研究型大学形成了共生关系

城市可以促进世界级研究型大学的发展，同时研究型大学也会促进世界级城市的发展。这种共生关系为双方带来了繁荣，实现了双赢。与之相似，全球的互联互通则与这种本地的共生关系相辅相成。拥有先进教育和科研能力的机构是联系它们所在城市与国际网络的重要门户，而拥有这些机构的城市区域是全球知识网络中非常重要的节点，因为城市区域的成功和繁荣不仅取决于是否能获取、使用本地生成的知识，还取决于是否能够获取和使用来自全球各地领军创新研究中心的相关资源。知识、理念和创新通过全球的血管、动脉流动和输送，这为我们提供了巨大的机遇、创新和动力，以便我们更好地参与各个城市区域未来的发展。因此，像多伦多和上海这样的全球网络中心发挥着越来越重要的作用，成为世界领先的经济中心。

图1展示了国际合作的领军城市，这是通过统计该城市发表的1名以上跨国作者联合署名的学术著作总量得到的。可以清楚地看出，这些城市都是世界最具有活力的经济中心。除此之外，风投和其他以移动互联网为基础的投资者也都在重点关注这些区域，因为这些地方拥有世界级的研究机构、人才和全球合作机会。

图1
2010—2015年总数排名前20位的城市地区的国际合著出版物

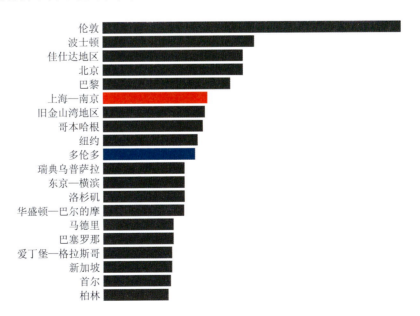

4. 注重非均衡投资和对创新的长期投入

在为城市制定经济发展战略时，我们必须认识到无论是在国家还是世界范围内，创新能力极强的经济活动并不是平均分布的，而是高度集聚在少数城市和区域中。因此，公共部门的投资也应该按照这种思路来分配，其目标应该是支持、帮助本地那些展现出独特能力和竞争力的企业、机构等，以及那些很难被替代或者模仿的核心资产。因此，很多国家和地方政府都将公共投资集中于那些脱颖而出的"尖顶"区域和机构，通过这种方式来扩大竞争优势。在世界范围内，我想大概中国将这一战略实践得最为成功。985 项目这一专项基金极大地提高了中国 39 所高校的国际竞争力，其中有 8 所学校在 2016 年泰晤士报世界大学排名中跻身前 100 名。

另外，创新不是一夜之间出现的，我们必须进行持续的、稳定的投资，我们需要耐心，同时还需要容忍犯错，需要冒一定的风险。在制定策略时我们必须认识到并权衡好独特的优势和竞争力，而这些优势和竞争力越来越倾向于集中在一小部分城市区域中。

就拿我最熟悉的城市和大学举例吧。你可能会惊讶，干细胞是 1961 年某个星期天的下午在多伦多大学发现的。但在这一伟大发现的半个世纪以后，直到最近，我们才在再生医疗方面有了重大突破，才把基于干细胞技术的新型治疗和医学介入方法应用于商业和临床。几十年间，我们始终都没有忽视再生医学的发展。在过去 25 年里，多伦多大学每年都会在干细胞和基因研究方面进行投资。图 2 中深蓝色部分表示研究经费，浅蓝色

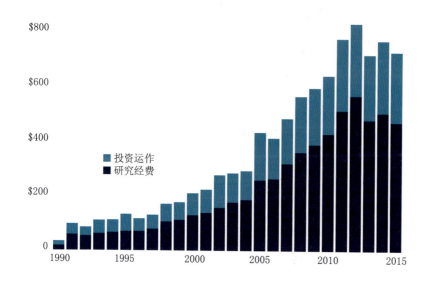

图 2
1990—2015 年多伦多大学可持续投资
（再生医学、遗传学）

部分包括工作人员的工资、福利、营运支出和资本投入，说明每一年在多伦多都有上百位研究者和上亿美元用于这项科研。这是一些里程碑式的事件，从历史角度来看，正是过去这些发现，使我们达到了现在的高度。这仅仅是一所大学里发生的一个故事，世界各地的领先科研集群都在发生着相似的故事。交通基础设施、文化资源、工业和智力的集聚等都遵循着同样一个规律，只有通过持续的、战略性的投资，才能建设出具有创新能力的成功城市区域。

5. 高度重视广义城市基础设施所发挥的价值

在探讨人才、高等教研机构以及连接它们和城市的纽带时，我们必须重视城市基础设施所发挥的价值。这里的基础设施是一个广义的概念。具有创新精神的劳动力大军精英成员，包括为城市创造着繁荣和机遇的人，以及大学的优秀师资和生源等等，这些人更倾向于选择在城市里生活，因为城市能够提供优秀的文化多元性和自然吸引力，包括活跃安全的社区、高质量的医院和学校，以及较强的包容力。所以整个区域交通运输系统的质量、文化艺术氛围和公共设施条件等，都是我们之前经常会忽视的支柱，它们支撑着经济的繁荣和创新的活力。

现在让我们看一下城市交通基础设施。考虑到多伦多是一个拥有600多万人口的城市区域而且人口还在快速增长，地铁发展成熟度显得远远不够。由于政府机构之间的角力和公共部门投资不足，多伦多平均通勤时间在北美是最长的。最近的研究表明，仅仅在多伦多这一个城市，这种低效率所带来的成本就高达每年110亿美元，甚至超出了城市每年的所有预算。

我听说上海也面临着交通运输的挑战。尽管如此，多伦多还是可以从上海的地铁系统学到很多东西。图3是上海的地铁交通图，由此看来上海和多伦多还是不太一样的，况且这还没有考虑上海的城际铁路，例如上海的金山铁路。另外，城市是否能提供高质量生活环境，一定程度上也决定了高等研究和教育机构能否吸引到人才。人才的流动性与日俱增，最抢手的人才往往可以任意选择自己想要居住的城市。这个时候城市的生活质量就显得非常关键，它决定了高等教育机构以及它们所在的城市能否获得长期的繁荣发展。

图 3
上海轨道交通网络示意图

    总体来说，上海和多伦多作为城市区域中的佼佼者，基本上融合了以上我所提到过的所有政策要素。通过持之以恒的、可持续的、战略性的投资，加快建设基础设施，吸引尖端人才，支持领军科研项目，促进不同领域和行业与全球领先地区进行沟通，相信这些城市区域一定会更加出彩。这正是全球领先的创新、创造城市区域的魅力之所在！希望我的讲演能让大家看到这些领先性的城市集群背后的成功要素，并使它们得到最大发挥，实现互惠共赢。

上海迈向卓越的全球城市

肖 林

时任上海市人民政府发展研究中心主任

中国城市治理研究院第一副院长

这次全球城市论坛的主题是"协同治理，共享发展"。这也是全球城市发展的重要特征之一。前不久，上海向社会公示的《上海城市总体规划（草案）（2016—2040）》提出了上海 2040 "卓越的全球城市"的愿景目标，从城市空间、区域格局、道路交通等方面对上海打造"卓越的全球城市"进行了科学规划。在 2040 上海城市总体规划编制的同时，按照上海市委市政府部署，上海市人民政府发展研究中心主持开展了"面向未来 30 年的上海"发展战略研究。2050 上海发展战略与 2040 上海城市总体规划的战略导向是一脉相承的，就是迈向卓越的全球城市。

1. 把握充满挑战和战略机遇的全球城市发展趋势

20 世纪 90 年代以来，伴随着科技创新，世界城市体系从垂直化的"等级秩序"进入扁平化的"网络时代"。处于核心地位的城市，从基于规模和首位度的"中心城市"进化为基于连通度和具有影响力的"全球城市"。未来 30 年，世界仍将处于深度大调整、大变化中，伴随科技革命和全球化的纵深发展，世界将进入以城市为中心的运行格局，全球城市将在自我重构中呈现新的特点和新的使命。

一是创新在城市功能中的地位更加突出。科技革命将深刻改变全球城市的运行脉络，全球生产网络向创新网络升级，创新在城市功能中的地位更加突出；全球城市从资本之都转向创新中心，知识经济跃升为全球的主导知识形态；人才成为全球城市的核心资源，能够为高技能劳动力提供高质量生活的城市将更具竞争优势；全球城市以更智慧的方式运行，城市在实体和虚拟空间中实现包容和可持续发展，成为全球城市提升治理能力的重要方向。

二是全球城市作为世界城市体系的核心节点功能更加突出。全球城市作为要素配置节点，体现更高的连接度的世界门户区域将更具竞争优势。作为产业技术策源地，全球城市定位从产业链转向价值链视角，成为高附加值环节的重要节点。作为经济活动中心，全球城市将吸引更多的非政府的新型治理主体加入，发挥国际合作交流的服务协调功能。作为全球治理的重要参与者，全球城市在高标准国际投资贸易规则的对接与制定过程中，承担着更多的协同治理和制度创新功能。

三是全球城市发展理念从注重硬实力转向以提高生活品质为核心，更加注重以人为本、包容和可持续发展。随着人类进入信息文明时代，如何更好服务人的全面发展，超越吸引资源与功能集聚，成为全球城市的发展方向。谋求生态文明进步是全球城市可持续发展的核心议题，提升居民的幸福感成为城市发展的重要目标。能否构建绿色低碳发展方式，能否构建公平正义价值理念、多元包容都市社会、文化融合与创新，都将成为全球城市发展和竞争力的关键。

四是作为人口、社会与文化多样化最为集中的地方，全球城市治理也将面临诸多挑战。全球城市老龄化问题更为突出，收入极化和社会分层更为显著，文化碰撞和利益博弈更为尖锐，容易引发中产阶层的不满与抗争。全球城市治理亟待在包容、有序、高效等多重政策目标和治理中构建新的平衡，公共政策面临深刻修正。

2. 上海发展战略导向和愿景目标是迈向卓越的全球城市

未来30年，全球发展大势和中国崛起前景为上海融入全球城市网络打开了更加广阔的空间，为上海形成具有全球影响力的城市功能提供更强大的动力。上海作为卓越的全球城市，将承担参与全球竞争合作和服务"一带一路"等国家战略的重大责任和使命。未来上海建设卓越的全球城市具有以下三重内涵。

一是具有全球竞争力和影响力的世界级综合性全球城市。在不同层面、不同维度上深度参与全球竞争，落实国家战略，引领区域发展。要强化全球都会地位，建设具有全球影响力的经济、金融、贸易、航运和文化中心，在要素定价、信息发布、规则制定等方面形成全球影响力；要强化亚太门户地位，建设并发展成为亚太航运中心和信息航运枢纽港，成为全球核心资源和战略要素在亚太地区集聚扩散的战略通道和关键节点；要强化国家战略先行者地位，成为中国对外开放战略的桥头堡和推动中国经济创新发展的先行者，代表国家参与全球创新与合作；要强化区域龙头地位，发挥长三角城市群首位城市的核心作用，带动长三角城市群发展成为世界最大的城市群。

二是全球城市网络体系中发挥枢纽功能的核心节点城市。在全球经济、文化、创新等领域承载全球性功能，具备全球领先的话语权。要发挥创新策源功能，推动全球重大科技创新取得突破，推进重大科学发展和创新技术的迅速商业化。要发挥投资管理功能，成为全球价值链、投资链、贸易链上的管理中心，对全球投资管理链上的高附加值环节、高端功能形成管控能力。要发挥资源配置功能，具有促进全球资源高效配置的开放性市场机制和功能平台，成为利用国际国内两种资源、两个市场的枢纽和跳板。要发挥人才集聚功能，成为具有影响力、吸引力和配置力的全球人才枢纽。要发挥文化交流功能，成为具有中国特色的世界文化大都会和世界文化交流中心。要发挥信息枢纽功能，成为全球信息网络中的信息流动性好、信息配置能力强、信息开放度高的战略枢纽。

三是彰显中国文化特质和引领现代文明的新型城市。对世界新兴城市发展具有积极示范影响和导向能力。科技创新的全球领先城市，在创新思想激发、基础科学研究、创新技术转化、产业应用开发等方面引领全球潮流。生产变革的全球引领城市，成为信息化时代生产组织模式和商业模式变革的引领城市，在资源节约、清洁能源等诸多方面建立全球领先的示范效应。智慧生活的全球示范城市，在带动智慧生活和智慧城市建设上走在全球前列，成为互联、智慧、智能的未来城市。文化融合的全球典范城市，凸显海派文化的学习力、继承力和融合力，成为大气谦和的文化吸纳之都、包容并蓄的文化聚集之都、深远睿智的文化创新之都和时尚繁荣的文化共享之都。

面向未来，上海将按照"创新、协调、绿色、开放、共享"的五大发展理念，塑造社会经济发展的动力，打造一座集中展示中国梦的全球城市，为所有人提供实现梦想的空间和全面发展的机会，提高全体市民的生活质量和健康水平，使生活在这座城市的人们拥有幸福美好的生活。

未来 30 年，在迈向卓越的全球城市的不懈追求和奋斗中，上海要努力建设成为一座创新活力之城。跻身全球重要创新城市行列，成为全球创新网络中的重要创新节点链接城市，成为创新氛围浓郁、创新资源密集、创新实力雄厚的创新枢纽城市，成为国际性重大科学发现、原创技术和高新产业的重要策源地，成为更具创新力和竞争力、能够应对各种挑战的活力城市。

上海要努力建设成为一座开放繁荣之城。集聚众多跨国公司总部等功能性机构，构筑高度发达、高度国际化、具有高度连通性的综合服务功能，在全球治理和国际事务协调中产生深远影响，成为功能更为多元、能够提供更多机会的繁荣城市。

上海要努力建设成为一座生态宜居之城。适宜于人们实现美好生活的聚居地，呈现清水环绕、绿意盎然、环境优美的城市风貌，为人们创造既舒适又便利、既生态又可持续、既安全又放心的居住空间环境以及自然生态环境，成为彰显世界标准、引领亚洲新生活的宜居城市。

上海要努力建设成为一座文化魅力之城。在海派文化基调上彰显中华文化的魅力，融合世界先进文化，成为多元文化思想的交流地，丰富文化产品的汇聚地，前沿文化创新的共享地，成为一座富有魅力、和谐多元的人文城市。

上海要努力建设成为一座包容共享之城。坚持以人为本，注重社会公平，将增强市民的幸福感和感受度作为城市发展的重要导向，为人们创造平等发展的环境、公平竞争的舞台，成为亲和包容、平等共享的包容城市。

上海要努力建设成为一座治理的典范之城。通过制度创新和模式创新实现社会善治良治，成为全球城市良好治理的典范，为我国其他城市和区域的发展治理提供示范，成为向世界展示中国国家治理体系和治理现代化的窗口。

3. 上海迈向卓越的全球城市需要转变发展方式和发展模式

上海城市经历了从计划推动模式到要素投入模式，再到效率驱动模式的转变，现已进入必须依靠创新转型发展的新阶段。未来30年，上海发展将面临人口规模、土地资源、生态环境和城市安全等多因素底线约束，也将面对因城市开放度提升、全球连通性增强、城市人口大规模流动等新情况所导致的外部性影响加大、多元文化冲突、城市非传统安全威胁增加等诸多挑战。上海要坚持创新发展理念，转变发展模式，走出一条中国特色、时代特征、上海特点的发展之路。

我们要走创新发展之路。坚持科技创新、人才驱动，提高劳动生产率。通过供给侧结构性改革提高要素供给质量，采取促进创新的战略和政策，实现更有活力、更高效率的经济增长。加快创新经济发展，推动新技术、新产业、新业态蓬勃发展，创造丰富优质的就业机会。

我们要走集约化发展之路。坚守底线约束，控制人口规模，优化人口结构，实现规划建设用地限制性增长，锚固城市生态基底，确保生态用地只增不减，确保城市生产安全和运行安全。推行集约紧凑、功能复合的空间利用模式，发展节能降耗的生产方式，倡导节约的生活方式，减轻城市过度的负载，为未来发展留足战略资源和战略空间。把环境魅力、绿色竞争力作为全球城市建设的重要方面，坚持自然资源和能源的永续利用，打造生态、可持续的城市和社区，营造绿色、安全、便捷的宜居环境。

我们要走韧性发展之路。针对人口变化、技术变革、重大事件、重大风险和灾害等不确定因素，构建富有弹性的城市系统和治理机制，实施战略空间留白，开展规划动态调控。强化对困难情境的预防、响应及恢复，建设品质可靠、恢复能力强的基础设施，打造海绵城市，果断处理气候变化和环境退化所带来的可能性威胁，关注和处理导致城市脆弱的核心问题，培育足够的城市储备能力。更加注重文化软实力，在尊重文化传统和保护文化多样性的基础上进行文化创新，增强城市人文竞争力，为城市发展提供持久动力。

互动对话

提问者：我有两个问题。第一个问题，请问格特勒教授，您在演讲中讲到了大学和城市可以彼此促进，我在想，大学能做什么工作，更好地参与到社区建设中，从而实现更美好的城市？这方面是否有些最佳实践？多伦多大学怎么更好地融入社区，促进城市更好地发展？第二个问题，请问肖林博士，是有关共享经济、城市交通的。最近上海摩拜单车很热门，我尝试了一下，从交大骑3公里到陕西南路。我根据百度导航走，在骑行过程中发现有些道路只是车行道，我不知道，就跟着导航，被交警拦下来，被教育了。现在摩拜单车在上海的年轻人中比较流行。之前我在伦敦生活过几年，在伦敦情况就不一样。上海市政府有没有考虑到摩拜单车跟车行道并行的这个问题？有没有可能在上海市中心设立更多的让自行车可以通行的道路？

梅瑞克·格特勒：在全球各地，大学领导也都意识到他们需要承担相关的责任，确保他们的机构是很好的城市建设者。首先，我们获得公共部门的支持，确实有义务回馈和反哺身边的社区、社会。另外，讲到利益相关者，大学领导如果让城市变得更美好，能做更多的贡献，让生活质量更好，最终也是帮助我们自己。因为这个城市的生活质量更高，整个环境更好，我们机构也能够吸引全国乃至全世界更高质量的师资和生源，并且能帮助我们留住这些人才。从这个角度来说，我认为有非常强的逻辑和理由符合你所提出的理念。

具体如何做？我们可以从以下几个方面着手开展。

我们鼓励老师和同学就城市问题寻找解决方案。我们有数百名老师对不同的城市和城市发展的维度感兴趣，例如物理的维度，社会公共卫生、环境和工程的维度，应对城市面临的问题。如何集聚这些专业的智力资源，更好地为城市服务？我在办公室设有一个新的职位，就是校长特别顾问，专门针对城市化问题的，是一站式的联系人。如果你是校外人士，可以找到他对接，你如果想找大学的专家，不知道怎么找，也可以找我办公室的校长城市问题顾问，他好比一个"媒人"，把大学和社区更好地构建和联系在一起。

除此之外，我们帮助老师、学生在社区找到一些合作伙伴，也是有一个合作机制。我们配对的相关中介机制，不仅非常有效，而且也很受欢迎。总体来说，我们的学生也非常希望能找到一些方案，解决现实世界中的一些问题。当然，我们学校也是社会的一部分，希望有更多学生能参与到社区项目。我们会助他们一臂之力，因为一旦他们参与，学生有很好的机会提高他们的经验和水平，最后对社区也是大有裨益的。

最后一点，我们现在更关注如何成为更开明的城市建设者。我们建设了很多楼，在多伦多大区有三个校园，正在施工的工程造价大概是 5 亿加元。通过我们学校的这些建筑项目，证明我们作为公立组织也是有能力为城市环境做贡献的。

肖林： 你的这个问题讲得很好，实际上这也是很多市民关注的问题。与其说这是一个交通问题，还不如说是一个发展理念的问题。2040 上海城市总体规划提出，要建设"卓越的全球城市"，"创新之城、人文之城、生态之城"。而"生态之城"的目标，体现在很多方面，包括交通和能源。在交通方面，除了规划发展公共交通之外，对自行车道和步行道也正在做更为详细的规划。比如黄浦江两岸，2017 年底全面打通 45 公里的滨江通道，里面就有自行车道、人行道和机动车道。这就是一个典范，除了现有的存量调整，也将重新做一些规划调整。

提问者： 上海希望成为一个全球的中心城市，她的区位很好，但上海的区位又受到周边的很多限制。我们发展全球城市，离不开跟周边地区的协调，就像任斌先生讲的城市群发展。我想问肖林博士，我们能不能建立一定的机制，使得整个地区能更好地协调发展。

肖林： 国家发改委发布的《长江三角洲城市群规划》对这个问题的定位、目标做了明确界定。2040 上海城市总体规划也已确定，要把上海建成"卓越的全球城市"与长三角城市群的联动发展结合在一起。所以，我们在进行机场、轨道交通等基础设施建设和布局中，都把整个长三角城市群作为世界第六大城市群整体来看待。上海跟周边三省已经有一些机制，比如说，每年我们有四个省市行政首长的交流机制，还有不同层面的一些例会制度。在长三角环境整治的一体化发展方面，中央也已经有明确要求。当然，现在我们还面临着一个客观的瓶颈，不同的行政区划如何跟城市群发展、都市圈发展的规律结合得更好？这也是一个课题。

提问者：我是同济大学的诸大建。请问任斌先生，刚才对PPP在中国的发展，您谈了很好的看法和评论。我的问题是，联合国和世界银行都把PPP与可持续发展联系起来，不是仅仅解决财政支付问题。您怎样看，为什么要跟可持续发展联系起来？对中国下一步您有什么好的建议？

任斌：为什么将可持续发展和PPP联系在一起？因为我们有不同形式的可持续性，包括财务、金融的可持续性。这方面，PPP会激发我们思考项目的创收、经济效益等等。做项目时，我们要考虑到财务的可持续性，从财政角度是可支付得起的、有经济效益的。

讲到环境的可持续性，确实值得我们思考。在这方面，PPP也能帮助我们推动环境的可持续性。总体来说，确实要构建一个关联。例如，过去中国地方政府发展的基础设施，总体超出了实际的能力需求，过多地设计和建造了道路、城市马路和其他设施。这个时候做PPP，地方政府也会反向思考。如果做这个项目，有哪些现金流？在设计的时候就倒逼你思考，地方政府不得不对未来的需求进行预测，从财政、融资等方面去考虑，如何把PPP架构优化，对环境容量优化，以便与可持续性有更好的关系。从这个思路而言，只有能够产生经济效益的资源才能得以使用。如果只需要四车道的高速公路，那么建八车道就没有必要了。不必要的资源投入，可能对环境是有影响的，这时就可以通过更好的对接避免资源浪费。因此，PPP对环境可持续性确实是有促进作用的。更好的财政管理、财务现金流能够使环境变得更好。

提问者：请问格特勒教授，我们大学生有些时候很难走出校园参与到城市或者是社区的活动之中。我的问题是，有没有什么政策或者课程，或者是特别的学分要求、项目安排等？多伦多大学可以鼓励更多的大学生走出校园，参与到社会活动中吗？

梅瑞克·格特勒：是的，我们确实有一些机会。我们的学生告诉我们，他们想有更多的机会参与到社会活动中。我们有一些提供实习机会的课程，在实习过程中，学生能与社区组织共同工作。另外，我们经常提供暑期实习的机会。我们大学和社区合作中心帮助学生找到实习机会，以便他们有机会接触社会。

我还要提两件事。在我们的员工中，有一些具有专业和行业经验。我们学生在第三、第四年的学习过程中，会有一整年时间在学校之外做专业实践，这给了他们更多的学习机会。然后他们回到学校，再花一年时间获得学位。还有一些项目，学生可以一个学期学习，一个学期工作，再回来继续学业。这些项目现在变得越来越普遍。

我们所面临的挑战就是学生告诉我们，他们还想要更多这样的机会。对我们来说，限制因素就是找到社区合作伙伴，不管是在私营部门，还是在政府事务领域，或者是非营利机构，帮助他们提升获利意识。这是一个双赢的局面，不仅有利于学生，也有利于他们。这是需要进一步教育和宣传的。现在我在国家层面也在进行一些工作，我们叫做商业高等教育圆桌会议，试图通过提升大家的认识来加强大学与社区合作伙伴之间的合作。

提问者：请问肖林博士，上海将如何看待在城市发展过程中政府与私人资本在提供公共服务上的关系？

肖林：这个问题提得很好。刚才任斌先生讲的 PPP 模式，实际上就是要大力推进政府投资与社会资本的融合，这也是推动基础设施建设的一个主要模式。我们长期的基础设施建设模式，是银行贷款、政府贷款、举债搞建设，现在债务也是到了要控制的时候。当然，公共产品、公共服务、基础设施下一步还是要大力发展，需要把政府的国有资本和民间资本、社会资本用好。国家发改委和财政部都有一个明确的关于推广 PPP 的标准范本，全国已经在大规模推行了。

任斌：我再说一下这个自行车项目。《中国日报》最近有篇文章，谈的是私营领域现在正带来一种自行车王国。我们知道，中国曾经是自行车王国，有很多人骑自行车，但在城镇化发展过程中，随着高速公路、道路工程的建设，自行车发展变慢了。通过分享经济，一种新的分享方式，中国好像要重新成为自行车王国。

梅瑞克·格特勒：从国际角度来讲，我们也看到了同样的现象，在伦敦、纽约、多伦多和其他大城市，我们看到骑自行车已经成为日益受人欢迎的一种出行方式。尤其被地方政府所鼓励，正在成为增加城市吸引度和宜居性的一种方式。因此，我们要面对的问题是如何提供更多的骑行空间和更安全的骑行环境。这样，政府出台改进宜居性的相关政策显得十分必要。

主持人：地方政府的举债现在备受国际社会关注，地方政府的债务现在似乎很大了。任斌博士以及刚才几个讲演者都提到了，社会资本是有兴趣进入这些领域的，这对我们地方政府的债务解决可能会提供不同的思路。

　　提问者： 刚才很多嘉宾在演讲过程中都提到了一个问题，就是连通性的问题。连通性问题，其实与集聚全球人才是息息相关的。当然，现在上海在全球化人才方面比例还相对较小，前面我看到数据是不到1%，但我想未来这个数据会有大幅度的提升。接下来可能有个问题，就是如何面对全球化人才的社会治理？我想听听格特勒教授的看法。因为加拿大也是一个全球化人才集聚的地方，接下来政府应该在哪些方面做一些服务全球化人才的措施？第三方包括NGO，未来在上海提供多元化服务方面，应该发挥怎样的作用？

　　梅瑞克·格特勒： 这个问题很好。可以从不同的范围来看这个问题。从整个国家和联邦层面来看，移民政策是非常重要的，这也说明加拿大为什么要实施开放的移民政策。这是一个积分制的移民体制和政策，我们吸引移民是基于他本身的资质和劳动技能，希望他能够成为我们有效的劳动力。这是加拿大通过实施移民计划，遴选高素质人才的非常有效的机制。

　　最近，我们正在国家层面讨论如何使移民政策更加灵活，更能满足尤其是知识密集型的行业和科学研究领域，乃至创新领域的人才需求。在竞争性的人才市场上，雇主往往要等候很长时间，才能等到一个他们需要的符合资质的工作人员，被允许进入加拿大境内工作。因此，在国家和联邦层面，很重要的一点就是要改进移民政策框架。在地方层面，回到刚才讨论的一个话题，就是如何建立一个满足新移民需求的宜居城市。

　　我们看多伦多利用多样化吸引人才的例子。现在我们大概有50%的居民都是加拿大境外出生的，这是一个令人吃惊的水平。这种多样化程度甚至高过了纽约和伦敦。更令人吃惊的是他们和谐共处，创造了一个和谐、稳定、宜居的城市环境。正如肖博士说到的，公共安全是社会安全的重要前提，是确保社区、邻里、学校安全的设施系统。同时，还要创造公平、公正、平等的教育环境。城市生活的这些方面会吸引人们到这个城市来居住和工作。还有就是高质量的交通系统，这是确保我们城市能吸引高水平人才的重要基础设施。

　　提问者： 放眼全球，从处于领先地位的城市可以发现，一个城市的软实力和生活质量是很重要的。可是在实际发展中却发现，有些城市房地产的开发项目实际上又破坏了上海的风景。比如外白渡桥附近，本来历史上有很多美丽的建筑，可是背后的高楼其实跟它很不和谐。

　　肖林： 上海在整个城市的开发建设过程中，对历史文化风貌和建筑保护的认识也在不断深化。现在上海市政府、上海规划部门，已经实施了最严格的历史风貌和历史文化建筑的保护。没有纳入国家保护建筑的，上海也在严格保护。在整个过程中，特别是上世纪90年代，在开发建设过程中，当时建筑、规划法规方面可能还不是很健全，在有的地方确实保护力度不够。但现在随着规划、历史风貌保护法律意识的加强，已经有非常严格的保护制度。甚至黄浦江畔的徐汇滨江，有些不是建筑，原来的起重吊车、轨道，都保留了。

上海在下一步的城市发展过程中，城市更新是主要的城市建设理念之一。城市更新就不是大规模搞土地开发、高强度建设，而是保护与开发相结合。这是最新的一个理念，也就是说紧凑型的、城市更新的理念将用于未来上海城市建设过程中。

Strategic Consideration and Suggestion on Building Shanghai into an Excellent Global City

Zhang Junkuo

Deputy Director General of Development Research Center of the State Council

1. The two trends in future global urban development should be highly valued

The history of human civilization development shows that communication and collaboration are the fundamental impetus of human progress. City, as the hub for people's production and living, plays a significant role in the division and cooperation of labor, the exchange of experiences, the sharing of knowledge, and the creation of wealth. Therefore, some academics refer to city as the greatest invention in human history. From the global perspective, the human society is still in the middle stage of the development of urbanization. Suffice it to say that the human society in the 21st century will continue to take on a spectacular look of urbanization.

Firstly, it is the continual increase of huge city or megacity. In 1950, only New York and Tokyo had a population exceeding 10 million, whereas now there are more than 20 megacities with a population of 10 million in the world. As is predicted by the United Nations, by the year of 2020, there will be more than 30 cities with a population of more than 10 million.

Secondly, newly-emerged megacities are mainly from developing countries, especially the emerging economies. These new megacities have witnessed not only rapid increase in population but also constant perfection of city function. In turn, their position and function in the global urban system is also rising dramatically, such as Beijing, Shanghai, and Shenzhen in China, Sao Paulo in Brazil, Mumbai, and New Deli in India, and their rankings are still climbing over the past years in the global city lists issued by different institutions.

2. It is of equal importance for urban development and governance of megacities in developing countries

As far as the development of megacities in developing countries, on one hand, through scale effects and centrifugal effects, it should help attract more and more population from the country into the city, to partake of the share of the fruition of modernity. On the other hand, it will inevitably bring about a series of problems concerning city governance, such as poverty in cities, social contradictions, environmental pollution, traffic congestion and cultural conflicts. These problems of city governance include both factors of the stages of development and of the time. For example, in the case of eco-environment management, the pressures confronted by developing countries in their city development and the technological measures they can draw on, are different from those of cities in industrialized countries at the same historical stage.

In the near future, it imminently becomes an important issue concerning how mega cities in developing countries perfect the city function, optimize urban governance, upgrade its capacity, maximize its productivity and efficiency, and come up with more sustainable methods of development. These will not only be the profound topics in the field of global urban development, but also realistic policy topics concerning the welfare of people in developing countries.

In the case of China, the development and governance of megacities is also a critical and imminent research topic. As the most important economic center of China, Shanghai is no doubt the most typical representative for discussions on megacities' development and governance. As is known to all, since 1978 when China embarked on opening up and reform, spectacular achievements have been made. In the city level, the achievements of Chinese cities are equally glamorous.

As a portal to China's opening up and reform, Shanghai, through 40 years of quick development, has made its transformation from a traditional industrial city to a modern international cosmopolitan. It has embraced tremendous changes in people's livelihood, social culture and urban landscape. The urban radiation level and global influence of Shanghai, in its capacity as a global economic center, financial center, shipping center and trade center, has been improved markedly. According to current development momentum, especially with the continuous growth of Chinese economic gross, Shanghai stands the chance of entering into the first echelon of the global city system in the near future. This requires Shanghai to further improve its urban function and competitiveness so that its resource can be better utilized and its ability in organization and coordination can be fully harnessed in the global process of division of labor.

In the newest Shanghai Overall City Plan, it is stated that, by the year of 2040, Shanghai will finalize the project of the construction of excellent global city, and the prospect of "a creative city, humane city, and eco-city". In order to achieve the strategic goal of building a global city, Shanghai still has a lot of chink to cover in its armor. Hence, we need to draw on the advanced experiences from other leading global cities and formulate corresponding strategies and policies.

3. Suggestions on building an excellent global city are given as follows from five aspects

Firstly, we need to promote the upgrade in structure of industry and employment, climbing higher to the value chain. Under the background of globalization, central cities of a country have to play a big role in the coordination and allocation of resources, based on its modernized industries ranging from finance, business, technology and information, in order to participate in global urban competition and governance. In the post-war period, faced with the loss of advantages in traditional industries like manufacturing industry and port transportation, London established its modern tertiary industry dominated by finance, business and real estate and reinforced the leading position of financial center of world economy through two rounds of financial reforms. In the 1990s, London brought out the potentials of talents and finance, and realized the development of its innovative industries with government encouragement, which won it the great fame of "the capital of innovation worldwide".

Compared with cities like London, Shanghai still has room for improvement in terms of industrial scale, economic structure and technical connotation. In the future, we should aim to improve our ability of global resource distribution and global urban competitiveness, enlarge the industry scale based on structural optimization, evacuate generalized manufacturing and service industries, promote the development of high-tech manufacturing and high-end service industry, and improve the technology level and quality of manufacturing industry.

Secondly, we need to accelerate the construction of innovation system and creative capability. In the era of knowledge-driven economy, innovation capacity is gradually replacing capital as a new driving force for global urban development. More and more attention has been paid to the innovative function of cities in recent years. New York is now constructing Silicon Alley in Manhattan compared to California's Silicon Valley, which has attracted more and more high-tech enterprises. London is building up its East London Tech City, aiming to develop it into the best science and technology business incubator in the world. Shanghai has the most wealth of innovative resources in China. However, there is a still long way to go before it can achieve the goal of "The Innovation Center for Science and Technology with global influence". For example, we are still in lack of high-level scientific research institutions and high-tech enterprises; the investment in fundamental research and application research is still far from enough; the allocation and coordination of innovative resources is not effective. In the future, Shanghai should make full use of the transition of technological innovation and reforms to outstrip other international cities, creating favorable innovative eco-systems and utilizing creative elements, so as to form innovative resultant for collaborative innovation networks.

Thirdly, it is necessary to build green and livable urban environment. It has become a new civilization mark for global cities to pay attention to the ability of sustainable development, explore the solution to bottleneck of resources and realize green development transforming from extensive development mode to intensive development mode. In New York's development plan for 2050, sustainable development is listed as one of the four core objectives, aiming to make New York the biggest sustainable development city in the world as well as the global leader of addressing climate change. As for London development plan, it mentions to take the lead in environmental improvement in the world, in the field of dealing with climate change and environmental pollution, developing low-carbon economy and high efficient utilization of resources.

In order to build green and livable city, Shanghai should promote high-quality industrialization and urbanization based on the optimization of the industrial and energy structure, so as to create more compact and reasonable urban spatial structure and add more urban green land and open space. At the same time, we need to accelerate the establishment of regional cooperation mechanism of ecological restoration, protection and governance, promoting the collaborative governance of Yangtze River Delta and the Yangtze River economic belt.

Fourthly, we must vigorously prosper the urban culture and boost its charm. Cultural development is an important part of human civilization. Cultural exchange can accelerate the recognition and trust between different groups of people, which is the bond of urban cohesion. Endowing the city with savor and soul, culture also serves as the visiting card to attract global attention. Nowadays, many global cities regard the cultural development as the basis for the urban prosperity and elevate the soft power of its urban culture through strategy making and policy leading.

For the purpose of building a global city, Shanghai also needs to treat cultural prosperity as an important strategy, accelerate the construction of cultural infrastructures and public goods, strengthen the excavation and preservation of urban historical and cultural heritages, develop the cultural innovative industrial clusters and actively promote the international cultural communication and exchanges, so as to make it into a charming city with Chinese characteristics.

Lastly, we have to realize the favorable urban governance, creating a safe, stable and harmonious urban society. Currently, inequality has become a prominent global issue. The huge polarization of different groups' interests has led to the great challenge to the formulation of public policy and interests coordination. Recently, terrorist attacks have frequently happened in cities like

New York, London and Paris. The underlying cause of these problems lies in the fact that the contradiction of different interest groups is not well coordinated.

In the future, Shanghai should learn from these lessons and experiences, actively exploring the system innovation and mode innovation of urban governance to maintain employment stability and further optimize the supply of the public service. Besides, it should accelerate the construction of urban legal system, improve its management ability and standard, make full use of modern means of information technology and strengthen the scientificity, efficiency and public participation of urban management. At the same time, the construction of social synergy of urban fine management should be accelerated in order to propel the modernization of urban governance. Cities are important places for creating material and spiritual civilization for modern society. It is also the spiritual and living home for many families as well as the place for young generations to pursue their dreams and achieve success. It is the yearn for people all over the world to build a vigorous, harmonious, stable, green and livable modern city. To make it happen, we need to innovate in the development concept and ideas and make active exploration in system and policy. More importantly, just as the theme of this forum—Collaborative Governance and Shared Development— goes, we should make joint and persistent efforts to promote the sustainable development of global city.

New Type of Urbanization in China: Recent Reforms and Innovation on Infrastructure Financing

Binyam Reja

Deputy Director，World Bank

Referring to the theme of the conference, "Collaborative Governance, Shared Development," we tend to think about best cities, urban governance and development. It is often left to us how we can finance these really great ideas that planners come up with. In the US, the economists usually pour cold water on planners and engineers, with the questions such as where to get the money or how to get financial support.

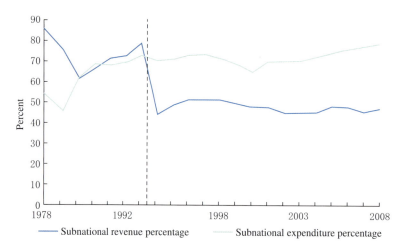

Fig.1 Revenue and expenditure of subnational governments in 1978—2008

My topic today is about how to finance the new organizations in China and how this issue is relevant to capital markets in mega regions or city clusters like Shanghai.

1. The financial support and impact of the infrastructure construction and financing framework of China

Firstly, I present you with some background information about the financing framework of China. The financing arrangement in China is governed by the Budget Law issued in 1994 and its subsequent amendments. At that time, the central government carried out major reforms that centralized most of the revenues to the central government but left the expenditure to the local governments, as a result of which an imbalance was created between local governments' revenues and their responsibility of spending. This means that 40% of the regional tax revenue should be handed back to the central government. At the same time, the Budget Law prevents the local government from borrowing money from their banks. As for the financing framework, local government is required or encouraged to develop economy and improve infrastructures. Therefore, the major question remains how they could do it. Megacities like Shanghai still have amazing infrastructures despite the lack of capital.

It turns out that local governments are ingenious to create additional revenue resources. This is different from other countries like US and India, which the central government has limit tax transferred. In the US, local governments do not send their revenues back to the central government, making huge difference from China.

The majority of funding source for infrastructures comes from the off-budget revenues, which refer to the fees levied on a variety of activities, such as water fees. Land-transferring fees, the option that the local governments choose to transfer the ownership of the land, is Chinese government's revenue stream. On the contrary, this represents how the other countries operate (Fig.2). The US federal government is responsible for the capital expenditure, because its operation and maintenance fee is very large.

Fig.2
Source of financing
in the US

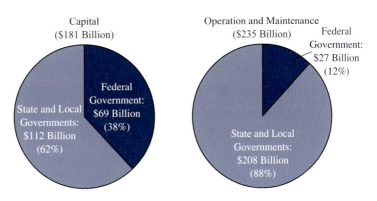

Source: Congressional Budget Office based on data from the office of Management and Budget and the Census Bureau.

So what is the impact of this traditional source of financing? Firstly, the local government has accumulated a huge amount of debt, because this revenue resource was sold by commercial banks. Since the financial crisis in 2008, the central government has announced a package of plans, which enabled local governments to borrow money for operation. The local government has racked up so many debts in five to six years, imposing a great impact on the stability of the regional tax structure.

The second impact of traditional financing is the urban sprawl. Many local governments relied on the financing of land and regarded it as a source of revenue. They first developed the peripheral areas, and then auctioned to raise the revenue so as to provide services for the cities. In terms of sustainability and city management, the expansion of city was not absolutely beneficial.

2. Financial needs of China's new urbanization and financing innovations of the local government

Hence, in the future, World Bank will make the investment projections based on the new urbanization. Basically, this new model of gentrification is supposed to take up 6% to 7% of GDP in the upcoming years, so the local government will continue to finance these infrastructures. Now appears a series of new reforms related to the government management, city public service, infrastructure, and social security. Since the beginning of 2015, the central government has been in the process of amending the Budget Law, to be more lenient with local governments and the debt transaction. It allowed the local governments to issue the bonds and then cancel the off-budget mode, so as to produce the local financing platform or achieve the investment cooperation of urban development. The new thing in the budget flow was the encouragement of PPP (Public-Private Partnership) and financing based on the revenue flows. It was the first time to be permitted to establish a private-public company that had its own cash flows, which enabled all parts to engage in infrastructure development. This was different from the previous mode of borrowing. In the past, the local governments borrowed the money by using the financing platforms, whereas now they provide a guarantee based on the cash flows and revenue, which can ensure financial stability. This reform has created the responsibility in terms of the incomes and revenue generated for specific projects. In general, PPP has experienced a series of ups and downs in China over the last 30 years. The programs of highways or water supply participated by some international companies have made some innovative progress.

Fig.3
New municipal finance reforms and infrastructure financing innovations

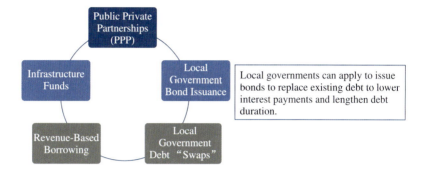

Shortly after the crisis in 1997, the PPP mode disappeared, and afterwards it was resilient. But the impact of PPP was different in 2008 because a package of stimulating programs discouraged PPP during the financial crisis. The local government seemed to borrow the money more easily through local banks to support the infrastructures. It was at this junction that they decided to abandon this difficult and challenging PPP. Comparatively, it was easier for local governments to borrow the money through regional banks.

Fig.4
Cost of urbanization as a share of GDP

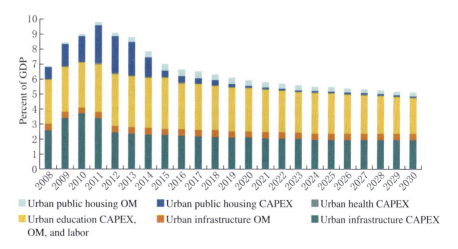

However, PPP has a new course now because it contains a wider conceptual frame which is not restricted to infrastructures as the single target to finance.

Primarily, it is an important policy shift from the government perspective. The government has been advocating the important impact of market since 2013, which was in line with what President Xi has endorsed, at the Third Plenary Session of the 18th Central Committee, that the market should propel newer forms of activities and reforms. Then the efficiency was also required to be improved, named as the supply-side structural reform that the Chinese government promoted. The local governments like Shanghai have been very successful in developing the infrastructures, but others were not very versed in performing an equally efficient job. Therefore, the local governments should get a better sense in how to both build infrastructures and maintain themselves.

In my opinion, many regional governments are better at construction than the maintenance, which needs the participation of private sector to improve the efficiency. PPP is the best choice as it can bring in the ability of the private sectors to operate. Besides, the local governments can also push PPP to help to reduce the local government's debts. In terms of attracting the investment from the private sectors, these sectors will be rewarded by the investments through users' fees or the resources that local governments would pay back to them. But some governments have mistaken private sectors for focusing on money rather than relevant cooperation.

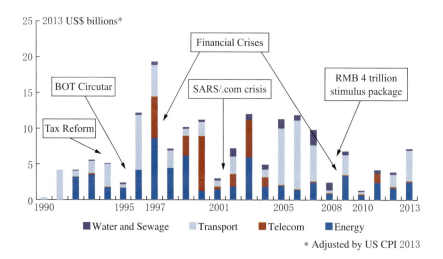

Fig.5
Private participation in infrastructure projects in China, by sector

We have conducted some statistical research in this field concerning the performance of the PPP project in China. It is a bit overheating now. According to the official statistic results derived from many PPP Center in China, over 10 000 PPP projects are now worth more than CNY3 000 000 000 000.

| 上海2050：协同治理与共享发展

The collaborative project covers all sectors including traffic, water supply, environmental application, and some social sectors such as health care, social insurance and education.

The local governments now continue to develop PPP as a way of financing. The PPP transaction is in the form of bidding and auction, which constitute 10% of all PPP activities. Under most circumstances, PPP is conducted through market mechanism and shares more pervasive appearances in more places. However, currently they are still in the initial process of acquisition and making a very sluggish progress. The reason will be explained later from the PPP and the private sector side.

For the conference, I present you with some of the examples in China such as the road construction PPP project in Anqing, "The Availability Payment Method," namely that the local government encouraged the private sector to participate in the development of roads and finance the project through the order of availability. Therefore, it was also called "The Government-Paid PPP," as supposed to "The User-Paid PPP." Another construction was made by Beijing Municipal Engineering Company that had the partnership with the local government. The Availability Payment Method helped to smooth the payment of the local government. By engaging the private sectors, the local governments had their fiscal responsibility spread out even though they had to pay for the private sectors. As a result, the local government considered whether the benefits outweighed the price paid for the private sectors. This type of PPP project is very cost-efficient and can also bring some better economic benefit. In an ideal world, the roads are always fixed by the government, but what if the government has no wherewithal and it is impossible to fulfill the money through taxation. Therefore, even though the cost might be higher when the project is finished by the private sector, it still has great value with the help of private sector. As a part of reform, the local governments could change the high and expensive loans into bonus through PPP.

Another World Bank project is in Urumqi, where the financing arrangement was based on the collaboration of the World Bank, China Development Bank, and the government of resources. The difference from the previous programs lay in how the CDB structure operated. Under the new Budget Law, the city can be used as a financing platform that allows local governments to borrow money, and the revenue flow be used to support CDB loan. The procedure was as follows. The local government raised the loan from the World Bank and also had its own tax. At the same time, Urban Transport Company could get revenues both from the bus services they offered and subsidies that the local government provided beforehand. With the transparency of municipal government's budget, the bus company could also go to China Development Bank to borrow extra loans. This is ubiquitous in many cities but still new for China, because in the past banks that only focused on the assets, regardless of the projects, were only allowed to borrow money based on allocations. The project financing, or the revenue financing, has specific purpose and methods to pay the loan.

The new Budget Law clearly prescribes the method to borrow and the revenue used to repay the borrowing. But this method is a new concept, in which the potential revenue, loan target, and the distribution of money are very closely related.

As for the implication of the subsidies, the local governments should meet the obligation ahead of the time and reach the agreements with the bus company. From our financing analysis, it shows that the local governments' subsidies supporting the bus company will increase (fig.9) after the implementation of BRT project, which will in turn induce better results.

3. Several suggestions for China to set up city clusters financing system

Now I return to the topic of "City Clusters". The city cluster refers to the Pearl River Delta, and the JING-JIN-JI (Beijing-Tianjin-Hebei Region). As for the question of how to finance these mega regions, China has no systematic financing system for such regions. Lack of central government's transfer, the challenge is how to finance regional transportation whose benefits are bigger than the individual city provides. The transportation program from Beijing to Tianjin tends to have more benefits than the single programs of Beijing or Tianjin, because the funds are targeted for specific programs of region. As a general rule to develop transport system, this is an example from the US. First of all, the planning has to focus on the regional level. The US has Metropolitan Planning Organization which aims to plan the transportation improvements at regional level. In this way, all different cities or countries can be brought into one planning organization so as to have an overall transportation plan which is also financed by the US federal government. MPO has built many branches in different areas of America since the establishment in 1970. Their responsibility lies in making a plan for transportation of metropolitan cities and taking the holistic federal picture into consideration when they receive the federal funds. Only through this collaboration and consideration can they get federal funding and eventually achieve their goals. The federal funding comes from a couple of resources including federal highway funds, supported by FTA. The local governments take the main responsibility for providing the funds matching with the federal funding. China is more decentralized-fiscal than the US, because different levels of Chinese government are required. The federal government fiscal system has the advantage that it can influence the policy and the final outcomes. As for the local governments in the US, the funding source is linked with the final local government performance. In the US, the income of most state governments stems from the tax revenue. But in China, the traditional source of funding such as tax revenue and the property transferred to private owners by the government cannot maintain the funding of the construction of megacities.

In terms of framework of financing city clusters, the traditional source of financing in China that the local governments used including land-lease revenue and small tax incomes is not enough to finance the programs in city cluster areas. Therefore, the local governments have to seek the help from the regional authority to raise funding and monetary resources, such as certain levies to generate funds for transportation improvements at the regional level. In China, the instances of fiscal transfer from the central government are few and less likely to happen within a short period of time. My recommendation is to take bottom-up approach to finance city clusters, having a type of organization like MPO, which can work together to generate the revenue, develop a collaborative construction plan.

As for the PPP plan in China, the central government has already provided the right policy on environment and mechanism, but it is up to the local governments to interpret the PPP, some of which will reach the standard but some may not. Hence, PPP requires a long time to prepare, slightly different from the method that the local governments generally rush to make the PPP projects. Basically, the private sectors tend to be involved in less capital and intensive projects. Thus, the lack of regulatory confidence prevents the local government from being enthusiastic about the PPP project in China. In other words, the PPP concession may take more than 15 years or even longer. As for mayors of local government, they often remain in service only for 5 years, then may get reelected again. In this case, the private sectors may lack confidence, or basically doubt whether the regulatory discipline exists to protect them against the changes in the government. If a dispute or disagreement occurs, an insufficient district reservation mechanism or third party arbitration mechanism cannot give the confidence to the private sectors in China.

Also, there is still the dominance of the state-owned enterprises for the last 20 years. The big SOEs have developed most of Chinese infrastructures. Now they are involved in PPP project and create the asymmetry of power. With huge capital, the SOEs have easy access to credit versus this private sector. Now, the SOEs represent the way that the policy defines PPP. Our local Shanghai SOE can go to Hunan province and compete for a water supply project under PPP but cannot do it in Shanghai. That is another mode of PPP.

In addition, some international companies show great interest in PPP, but have the same issue as the domestic private sectors in terms of regulatory confidence, competition from SOE, etc.. But China will take the step to initiate the infrastructure development, and more improvements in the financing system are expected in the future. This is my presentation.

The Five Key Elements to Successful Global Spiky Urban Regions

Meric Gertler

President，University of Toronto

Shanghai is doubtless one of the most dynamic and innovative urban regions in the world. Today, I would like to share with you what makes urban regions like Shanghai so successful. And there are many answers, of course, but I would like to suggest five ingredients that are shared by many successful cities. But before I do that, let me start with some contexts. Some of you may be familiar with the work of Thomas Friedman of the *New York Times*' best seller a few years ago which argues that the world is flat, and I use that image to convey the declining relevance of geography and international borders that thanks to the Internet and increasing rich of global cooperation. In response to this view, one of my colleagues in University of Toronto, Professor Richard Florida, argued in a widely cited essay in The Atlantic that the global economy is not flat, but "spiky". Florida persuasively described an emerging geography and believed that the importance of major urban regions is growing, not weaning. Urban regions are increasingly recognized by both academics and policy makers as vital contributors to local and national prosperity, the source of creativity and innovation, and engines of local economic growth and resiliency. Shanghai exemplifies this point better than perhaps anywhere in the globe. Shanghai has reinvented itself many times and helped China transform in the process. Similar stories could be told of cities like London, San Francisco, Berlin, Toronto and other successful city regions. So in this context it is important to observe that the successful urban regions are privileged sites for innovation, entrepreneurship, and the generation of new ideas and opportunities. Their successes are not accidental. So one of my aims this morning is to help make sense of the forces shaping the successes and to offer a few suggestions so as to help my partners to take full advantage of these forces.

1. Spiky cities can attract and retain a critical mass of top talents

These are also typical places where people can get together and share knowledge easily. People around the world may use different approaches or from various perspectives to deal with the same or similar things. Some documents called this characteristic as agglomeration effects.

The reasons underlining this connection are many and varied, originating from both the supply side (the environment that the cities offer), and the demand of the generator. This relationship is really at the very heart of successful urban regions. Clustered with talents, urban regions offer a geographically-concentrated pool of resources, including human capital, the most important resource, as well as a wide array of specialized services. All these resources support entrepreneurship and the development of new products. Furthermore, cities foster innovation particularly well since innovation frequently arises from the close and sustained interaction between the users of technology and the producers of those technologies; they bring together technology producers and customers in a close and creative dialogue.

Jane Jacobs, a writer focusing on the topic of cities. She first lived in New York City and then moved to Toronto. As an eminent urbanist, Jane Jacobs pointed out that cities excels in circulating knowledge among firms, including those in the same or related industries as well as those seemingly unrelated industries. And cities have the capacity to facilitate such knowledge spillovers and localize learning to provide tremendously fertile conditions for innovation, even in a time when information technologies make it so easy for information to be shared instantly over long distances.

How to produce, attract and retain highly-qualified talents should indeed be a top priority for public policy and the innovative capacity of city regions. Urban transformation is inevitably attributed to many factors. Geographical and physical capitals are important, but human resources, creative, educated and innovative people are truly fundamental. As former New York City mayor Michael Bloomberg stated, "I have long believed that talent attracts capital far more effectively and consistently than capital attracts talent". Highly educated creative human capital is the preeminent factor of production, shaping the competitive advantage of different firms. Moreover, because this kind of talents are increasingly sought-after, cities that aspire to be economically dynamic need to embrace their ability to generate talent in sufficient numbers, or to attract talents from other locations, nationally and globally, and then to keep them firmly rooted in place once they arrive.

University of Toronto graduates more than 16 000 students into the community every year. Universities like Toronto and Shanghai Jiao Tong excel in producing talents. Indeed, I would say that this is their most important contribution to the success of their host regions, but they also play a major role in attracting talent through their national and global recruitment of students and faculty. Fully 50 percent of the faculty of the University of Toronto and more than 25 percent of our students are recruited from outside Canada, so we are the backbone force that brings talents to Canada.

2. Spiky cities have great connectedness with outside world

At the same time the talent and successful urban regions are highly clustered and highly interconnected. Cities, when they are successful, are gateways to global networks: knowledge-producing networks, business networks, political and cultural networks. Insights into the big challenges or the solutions to those challenges shared through these networks naturally stimulate new ideas, products and services at home.

Here you can clearly see the role that major urban regions play in anchoring global knowledge networks. Connections are really the global arteries carrying ideas and opportunities between leading city regions and filling creativity and innovation.

These observations about the forces shaping successful urban regions also suggest some ideas that may be useful on helping build successful urban regions and innovative city clusters. There are dozens of examples to learn, not the least

I would argue the cities we are privileged to be in today.

3. Spiky cities form symbiotic relationship with research universities

Cities foster the development of world-class research universities, while at the same time research universities foster the development of world-class cities. The leveraging of this relationship creates a mutual advantage leading to prosperity for both partners. Similarly, this local symbiotic relationship is complemented by critically important global connections. Institutions of advanced education and research are important gateways connecting their host urban regions internationally. Urban regions that host leading institutions of education and research are highly connected knots within global knowledge networks. Because the prosperity of city regions depends not only on their ability to access and use the knowledge that they produce locally, but also on knowledge that is produced in other leading centers of research and innovation around the world. The flow of knowledge, ideas and innovations through those global arteries is a tremendous source of opportunity, innovation and dynamism for participating urban regions. As a result, well-connected global network centers of knowledge production, like Toronto, like Shanghai, are increasingly coming to the fore as the world's leading economic centers.

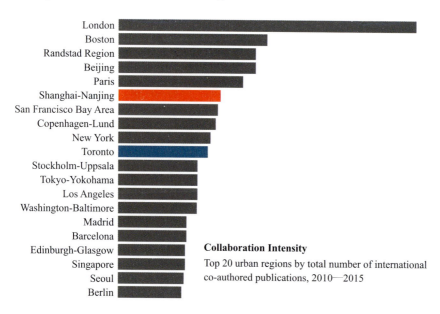

Fig.1
Top 20 urban regions by total number of international co-authored publications

Collaboration Intensity

Top 20 urban regions by total number of international co-authored publications, 2010—2015

This picture shows the world's leading centers of international collaboration as measured by the total number of scholarly publications written with one or more international co-authors (Fig.1). These are places that are clearly recognized as the world's most dynamic urban economies. They're also places that have been sought out by venture capital and other forms of mobile investment, since these special places have world-class research institutions, human capital and opportunities of global collaborations.

4. Focusing on the unevenly investment and long-term investment in innovation

Urban economy development strategy must know and suppose that activities with the greatest innovative capacity are not evenly spread across the national or the global landscape, but are highly concentrated in a relatively small number of city regions. Thus, public sector investments that are designed to stimulate innovation ought to be similarly targeted. The goal should be to enhance and support those local firms, sectors and institutions that have demonstrated unique capabilities and competences, as well as assets that are difficult to be replaced. Consequently, many national and sub-national governments have clustered their public investments in research and innovation, building upon spikes of institutions in selected regions and amplifying their competitive advantages. I think this strategy has been more successful in China than anywhere else in the world. As part of the Project 985, targeted funding has dramatically lifted China's 39 top universities, 8 of which now rank among the world's top 100 most respected institutions in the 2016 Times Higher Education World Reputation Rankings.

In addition, innovation does not happen overnight, patience and sustained investments are the often overlooked factors. Success requires commitment as well as tolerance of risk-taking and failure as part of an overall strategy. This strategy must recognize and leverage those unique and competitive advantages that are increasingly clustered in a relatively small number of urban regions.

Let me give you an example from the region and university that I know best. It may surprise you that stem cells were discovered in the University of Toronto on a Sunday afternoon back in 1961. But it is only recently, more than half a century later, after that transformative discovery that we find ourselves on the verge of a revolution in regenerative medicine. New therapies and medical interventions based on stem cell technology are only just being developed for commercial and clinical applications. We never neglect regenerative medicine for decades on the contrary. In the past 25 years, University of Toronto invested in stem cell and genetics research annually (Fig.2). Dark blue represents research fund; light blue represents salaries, benefits, the operating expenses and capital investments, which shows that hundreds of researchers have been employed and millions of dollars have been spent every year in Toronto. Here I've highlighted a few milestones and discoveries along the way to give you a sense of what's been happening and the historical trajectory that has led us to where we are today. It's just one story at one university. There are still some of the stories could be told in leading research clusters around the world, and through the global knowledge networks, not least here in Shanghai. Transportation infrastructure, cultural resources, industrial and business clusters, they all follow a similar pattern. Innovative, creative and successful urban regions are invariably the product of sustained and strategic investment over many years.

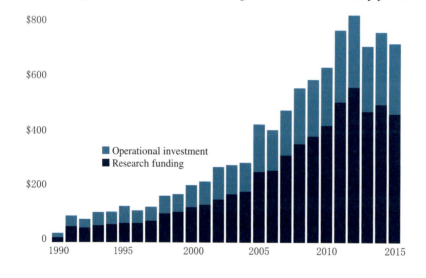

Fig.2
Sustained
investments,
1990—2015

5. Paying attention to the value of urban infrastructures that are broadly conceived

When thinking about talents, research institutions of higher education, and the connection with cities, it's important to appreciate the value of urban infrastructures that are broadly conceived. The most talented, creative members of the labor force, including the faculty members and university students as well as those who generate opportunity and prosperity, prefer to live in urban cities, because cities are culturally dynamic and physically appealing, for example cities have vibrant and safe neighborhoods, high-quality schools and hospitals. Comparatively, cities are more open to new comers and new ideas. Hence, the pillars that support our economic prosperity and innovative dynamism are actually the quality of the whole region's transportation system, the environment of culture and arts and public facilities, which are often overlooked.

Let's take a look at our urban transportation infrastructure. It's a remarkably undeveloped system given that Toronto's population has come to more than six million, which is still rapidly growing. Decades of delay, intra-governmental gridlock and insufficient public investment have resulted in Toronto becoming the longest commuting times to work among North America. The recent study shows the cost of this inefficiency accounts up to 11 billion dollars a year in

Fig.3
Shanghai railway

Toronto alone, more than the city's entire annual operating budget.

I have been told that Shanghai is also being faced with transportation challenges. However, I still think Toronto could learn a lot from Shanghai's subway system. Look at the map here (Fig.3). By comparisons, there exist some differences, not alone Shanghai's high-speed rail options, such as the Jinshan railway. In addition, the high quality standard of life in the city can determine whether those higher education institutions are able to attract and retain talents. Talents are increasingly mobile, and the most sought-after people can choose alternatively where they live. They have many options, so quality of place is a crucially important determinant of a long-term prosperity of those higher education institutions as well as their urban regions.

Generally speaking, Shanghai and Toronto are the best of urban regions that combine nearly all of policy ingredients that I've mentioned. Extraordinary things can happen when investments in infrastructure become more sustained and strategic, attracting extraordinary talent, funding leading research, and facilitating communications between different fields, industries and leading global regions. This is the allure of the world's leading innovative and creative urban regions. I hope my remarks will offer some insights into the factors behind these successful urban regions and how we might harness them to our mutual advantage.

Shanghai on the Way to an Excellent Global City

Xiao Lin

Then Director General of the Development Research Center of
Shanghai Municipal People's Government

The theme of this forum is "Collaborative Governance, Shared Development". It is also one of the main characteristics of global urban development. Lately, Shanghai municipal government publicized "Draft of the Overall Plan of Shanghai (2016—2040) ", in which it put forward the objective of building Shanghai into an excellent global city by 2040 and made scientific planning from aspects including urban space, regional structure and transportation. With the overall plan of Shanghai 2040 being made at the same time, according to the deployment of Shanghai municipal party committee and municipal government, Shanghai Development Research Center initiated the research of development strategy for the next 30 years. The development strategy of 2050 shares the same strategic orientation with the overall city plan, which is to move towards a global excellent city.

1. Staying tuned to the development trend of global city，which is mixed with challenges and opportunities

Ever since 1990s, accompanied by technology innovation, world urban system has shifted from the vertical "hierarchical rank" to the flattening network era. Cities at core status, which were "central cities" based on the scale and primacy, have now evolved into influential "global cities" based on connectivity. There will still be great adjustments and changes in the next 30 years. With the revolution of technology and in-depth development of globalization, the world will enter into a city-centered running pattern which will enable global cities to play new roles in this reconstructing age with new characteristics and responsibilities.

Firstly, the status of innovation in urban function is more and more outstanding. The scientific and technological revolution will deeply change the operating pattern of global cities and global production networks will upgrade to innovative networks, which makes the role of innovation in urban function more prominent. Global cities have made their transformation from capitals of capital to innovation centers; knowledge economy occupies the global fulcrum, and talents have become the essential resource in the global economy. Cities which can provide high quality life for high-skilled workforce will be more competitive worldwide. Operating in an intelligent manner, cities will realize its inclusive and sustainable development with sound governance in both the virtual space and reality, which turns out to be an important aspect for global cities to improve governance capacity.

Secondly, the function of being the core node of world urban system is more and more highlighted for global cities. As the coordinator of all resources, global cities will have more advantages in connectivity as the portal towards the world, transforming from industrial chain to value chain as the source of industrial technology. As a result, global cities will better serve its coordinative function of cooperation, with the participation of non-governmental organizations. Carrying a significant impact on the global development, global cities will play a mediating and creative role in the process of prescribing the standards of international trades.

Thirdly, the purport of the city's development centers around improving life quality, and it puts more emphasis on the people-oriented, inclusive and sustainable development. As the society is going through the age of information civilization, this ideology can conduce better to the comprehensive development of human society than traditional resource attraction, becoming the predominant trend of the society. The quintessential topic of sustainable development boils down to a collective hope for ecological amelioration, and an objective of achieving higher level of happiness for the residents. It counts as a competitive edge if the city can attain green low-carbon development style, fair and equal value, and intercultural integration and creativity.

Fourthly, global cities are also confronted with multi-pronged challenges as a hub of a highly concentrated variety of population, society and culture. The aging trend of population, income polarization, social stratification, cultural clash, and conflict of interest are all becoming salient problems in the society, which can easily stir up dissatisfaction and protest within the middle class. It is imminent for global urban governance to create a new form of balance within the confusion of multiple targets and rules and to make profound amendment on public policies.

2. The orientation and vision of the development strategy of Shanghai towards an excellent global city

In the next 30 years, the global and Chinese development trend will pave the path for Shanghai to be better assimilated into global urban network and provide stronger impetus for Shanghai to form urban functions of global influence. As an excellent global city, Shanghai will undertake the responsibilities and mission of participating in global competition and cooperation as well as serving national strategies like "the Belt and Road". Building Shanghai into an excellent global city can be interpreted from the following three aspects.

Firstly, it should be a global city of global competiveness and influence, participating in global competition in different aspects and latitudes, implementing national strategies and leading regional development. The status of global cosmopolitan should be emphasized in order to be built up as a center of economy, finance, trade, shipping and culture, and be globally influential in aspects like pricing elements, distributing information and making rules. As the portal for the Asia Pacific Gateway, Shanghai needs to transform into the shipping center and information port hub of Asia Pacific, serving as the strategic channel and critical node of gathering and spreading the global core resources and strategic elements in this region. As the pioneer of opening up and economic innovation in China, Shanghai should participate in global innovation and cooperation in a leading position on behalf of the country, utilizing the core effects of city clusters of Yangtze River Delta to make it the biggest one in the world.

Secondly, it should be a crucial node city that occupies a fulcrum in the global urban network, bearing global function in fields like global economy, culture and innovation and having a leading voice in the world. Efforts should be devoted to promoting global scientific and technological breakthroughs and quick commercialization of innovation. Capabilities of investment management can be utilized to make Shanghai the management center of the triumvirate of global value chain, investment chain and transaction chain so as to take control of the high-end features of global investment management chain. For the allocation of resources, it should accelerate the establishment of market mechanism with global openness and serve as the pivot of using two kinds of resources and markets both at home and abroad. Besides, functions of gathering talents, exchanging cultural and informational communication should be given full play in order to make Shanghai a global talent hub with global attraction and configuration, a global cultural communication center with Chinese characteristics, and a global open strategic pivot with fluent information fluidity and strong capacity of information allocation.

Thirdly, it should be a new modern city which demonstrates Chinese cultural characteristics and leads modern civilization, exerting exemplary influence on the development of global emerging cities. As a global leading city in scientific and technological innovation, Shanghai takes the lead in global trend in many respects including inspiration of creative ideas, basic scientific research, transformation in innovative technology and development of industrial applications. As a global leading city in production transformation, Shanghai sets excellent examples in saving resources, clean energy as well as reform of organization and business modes. As a global leading city in smart living, Shanghai is moving towards a connective, intelligent and smart city with leading steps in smart living and construction of smart cities. As a global leading city in cultural integration, Shanghai features public wisdom and boosts absorptive, profound, innovative and fashionable captivity.

In the future, Shanghai is going to develop itself following the developing concept of "innovation, coordination, green, openness, and sharing", so as to become a global city manifesting the Chinese dream, which provides opportunities for everyone to realize their dreams and achieve all-round development and improves the living quality and health conditions of all citizens in order to enable people living here a happy and beautiful life.

In the 30 years to come, Shanghai will keep marching forward toward a global city with excellence. We need to spare no efforts to build Shanghai into an innovative and vital city and join the procession of innovative cities with global significance. To be more specific, it should be an important node city in the global innovation network, a pivot city of favorable environment, intensive resources and great potentials for innovation, an important source of scientific findings, technologies and industries, and last but not least, a dynamic city full of creativity, competiveness and capacity to confront various challenges. In order to build a city full of prosperity and vigor, Shanghai needs to build up the comprehensive function which is highly developed, international and connected by assembling headquarters of multiple multinational corporations. It is expected to have a far-reaching influence in the global governance and coordination and become a prosperous city with more diversified functions providing more opportunities.

In order to build an ecological and livable city, which is suitable for people to live a better life and presents the beautiful landscape of clean water and green scenery, we need to build Shanghai into a livable city which is comfortable, convenient, ecological, sustainable and safe, demonstrating the global standard and leading new lifestyle in Asia.

In order to build a city of cultural glamour, Shanghai should demonstrate the charm of Chinese culture based on its local cultural features and exchange with other multi-cultural ideas at the same time, so as to enrich its culture and become an inclusive city featured with human-orientation, and social fairness. Driven by the happiness of civilians, Shanghai is supposed to become an affiliative and inclusive city which offers opportunities for equal development and fair competition.

We will work hard to establish a model city of governance. Through institutional innovation and modal innovation, Shanghai will set a good example for other counties in China and the world for its well urban governance, which showcases the country's governance system and modernization of governance.

3. Shanghai needs to transform its development mode and pattern towards an excellent global city

Shanghai has experienced the process from the promoting pattern driven by plan to efficiency, which should depend on innovation. In the next three decades, Shanghai will face a series of problems restricted by population scale, land resource, eco-environment and urban security. As the same time, the increase of external impact, multicultural conflict and untraditional urban safety threats caused by the growing urban openness, global connectivity and large-scale flow of urban population will also pose great challenges. Shanghai should always adhere to the five development concepts to transform development pattern, embark on a road with characteristics of the times, Shanghai and Chinese features.

We should take the path of development triggered by innovation. We need to stick to improving labor efficiency driven by innovation and talents. Through structural reform from the supply side, we can improve the qualities of all factor productivity so as to achieve economic development with higher vigor and efficiency through innovative policies and strategies. We can promote the development of new technology and industry, which also generates more opportunities for the job market.

We should have an intensive pattern of growth. We need to hold fast to those bottom line constraints and control the population size to optimize the demographic structure and to realize the restrictive growth of planned urban construction land. We should ensure the ecological land preserved, urban production saved, and operation safety guaranteed. We can intensively use multifunctional special structure of land-use to develop the production mode of energy-saving and cost-reducing. We also need to promote the frugal type of lifestyle to relieve the city from overburden. As a result, we can leave adequate strategic resources and energy for future generations. We should also regard environmental enchantment and green competency as an important part of global urban construction and persist in the sustainable use of natural resources and energy in order to make the city and community ecological and sustainable with livable environment of greenery, safety and convenience.

We should take the path of tenacious development as well. Faced with uncertainties like demographic change, technological transformation, big events, major risks and disasters, we should have a flexible and elastic urban system and governance mechanism so that we can carry out dynamic control of planning with prevention, response and recovery to contingency. We need to build a sponge city of reliable and resilience infrastructures to deal with potential threats in case of climate change and environmental degradation. We should also pay attention to the core issue leading to urban vulnerability and the nurture of urban accumulating capacity. With more attachment to soft power of culture, we need to respect cultural traditions and preserve cultural diversity to promote cultural innovation, which will strengthen urban humanity competitiveness and provide permanent power for the sustained development of society.

Dialogue

Audience: I have two questions. The first one goes for Professor Gertler. You have mentioned that universities and cities can promote each other. But I was wondering what universities can do to engage more in community activities in order to build a better city. Would you like to share with us some of the best practices in this respect? How can University of Toronto get involved in the community and contribute to a better country's development?

The second is for Dr. Xiao Lin. My question is about sharing economy and urban transportation. Mobike is very popular recently in Shanghai; my first riding experience is from Shanghai Jiao Tong University to South Shaanxi Road, around 3 kilometers. I followed with the Baidu navigation system. During my riding, I found that some roads are just motorways but I don't know, thus stopped by traffic police and was educated. As we all know that Mobike is very popular among the youth in Shanghai. I lived in London for few years where bicycles can be ridden on roadways, which is quite different from Shanghai. So it seems that Shanghai Municipal Government has not considered that riding Mobike on roadway is banned. Is it possible that Shanghai government can set up more bicycle lanes in the downtown area?

Merrick. Gertler: I think that a lot of principals from many countries have recognized that they have the responsibility, to make sure their institutions are good urban builders. There are several reasons behind.

First of all, we have gained a lot of support from our society, so we have the obligation to give back to our community and society. In addition, it is also a matter of self-interest, because what we can do is to make the city, such as

Shanghai and Toronto a better place. So actually it is helping ourselves. Because the higher the quality of city life, the better the environment. Thus we can attract and retain the talent teachers and students who have great quality from the nation and even all over the world. From this perspective, I think your suggestion is quite logic and reasonable.

How to do that, specifically? We have several ways to the ground.

We encourage our teachers and students to work on city's problems. Hundreds of teachers have great interests in different dimensions of urban development, such as physical, social, political, public health, environmental and engineering perspectives and more. So how can we make use of these experts to contribute to our urban development? I have a new position in my office, which is the special adviser for urban issues who is an one-stop shopping contact person trying to find experts inside the university. They help to connect the citizens or organizations with the experts inside our university. What's more, they also help our faculty to find some partners in the community. It is also a search mechanism.

More generally, I think our students enjoy the opportunity towards real-world problems, because many of our tutors are finding more ways for our students to engage in the urban projects. What we are doing is to help our students to accumulate more experiences and contribute to their communities as well.

The last thing I want to talk about is how we can become more liberal city builders. We build a lot of lovely buildings; we have three campuses in Toronto region and some construction of 500 million Canadian dollars underway. We want to make sure that what we have built can raise the design quality of our city. So we can demonstrate the ability to contribute to the environment as a public organization through buildings of our school.

Xiao Lin: This is a very good question, which is concerned by a lot of citizens. Actually it is about the concept of development rather than a transportation issue. In the overall plan of 2040, we envision Shanghai, in the year 2040, will become an excellent global city, a city of innovation, humanity and ecology. An eco-friendly city can be manifested in many aspects including transportation and energy. In terms of transportation, we will make a more detailed plan in terms of both bicycle lanes and footpaths besides developing public transportation. We have been working on the relevant plans including the routes. Take the roads along the Huangpu River as an example, the reconstruction of the roads around forty-five kilometers will be completed by the end of 2017, which will include bicycle lanes, sidewalks and motorways. This is a typical example in which we will make some adjustments besides the existing routes.

Audience: I'm very glad to be here today. Shanghai hopes to become a central city of the world because of its geographic advantages, but China itself is a very large market which set certain restrictions to Shanghai's development. In this sense, Shanghai should pay more attention to collaborating with its neighboring or surrounding areas on the way to building an excellent global city, which is related to the development of city clusters mentioned by Mr. Binyam Reja. Therefore, my question is for Dr. Xiao Lin. I'm wondering that how we can establish certain mechanism for Shanghai to achieve shared development with surrounding regions.

Xiao Lin: Thank you for your question. Actually, National Development and Reform Commission has made a clear definition on the orientation and objective of this problem in the plan for the development of the Yangtze River Delta. In the overall plan of Shanghai 2040, it is ascertained that the efforts to building an excellent global city should be closely combined with the linkage development of the whole Yangtze River Delta. If you look at our infrastructure layout concerning airports and rail transportation, you can find that the whole Yangtze River Delta is aimed to be built as the sixth largest city cluster in the world. There has already been some mechanism created by Shanghai with surrounding three provinces and one city. For example, we have communicative mechanism between chief executives of 4 regions every year and regular meetings at different levels. As for the environmental renovation in the Yangtze River Delta, the Central government has also made clear requirements for its integrated development. Of course, we are now still facing the objective bottleneck concerning how to combine different administrative divisions with the general development of those city clusters effectively. That's the problem we've been thinking about.

Audience: I am Zhu Dajian from Tongji University. My question is for Mr.Binyam Reja. You have given us very good points about the development of PPP in China. We know that both the United Nations and the World Bank have emphasized the combination of PPP projects with sustainable development, which is definitely not only to solve the problem of financial payment. So I'd like to know why should PPP be connected with sustainable development and how to achieve it? Do you have some suggestions for China in the future?

Binyam Reja: How to relate sustainable development with PPP program? From this perspective, we have different kinds of sustainability, including financial and economic one. In this part, the PPP will inspire us to consider the project revenue, economic benefit, etc.. When making projects, we should consider the financial sustainability. If it is operated in the right way, a financial sustainability should be affordable and economical from the perspective of fiscal.

When it comes to the environmental sustainability, it is also worthy of our consideration. In this regard, the PPP can also help us to promote environmental sustainability. In general, we must create a link. For example, the Chinese local governments designed and constructed too much infrastructure in the past, such as roads, city roads and other facilities, which were beyond their ability to actual demand. When the PPP is engaged, the local governments will also reverse consideration. If they do this project, how is the cash flow? The cash flow will be reversed transmission at the time of design. The local governments have to make prediction on future demands. They should consider, from the point of financing and capital, the means of structure optimization, the optimization of the environmental capacity, and its better relations with sustainability. From this way of thinking, only resources that can bring the economic benefits should be used. If a four-lane highway is enough, there is no need to build an eight-lane one, because the unnecessary resources have an impact on the environment. At this time they can avoid it by better docking. From this perspective, the PPP really make a contribution to environmental sustainability. The better fiscal management and financial cash flow can also do well to environment.

Audience: I want to ask a question for Professor Gertler. It is often the case that university students can hardly find some opportunities to engage in community activities outside campus. So I want to know about whether there are some policies, courses, special requirements on credits or project arrangement which help encourage your students to participate more in social activities in your university.

Merrick Gertler: Yes, there are quite a few opportunities and our students are always telling us that they want to have more opportunities to participate in social activities. Actually, we have a number of courses which provide practical internships where they can work with the community organizations. In addition, we often provide some internship opportunities during summer when our students can work full time. Our university and community cooperation center help students find internships so they have a chance to contact with the society.

I also want to mention two things. Some of our faculties have professional and industrial experiences. In the third or fourth year of study process, our students have a whole-year time to do professional practice outside school, which gives them more learning opportunities. Then they can return to our university, spending a year for the degree. We also have some programs that students can learn a semester and work a semester, then come back again to continue their studies. These programs are becoming increasingly popular. The challenge is that students told us that they also want to have more such opportunities. For us, the limiting factor is how we can find the community partners, no matter in the private sector, or in the field of government affairs, or nonprofit organizations, and improve their awareness of gaining benefits. This is a win-win situation because it is not only advantageous to our students, but also beneficial for them. It needs further education and propaganda. Now I'm doing some work at the national level, we call them higher education business roundtable, which is trying to strengthen the cooperation between universities and community partners by raising their awareness.

Audience: I'd like to ask Dr.Lin Xiao, how do Shanghai Municipal Government treat the relationship between those public services provided by the government and by private sectors in the process of urban development?

Xiao Lin: That's a very good question. The PPP mode mentioned by Mr. Binyam Reja just now actually advocates public products provided by both the public and private capital. It is also a major mode for promoting the construction of infrastructures. Our long-term infrastructure construction pattern consists of bank loans, government loans and debts that should be controlled nowadays. Of course, our public goods, public service and infrastructures still need to be developed further. In this sense, how can we make full use of state-owned capital, private capital and social capital? We know that the National Development and Reform Commission and the Ministry of Finance both have a clear standard and guideline to promote PPP program which is already widely carried out throughout the country.

Binyam Reja: I want to discuss about the bicycle project again. The article published in the China Daily has proposed that the private sectors have brought about the kingdom of bicycles. As we know, China used to be the kingdom of bicycles because there were quite a lot people riding bikes; but in the process of urbanization characterized by the construction of highway and road engineering, the development of bicycle becomes slow. By sharing economy, a new sharing way, China is more likely to go back to a kingdom of bicycles.

Merrick Gertler: From the international perspective, we can see the same phenomenon, in London, New York, Toronto and other cities where cycling is increasingly popular when we are traveling. And riding bikes has also been encouraged by many local governments as a oneway to increase its habitability and attraction of cities. So what we are faced with is how to provide more space for riders and ensure their safety. By doing so, it's quite essential for the government to enact relevant policies to improve the livability of a city.

Moderator: Now the international communities are paying more attention to the debts of local governments, which is well connected with the topic that Dr. Binyam Reja and several speakers have mentioned. Actually, the involvement of private sectors may offer a solution for the debts of local governments.

Audience: My problem is about the connectivity that many guests have mentioned. In my point of view, the topic of connectivity is closely combined with gathering global talents. Obviously, the proportion of global talents is still relatively small in Shanghai, lower than 1%, but I think it will be greatly improved afterwards. So the following question is how to manage those global talents. I want to know the opinions from Professor Gertler, because Canada is a place converging global talents. For your government, what services will you provide for this group of talents? In addition, what role should the third party like NGOs should play in providing diversified services for these talents in Shanghai?

Merrick Gertler: This is a good question. You can look at this from different scales. In terms of the national level and the federal level, immigration policy is very important, that's why Canada has relatively open immigration policy. This is a points-based immigration system and policy; we attract immigrants based on their own qualifications and labor skills, so they can become our effective workforce. This is an effective mechanism for Canada to select high-quality talents through the immigration project.

In terms of nation, we have been discussing about how to make immigration policy more flexible and accommodating to meet the needs of talents in knowledge-intensive industries, the field of scientific research and even technology innovation area. In the competitive talent market, many employers have to wait for a long time until those qualified staffs have received permission to work in Canada. At the national or federal level, therefore, it is important for us to improve the framework of immigration policy. At the local level, back to the topic discussed before, the problem lies in how to build a livable city which can meet requirements of new immigrants.

For example, Toronto is attracting talents through diversified ways. Half of its population is in foreign-born individuals, which is quite surprising. The degree of diversity is even higher than that in New York and London. What is more surprising is that these people can live in harmony, thus creating a harmonious, stable and livable city. As Dr. Xiao has mentioned, public safety is the important premise of our social security, which ensures a safe facilities system for our community, neighbors and schools. At the same time, we need to ensure education fair, just and equal. These positive aspects of city life can attract people to work and live in this city. Another factor is high-quality transportation system, which is crucially important for the urban infrastructures because its level and quality can help our city to attract talents.

Audience: Around the globe, it is well acknowledged that a city's soft power plays an equally important role as its hard power. But it can also be found that some developers have damaged the city's beauty in their real estate development projects. For example, many new skyscrapers have been built near the Wai Baidu Bridge, in sharp contrast to those beautiful historical buildings.

Xiao Lin: From the current conditions of Shanghai urban physical development, the protection of historic buildings and cultural heritage is always being extended and deepened. Nowadays, Shanghai's historic character and buildings are stringently safeguarded by the Shanghai municipal government and Shanghai planning departments. Those which are not listed as national conservation building are also strictly protected in Shanghai. In the 90's, the lack of laws and regulations in building and planning led to the insufficient architecture protection in some places. However, strict protection systems have been formulated with the reinforcement of public's legal awareness of historic protection. For example, the original lifting crane and rail transit are retained along both sides of the Huangpu River.

In the new round of urban development, Shanghai will implement the new concept of "Urban Renewal", which will depend less on large-scale land development and intensive construction and pay more attention to the combination of protection and development. The concept of compact urban renewal, which is the latest concept, will be applied in the future urban construction of Shanghai.

PARALLEL FORUMS

平行分论坛

FORUM I

分论坛一

Innovation of Urban Governance
城市政府治理创新

主持人·HOST
钟杨·Zhong Yang
上海交通大学国际与公共事务学院院长
Dean of School of International and Public Affairs
Shanghai Jiao Tong University

城市政府治理创新分论坛现场嘉宾聆听演讲

Guests are listening to the speeches attentively at the Innovation of Urban Governance Parallel Forum I

上海交通大学国际与公共事务学院院长钟杨主持平行分论坛一

Zhong Yang，Dean of School of International and Public Affairs，hosts the Parallel Forum I

经济合作与发展组织城市政策项目主任鲁迪格·阿伦德在平行分论坛一上作专题演讲

Rudiger Ahrend，Head of Urban Policy Program of OECD's Directorate for Public，delivers a speech at the Parallel Forum I

德国达姆施塔特工业大学教授休伯特·海纳特在平行分论坛一上作专题演讲

Hubert Heinelt，Professor of Darmstadt University of Technology，delivers a speech at the Parallel Forum I

韩国公共管理学会会长、高丽大学教授崔兴硕在平行分论坛一上作专题演讲

Heungsuk Choi，President of Korean Association for Public Administration and Professor of Korea University，delivers a speech at the Parallel Forum I

哈佛大学肯尼迪政府学院韦瑟赫德教授史蒂芬·卡尔曼在平行分论坛一上作专题演讲

Steven Kelman，Weatherhead Professor of Public Management at Harvard University's John F. Kennedy School of Government，delivers a speech at the Parallel Forum I

清华大学公共管理学院教授蓝志勇在平行分论坛一上作专题演讲

Lan Zhiyong，Professor of School of Public Policy and Management of Tsinghua University，delivers a speech at the Parallel Forum I

上海交通大学凯原法学院教授叶必丰在平行分论坛一上作专题演讲

Ye Bifeng，Professor of Koguan Law School of Shanghai Jiao Tong University，delivers a speech at the Parallel Forum I

美国中佛罗里达大学公共管理学院院长南姆·卡朴库在平行分论坛一上作专题演讲

Naim Kapucu，Professor and Director of School of Public Administration at the University of Central Florida（UCF），delivers a speech at the Parallel Forum I

大都会治理为什么重要:
来自OECD国家的经验

鲁迪格·阿伦德

经济合作与发展组织城市政策项目主任

在经合组织（OECD）国家，大都会的治理是 20 世纪 60 年代大家关注的话题，后来大家没有兴趣了，90 年代大家又开始考虑这个话题。现在看到很多大都会的区域都在进行治理结构的改革。如澳大利亚、土耳其、英国、法国、意大利都对架构进行了改革。每个国家在如何改进治理体系方面的改革都不一样，目的就是要让大都会的治理结构得到改善。为什么突然这么多国家开始对大都会的治理改革这么感兴趣？首先大家越来越多地认识到，行政干预已经过时，已经不符合现实需求。还有越来越多的证据表明，大都会碎片化阻碍了区域城市的发展。

1. 大都会区域的内涵和 OECD 行政分区

请看图 1，左图是大巴黎，中心点是巴黎的行政中心；右图是罗马行政区域，中间是不同的行政区域，一般我们说的数据都是针对行政区域。对比罗马、巴黎，罗马还有很多空地，巴黎和罗马的稠密度完全不一样。对比稠密度的时候，肯定要对比整个区域，不能用巴黎整个区和罗马中心区的稠密度进行对比。还有一些人口指标，比如 25% 的巴黎人是最富有、

图1
大都会行政区域

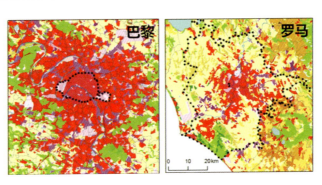

受教育程度最好的人，我们对比的时候不能用巴黎 25% 的人和罗马的所有人口进行对比，这种对比是没有意义的。

因此，我们考虑另外一个词，就是功能区域。首先看一个城市的市中心稠密度最高的地方，然后看人口密度最低的地方，接下来研究一下大家的通勤方式，找出这些功能区域，再用功能区的层级进行对比。只用行政边界对比，不管是国际国内的对比，都是没有意义的。

我们可以把这个定义放在中国使用，但有的时候我们要做一些改变。中国的情况不太一样，因为城市结构不太一样。首先就是人口、功能区，增加得越来越快。比如北京的行政管理区和功能区不太一样。我们有很多相关的数据，在其他国家也有类似的方法论。我觉得 2030 年全球会有超过 30 个超大型城市。如果我们使用大都会区域来统计，世界看起来会更有组织一点。

2. 重视大都会区域治理的原因在于行政的碎片化

整个城市的经济、社会实体，分布比较广泛。因为现在城市发展很快，已经超出了历史的边界。比如，拿破仑在 200 年前上台的时候做了一件很出名的事，他把法国划分成省（département），建造方式就是这个省到首都的距离可以保证区域里的每个公民可以在早上骑马到首都去，晚上可以回来。他的做法很聪明，200 年之后，我们有了车、有了飞机，但法国省的边界依然存在。还有很多小村庄，是围着城市分布的，可能离城市有二三十公里远。现在城市群已经很大了，但行政结构还是一样的，这就会造成问题。城市之间的合作需要通过城市群来完成很多事情，而不是把自己不想要的东西扔出城市边界。这是过去的方法，现在已经不可行了。

举个例子，一个 OECD 国家的富有城市，我们到那儿后，发现竟然没有公共交通连接机场和市中心，我们很惊讶，问这里为什么没有现代公共交通。他们说，"哎，没钱啊"。但是，这是个非常富有的国家，钱不是问题。问题在于如果想建立像火车的公共交通系统，就需要沿线各个城市市长们的同意，这会非常复杂。靠近机场的市长就会说，他们不需要火车连接都市和机场，因为非常近，市民不会用到火车。事情就到此为止了。对于这个市长和他的市民来说，这样似乎是理性的决定，但对于城市化而言却是一场灾难。另外一个例子，你坐地铁去一个城市，到地铁终点时出去，你以为你在市中心，但是并没有停在那里，而是停在了行政边界，而不再往前延伸。因为建设地铁会涉及不同的、小的市政区域的决策，需要很多人做出决定才可以完成，到目前为止他们还没有就继续扩建地铁达成一致意见。这样的例子还有很多。我们不禁会问："这些都是特殊案例吗？还是我们真的很幸运，直接发现了有问题的地方？"我们一直在收集一些数据并作出分析。

如果人口一定的话，行政碎片化越高，城市区域越多，生产效率就下降得越厉害。人口不变，市政区域的数字每翻一倍，生产效率会降低 6%，也就意味着，每年 GDP 都会降低 6%。我的一个同事说："城市得多有钱才能负担得起这样的损失啊。"这并不是一个理论方面的问题，其实会对城市产生负面的经济影响。

我们看一下经济增长的数据，在 OECD 国家碎片化不那么严重的地区，增长率在过去十年上升了。而生产效率并不是唯一的一个问题，行政碎片化也会产生一些不理想的社会结果。因为可能有钱人都会住在同一个地方，而穷人集中在另一个地方。对 OECD 国家来说，穷人聚集的地方可能会有更多的社会问题，教育资源不好会产生很多的不公平，在这些地方成长的孩子，之后接受教育的机会越来越少，他们的人生从一开始就落后一大截了。

3. 建立大都会政府部门是一个可行的选择

那我们可以做一些什么事情？其中一个可能性，就是建立一个大都会的政府部门。这有一定的可行性。当然，我们不需要大都会具有所有的功能，有些功能最好可以分配给当地政府。可以设立一些地方区域，把这些功能转移过去。但很多 OECD 国家，我前面也提到过，主要是政治方面的问题。政府官员都不愿意讨论这个问题，因为他们很可能会很快丢掉工作。

对大都会来说，真正重要的是哪些功能，然后按照具体情况创立这些功能性的部门，这个就是大都会政府，或者叫大都会管理机构。很多城市都有这些机构。我们在 OECD 国家作了一个调查，发现 1/3 的大都会区没有大都会政府功能，剩下的 2/3 有，但是很多比较弱，可能就市长每年开两次会，解决一些问题。只有 20% 的大都会政府部门有比较强的监管权。非常有意思的就是这些大都会政府部门会有非常多不同的功能、不同的任务。他们有非常多的工作，如改善文化、环境、社会福利等。但有三个最为关键，即：空间规划、交通、区域发展。空间规划、交通是主要的功能，基本超过 2/3。这是大都会政府要实施的关键核心功能。我们可以看到，这些功能在大都会层面实施会产生很多外部性，是非常合理的。

现在让我们看一下，大都会政府部门是不是真的有积极影响。在很多 OECD 大都会区域里，如果没有治理机构，城市密度非常高，会有很多无计划扩展的情况。如果有大都会政府部门，则会进行空间规划管理，城市密度降低。另外我们看到，大都会政府的存在也会改善社会福利，可以看到交通系统改善，人口减少，生产力也会增加。因为有了大都会政府，沟通也更加方便，可以有效减少碎片化带来的负面问题。

城市治理的不同模式
——特定部门间的利益协调与合作

休伯特·海纳特
德国达姆施塔特工业大学教授

非常高兴可以从更一般意义上谈治理。我将集中阐述治理的不同模式演变，及其与城市协同治理特别是创新协同治理的相关性问题。我会简述一下关于治理方面的一些辩论，因为这方面的辩论非常广泛。另外，我会大概介绍一下不同的治理模式，以及这些模式如何进行融合，这些融合又如何影响到创新。

1. 关于治理方面的辩论

首先是关于从政府管理向治理转变。Vincent Kauttman 1986 年出版了一本书，这本书的编辑花了很长时间，上世纪 80 年代初就开始了。这本书在当时就提到，我们需要指导和控制。这本书的作者们反映了现代社会中协调社会各类资源的困难，我们能否很好地指导并控制现代社会的各项社会活动。在那个时候，我们就很清楚地看到，有一些非市场因素在协调个人行为。当然，从经济学假设来看存在外部性问题，因此需要国家和行政层级的干预。但是，这些就足够了吗？是不是还有一些超越政治等级形态的因素，可以确保各种社会活动的协调抑或谈判和治理？我后面会继续回到这一点。

其次是关于政策网络方面的辩论，主要是在政治科学方面的内容。有一种反映是国家和社会之间的关系，即传统的多元论，包括不同的利益集团都想影响到国家，或者通过不同政治层级的干预来影响社会。还有新社团主义，各个利益集团对社会进行等级式干预，从而影响社会协调的运作方式和整个社会的发展。

在这些辩论中，传统治理方式都太普遍了。当你接近这些参与者群体和决策者时，你可以问他们在有干扰的情况下如何协调各种互动的活动。在这些辩论中，我们看到不同的协调模式。我们需要谈判（bargaining），而不是政治的，是一种通过温和方式来进行的协调。当然，基于服从多数决策的西方民主社会，也会有等级式的协调方式。

还有一种比较新的即所谓治理核心，就是既通过沟通互动又通过谈判和论理的方式来进行协调。

John Einstein 有一个研究，强调谈判是一种沟通方式。但这里沟通的参与者都比较坚持自己的立场和利益，要达成一致就要进行妥协，没有妥协是不行的。有时这不容易，但这就是博弈。进行谈判的人告诉我们，对于自私的参与者是可以通过谈判协调他们的行为的。

论理则不同，参与者必须开诚布公地讨论是不是有问题，问题在哪里。如果我们有问题，可能是你有问题，而我没有问题。那解决问题的方法是否适合我们所有人呢？什么方法对双方来说是都说得过去的？不管是从常识的角度看还是从达成共识的角度看，什么样的解决方案更说得过去？首先大家都是自私的，自私的参与者要找到共同解决方案，还要讨论共同的问题，就共同的目标和解决问题的方式达成共识。

那结果是什么呢？我们可以看到在政府安排、大都会政府安排、城市治理方面，混合使用这五个协调方式来协调社会行为。有的时候更多是市场的，有的时候更多是等级式的，有的时候是谈判式的，有的时候又是开放式的论理。很重要的一点在于，政府治理的安排能够给我们带来创新，带来一些新的东西，同时让大家实施一些新的想法。

2. 关于三阶治理层级理论及其执行

在这里，引用 Jan Kooiman 的一个概念，同时从 Elinor Ostrom 的著作中可以看到。她区分了三个选择，即制度选择、集体选择、操作选择，Kooiman 则区分成元治理、一阶治理、二阶治理（图1）。

什么叫元治理？这是一种互动的层级，是指城市、城市集聚区、政策区里的行为人，要就某一个特定问题的定义以及寻求表达和解决问题的合适方法达成共识，他们寻找问题存在的原因并吃透它。这里认知过程非常重要。这就是一种对想法的思考，从我们认为最佳的方式来看，哪一种概念能够解释这个问题。这里主要靠论理的治理方式，因为一般来说你不可以用等级式的方法去假设问题是什么，参与者必须一起参与进来，这样才

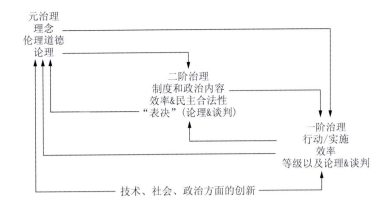

图 1
Kooiman 的不同治
理层级

元治理
理念
伦理道德
论理

二阶治理
制度和政治内容
效率&民主合法性
"表决"（论理&谈判）

一阶治理
行动/实施
效率
等级以及论理&谈判

技术、社会、政治方面的创新

能用主导的概念表达问题。接下来就是二阶治理，也就是集体选择。需要建立一些规章和政策，同时还要对一些问题建立有约束力的决定。谈判和论理是相关的，最重要的是拟定和执行决策。一阶治理是一个行动的世界，把其他层级达到的决定执行下去。这里需要用一些等级式的行政行为，也需要加上谈判和论理的方式才能达到理想的目的。

总结一下，这三阶是互相连接的、相互影响的，是一个闭环。要获得技术创新、社会创新、政治创新、城市治理创新，首先要对元治理等级达成共识。如果不能让论理的潜力释放出来，那就不可能达成任何一种形式的创新。因此，必须有约束性的决定，同时还要有执行。因为有的时候必须动员相关的资源和知识，这样我们才能对某些行动内容在更大的城市范围内予以具体的执行。

在关于治理的辩论中，我们想提出这样一个问题，这也是大家经常讨论的，就是关于有效执行的问题。也就是说是不是能达到你想要的效果？要把其他参与者的动机考虑进去，要确保他们愿意一致行动，同时，还要动员他们的知识和资源。在元治理层面和在执行层面达成一致同样重要。如果你不能解决社会可治理性这个关键层面的问题，你就不可能创新。这对国家、政治系统来说，都是非常正确的。如果一个国家不能形成一种开放的局面，不能开放地对一些想法进行公开的辩论，那么就不可能带来新想法、新视角以及创新。刚才我们讲到了，一定要有沟通的空间，还要通过论理、谈判达成共识，然后才能进行到执行的层面。要让行为人心甘情愿地执行所达成的共识。

从首尔市政府电子参与系统看市民参与的治理

崔兴硕

韩国高丽大学教授、韩国公共管理学会会长

今天我们讨论大都会治理和全球化治理，这里面有一个全球等级体系的概念。在国家层面上有一个城市等级体系，那么在全球层面上也有一个全球城市等级体系。在这些全球城市中，公司总部、国际金融、全球交通和通信、高端商务服务业等功能正在推动整个城市的发展。这同样发生在上海和首尔。

1. 亚洲金融危机后首尔市治理转型的压力增大

1997 年，亚洲金融危机之后，首尔市在全球城市等级中进行了重新的定位，这是一轮面向全球的第二次开放。首尔从 1997 年开始发生的重大变化已不能只用国内的因素来解释，而要用全球的变量来解释。在全球城市等级中，纽约、伦敦、东京等中心城市被视为命令和控制的最高等级。但是，我个人认为，东京不在这个等级。首尔、香港、新加坡、上海、北京等都是区域性大都市，它们之间的竞争越来越普遍。很多学者提出假设，比如微软在新加坡有亚洲总部，有人想让一个分支机构从新加坡搬到首尔，总部就要讨论，员工的孩子在新加坡能上很好的国际学校，那在首尔能不能上到很好的国际学校？因此，这些大都市之间都在进行竞争。全新的城市功能推动了城市的发展，但同时也对城市治理构成了很多压力。在首尔，很明显可以看到一些重大的变化，对首尔大都会的治理形成了压力。

在首尔，还出现了分极化。很多人失去了工作。一些好工作漂移到其他国家了，比如越南、泰国。一些高工资的工作岗位正在增加，他们的年薪可能是数百万。同时，一些低端的服务行业岗位也在增加。还有跨国的资本主义阶层，他们特别喜欢顺畅的、功能性的、全球性的系统集聚，他们崇尚消费主义，和本地的阶层存在一些冲突。从首尔治理的角度来看，有两任市长对首尔的全球化发展有重要影响。朴元淳市长更多关注的是增长管理，就是必须对增长进行控制，比如新的城镇发展、老城区的重建。在城市区域，过去可能有10 000户，在再开发之后只有6 000户，其余的4 000户需要在首尔城的外部找到居住的地方。目前的市长不喜欢这样做，取消了很多这样的项目。由于全球化带来的压力，当然冲突管理也是需要的。就像上午我听到的上海发展的介绍，上海其实也需要应对这样一些治理方面的压力。首尔市政府想做更多的工作。当然，他们正在重新选举，同时也在促进发展。他们希望获得良好的声誉并和市民建立很好的关系。

2. 开发电子参与系统来改善治理

我今天要讲的一个案例就是"世代绿洲"（Sangsang Oasis）——市民电子参与机制，另一个案例——首尔的大山呼叫中心可能没有时间介绍。我们有好几个类似的举措，来改善市长或者市政府和首尔市民之间的关系。现在首尔房价出现两极分化，江南区的房价是均价的2倍，与最便宜地区的房价相差2倍以上。有人开心，有人不开心，我们必须应对这些不开心的情况。

下面我具体讲讲这个电子参与举措的有关内容。电子参与和传统的线下政治参与有什么区别？这是"世代绿洲"的屏幕截图（图1），非常漂亮。图中照片是目前的市长，他想与更多市民建立联系，想让市民觉得他

图1
"世代绿洲"屏幕截图

是非常友好的。

然而，这是一个过程。市民会提出一些提议或者他们想做什么，然后会有一个市民初步的投票，之后举行官方会议，再通过一个市长参加的大型会议进行选择。这就是市民提议和参与的机制。下面是市民电子参与的流程图（图2）。

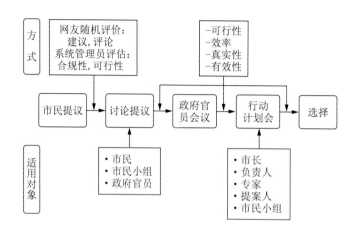

图2
市民电子参与流程图

基于线上参与可作些调研，我们使用很多数据，里面包含样本的特征。我觉得这个分布比较能代表首尔的情况。这是他们使用这个系统的方式，比如说，他们会提出一些建议、评估别人的意见或者浏览别人的意见等。这里有一些组群的分析，包括线上参与、线下参与两个维度；分四个不同的组群，第一组群是线上线下都非常不积极，第二组群只有在线上非常活跃，第三组群在线上线下都非常活跃，第四组群只在线下是活跃的。当然，也会有一些群体的差异，比如说他们对城市发展的知识，还有对城市情况的了解，对城市的信任度、年龄、受教育程度以及职业、收入都会有一个相关性。

当然，我在探索这些分析的现实意义。第一组，不活跃的市民组群，他们对城市的情况不是很了解，对反腐败的举措持怀疑态度，对城市信任度比较低，也比其他组群年轻。最活跃的组群，通常他们非常了解城市的情况，有非常高的信任度。只在线上非常活跃的组群，知识情况非常好，了解城市，也比较积极，相对而言他们对城市的信任度更高，平均年龄会比线下的活跃组群大一些，也会有更多的白领人群。线上活跃的人群、仅在线下活跃的人群、线上线下都不活跃的人群，他们之间有些不一样。

对这些组群内部的研究讨论，主要有四个预测模式。不同组群市民的线上参与，和不同的变量相关。从线下活跃的和大多数不活跃的市民来看，他们的年龄变量和在线上的活跃度相关。但是对其他的市民组群，年龄不是非常重要的影响因素。

　　总而言之，电子参与系统为市民参与提供了另外的渠道。电子参与系统其实和线下参与是一样的，可以让不同类型的人群参与。我和我学生的文章写到，这可以减少偏见、减少官僚政治。某种程度上，线上参与和线下参与是类似的，对那些最活跃的组群是互补的效果，对那些线下活跃的组群也有补充性的影响。这就在线下和线上参与之间建立了某种联系。像市民的满意度测评、对政府的了解程度和评价意见、甚至信任等线下参与方式和结果，可能会影响到线上参与的方式和结果。

城市治理绩效评估创新

史蒂芬·卡尔曼
哈佛大学肯尼迪政府学院教授

　　我向大家介绍一下美国城市绩效测量。绩效测量在美国政府所有层级都会使用到，但主要应用在美国城市评估方面。说到绩效评估，你们对政府方面的使用可能不熟悉。这是一套测量指标，通常来说是数字，但不一定是数字，可以看到一个机构给公众提供价值的水平。在中国和美国，最常见的政府绩效测量指标就是 GDP 增长率、空气污染指数，还有急性食物中毒时送医院的就诊人数、癌症死亡率，等等。

1. 美国城市绩效评估的背景

　　城市绩效评估的背景是美国城市复兴。经过几十年的城市人口下滑，美国很多人迁移出去，城市没有什么发展，很多美国城市在 20 世纪 90 年代开始出现复兴。图 1 是 20 世纪 80 年代初的时代广场，有色情电影院、色情书店。今天的时代广场是图 2 这个样子。通常来说有非常多的人，但因为下雨，这张照片里人少一点。还有另外一张照片，是 80 年代初的曼

图 1
20 世纪 80 年代初美国的时代广场

图 2
现在的美国时代广场

图 3
20 世纪 80 年代初的曼哈顿

图 4
现在的曼哈顿

哈顿（图 3），以前有条铁路线，把肉从西部运到纽约市来，还有一些肉联厂，这周边除了铁路线，什么都没有。而现在（图 4），曼哈顿已经成为纽约主要游客观赏地。我有一个 NGO 的朋友，她告诉我，夏季的每个周末，她就会到曼哈顿高线公园去读书。这是美国城市的故事。

城市也是美国政府管理创新的核心载体。这是我在肯尼迪学院的同事写的两本书，是关于美国的城市如何改善管理和治理的。

图 5
两本书的封面

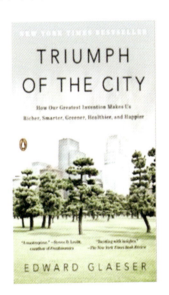

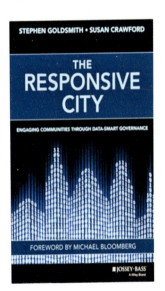

大家可能听说过迈克尔·布隆伯格，他是亿万富翁，通过将信息技术应用到金融服务业赚了很多钱，有些产品也卖到了中国；后来成为了纽约市长。他通过慈善活动，想寻求进一步改善美国城市治理创新方面的绩效表现，用他们的方法论改善美国城市的管理和治理方法。进而挑出一些典范城市，让其他城市向这些典范城市学习。他还发起市长挑战，挑战美国

其他城市的市长，建立各种各样的城市治理改善机制。

2. 美国城市绩效评估的特点

说起绩效指标，它很大程度上为美国城市的复兴带来了推动作用。大家对高质量公共服务的要求越来越高了。我们现在讲美国城市绩效测量的特点。第一，与公职人员的升迁决策不挂钩。第二，这个测量不是讲 GDP 的增长，而是犯罪、社会、健康、环境方面的测量方法。这是纽约城的一个评估方法，包括犯罪、健康、基本服务、教育、基础设施，根本不提 GDP 的增长。评估这些官员的时候，一般不会和更高级的官员沟通，而是向下跟下级官员积极沟通，改善他们部门的绩效。还有就是透明度，美国很多城市都在网上公布了绩效的测量方法，包括绩效是否达到了目标。

图 6 是纽约的年度绩效考评情况，可以看到整体犯罪率和不同类型的

2016 财年绩效

服务 1 管理与犯罪活动有关的公共安全计划
目标 1a 降低犯罪率

纽约市警察局正在实施新的社区警务模式。缩减了特种部队，提供更多的巡逻人员，这样警官有时间和自由更多地与社区成员会面，并与他们合作，查明反复出现的问题，并努力解决他们发现的问题。巡逻人员与当地社区论坛紧密合作，就特定群体面临的最关键的问题和犯罪类型达成共识，以有效确定并调整警察行动的优先顺序。

与 2015 财年相比，2016 财年期间的重大犯罪总犯罪率增加了不到 2%。与 2015 财年相比，2016 财年谋杀案减少了 2%。与 2015 财年相比，城市公立学校的重罪犯罪率下降了 13%。

基于联邦调查局城市犯罪总指数统计半年度数据（已汇入 2015 年日历），纽约市依然是美国 10 个最大城市中人均犯罪率最低，最安全的大城市。

绩效指标	年度					目标		期望趋势	5年趋势
	FY12	FY13	FY14	FY15	FY16	FY16	FY17		
★ 重大犯罪	109,299	110,099	110,023	103,872	105,614	⇩	⇩	下降	持平
★ - 谋杀和非故意杀人罪	474	369	320	348	341	⇩	⇩	下降	持平
★ - 强奸	1,098	1,196	1,064	1,064	1,164	⇩	⇩	下降	持平
★ - 抢劫	20,291	19,319	18,208	16,428	16,670	⇩	⇩	下降	下降
★ - 严重人身攻击	18,762	19,616	20,517	19,544	20,877	⇩	⇩	下降	持平
★ - 盗窃	19,162	18,360	17,140	15,828	14,463	⇩	⇩	下降	下降
★ - 重大盗窃	40,642	43,622	45,238	43,112	45,164	⇩	⇩	下降	下降
★ - 盗窃汽车	8,870	7,615	7,536	7,548	6,935	⇩	⇩	下降	下降
★ 房地产业的重大犯罪	4,771	5,018	5,328	4,858	5,205	⇩	⇩	下降	持平
★ 交通系统中的重大犯罪	2,741	2,535	2,488	2,283	2,520	⇩	⇩	下降	下降
与家庭暴力相关的犯罪 - 谋杀	75	71	56	61	53	•	•	下降	下降
- 强奸	535	464	471	481	526	•	•	下降	持平
- 严重人身攻击	6,781	7,420	8,335	7,771	7,986	•	•	下降	上升
★ 学校安全 - 重大重罪	812	699	654	614	532	⇩	⇩	下降	下降
- 谋杀	0	0	1	0	0	•	•	下降	持平
- 强奸	5	4	2	6	2	•	•	下降	下降
- 抢劫	148	106	94	55	66	•	•	下降	下降
- 严重人身攻击	250	200	172	176	148	•	•	下降	下降
- 盗窃	81	81	53	51	33	•	•	下降	下降
- 重大盗窃	326	305	331	325	279	•	•	下降	持平
- 盗窃汽车	2	3	1	1	4	•	•	下降	上升
学校安全 - 其他犯罪类别	3,295	2,626	2,485	2,286	2,219	•	•	下降	下降
- 其他事故	5,365	4,350	3,811	3,975	4,092	•	•	下降	下降
帮派动机事件	310	264	225	328	349	•	•	持平	下降
枪支逮捕	5,835	5,581	4,776	4,776	5,194	•	•	持平	下降
重罪逮捕	NA	40,258	42,444	41,599	43,516	•	•	持平	NA
毒品逮捕	99,344	81,737	75,389	61,007	56,320	•	•	持平	下降
青少年重罪逮捕	3,450	3,016	2,883	2,671	2,495	•	•	持平	下降

★ 关键指标 "NA" - 表示不可用于本报告中   ⇩• 表示期望趋势

第60页 | 市长管理报告

图 6
纽约的年度绩效考评

犯罪情况，比如抢劫、杀人。还有过去五年数字的比较，目标是多少，数字是往下走还是往上走，什么方面没有改善，什么方面更糟糕了。即便没有什么改善，也要跟公众分享相关信息。

3. 美国城市如何利用绩效评估来改进管理和治理

接下来我讲一下城市如何使用绩效评估方法，把它当成一种管理工具来改善绩效。一般用三种方法：一是激励，二是聚焦，三是学习。我会一一简单介绍。

首先，激励。你给员工设立一个明确的绩效目标，而不仅仅是说"要全力以赴"。很多证据表明，设立明确目标可以显著提高绩效。社会科学有近百种研究都表明，绩效衡量法是很有效的激励员工的方法。甚至没有金钱的鼓励，也能让员工有很好的绩效改善。

其次，聚焦。就是每个员工每天有很多工作要做，我们用绩效评估告诉员工，要把重点放在这个工作上，而不是放在那个工作上，这就是聚焦。一般来说每件事都很重要，就没有什么事是重要的。要聚焦，要挑几个重要的事做，不然没有什么事对你来说是重要的。还有，一般来说有了测量，才会有成绩，有了评估之后才会有成功的概率。

最后，就是鼓励学习来改进绩效。测量本身就是一种反馈。这是一种循环，首先要测量绩效，这是第一阶段，看做得怎么样。接下来就是发现你想做好而结果没有做好。第二阶段就要找到问题在哪里，然后进行一些改善。比如找到问题，尝试着改变，然后形成一个闭环，进行再次测量。一开始是测量，最后也是测量，中间做一些改变，这样我们才能慢慢改善绩效。我们用绩效评估来让大家通过学习去改善。假设你想学习如何投飞镖，得有一个具体的目标。如果不知道目标在哪，那工作就很难做。首先要知道飞镖可能会落在哪里，这样才能知道接下来该做什么，从而改变绩效。

总结一下。我们这些技巧如何帮助改善结果？使用绩效考量，我们就能激励员工，让他们工作更努力，这样他们就能达到目标。另外，聚焦就能让大家做正确的事。用绩效评估让大家学习，可以让大家用正确的方法做事情。聚焦是做正确的事情，这是两个不同的概念。学习是用正确的方式做事情，让我们的工作变得更聪明，鼓励让大家工作更努力。

下面转到城市要用制度性方法来改善绩效。过去十年中，我同事写了一本书，也就是我们所说的绩效表。很多城市管理者都和他们的上级、下属定时开会，评估绩效结果，讨论什么地方做得好、什么地方做得不好，什么地方可以进一步改善，很多城市已经建立了这种机制。这就是所谓的绩效测量表会议。美国有大量的城市在使用这种方法。纽约是最先开始用这种方法的城市。警察也参与其中，比如犯罪率什么地方上升了、什么地方下降了。在上世纪90年代抢劫率占第七名，使用了这种机制之后，抢劫率下降成为了美国的第二十四位，得到了很大的改善。

此外，还有洛杉矶的会议机制。官员坐在会议室里讨论垃圾清运问题，这是他们使用的一些图表、数据（图7），可以看到洛杉矶某个区的街道清洁工作。绿色的区域是做得还不错的，红色的是做得不好的，这都有一系列的打分方法。看这些数据，就可以提出建议，说这方面可以做得更好一点，然后定出下一步的策略，这是非常实用的一种方法。

图7
洛杉矶第9议会区清洁数据信息

专家点评

蓝志勇（清华大学公共管理学院教授）：鲁迪格·阿伦德教授谈论了非常重要的话题，现在城市发展特别快，我们大都市的发展已经处于全球首位。那我们对城市如何进行划分？这是很不容易的。这有助于协调它们之间的功能和合作，以及在不同的区域之间缩小贫富差距。鲁迪格·阿伦德先生告诉我们，行政的边界不那么重要，对中国来说，这个经验非常重要。美国之前也是努力整合城市区域之间的合作，修建了很多公路。对美国来说，他们也要建立一种机制，分享税收。就像自豪感一样，像上海是这个区域中最大的城市，相对来说就比较容易牵头。但在京津冀地区则不同，北京之外还有天津等其他的大城市，协调起来的工作量就比较大。最重要的一点，不能单纯只靠行政指令，而要让这些城市通过市场化的方式来协调合作。钱是一个很重要的因素，另外一个就是谁牵头。

休伯特·海纳特教授讨论了治理的方法。协调机制，一个是等级的，另外一个是市场的，还有谈判的，也有通过宗教的方式进行说服。今天提到谈判和论理，其实更多的是后现代思维方式和内容。在谈判和论理过程中，还是有些人会比其他人在谈判力方面更弱势，实际平等的情况并不是特别理想。即使在城市之间互相竞争的情况下，我们必须解决这个问题。领导力也是一个问题，如何确保指令是得到服从的，要有持续性的等级性。另外，要有一个底线，如果不听，要么会给你指令，要么采取其他的措施。所以在谈判方面，也应该有个底线。

崔教授的发言非常有意思，是一个非常实验性的研究，介绍了市民的电子参与。我们看到电子参与其实可以成为一个真正的都市治理的渠道，他还提到了方便使用的关键性。我去过很多城市，其实他们不太喜欢使用非常复杂的技术，更多使用社交媒体。这是非常重要的一个设施。在美国他们会说唯一的一个技术就是微信，微信是唯一可能影响到美国高科技的一个威胁，因为它有非常高度的结合，结合推特、脸书这些功能，所以不需要很多其他的应用。

卡尔曼教授提到绩效测量，我觉得这个非常有意思。对我来说，这是一个非常不一样的角度。我其实也参与到了很多政府的绩效评估工作中，我也在市长办公室工作过。首先我非常喜欢您说的美国城市复兴的那一段，非常有意思，我也很想了解，这些美国城市复兴背后的原因到底是什么？通过市政的改革之后，应该可以让城市有很好的发展。另外我们看到一些城市，应该也会有不同的增长。所以我很想知道，为什么上世纪80年代美国的一些城市有重新发展的动力？我看到洛杉矶和凤凰城从90年代开始，增长达到30%，对绩效测量真正的推动力是1991年，就是戈尔出版《国家发展评估》。他提到促进绩效测量的主要因素是政治方面的因素，也许一部分是运营方面的原因，他们希望国会或者政府来证明绩效测量的原因。另外，他想展示出传统的官僚机制其实是做得不错的，想用这种方式激励人们更好地工作。所以绩效测量在城市的应用，在联邦政府采用绩效测量之前，其实很早就开始了。凤凰城60年代就已经开始了，他们有非常好、非常细化的方式来评估每个工作人员的绩效。不仅仅是简单的一个服务，而是将所有的绩效和年终的薪水相结合。比如说，有一个5%的绩效工资，管理人员可以决定3%—8%的区别。其实我也参与到了这个工作中。在凤凰城，他们用到了城市中，很多人都想学习凤凰城的经验。他们是绩效和工资相结合的。

除此之外，我也看到了一些照片，因为我也在警察部门工作过。我看到一个学生的数据，运作了很长时间，但并没有运用到这些数据，因为他们没有足够的科技来提取这些数据进行分析。所以我觉得这就是为什么很多年以来，他们并没有使用这些数据进行评估的原因。第二点就是进行评估之后，在很多部门，甚至很多城市，雇用很多高水平的分析师进行绩效测量。他们必须付非常高的工资，也许比平均工资高15%。有的时候甚至花很长时间来进行绩效测量，甚至出现马鞍比马还贵的情况。这些问题如何解决？我觉得这也是值得讨论的。

休伯特·海纳特：我觉得您说得非常对，就是谈判和论理可能有不平等的危险。说到政治或机构的设计，我们应该更好地支持平等性，支持弱势人群。他们表达的时候可能会比较弱势，或者没有足够的资源进行谈判，我们要支持这些人。我们有很多例子。我自己也参与到了德国市政的工作中，也看到了不平等的情况。比如，要提供机会给受过高等教育的人工作机会，或者更多政治参与的机会。另外一个就是等级。

其实，我们需要一个结合、一个混合。通常来说，取决于你要怎样的综合性，等级肯定是要在的，等级会有一定的帮助，它可以帮助我们达成共识，如果没有办法及时达成共识，那我就做这个决定，其实还是有必要的。

另外就是公众的力量。通过谈判、论理的方式，这个应该在公开的场合来开展。这和自私也有一些关系。所以，如何激活不同的治理方式的潜力，如何更好地进行政治和机构的设计，这是非常重要的。

史蒂芬·卡尔曼：为什么这些城市会复兴？我不是城市方面的专家，但是我可以给一个假设。前面提到很多城市人口在下滑，很多人都在离开，政府想阻止下滑，其实这是他们工作的一个方面。我假设，因为这些城市下滑得太多了，所有价格都很低了，几乎已经崩溃了。很多城市有非常漂亮的老房子，有近百年的历史，突然之间情况非常糟糕，所以在20世纪70年代初，有一个都市先锋运动，这些都是非常专业、接受了良好教育的人士，他们可以免费获得这些房子，所以他们开始慢慢回来、开始重建，然后城市就慢慢复兴起来。我的猜想是城市已经下滑到最低点，东西都很便宜，这就很吸引人搬过来，然后城市就可以逐渐自给自足了。另外，文化可能也发生了变化，这些年轻人进入城市以后，非常喜欢城市。这是我的一个猜测。

说到绩效评估，最早的时候，甚至赫伯·西蒙1930年就写了一篇文章，是关于绩效评估的。刚才提到凤凰城，这是一个比较小的城市，现在慢慢向主流城市靠拢。

互动对话

主持人： 今天我们想听到来自不同的利益相关者的不同声音。我想问一个问题，阿伦德先生，您刚才讲到用 GDP 作为衡量经济绩效的指标，为什么？

鲁迪格·阿伦德： 我们有很多数据，要看很多其他的变量。对政策制定者，如果你告诉他们生产率降低了，那他们可能只会一直讲治理，但如果告诉他们数字，说生产率降低了 60%，他可能马上就注意了。这是我们希望 OECD 的政治家们注意到的方面。当然 GDP 不是唯一的指标，我们有一些评估的指标，也有相关的结果。这能提醒他们注意。

提问者： 我想请问史蒂芬·卡尔曼教授，刚才您讲到纽约犯罪率的下降，分成不同的方面。我很惊讶第一次详细地看到这些数据，请给我们描述一下，政府如何使用这些数据，为了改善自己的绩效，怎样使用数据来预防犯罪。

史蒂芬·卡尔曼： 我想他们使用数据是想知道怎么改善。请看这张表，有分成 15 种犯罪类别，各个类别的犯罪趋势有上有下，如何比较他们的目标呢？比如说杀人犯，两年前美国纽约时报报道，纽约的犯罪率从这个绩效评估机制开始之后，下降了 80%。现在的犯罪率是上世纪 90 年代的 1/5。也就是说，如果纽约的犯罪率还像上世纪 90 年代那样高，每年纽约会有 400 个人遇害，正因为实施了绩效评估，这 400 个人都得以幸存。这是一种戏剧性的变化。纽约时报说，谋杀率下降意味着杀人犯在减少。警察就在想这是如何发生的。现在纽约警察对每一起谋杀案进行分析，发生在哪里，属于哪种类型。掌握是什么造成了犯罪事件，用数据分析出一些预防措施，从而进一步降低犯罪率。用习语来表达绩效评估，就像在潜水，潜到最深处找到根源，这就是纽约和其他城市所做的事情。他们有原始数据，但是他们没有停留在原始数据。他们在做"深潜"，试图了解原始数据背后的信息，然后草拟路线图，如何使自己的工作做得更好。

大都市区发展中的城市合作：以京津冀为例

蓝志勇

清华大学公共管理学院教授

上海是一个非常大的大都市。很幸运，因为她是这个区域唯一的大城市，所以不会有很大的问题，因为大家都围着她转。但是北京的情况就不一样。这就是我今天要讲的，包括城市群和城市间合作的需求。另外，讲讲国家战略，提提目前的一些情况、背景和问题，以及未来的挑战和战略。

1. 什么是城市群

我们说的城市群或城市带、城市区域，主要是指相毗邻的城市的空间结合。非常有意思的就是亚洲很多城市人口非常多，所以城市的特征就是人口非常多，以及住房非常密，尤其是中国。18 世纪之前，世界上有一半的人口住在亚洲。现在这个趋势正在回来。

现在中国有 11 个城市群，最大的城市群，包括珠三角、长三角和京津冀，还有其他一些城市群。珠三角的特征比较有意思，因为它是和香港、澳门跨境的一个区域。长三角城市群里，上海最大，南京、杭州比较远一点。京津冀情况比较特殊。

美国波士顿–华盛顿大都市区主要有 5 个大城市，包括波士顿、纽约、费城、巴尔迪摩和华盛顿特区，还有 40 个中小级的城市。这里是美国密度最高、人口最多的区域。还有芝加哥–匹兹堡、圣地亚哥–旧金山占美国超过一半的 GDP，其中圣地亚哥–旧金山占美国经济的 21%。

这也是我的一个猜测，可能是中国的工业化还没有达到这个水平。中国的工业化如果完成，我相信很多的经济活动和金融活动也会像美国那样集中。中国的城市群在接下来会越来越重要。

2. 京津冀区域协同发展是国家战略

中央政府希望京津冀三个行政区域有很好的协调和合力，也就是说，非首都核心功能的行业、产业和人口都可以调出北京，而让河北接纳这些人口。北京如果把非首都核心功能挪到河北，河北是很高兴的。天津也正在等待，它本身就是枢纽，而且有自己的行业优势和金融中心，很久以来都是独立城市。因此天津不愿意和北京合作，不愿意成为二级城市。北京行政中心现在已经搬到通州，通州要进一步明确自己的城市功能，比如是为北京提供服务，还是成为北京本地的行政中心？三个区域的协调由谁做？目前并没有一个答案。他们一直在讨论，每个地方的意见都不一样。

这是协同发展的一个背景，天津经济实力急速上升，和北京形成了竞争。北京因为可持续发展要求越来越高，很多产业搬出去了，但不想搬到天津，想搬到河北，这样北京可以管理。这样一来就把所有问题转移到河北，北京还是中心，而且也有很好的收入。河北说，你得给我钱，我才能接纳这些工业，而且很多工厂搬到河北，成为了污染源。北京把这些工厂管理得很好，但一旦搬离北京，就没有办法管理了，污染物还是会飘到北京去。因此把问题挪到其他地方，问题也会失控。河北的问题如果越来越多，这些问题还是会回到北京。北京目前协调非常积极，想付出行动。天津在观望，不知道自己从中能获益多少。河北也在等待支持。

这是一个国家战略，大家讲城市规划、战略规划，目前中央政府也制定了计划，核心就是要疏散北京的一些非首都功能，推动北京生态环境保护、产业升级转移等。未来要对城市功能进行更加清楚的定位，未来北京还是全国的政治中心、文化中心、国际交往中心，天津会成为全国的一个先进制造研发基地、北方国际航运核心区，而河北是一个重要的物流基地等。北京很大，是超大城市，有自己的金融中心。现在想把天津作为金融中心，那么北京原来的金融街怎么办？还有河北唐山，也是一个现代城市，有非常好的港口区和行业。要推动天津的发展，那河北怎么办？说到这些超大城市，最好是自然而然形成自己的功能，而不是说强制推行特定功能。有了这些规划，我们还是不能解决很多问题，很多基础设施还是在原地，如果不把这些问题解决，这些规划恐怕没有什么用。

3. 协同治理是京津冀协同发展的核心

大家可能会觉得这是一个规划问题，其实有很多管理和治理问题没有解决。这个过程中，谁应该做规划？中央政府已经迈出了第一步，北京想成为领头羊，而天津不服气。这就又回到我们治理的原则，就是层级应该怎么安排，最重要的一点，谁应该是领头羊，基础设施投资来自哪里，成本怎么分担，收入、发展利益该怎么分配？这些问题应该怎么解决？目前多数的重点是放在技术层面，比如建桥、盖楼、交通。最终这些区域到底应该做什么？应该怎么安排？功能的重要性该怎么排序？这些问题都没有解决。城市区域需要有综合的投资平台，目前并没有这样一个平台，中央政府给了一些钱，这些城市在犹豫，不想做自己这份投资。

有一个新理论，叫做综合城市化，就是说让大的都市区建立一个高速的交通系统。我想他们可以考虑这一点。这样就会有连接性、混合性和可穿透性。

法国城市合作机制

叶必丰

上海交通大学法学院教授

我关注的是中国的城市群建设。这就需要跟踪一个国家。以前，我跟踪过美国，但后来发现，法国国家结构跟我们更接近。所以我跟踪法国。2016 年 5 月份我去巴黎、勒芒两个城市做了访问，今天我要报告的就是关于这个访问的中国式观察和从法律角度的观察。

1. 法国行政观念正在变革

从原来的统治、管理到治理这样的一个发展过程，现在更多地强调多方参与的治理。从观念上讲，统治更注重和强调的是等级、阶级、社会的对立。有暴力和专政，没有法制的贯彻，仅仅关心的是政权以及政权私有化的观念。当时法兰西封建时期，国王仅仅关注政权是不是稳定，对公法上的事情比较关心，对私法很少加以关注。后来近代发展到公共权利为特征的管理，强调的是秩序行政、守夜政府，强调公共权力，近代意义上的法制得到了发展。但还是一种消极的人权，公权和人权仍然对立。后期发展到公共服务为特征的公务理论，强调积极行政、福利国家，强调公共服务，现代意义上的公法得到了发展。我们国家也讲社会和谐，但是法国 19世纪末团体主义兴起时，就是我们今天所讲的社会和谐的问题。

20 世纪 80 年代开始到本世纪初，法国对国家行政体制进行了一系列的改革，旨在实现国家治理体系和治理能力的现代化。在这一系列的改革中，最主要的内容是四个方面：第一是国家结构现代化，尤其强调了城市的自治；第二是强调简化行政程序，改善与被管理者、被治理者之间的关系；第三是公务管理的现代化，尤其是电子数据化；第四是国家股东制，为此专门建立了公众参与办事处。

2. 法国城市合作的路径

关于城市群建设的路径，基本有两条：一是层级的路径，包括传统的命令性的城市群建设路径和 20 世纪 80 年代以来形成的非命令性的城市群建设路径；另一种是平行的路径，就是城市之间相互合作。我这里所关注的，是城市相互间的合作，也就是平行路径上的城市群建设方案。目前，法国的城市合作有三种模式：第一种，城市联盟；第二种，城市合作区；第三种，专项合作。

第一种形式是城市联盟。城市联盟是一种实体性的城市群组织模式，主要适用于中等城市与周边小城镇之间的一种城市群建设。这种模式是以人口密集的中等城市为中心，把周围分散的城镇联合起来，构成一种卫星城。

由于历史上的原因，在 6 600 万人口的法国国土上分布着大约 3.6 万多个城镇，是欧洲之最。其中有的城市人口很多，在 2 500 万左右，也有只有几百人的小镇，还有比较大的城市。众多的小城镇同样需要良好的交通、教育、科技和卫生等公共服务，但是自身无法得到满足或解决。而中等城市又需要发展，需要实现对周边的辐射，所以 1971 年法国政府曾经尝试对城市进行合并。但遭到了强烈的反对，大量市民进行游行示威抗议等等，认为这破坏了历史和文化的延续。然后法国转而进行城市的联盟建设。目前法国共有 13 811 个市镇结成了 1 241 个城市联盟。

城市联盟不是国家强制，而是各城市自愿组成。加盟的城市要将部分的税收权、规划权、公共网络服务建设经营权、工业小区的开发权等移交给城市联盟。城市联盟还依法享有向所有加盟城市辖区内企业征收特别税的权利。城市联盟的财政收入如果有盈余，原则上还应按人口比例，对各加盟城市进行分配，当然还应参照经济的发展状况。各城市仍然独立存在，负责公共福利事业。城市联盟设有自己的管理机构，行使上述权力，负责运营。管理机构领导层为联盟委员会，设有主席 1 人，委员若干人，均为加盟城市市长。但并非每个城市的市长都能成为委员，那些人口非常少的城市市长不能参加到委员会。他们需要以会议形式工作，只有一致同意才能通过，有反对票，就由投票委员所在的城镇全体公民公决。管理委员会还设有若干个工作机构。这是城市合作的一种形式。

第二种形式就是城市合作区。城市合作区是一种紧密型的城市群组织形式，适用于大城市间的协同建设和发展。著名的有大巴黎区，还有马赛、里尔、南特和波尔多等大城市。法国的城市不像我们国家有行政级别，只有大小之分，没有行政级别的高低，因而没有互相的隶属关系。法国的城市也与法国的大区和省不一样，大区和省代表中央，城市代表地方，大区和省是在各地代表中央的监管区，行政首长由中央任命；而城市因为是地方共同体，市长是选举的。同时城市与省、大区都有明确的权限分工，比如小学属于城市事务，中学属于省的事务，大学属于大区事务。对城市规划建设也分工明确，因此不仅小城镇，大城市的发展建设，都需要通过合作实现，不是通过隶属关系就能实现的。

城市合作区设有市长联席会议，市长联席会议由各合作城市市长组成，选举其中一名当主席。它是一个协调性机构，不具有城市联盟的职权。据现任大巴黎区主席介绍，大巴黎区市长联席会议每月举行一次，以协商一致为决策原则。基于城市间没有隶属关系，市长并非上级或中央任命，而是民选，并不存在协调中的不平等现象。这些都是我根据中国的问题去观察的。市长联席会议下设若干日常工作机构，有几十名工作人员，日常工作机构的任务是与各城市的相关部门进行反复沟通，起草各种文件，准备会议方案。城市合作区的一项重要任务，是协调城市规划与城市建设，包括城市规划编制、土地储备、城市交通管理，道路、标牌和停车场的建设和管理，以及共同建设开发区等等。

第三种是专项合作。专项合作是指通过合作协议，实现单一任务的城市合作形式。城市联盟和城市合作区都是相邻城市间的合作，专项合作不限于相邻城市，可以适用于全国甚至外国城市间的合作。合作内容可以是环境保护、文化、教育、经济发展、旅游开发等各个方面。合作协议也是一种合同，但不是民事合同，而是行政合同，目的在于实现城市政府的公共服务任务，对各城市具有法律约束力，不仅对政府具有约束力，甚至对公众也有约束力。这方面著名案例就是贝兹城案。1986年10月10日签订了无固定期限的经济合作合同，双方共同在贝兹新城建设一个经济区，约定按一定比例分配区内税收。后来贝兹新城提出1993年9月起取消合同，贝兹城向行政法院提起诉讼，要求贝兹新城赔偿380万法郎的违约金。行政法院判决合同对双方仍有约束力，双方应该继续履行。

最新的例子是里昂市政府资助阿尔及利亚某个城市修缮教堂的案件。案件的争议焦点是，原告认为里昂市政府资助一个教堂，违反了政教分离的宪法原则，但行政法院判决，这属于对文化事业的资助，回避了政教分离的宪法问题。这个案件也是非常有意思的，里昂市政府多数票通过了这个资助，而投反对票的少数政府官员到行政法院提起诉讼。尽管城市合作协议是合同，引发的纠纷可以诉诸行政法院裁判解决，但是这种情况很少发生。为了合作继续，有关纠纷多通过协商解决，达成和解协议，终结纠纷，并避免今后再次发生纠纷。

目前，京津冀、长三角、珠三角很多人都在呼吁，要有一种解决区域纠纷的法律机制、制度机制。法国有，但有了也很少用。大多数都是通过协商解决。和解协议同样是行政合同，必须合法，不能通过和解减免缔约一方法律规定的应尽责任，不能将法律禁止的内容合法化。为了合作协议的顺利履行，避免因合作协议违法而发生合作纠纷，法国法律要求大区行政首长介入城市合作协议的缔结、签署。我们民法上提到不仅合同履行时候有违约责任，而且合同缔结时也有过错责任问题。行政合同中也会存在这样的问题，所以这就要求大区行政首长介入这种行政合同的缔结来进行监督。同时，大区行政首长也可以协调各个城市的合作纠纷。

3. 法国城市合作的启示

中共十八届三中全会提出了推进国家治理体系和治理能力现代化的问题。这对我们国家是非常重要的一个问题，是我们各项改革目标的一个关键点。在这个提出以后，国务院又推出了《关于中央和地方财政事权和支出责任划分改革的指导意见》，明确了要合理划分中央和地方财政事权和支付责任的界限，要推进国家治理体系和治理能力现代化。这份文件非常重要。文件总体要求之二讲到，要最大限度减少中央对微观事务的直接管理，发挥地方政府因地制宜、加强区域内事务管理的优势，调动和保护地方干事创业的积极性和主动性。

同时，今年（2016）6 月份国家发改委颁布了《长三角城市群规划》，一共包括 26 个城市。城市群建设源于区域经济一体化和城镇化这两条线，现在已经是我国实现治理体系、治理能力现代化的重要内容，与法国的改革和城市合作有很多相同的地方。根据我国的国情，城市合作恐怕不能照搬法国的城市合作模式。通过我的观察发现，他们是城市自治，我们最多讲地方自主权、城市自主权，尽管有国务院的文件，但远远达不到城市自治的程度。在城市自治情况下，城市跟中央体系是两个体系，互补连通的。我们恐怕达不到这个要求，但还是有很多共同的地方。而且国务院的这份文件，在很多国家是议会通过的宪法性文件。目前我们是国务院的一份指导性文件。但我觉得，还是有很多可以借鉴的地方，关于协调机构、合作协议、纠纷的解决机制等等。

都会区灾害恢复的协同治理

南姆·卡朴库

美国中佛罗里达大学公共管理学院院长

我今天要讲的主题是提得比较少的"大都市地区的灾害恢复协同治理"。所有发言人都提到了大城市的安全问题，但大多数时候，要么是因为缺乏资源，要么是因为灾害很少，我们很少去投资人为灾害或自然灾害的协同治理。除非有大事件发生，通常情况下投资者、公众或个人都不会注意到灾害。我今天的演讲就侧重于开放政府的协同治理、创新或救灾作为。

1. 集体治理的内涵及在美国的应用

"集体治理"很难定义，简而言之，就是让我们的公民以整个社区为单位作好应灾准备，如果发生任何事情，他们至少可以作为公民、行业代表甚至作为整个社会的代表应对灾害带来的损失。我将简要强调美国救灾中的一些经验教训，希望对别的国家或大都市地区有所帮助。

根据我的研究，同时基于一些在美国灾害管理方面有很多经验的朋友的反馈，美国有世界上最好的灾害管理系统。在美国，佛罗里达州因其丰富经验，拥有全国最好的灾害管理系统。几年前，我们经历过几次飓风，但并没有看到很多人员伤害，有 8 人不幸遇难，但经济损失超过 250 亿美元。即使有飓风预警，我们知道了飓风的路径，但飓风造成的破坏对城市来说可能是毁灭性的。大部分的损失发生在北卡罗来纳州。

2. 美国灾害恢复的协同治理机制

我的演讲会强调协同治理和协同网络的意义，以及在应对灾害中如何实施，并举一些在美国使用的例子，其中一些是基于灾害响应和政策变化的关键问题。

大都市治理的精髓包括灾难管理、灾难协调、资源整合的综合治理。在佛罗里达大学，我们经常邀请专家进行灾难管理的主旨演讲。我经常问他们，灾难管理最关键的因素是什么，他们的答案是：协调，协调，协调。所以在协同治理中，最关键的因素就是协调。在美国我们有一些方案在地方、州、国家级别协调资源。我们学到最宝贵的经验就是建立灾难准备、反应、恢复及减灾的政策框架。每个框架都可以作为地方政府减灾应急的参考。政府必须协调资源。我会提供一些灾难应急框架的背景，以及灾后恢复的框架，后者在经济恢复、社区功能恢复上，都能反映出资源协调的重要性。

传统的灾难反应／管理有五个阶段，本来是四个阶段，"9.11"之后，我们又加入了第五级。主要是预防人为灾难如恐怖主义等。救灾、恢复、备灾、减灾是传统灾难管理的四个阶段。

前面提过佛罗里达在灾难恢复方面有最好的机制。在没有灾难的情况下，佛罗里达州的紧急指挥中心只有几个人。一般只有五个人，在他们当中，只有三个人是灾难管理专家，其他都是秘书或行政人员。设想一下，如果一个有 250 万人口的大都会地区突发灾难，这五个人该如何应对紧急情况？上海这样的大都市，一般都有报警热线，但不一定会有紧急指挥中心。我也看到有一些这方面的培训，他们非常希望能够有创新方法应对灾难，但过于依靠来自中央政府的拨款。所以关键在于，一旦发生灾难，大家该怎么做？需要做好准备，进行演习，知道资源在哪里，相关负责人在哪里，他们各自的职责是什么。在美国有句话叫做：灾难发生的时候，根本没有时间换名片。因此要确保大家在灾难发生之前就对整体情况有所了解。

图 1 是 2004 年佛罗里达州的飓风路径图，可以看到佛罗里达大学处在飓风的中心。短短四周之内发生了三次飓风袭击。在这栋建筑里是我们的应急指挥中心五人小组，这栋建筑里一共有 180 人。试想，如果飓风或其他灾难发生之前，这五个人对所有情况一无所知，飓风发生时他们也不可能知道各自的合作伙伴，以及他们的文化、对灾难的了解程度和各自的能力。无论有没有发生灾难，人与人之间的这种协调与合作都至关重要。

在过去，美国的政策、框架、组织架构、紧急指挥中心都发生了很多变化，这些变化主要是自下而上的一个机制。在美国，郡和市政府是主要

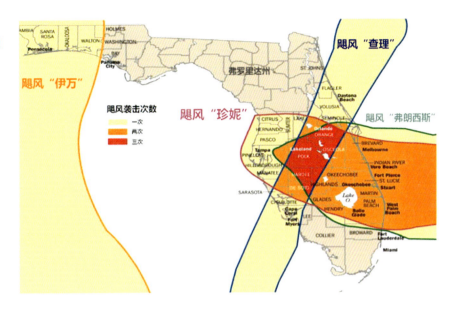

图 1
2004 年佛罗里达州
飓风路径

决策者，从法律上讲，地方政府对灾难准备和灾难响应负责。所以这是一个自下而上的体系。郡级政府做决策，州政府如果觉得有必要，就会请求联邦政府参与。但只有国会才能做决定投入几十亿甚至几百亿美元进行救灾。如果没有走这个流程，相关的应急反应预算只有几百万美元，远远不够应对任何重大灾难。但自下而上应急决策的关键在于，地方政府要达成协议，同时州级政府紧密合作，多方协调。

3. 美国灾害恢复的治理网络

我在研究发现中提到，治理网络中有一些概念十分关键，我自己也把治理网络作为一种方法论来理解灾难响应，这样做也确实行得通。最近我研究了过去 30 年发表的文献，想知道他们对治理网络中的合作是怎么定义的。我一共读了 1 800 篇文献，其中只有 30% 对合作给出了定义。如果没有对网络合作给出定义，那就不能对网络里的各项内容之间的关系做出详细描述。只有 70 篇文献使用了"治理网络"这个词组。我想强调的是网络分析是很好的方法论，希望人们可以使用网络分析的方式。这是我和我们的工程师和建筑师合作做出来的一张图（图 2）。一旦有灾难的时候，不会有这种复杂的展示，可能你都找不到灾难管理的相关负责人。在灾难发生的时候可能也找不到这些市民或者郡负责人。我们该如何调动资源、沟通协调、达成一致，以保证市民可以找到应对灾难的解决方案？比如在"9.11"非常时期就使用了非常手段，因为灾难规模太大，纽约市市长直接和总统沟通，而没有遵循通常使用的沟通机制。市长和总统之间直接联系，这样总统就可以迅速做出决策。

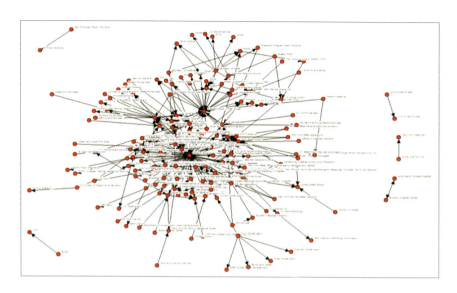

图2
9.11 响应网络

最新的研究进展是我们可以改善整个社区、市民、非政府组织以及地方政府灾难响应机制，关键在于建立一种框架，以帮助形成基于社区功能的合作网络和协同机制。对于灾难管理框架而言，不同职能部门在交通、沟通机制方面，要进行全面合作、整合资源。这也让我有机会看到灾难响应和灾后恢复的整体情况，也让我有机会评估交通和沟通在其中起的作用，有哪些可以改进的地方。还有很多可以研究和进行实践的空间。一个组织将哪一个功能视作其主要功能也会有很大不同。和组织架构图一样，人们的实际操作可能和组织架构上显示的有很大区别。比如"9.11"事件就十分强调正式和非正式的区别。在美国我对3 000多个人做了调查，问他们协作中最关键的因素是什么，85%的回答是信任，这就意味着如果你没有事先打好信任的基础，就无法在应对灾难时顺利进行协作、相互合作或发挥职能。

图3代表着大都会的社区复原韧性，可以按地理、民族或人口来定义社区。作为组织、政府实体或市民组织的组织能力都包含一些因素。我们的研究关注的是社区复原韧性，而社区能力指的则是诸如金钱和其他资源等的外部因素。在美国的联邦系统中，国家层面有联邦政府，下面有区域应急管理体系、州应急管理体系以及社区层面的组织。每个组织都有其不同的系统。这也是为什么要把注意力放在区域层面以提高协作及合作水平，因为大部分灾难都不会局限在一个地方。比如飓风袭击了地处边界的

城市或郡，这时候就需要进行区域合作。新的框架体系强调社区这个概念，同时注重发挥非政府组织的作用，帮助并维持社区的复原韧性。我认为治理网络是协作的一个重要因素，可以保证及时协调资源并传递信息，从而进一步确保良好合作和及时响应。

图 3
治理网络和社区复原
韧性

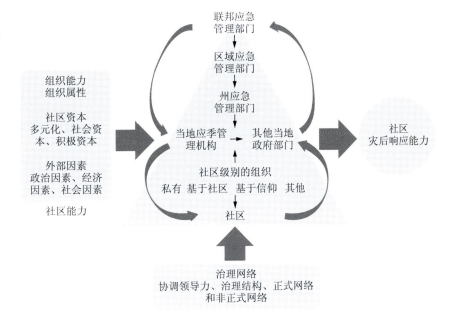

互动对话

提问者： 请问叶教授，法国的城市安全保障能力怎么样？有什么好的做法？第二，请教一下美国的南姆教授，您认为美国有哪些重要的城市安全保障方面的经验？最重要的是什么？尤其是从管理视角、政府的管理方面，有什么好的做法？城市政府官员应该加强哪方面的教育？

蓝志勇： 前不久法国出了好几个事件，恐怖分子事件，是因为市和镇分得太小了，外头人根本进不去，警察都进不去。这个问题我不知道是怎么解决的。另外请问卡朴库教授，在国土安全部建立之后，美国在应急管理方面有什么变化？

叶必丰： 法国在法律上对城市合作有哪些形式？这些法律能不能值得我们借鉴？我们立法的时候，有没有可借鉴的地方？我是做这方面的研究。当然你的问题，治安和安全保障的能力，这可能更多是公共管理方面的一项课题，这个课题我没有跟他们进行过交流。所以你的问题我也很难给你满意的回答。

这次我考察了两个地方。一个是大巴黎区，另外一个是勒芒城市联盟。所以是考察了两种形式。我还没有深入到您说的具体分得很细的安全方面的议题，比如，在紧急情况发生时，警察怎么介入的问题上。城市联盟我最关注的是地方自治。为什么关注地方自治？我们国家治理体系、治理能力现代化当中，很重要的一个问题，就是我们的地方自主权能不能跟法国的地方城市自治有借鉴的地方？法国以前也是没有地方自治的，是改革以后确立了城市的完全自治地位。我们城市要是合作，恐怕要有相应的自主权，才有合作的空间。如果说跨区域的问题都要由上级政府、中央政府解决，那城市之间的相互合作，恐怕空间非常小。

南姆·卡朴库： 第一是关于安全方面。美国应对恐怖主义、自然灾害的时候，是不是安全？当然，我们有很多变化。尤其是"9.11"和卡特里娜飓风及其他的灾害之后，我们组织结构和特定需求方面发生了变化。但是，我们肯定没有办法说做好了100%的准备，这是不可能的。我们在准备标准方面有了一些举措。我们有非常重要的机构，为州以及县做好相应的应急准备提供专业的说明，这对州和郡政府来说非常重要。在美国，联邦中心有非常棒的教育计划和应急管理的研究机构。他们为警察、消防员和每个应急管理人员提供定期的教育和培训。在应急管理系统里，只有获得一定的培训量才能晋升职务。应急管理机构也有一些线上领导力课程，包括协调、志愿者管理工作等。还有一些教育培训方面的机制，确保大家都可以做好准备。在佛罗里达，我们也有一些税收收入是直接用于灾害预备的。我们针对灾害要有一些资金方面的准备。通常来说，灾害其实给决策者和政策制定者提供了一些投资机会。

另外一个非常大的变化，就是DHS，这是针对"9.11"所创建的，这是一个非常重大的事件，这是之后国防部最大的一个机制，是美国政府非常大的一个变化，大概有差不多22个机构结合起来。还有文化等各个方面的一些区别。在DHS中有两种不同的文化，包括持枪和反对持枪的文化，这往往导致工作不太好协调。大多数是关注于预防恐怖主义的袭击。卡特里娜飓风之后，我们希望有个平衡，不仅要关注恐怖主义，还要关注自然灾害。此后的主要变化是，联邦政府不再包办一切，只给州和地方政府提供指南，地方政府则制定并实施应急管理方案。

Why Metropolitan Governance Matters: The Experience of OECD Countries

Ahrend Rudiger

Head of the Urban Programme in the OECD's Directorate for Public Governance and Territorial Development

When it refers to OECD member countries, we can find that the metropolitan governance was a subject in 1960s and then the interest went away. However, in the 1990s the interest came back again. There are a huge number of metropolitan areas and counties that have recently seen many efforts to change the metropolitan governance structure. This is happening in different countries in OECD from Australia, over Turkey, UK, France and Italy. These are all countries that have recently undertaken major reforms of metro governance structures. And what's interesting is that these reforms are very different in how exactly the countries are trying to model their systems, but for all that they are trying approaches to have the governance of the urban areas and countries work better. Why there are so many countries suddenly interested in metro governance reform? The first reason is that there is a growing understanding that administrative borders that you have in metropolitan areas are outdated and aren't working anymore. And there's also increasing evidence that fragmentation of metropolitan areas, the municipal fragmentation is really hampering the wellbeing and performance of metropolitan areas.

1. Meaning and administrative area of metropolitan areas

These two charts (fig.1) show you the Paris administration, the city of Paris, and the administrative center of Paris. In contrast for this, this is the administrative city of Rome where you see the urban administration is only a small part of it. When you have data, you typically have the data of the administrative cities. And when you compare the city of Paris with the city of Rome, what you actually do is that you are comparing 25% of the urban area which everybody lives in Rome plus a lot of empty space. It has several problems, the first problem is calculating density-the population per square kilometer, obviously the density of the two is very different. If you want to compare density, you compare either the whole city, or the administrative center, but comparing this small part with this large part is obviously nonsense. Also when you compare indicators of population, the problem is, these 25%, and not randomly, are by and large the 25% most educated and richest people in Paris. Comparing the 25% happy few in Paris with everybody in Rome and many other cities isn't very useful.

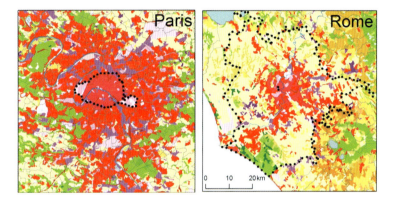

In the OECD (Fig.1) we have been calculating what we called Functional Urban Areas. The way is that we are looking at city's core to look at the minimal density, and then We're looking at commuting patterns where are the areas that people live, the way they commute each day to the city that they are working. This definition is called Functional Urban Areas, and then we can meaningfully compare the urban administration with this given definition. When you are just using administrative boundaries, whether national comparisons or international comparison, they are often not very meaningful.

And We've also been applying this definition to China, but slightly change definition because when you are doing this, you often get quite different picture of the urban structure in China. First, in functional area, population size probably increases. If we start from Beijing, the view of the urban system on the function of areas, and on the urban agglomeration is very different. If you look at that administrative data, we have already a lot more mega-cities in the world than we think. It is probably already more than 30 megacities we expect by 2030. When measuring it, we are really measuring on metropolitan areas; you will see that the world is more organized today than what we think.

2. Administrative fragmentation as an important factor or metropolitan governance

When we look at a functional area, We're looking at a whole urban area, the social, economic entity. And cities have been growing and outgrowing their historic boundaries. For example, when Napoleon took power more than 200 years ago, he did something that was really smart at the time. He found the department, or small region. And he founded them in a way that each citizen in the département in the morning get to the horse, ride to the capital and in the evening ride back. So that was the boundary of the department. That was really smart at the time, about 200 years later, we have cars, we have planes, we have still the same boundaries in France. That's also true for many cities. Many city boundaries are dating back to a long time ago when you had small cities and villages like 20, or 30 kilometers away from city which were really separate at that time. These days we have a large urban agglomeration but are still having the very often same administration structure. That's creating lots of problems. Often you need cooperation between municipalities when you do something in urban agglomeration. You don't jump in putting something undesirable directly out of the border. That's the old thing.

For example, a very large airport in a rich OECD country, so we want to get there, we try to take public transport. There is no decent public transport connecting the airport and the city center, so we're really surprised that we asked people why we don't have modern public transport system here. They would say, "Yeah, you know, it's about money." Well, it's a rich country. It really isn't money. The problem is if you really want to build public transport system here like the train, you need to get mayors who are on the way. They all need to agree. The mayors who were close to the airport would say, "my voters they don't need the train. They are close to the airport, so the train system wouldn't be employed. So I think you shouldn't do it." And that's where it stopped. That obviously may be rational from the point of view of this mayor or his voters. For the urbanization it's a disaster. Having the voting system is not very good. In another city, you take the metro, and then you go to the end of the metro line, and get out. You think you are in the middle of the city, but you don't really think why the metro line stops there. We actually find out where it stops is the administrative border of the city and it just hasn't been growing ever since. Somehow the city and the municipality haven't agreed on how to continue the metro line. There are a lot of these examples. They are really abounding. So we ask ourselves, "Are these isolated case studies? Or you are lucky and you just go to places where this problem is or these are just general problems? " So we have been collecting some data, and clenching some numbers.

When there is a high administrative fragmentation, at a given population size, the productivity actually goes down. And when you double the number of municipalities for a given population size, your productivity goes down by 6%. That means each year, you are losing 6% of your GDP. As a colleague of mine once said, "You should be really rich to be able to afford doing that." This is not just a theoretical problem, this is a problem that has very strong negative economic consequences.

And we also look at economic growth rate, in the OECD, in a less fragmented metropolitan area, their growth rate actually go up for the last ten years. Productivity is not the only problem that's created by municipality fragmentation. Municipality fragmentation also leads to undesirable social outcomes because it leads to more fragmentation. Basically it facilitates all the rich people live in one place and all the poor people live in the other place. That may not be a problem as such. But typically in these OECD countries, the areas where the people live have more social problems. There are bad schools, bad traffic and social structure which create a lot of inequality. Also in the senses that kids who are born in these areas only have the opportunity to cheaper educational level, and have a bad start in their lives.

3. Creating a big municipality is one option

What can you do about it? One possibility is that you can create a big municipality, which makes some sense. Also, you don't necessarily want all functions at metropolitan level. There are certain functions which are better at local level. You create some municipalities and transfer some functions there. But the problem that we have in many OECD countries, like I mentioned, is the political. In many countries, politicians are not going to touch it because if you don't like the idea of their mayors, when they try to do that, they will be voted out very quickly.

Another way to get around the problem is what are the functions that are really important at metropolitan level, what should not be decided at metropolitan level and then to create an situation which is actually taking care of those functions. That's what we called metropolitan authorities, or metropolitan governing bodies. The example is we create a lot of authorities. What we were trying to understand a lot of cities actually have that kind of metropolitan governing bodies. And we did a survey for the OECD, and we found that there are roughly 1/3 of the OECD metropolitan areas, they don't have any metropolitan authority. There is 2/3 who have one but a lot of them are weak one, if you have something where the mayors can meet and decide where they can be generous. And there is only less than 20% have relatively strong metropolitan governance approaches. What's interesting is that these metropolitan authorities have a lot of different parts of functions. But three functions are standing out. They do all kinds of things: improve culture, environment, and social welfare. But these three dimensions really stand out-spatial planning, transport, and regional development. Regional development is often a secondary function but spatial planning and transport are more than other metropolitan areas. These are really important core functions that are undertaken at the metro level. And it's also relatively easy to understand because there are a lot of externalities and street level functions, so it makes all sense to have these functions taken over by the metropolitan authorities.

Then we can show that these metropolitan authorities have positive impact. And we were able to show in those OECD metropolitan areas without the governance body, the density went up when there is actually sprawling. As to those with one, their density went down so there is much better spatial planning when the municipal system takes place. We also show that wellbeing increase when you have metropolitan authorities, which means better public transport system, lower level of pollution and last but not least, when it comes to productivity, we can also show that in average, the metropolitan authority reduces the externality from the fragmentation as we have been talking about earlier, reduces it by half. And we think that when you have more powerful metropolitan authorities, communication can be much larger which actually mitigate all negative effect of fragmentation.

Different Modes of Governance and their Particular Relevance for Specific Sectors of Interest Intermediation and Collaborative Urban Governance

Hubert Heinelt

Professor of Public Administration，Public Policy and Urban Research at the Institute for Political Science，TU Darmstadt

It's a pleasure for me to continue the presentation on governance in a more general sense. As the draft was quite long, I will concentrate on presenting the development of different modes of governance and their relevance for collaborative urban governance, particularly in respect to innovation. I will briefly reflect on specific approaches in the debate about governance as it is quite broad. Then I will outline different governance modes, and how they are mixed together and how the mixtures of these modes can impact on innovation.

1. The debate on the governance

I am referring to two different approaches in academic governance debate. The first one you would know is the shift "from government to governance". In my opinion, the book edited by Vincent Kauffman is very influential. It was published in 1986. It took a long time to edit the book since it started in the early 1980s. And the book was telling that we need guidance and control at that time. The authors of this book reflected on the difficulties of coordinating society's interactions in modern society. Are we really able to guide and control the activities taking place in modern society? It became clear already at that time that there was something more than the market which is coordinating individual activities. But assuming from economics, there are some externality therefore we need a state and a hierarchy intervention. But is it enough? Isn't there something else beyond the hierarchy political forms of reassuring the coordination of society interaction, bargaining and governing? I will come back to it.

The second part of this debate is about the policy network, particularly located in political science. One reflection was on the relationship between state and society, that is the old approaches of pluralisms, which includes the competition of interest groups trying to influence the state and hierarchal political interventions trying to influence society. Neo-corporatism is also included. The collaboration between interest groups as a state is intervening hierarchal in society to coordinate what's going on in societies.

In this debate, these old approaches arc too general. When you get close to these particular actor constellation and policymakers, you may ask them how to coordinate the interactive activities when disturbed. And what came out of this debate are reflections on these different modes of coordinating society interaction. We have to bargain, not in a political way, in a mild attempt to coordinate interactions. We have hierarchy based on majoritarian decisions in western democratic society.

And what is new, what is really at the heart of governance is the coordination by communicative interaction either by bargaining and arguing.

Here I think the work of John Einstein was very influential. He emphasizes that bargaining is a way of communicating. But the actors involved in this communicative interaction are sticking to their preference, to their interests. If we need to achieve an agreement, some kind of compromise has to be achieved, which is sometimes hard. But here, game theory and colleagues engaged in this debate show that it is possible that selfish actors can coordinate their activities by this mode. Arguing is different. Here actors have to be open. What is our problem? If we have a problem, maybe it's your problem, not mine. What are the perspectives of solving this problem which seem appropriate to all of us? Not only in a common sense, but in the sense we develop a common understanding about the causes, what kind of approaches can be accepted? On the one hand, selfish actors are part of the solution. On the other hand, selfish actors need to talk about common problems and agree on common objectives and common ways of solving these problems.

What is the outcome? The result is that we can find in terms of government arrangement, metropolitan government arrangement, urban governance, the use of the mixtures of these five modes to coordinate social interactions. Sometimes more market, sometimes more hierarchy, sometimes more selfish bargaining, and sometimes more open-minded arguing. One key point lies in the governing arrangement can bring about innovation, something new and some new ideas.

2. The Theory and Implementation of Second Order Governing

Here I am referring to a concept of Jan Kooiman (Fig.1), and we can also find it in the work of Elinor Ostrom. She distinguished three collective choice levels: constitutional choices, collective choices and operational choices. While Kooiman distinguished them as meta governing, second order governing and first order governing.

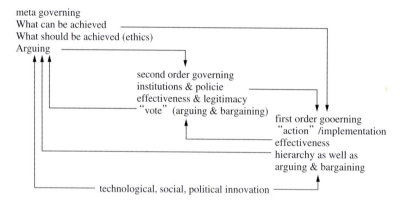

Fig.1
Innovation
and different
governing orders
(Kooiman)

What is meta governing? It's a level of interacting in which actors in a city, in an urban agglomeration, in the policy area try to agree on a specific problem definition and look for appropriate solutions to address and to solve this problem. Sense-making processes are important. It's a struggle over ideas, which concept can explain the problem from our perspective of the best way. Here you have to rely mainly on the governance mode of arguing because you cannot use hierarchal mode to decide on one specific understanding of the problem. You have to take all the other actors with you, so that you can use the dominant concept to address problems. Then is the second order, which is also called collective choices. You have to establish institutions and policies, and then take binding decisions on problems. Bargaining and arguing are relevant, and the most important part is to take and enforce specific decision. A first order governing is a world of implementation. It brings about the effects which are intended by the other levels. Here hierarchy mode, combined with the modes of bargaining and arguing, is necessary to achieve the intended goal.

To summarize, these three levels are inter-connected and interactional. They are feedback loops. And I think to achieve technological, social, political innovation, metropolitan governance innovation; first of all, we have to agree on specific concept of the meta governing. If we are not able to mobilize the potentials of the governance mode of arguing, we are in a bad position to achieve any kind of innovation. Here binding decision must be taken, together with the implement of innovation. It's important because we have to mobilize the specific resources and knowledge therefore we can make sure the implement of the program in a specific context in a bigger city range.

As for innovation and governability, in this debate about governance, I'm referring to a question we have often discussed, a question about implementation. Effective implementation is really governability that you achieve the effects you want to achieve. You need to take the motives of actors into account. You have to secure the willingness of actors to comply and you have to mobilize their knowledge. Agreement is both important at meta governing level and implementation level. If you are not able to solve this crucial aspect of social governability, you will not be able to innovate. This is true for the country and its political systems in general. If one country is not open for the struggle over ideas at meta governing level, they are not able to create new ideas, new perspectives, and innovation. As we have mentioned, a space of communication must be firstly gained. Next is the the consensus through bargaining and arguing. Then we can come to the level of implement. It's important that the actors will implement the consensus with their willingness.

Governing Thru Citizen Engagement: E-Participation in the Seoul Metropolitan Government

Choi Heungsuk

Professor, Korea University; The President-elect of the Korean
Association of Public Administration

Today, we are going to talk about governance of mega cities and globalization. As there exists the concept of the urban hierarchy at the national level, we also have a much similar concept as the global hierarchy at the global level which plays a very important role in today's lecture. Nowadays, corporate headquarters, international finance, globalized transportation system and high-level business services all contribute to the development of mega cities, as what is happening in Shanghai and Seoul.

1. Growing pressure in governance transition of Seoul after the Asian financial crisis

In 1997, after the Asian financial crisis, Seoul started on a reopening to the world by repositioning itself in the global urban hierarchy. Actually it wasn't just in Asia. In Seoul, the changes that have been made from 1997 cannot be explained by domestic factors, but global. New York, London and Tokyo are regarded as command and control centers. But I don't think these include Tokyo. Seoul, Hong Kong, Singapore, Shanghai, Beijing, etc. probably are regarded as regional cities. The thing is that they are competing; they are becoming similar. These are some hypotheses that have been suggested by several people. For example, Microsoft has their Asian Headquarters in Singapore. If some want to move a branch from Singapore to Seoul, those from Asian Headquarters will be asking questions like: can I have my kids send to the kind of international schools like these here in Seoul. These megacities are competing with each other. Although new urban functions become driving forces for city growth, they, at the same time, put more pressure on urban governance. In Seoul, changes are obvious and they lead to much pressure on urban governance.

Then we have polarization in Seoul. There is an obvious loss in decent jobs and they are flowing out to other countries like Vietnam, Thailand etc. But jobs with high annual incomes are increasing, some of which are of millions. We do not see that kind of jobs much before the financial crisis. At the same time there is a growth of low-paid jobs in the service sector. Also we have this transnational capitalist class, they want to have smooth, functional and global accumulation of systems; they advocate consumerism. They have conflicts with local classes.

In the context of Seoul governance, former two mayors realize the importance of globalization development. The incumbent president Park Won-soon is more interested in growth management, the control of growth, such as development of new cities and towns or reconstruction of old parts in cities. In cities, there may used to be 10 000 households. Yet after redevelopment, only 6 000 remain; the rest 4 000 have to find living places outside the city of Seoul. Park Won-soon doesn't like that. He has cancelled many of those projects. Thanks to pressure from globalization, conflict management is also necessary. The lecture I have heard this morning about Shanghai proves this. The municipal authorities definitely plan to do more. Now they are engaged in reelection and promoting urban development. They hope to win a good reputation and establish a close relationship with citizens.

2. Improving governance by developing Sangsang Electronic Participation System

Today, I would like to talk about Sangsang Oasis—a electronic citizen participation mechanism. Another example is the Seoul Call Center which I may not have time to introduce, but actually we have many measures like this to improve the relationship between mayor, or the municipal government and citizens in Seoul. This is about the polarization of housing prices in Seoul. The housing price in Gangnamis actually twice the average. And more than twice the price in cheapest region. Thus some people are happy, and some are not. This problem must be solved.

Then I will talk about e-participation. How is e-participation different from traditional offline political participation? This is one screen shot of Sangsang Oasis (Fig.1), quite pretty. This guy is the current mayor. He is really trying to reach out, to have people feel his friendliness.

Fig.1
One screenshot of
Sangsang Oasis

And then this is a process. Citizens make proposals. Then there will be initial vote by them. Followed by official meetings, and then a conference with the presence of the mayor. This is the mechanism proposed by citizens. This is a diagram (Fig.2).

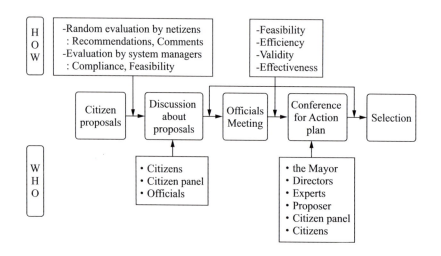

Fig.2
Process of
selecting
proposals in
Sangsang Oasis

They do researches on offline participation and use many statistics including characteristics of samples. I think it represents the situation in Seoul. These are ways that they are using the system. They use it to make suggestions, comment on ideas, evaluate other people's views, or just watch other people's opinions. For the surveyed groups, I have two dimensions, on-line participation and off-line participation. There are four groups. The first group of people are inactive in both dimensions. The second group of people are just active in online participation. The third group of people are very active on both dimensions. The last group of people are just active offline. Of course, differences between groups cannot be avoided, such as people's knowledge about this city, its development, their level of trust in this city, their ages, education level, occupations and incomes.

Surely, I am going to find practical meanings of this research. Citizens in the inactive group, the first group, they are less informed. They are skeptical about government's anti-corruption action and have a low sense of trust in city. They are the youngest of course. The most active group is well aware of this city and put much trust in it. Those only active in online participation are well informed, knowing the city very much, relatively more active and having more trust for this city. Their average age is slightly older than that of the fourth group and this group has more white-collar workers. What I'm suggesting is that the people who are active in the online participation are a little different from those who are active offline or those who are inactive.

Following this analysis, we have four prediction models. To summarize: online participation of different groups of citizens is associated with different variables to some extent. As for the offline active and the most inactive groups of citizens, the age variable has turned out positively associated with their level of online participation. For other citizen groups (i.e., online active and the most active groups), however, age has no statistical significance.

In conclusion, the e-participation is actually making another channel for citizen participation. E-participation is the same as off-line participation, meaning that it provides another channel for different groups of people. In another article I and my student wrote, e-participation can reduce bias and bureaucratic politics (Choi & Lee, 2014). E-participation, to some extent, it is equivalent to offline participation. It is supplementary both for the most active groups and offline active groups. Therefore, a relationship has been built between online and offline participation. And then online participation can be affected by some variables considered to be associated with offline political participation, such as sense of fulfillment of citizens, knowledge and evaluations about government, and trust in government.

Innovations in Performance Measurement in Cities

Steven Kelman

Weatherhead Professor of Public Management at Harvard
University's John F. Kennedy School of Government

I'm going to talk about Performance Measurement is US Cities. Performance measurement is used at all levels of the US government, but the most aggressive and prominent use is occurring in US cities. When it comes to performance measurement, may be you are not very familiar with those in government. Performance metrics or measures are defined as metrics, that usually are numbers but don't have to be, that indicate how well an organization is delivering value to the public. For example, examples of performance measures, most of which are relevant to China as well as to US: GDP growth rate, Air pollution index, Number of hospital admissions for acute food poisoning, Cancer death rates, etc.

1. Background of performance metrics in US cities

A background to the use of performance measurement in cities is the revival of American cities. After several decades of decline in the US cities—people moving out, the economies not improving in cities—many American cities began to revive during the 1990s. This is Times Square's night in early 1980s (Fig.1), with pornographic movie theater and pornographic bookstore. Times Square today looks like this (Fig.2). It's actually raining, not huge amount of people there. Another example is Manhattan in the early 1980s (Fig.3). Before there was a railways line that took meat that were coming to New York City from the western part of the US. There was nothing here then. Today it's the Highline (Fig.4), a major tourist attraction in New York City. One of my friends in the NGO that supports the Highline told me every weekend during the summer, she will go there

Fig.1
Times Square's night in early 1980s

Fig.2
Times Square Today

Fig.3
Manhattan in 1980s

Fig.4
Highline Park

and read a book all day and enjoy the Highline. That's the story of US cities.

And cities are also a central location for management innovation in US government. Two books (Fig.5) written by colleagues of mine from Kennedy School, about the revival of US cities basically are saying that, here are ways that US cities are improving their management and improving their governance.

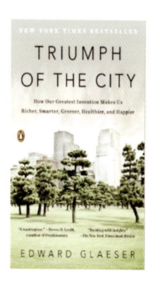

Fig.5
Cover of the books

On the philanthropic area, many of you have probably heard Michael Bloomberg. He is a billionaire who made a huge amount of money based on developing information technology for the financial service industry, a lot of it is sold to China. He later became mayor of New York and now is spending a lot of his time to his philanthropies on looking for ways to improve innovation and quality of performance in the US city government. For example he has one project called "What Works Cities" where they take different experiments for improving performance in US cities and develop information about which of the direction is working and try to spread the knowledge of those changes to other cities as well. Another thing is called "Mayors Challenge" where he challenges mayors of big US cities to develop various changes and to spread those as well.

2. Features of performance measurement in US cities

Interest in performance measurement in cities has grown mostly after cities' revival—as conditions have gotten better, people coming to demand more in terms of the quality of public services. Here are a few major features of performance measurement in US cities. First, it is not associated with promotion decisions of public officials. A second is that the most important performance measure is not GDP growth, but rather various crime/social/health/ environmental measures. For example, this is the performance measurement of New York City, including metrics such as crime, health, basic services, education, and infrastructure. It does not even mention GDP growth in the performance measures in New York City. Also the officials whose performance have been measured generally do not spend their time talking with more senior officials above them, but rather with more junior officials below them trying to improve the performance of the organization. And the last is transparency: most cities that have performance measurement in the US publish these metrics on the Internet, often including whether performance has met a certain target.

Fig.6 is about the Mayor's Management Report regarding the performance measurement in New York City. There are all different types of crimes, murder, robbery, burglary, the actual numbers of the last five years, the target, and the five-year trend. Going up indicates some are getting worse. Even their

HOW WE PERFORMED IN FISCAL 2016

SERVICE 1 Manage public safety programs related to criminal activity.

`Goal 1a` Reduce the incidence of crime.

The Department is implementing its new neighborhood-policing model. Specialty units have been scaled back to provide more patrol personnel so that officers have the time and latitude to meet and work with more community members to identify recurring issues, and to work on the remediation of the issues they have found. Patrol officers are working with local neighborhood forums to reach a consensus on the most critical issues and crimes facing that particular community, in order to effectively prioritize and adapt police operations.

Total major felony crime increased by less than two percent during Fiscal 2016 compared to Fiscal 2015. During Fiscal 2016 murder decreased two percent compared to Fiscal 2015. Major felony crime in the City's public schools decreased 13 percent compared to Fiscal 2015.

Based on preliminary semiannual FBI total index crime statistics for cities that have reported data for Calendar 2015, New York City remains the safest large city with the lowest rate of crime per capita among the 10 largest U.S. cities.

Performance Indicators	Actual					Target		Desired Direction	5yr Trend
	FY12	FY13	FY14	FY15	FY16	FY16	FY17		
★ Major felony crime	109,299	110,099	110,023	103,872	105,614	⇩	⇩	Down	Neutral
★ - Murder and non-negligent manslaughter	474	369	320	348	341	⇩	⇩	Down	Down
★ - Forcible rape	1,098	1,198	1,064	1,064	1,164	⇩	⇩	Down	Neutral
★ - Robbery	20,291	19,319	18,208	16,428	16,670	⇩	⇩	Down	Down
★ - Felonious assault	18,762	19,616	20,517	19,544	20,877	⇩	⇩	Down	Neutral
★ - Burglary	19,162	18,360	17,140	15,828	14,463	⇩	⇩	Down	Down
★ - Grand larceny	40,642	43,622	45,238	43,112	45,164	⇩	⇩	Down	Neutral
★ - Grand larceny auto	8,870	7,615	7,536	7,548	6,935	⇩	⇩	Down	Down
★ Major felony crime in housing developments	4,771	5,018	5,328	4,858	5,205	⇩	⇩	Down	Neutral
★ Major felony crime in transit system	2,741	2,535	2,488	2,283	2,520	⇩	⇩	Down	Down
Crime related to domestic violence - Murder	75	71	56	61	53	•	•	Down	Down
- Rape	535	464	471	481	526	•	•	Down	Neutral
- Felonious assault	6,781	7,420	8,335	7,771	7,986	•	•	Down	Up
★ School safety - Major felony crime	812	699	654	614	532	⇩	⇩	Down	Down
- Murder	0	0	1	0	0	•	•	Down	Neutral
- Rape	5	4	2	6	2	•	•	Down	Down
- Robbery	148	106	94	55	66	•	•	Down	Down
- Felonious assault	250	200	172	176	148	•	•	Down	Down
- Burglary	81	81	53	51	33	•	•	Down	Down
- Grand larceny	326	305	331	325	279	•	•	Down	Neutral
- Grand larceny auto	2	3	1	1	4	•	•	Down	Up
School safety - Other criminal categories	3,295	2,626	2,485	2,286	2,219	•	•	Down	Down
- Other incidents	5,365	4,350	3,811	3,975	4,092	•	•	Down	Down
Gang motivated incidents	310	264	225	328	349	•	•	Neutral	Up
Gun arrests	5,835	5,581	4,776	4,776	5,194	•	•	Neutral	Down
Major felony crime arrests	NA	40,258	42,444	41,599	43,516	•	•	Neutral	NA
Narcotics arrests	99,344	81,737	75,389	61,007	56,320	•	•	Neutral	Down
Juvenile arrests for major felonies	3,450	3,016	2,883	2,671	2,495	•	•	Neutral	Down

★ Critical Indicator "NA" - means Not Available in this report ⇩⇧ shows desired direction

Fig.6
The performance measurement of New York City

performance is not good; they share that with the public.

3. How US cities use performance measurement to improve organization performance

Next I will talk about ways that cities are using performance measurement as a management tool to improve their organization performance. There are three ways they do it, one is to motivate their staff, the second is to focus their staff, and the third is to learning. I will discuss each of these very briefly.

Turning to motivation, if you give your employee a specific performance goal, rather than just saying "Do your best.", there is a huge amount of evidence, just doing that improves the performance of the employee. There are nearly hundreds of studies, very well-established findings of social sciences that demonstrate that, performance metrics motivate people. And that motivation occurs even without financial rewards.

The second is focus. The basic idea here is that there are many things that employees could do when they come to work every day, and focus is a usable performance to tell the employees "I want you to work on this rather than on that". You want to focus on a small number of priorities or else your actions are diffused. "What gets measured gets done." Again, having a measure increases the chances of getting things done.

The third is to promote learning. The basic idea here is feedback. Performance measurement we use as itself is feedback, that what we do is a cycle, in which is you start off by measuring your performance, that's stage one, how well are we doing? And then you discover you are not doing well as you wanted to, then phase two becomes you see where your problems are, then the important phase is that you try some organizational change designed to improve performance. You measure to see your problem, you try out to change, then close the feedback and you measure again. Measure at the beginning and the end and in between all make changes. And that is a way overtime you improve your performance. Imagine if you were trying to learn at a throw darts battle. Imagine how hard it would be to learn, to get better, to do a better job, if you don't see where the darts landed. That image of where the darts landed is very helpful to figure out what I need to do a better job.

To summarize, how do these techniques improve results? Simple version is, if you use performance measurement to motivate, you are getting people to work harder, when they work harder, they get their goals; if you use performance measurement to focus people, get them to do what we're interested, that is to do the right things, to do this rather than that; if you use performance measurement to learn, you get people to do things right, as opposed to do the right things. Those are two different concepts. Focus is to do the right things; learning is to do things right; motivation is to work harder; learning is to work smarter.

And turning to institutional ways that cities had in place to improve performance. There is a book my colleagues wrote ten years or so, they called performance stat. Stat is short for statistics. A number of cities have regular meetings where senior officials meet with staff of lower levels of the organization to go through the various performance measures, their part of the organization to discuss where they're doing well, where they're doing badly, how to do a better job. That is called a performance stat meeting. A large number of cities in the US how have this. This started in New York. This is a real staff meeting involving police that are going over where the crime is going up, where it is going down, how can we do a better job. And Using stat during 1990s which when it was introduced, the murder rate in New York went down from the second highest in the US to 24th. It's second high-test in the 1990s, ten years later it's 24th high. So they really improved their performance a lot using this kind of staff meeting.

And to finish up with a similar thing in Los Angles called the LA stat. Its officials are sitting around the table and talking about performance in this case involving sanitation, which is keeping the garbage off the city. This is something that the charts and data they use in meeting. Taken a certain district of LA. This is a map (Fig.7) that shows data which part of this district is green, that are doing well; which are yellow that are in between; and which are red, that are doing badly. There are a whole bunch of measures they do, and they have recommendations. Based on these data, they develop recommendations to see how they can do a better job and the strategies moving forward. This isa very practical method.

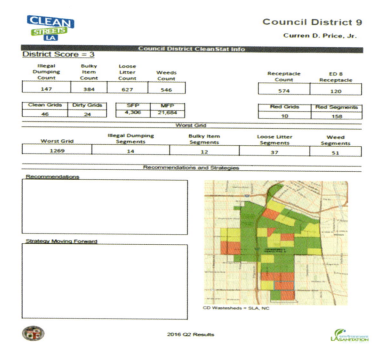

Fig.7
Clean Street LA,
Council District 9

Remark

Lan Zhiyong (Professor of School of Public Policy and Management of Tsinghua University): Prof. Ahrend brought very important message to China in this time of need, because right now China's cities are growing very fast. Presumably, its metro-centers are probably growing on top of the world. But if we look at it, we do have problems in dividing our many regions and districts even within one city. It is a harsh job to coordinate their activities, and also we have disparity between rich and poor areas. Your message that administrative boundaries are less important is very significant to China. I remember in the US they worked very hard to consolidate the cooperation of those cities working around. Together they built high roads. But the real question is for China, even in the United States, that they have to work out a mechanism to share the tax revenues, like the sense of pride, who is the bigger guy in town. In certain places like in Shanghai, it's the only bigger city, it's relatively easy. But move to Beijing area, it has Tianjin and other big guys; this involves a lot of work. The real thing is, how they, other than using metropolitan authorities associations, are really working together to make it possible. Money, very important, is a very important issue, and who will take the leadership.

Prof. Heinelt's presentation is interesting in a way to discuss governance mechanisms. When it comes to mechanism of coordination, one is political power, hieratical, another is market power using bargaining and purchasing, and another one is persuasion through religious ideas. The one you are talking about, bargaining and arguing is associated more with what we call post-modern thinking. But the real criticism for post-modernism is, even in those bargaining and arguing processes, some people are more equal than others, they have more bargaining power than other people. So that kind of discourse is never equal. That is the problem that needs to be resolved, even among those cities competing with one another. When it comes to leadership, one big issue is how to ensure your orders are obeyed, you need communicate and talk to people, they constantly have a system of hierarchy and have a bottom line, if you don't really listen either way, I will vote you out. I will give you orders, so I will buy you out. What would be the bargaining line or whoever shouts the loudest or whoever has the dominant power.

For Choi, yours is also very interesting. You did empirical studies to see right now, whether electronic participation can really be a political process in governance, and the ease of use was mentioned. I visited a few Chinese cities in the process of doing smart cities. They don't really find it fun to use complicated technologies so as with social media, which goes a long way, probably is much better than any of the conventional devices. So I view that as an important device. Even in the United States, they say that Wechat is the only technology that may pose a threat to US hi-tech companies because it combines or integrate the advantages of Twitter, Facebook, so you don't need a lot of applications.

Prof. Kelman's performance discussion I found interesting and to me I thought it really came from a different perspective. I participated a lot in local government performance evaluation, and I worked in the city mayor's office in the City of Phoenix. Number one, I really like your discussion of the renaissance of American cities. I thought that was really interesting. I'd really like to know what are the reasons behind those reactivation of American cities. After the municipal reform in the progress years, that was a big time for cities to grow. I wonder why in the 1980s they started to have this momentum of city redevelopment. Because I mostly based on the west, I watched the city of Los Angeles and Phoenix city, and those have been growing by 30% starting from the 1990s. But for performance measurement, I thought the real push started in 1991 when Gore was publishing his National Performance Review. He made it clear the objective of promoting performers' measurement is political, rather than, probably part of the reason is operational. Firstly, he wanted the Congress the politicians to clarify objectives they use to evaluate the executive function of government. Secondly, he wanted to use that to demonstrate that traditional bureaucracy actually has been doing a good job. And thirdly, he would use that as a performance yardstick to motivate people to work. However, performance measurements in cities started much longer before the federal government adopted performance review, so I knew like the City of Phoenix they started in the 1960s, PVB. They have very good detailed yardstick to evaluate the performance of each of their workers. Actually it's not just lip service, they associated it with every of those performer's pay by the end of the year. Their average budget allocation is 5%, but the manager can really decide in between 3% to 8%. I participated in their performance. Each time when the City of Phoenix manager was introducing their use in the legal cities, ICMA, usually the room was crowded because people came to learn the city experience which was rated very high in its performance. And one city manager mentioned: because we associated performance with pay.

Other than those, I saw the pictures because I also worked in the police department with one of my students. And they had their data running for many years and every year over a million US dollars running. But they didn't use their data because they don't have enough technology to pull those out for good analysis. I did some of those. That was part of the reason, for many years, they actually didn't use their data for evaluation. Number two, after the performance evaluation campaign, actually many units, even their cities, actually hired many high-level analysts, they had to pay them very high salary, probably 15% more than average in order for them to have those performance done. So sometimes I joked about it that they spent too much time on evaluating the performance to the point that the saddle is more expensive than the horse. But how those problems can be resolved, sometimes also worth discussion.

Hubert Heinelt: I think you are absolutely right that this mode of bargaining and arguing implies the danger of inequalities. But I think it's a question of political or institutional design to support the situation of those who are weak to articulate themselves, for those who don't have the resources to bargain. I think there are a lot of examples. I myself am involved to develop guidelines for citizen participation in German municipalities and where there are imbalances, you can strengthen the weak. For example, offering the opportunities to higher educates to articulate their position, or to organize the processes of the political intellect.

The other point is hierarchy. May be it's not clear. I spoke about a mixture of those modes. I think, talking about mixture means that these modes are mostly over there, it depends on the mixture. Hierarchy should be there, hierarchy can be helpful, the shadow of hierarchy, as it is blamed, can help to come to an agreement. If you are not coming to an agreement in time, I will take this decision, it can help a lot.

And also what it's called the light of the public. In argument, in exchange of good reasons, struggle over ideas should take place publically and then those who are still sticking to selfish position can be blamed for this position. The question of how to mobilize the potentials of different governance is about the institutional design.

Steven Kelman: Two reaction to why the cities come back. I'm not an expert on cities, so this might be hypothesis. You mentioned there was a period when the city was really collapsing, and people were leaving. At that time, the government was trying to fight back a little bit, trying to hold back a tsunami coming to cities that destroy everything may be with one piece of wood. The reasons cities came back I guess, my hypothesis would be, the cities had got down so far, the price of housing, the price of everything have totally collapsed. In many cities there are very beautiful old houses. It was beautiful when it was originally built over a hundred years have become terrible and near to collapse. In the early 1970s, the first movement called urban pioneers, these were well-educated, professional people. Some of these people could actually get these houses for free, that were abandoned. They started moving back in and building them up again. So my guess is at the beginning of the revival, because the cities came down so low, they finally reach a point it became economically attractive move back again. Then it started to feed on itself. Then the culture changes, these young people coming to cities started to say, we loved cities, so the cultures have followed in some ways as the economies. It's just a thought.

Earlier you said measurement, in some tradition of performance measures in the US cities go back to the 1930s. Some of you might know the very famous American social scientist Herbert Simon who wrote in the 1930s about performance measurement. And you mentioned Phoenix, that's a very small city, was one of a kind of thing. It now becomes more and more into the mainstream of what people trying to do.

Dialogue

Moderator: What we need is really discussions between different stakeholders. Maybe I have a question to Mr. Rudiger. I'm wondering why you use economic performance as your dependence of those, and most importantly, you use GDP as your measurement, why?

Rudiger: We have a lot of data and we should look at all the variants. For policy makers, if you simply told them that the productivity drops, they might only talks about governance. But if you told them that the productivity reduces by 60%, they will pay attention right away. This is an area we hope politicians in OECD countries can notice. Of course, GDP is not the only indicator and we also have other performance metrics and corresponding evaluation results. So GDP can get them pay attention to the issue.

Audience: My question goes to Prof. Kelman. You talked about the separation of different crimes in New York City. It's very impressive for me because it's the first time for me to witness such data in detail. Can you describe how these data function and how the government use the data for? And further improvement to crime prevention, how they use these data to do it?

Steven Kelman: I think they are using it to figure out how to do a better job. Let me give you one example. You are absolutely right. If you look at the chart that I showed, it shows 15 different kinds of crime, the trend going up and going down, how it is compared to its target. But if you take a specific example of homicide murder, there is a very interestingly-written article by The New York Times two years ago. Since the beginning of their concept, their performance measurement system, murders in New York has gone down

80%. So there are one fifth as many murders today as there were in the 1990s compared today. One way to think about it in very practical human terms is that every year now in New York 400 people are alive who would have been dead if New York still had the murder rate at the beginning of the 1990s. This is very dramatic change. What The New York Times said is that now the numbers have gone down so much, there are fewer murders left. The police, they really want to target it to see why they take place. For every murder in New York City, they are now doing an analysis after the murder, trying to get all the information to see why this murder take place and look for patterns. And when you learn about patterns of what kind of things are causing murder, they are basically analyzing and using it to come up some interventions, what we should do to try to bring down the number of murder even further. Again I will use an idiomatic expression, within the performance measurement movement in US. They are making deep dive, go deep down to the bottom. That's what New York and other cities are trying to do. They have the raw data, but they don't stop with the raw data. They do a deep dive to learn what's behind that data, and draw figures to see how we can do a better job.

Inter-city Collaboration among Mega Cities in Regional Development
—the Case of Beijing, Tianjin and Hebei Region

Lan Zhiyong

Professor of School of Public Policy and Management，Tsinghua University

Shanghai is also a big city. Luckily, it's the only big city in the region. So, there will not be any problems because everybody works around it. Beijing's situation is different. This is what I'm going to talk about: urban clusters in China and the need for inter-city collaboration, national strategy, the background of the policy; current situations of the collaboration; issues and challenges.

1. What is urban clusters ?

The so called urban clusters, city belt, or metro area is a simple definition of spatial areas where more than one cities reside adjacent to one another. The interesting thing is that cities in Asian countries have large population size. Thus, they are characterized with large populations and the density of housing units, China in particular. Before the 18th century, half of the population lives in Asia. And now it looks like this trend is coming back.

As of now, China already has 11 urban clusters. The biggest clusters include the Pearl River Delta region, the Yangtze River Delta Region, the Beijing-Tianjin-and Hebei region, and some other regions. Pearl River Delta region is interesting because it works across the borders with Hong Kong and Macau. In the Yangtze River Delta region, Shanghai is the biggest while Nanjing and Hangzhou are a little remote. Beijing, Tianjin and Hebei region is a special case.

In the United States, Boston-Washington Metro area centered around five large cities such as Boston, New York, Philadelphia, Baltimore, Washington D. C., with about 40 medium and small sized cities scattered around. It has the highest density in the US with the largest population. And other three clusters, including Chicago-Pittsburg area and San Diego-San Francisco occupy more than half of the US GDP. For example, San Diego and San Francisco account for 21% of the US economy.

Presumably it is because the way I look at it. China's industrialization is not quite up there yet. If it has realized industrialization, I believe a lot of economic and financial activities will be highly concentrated and gathered. With those in mind, we will know that urban clusters in China are going to be more and more important in the years to come.

2. The collaborative development of Beijing-Tianjin-Hebei region is a national strategy

The central government wanted these three regions to coordinate and cooperate with each other. That is to say to move the non-capital functions, such as the industries and population, out of Beijing and place them in Hebei. Hebei will be happy about it. Tianjin is waiting. It's a hub with its own harbor, industry and financial center, so it's an independent city with long history. Thus, it is not willing to cooperate with Beijing and become a second-tier city. Now Beijing is moving its administrative center to Tongzhou, one specific area. Tongzhou still has to clarify its urban function, whether it becomes a service unit for the capital Beijing, or becomes an administrative unit for the local Beijing, or becomes a center to coordinate the activities of all these three regions? It has become an issue which they don't have an answer. They were discussing and they all have different opinions.

This is background information for collaborative development. Tianjin's economic power is rising quickly and competes with Beijing. Beijing, in the process of becoming a more sustainable city, is transferring many of its factories out. But it does not want to send them to Tianjin whichhas a good industrial base. Because Beijing does not want Tianjin to upgrade further. Thus, the movement to Hebei is more manageable for Beijing. After transferring those problems to Hebei, Beijing would still be headquarters with good financial revenues. However, Hebei says we won't accept those factories unless you give us money. Besides, once those factories moved to Hebei, they will become the polluters. And all those factories were very well managed in Beijing, but once they were moved out of Beijing, they can't be managed by Beijing. But the pollutants will still coming to Beijing. Thus, when you were thinking of sending your problems to other places, you must realize the biggest problem for yourself is whether it is controllable. If Hebei has more problems, those problems will coming back to Beijing. Beijing is highly motivated and is eager to act, because it is hoping to benefit from this new collaboration. And Tianjin is standing by and on-looking to see what happens because it doesn't see what can get out of this relationship. And Hebei is waiting for financial support.

Then we have the National Strategy. Everyone is talking about urban planning and strategic planning. And the central government does make a plan. The key is to evacuate the non-capital functions of Beijing, and then it will help to push the integration of transportation, ecological and environmental protection, as well as industrial upgrading. In the future, it's trying to define the city functions. Beijing will still be political, cultural, international and science center. And Tianjin will become the national research base for manufacturing, international navigation center, and financial innovation center. And Hebei will be the industrial, transportation and logistics base. Now the issue is Beijing is a mega city with its own financial center. Now if you want to create Tianjin as a financial center, what will happen to Beijing's financial street? And Tang Shan in Hebei province which is also a very modern city with a wonderful harbor area and industries. If you want Tianjin to further develop these industries, what happens to Hebei? For mega cities, it is better for them to have their own functions rather than implementing those functions deliberately. Even though you have those guidelines, you still can't work out a lot of problems because many of the existing infrastructure and possibilities are already there. If you do not solve it, all those guidelines will be there in vain.

3. The collaborative governance is the key to the collaborative development of Beijing-Tianjin and Hebei region

A lot of us think this is a planning issue. Many of the managerial and governance issues haven't yet been resolved. So in this process, who are the ones that are supposed to do the planning? The central government already made its first move. What about the role of Beijing, it wants to be the leader, but Tianjin is not complying. It really goes back to your governance theory about hierarchical arrangement. The most important thing is who should be the major person leading this change? Where would the infrastructure investment come from? How to bear the cost? And how developmental benefits will be divided? How those things are supposed to do? Currently most of the efforts have been emphasized on the technical side. How to build bridges, transportation and buildings? But as to eventually what those areas are supposed to be? How they're going to prioritize their urban functions? Actually all those problems have not been very well resolved. I think they need to have more integrated platforms which they don't have yet. The central government gives limited amount of money. These cities are hesitating to make their own investment.

There is a new theory called integrated urbanization which allows big urban areas to have multiple functions with a high-speed transportation system in between. I think the Beijing-Tianjin and Hebei region can take it into consideration which shows: hybridity, connectivity as well as porosity among cities.

Cooperative Mechanism of French Cities

Ye Bifeng

Professor of Koguan Law School at Shanghai Jiao Tong University

My focus is also on the construction of urban clusters in China. This requires tracking the experience of another country. Previously, I tracked cities in the United States, but later I found that the French national structure has more resemblance with China. So I turned to French cities. This May I went to two French cities Paris and Le Mans to conduct a visit. And today I'd like to report this visit from the perspective of a Chinese observation and from a legal point of view.

1. Governance concept in France is changing

The development process is from the original ruling and management to governance which puts more emphasis on multi-party participation. From the concept perspective, ruling focuses more on hierarchy, class and social opposition. There were violence and dictatorship, but no implementation of the rule of law. They only cared about the regime and the privatization of government power. At that time the French king was only concerned about the stability of his regime and public law, rather than private law. Later, modern management with the characteristics of public rights, put more emphasis on the order of administration and vigil government, which spurred the development of modern legal system. But it was still negative human rights, public rights and human rights are still opposed to each other. Then there emerges the public service theory which is characterized by public service, emphasizing active administration, welfare state and public service. Since then modern public law has been developed which stresses group and social cooperation. China also stresses social harmony, but the rise of French corporatism in the late nineteenth century is also a kind of the social harmony we are talking today.

From the 1980s to the beginning of this century, France has carried out a series of reforms on the national administrative system, aiming at modernizing the country's governance system and governance capacity. In the process of these reforms, four aspects are the most important: first is the modernization of state structure with an emphasis on urban autonomy. Second is to emphasize the simplification of administrative procedures and to improve the relationship with the governed group. Third is the modernization of public administration, especially electrification. Fourth is the state shareholder system for which a public participation office was especially established.

2. The ways of French cities collaboration

There are two paths of urban agglomeration construction: First, the path of level. The path of level has the traditional order construction path of urban agglomeration, at the same time since the 1980s, a kind of non-order construction path has been formed. There is also a parallel path, that is, the cooperation between cities. What I am concerned is the cooperation between cities, which is the schemes of parallel construction path of urban agglomeration. Currently, there are three modes of urban cooperation in France: first, urban alliance; second, urban cooperation zone; third, special cooperation.

The first one urban alliance is a kind of entity urban agglomeration model, which is mainly applied to the construction of city alliance between medium-sized cities and the small cities and towns surrounding it. This model is to centralize the densely populated medium-sized cities, while uniting the towns scattered around it, to constitute a satellite city.

Due to historical reasons, France, with a population of 66 million, has 36 000 cities and towns in its territory, the most in Europe. Some of the city population is at 25 million, while there are towns with only a few hundred people. And there are relatively large cities. These small towns also need good transportation, education, technology, health care and other public services, but their needs can not be met by themselves. And medium-sized cities have to develop and to extend to the small cities and towns surrounding it. So in 1971 the French government tried to merge some cities. But there were strong opposition, demonstrations and protests, holding that it had destroyed the continuation of history and culture. So the government then turned to city alliance. At present, France has a total of 1 241 urban alliances formed by 13 811 municipalities.

The city alliance is not national compulsory, but formed voluntarily by the members. The city members should transfer part of their tax rights, planning rights, construction rights of public network service and industrial development rights to the city alliance. The city alliance also has the right to levy a special tax on all members within the jurisdiction. If there is a surplus of the revenue of the city alliance, the revenues should be assigned to its member cities according to the proportion of the population and the economic conditions of the cities. The cities are still independent, responsible for their own public welfare undertakings. The city alliance has its own governing body, which exercises these powers and is responsible for its operation. The management leadership of the city alliance should be a committee with a chairman, a number of members who should be mayors of the member cities. But not every mayor of the member cities can be on the committee, such as those mayors of cities having few populations. They need to work in the form of meetings; the proposal can only pass through unanimous consent. If there is a veto, it should be decided by referendum of the city whose mayor votes. There are also a number of working bodies of the executive committee, which is a form of city alliance.

The second form is the urban cooperation zone. Urban cooperation zone is a compact form of urban agglomeration, which is suitable for the collaborative construction and development of large cities. The famous cases are Grand Paris area, as well as Marseille, Lille, Nantes, Bordeaux and other big cities. French cities do not have the administrative hierarchy like we do while they just differ in size. Hence there is no affiliation between cities. The French cities are not the same as the French regions and provinces. Regions and provinces represent the central government. The cities represent the localities. The regions and the provinces are representatives of the central supervision at local areas. The executive heads are appointed by the central authorities, while the mayor is elected. At the same time, the city, the province and the region has a clear division of powers, such as primary schools belong to city affairs, secondary schools belong to the provincial affairs and the universities belong to the regional affairs. Urban planning and construction in France also has a clear division of power, so the development of small cities and towns, large cities all need to be achieved through cooperation rather than subordination.

The urban cooperation zone has a joint meeting of mayors, which is composed of the mayors of the member cities and one of them will be elected as the chairman. It is a coordinating organization of the alliance with no executive powers. According to the current president of the Greater Paris area, the Greater Paris Mayor Joint Meeting is held once a month, working in line with the principle of consensus decision-making. As there is no affiliation of cities, and the fact that the mayors are not appointed by superior departments or the central government, but are elected by citizens, there is no inequality in the organization. I noticed these based on China's issues. The task of Mayor Joint Meeting consisting of a number of offices with dozens of staff is to communicate with the relevant departments of the member cities, draft various documents and prepare meeting plans. One of the important tasks of the urban cooperation zone is to coordinate urban planning and urban construction, including urban planning, land reserve, urban traffic management, construction and management of roads, signs and parking lot, and joint construction of development zones etc..

The third form is special cooperation, which is to achieve a single task of urban cooperation through the cooperation agreement. City alliance and urban cooperation zone are cooperation between neighboring cities, while special cooperation is not limited to neighboring cities, but can be applied to national and even overseas provinces and foreign cities. Cooperation can be on environmental protection, culture, education, economic development, tourism development and other aspects. Cooperation agreement is an administrative contract, but not a civil contract, whose purpose is to achieve the city government's public service objectives. It is legally binding to member cities, not only binding on the governments, but also on the public. A famous case is the Betz City case. On October 10, 1986, the city signed an unfixed-term economic cooperation contract to build an economic zone—Betz New Town, and agreed on the distribution of taxes revenues by a certain percentage. Betz New Town proposed in September 1993 to cancel the contract. The city of Betz sued it to the Administrative Court, and required Betz New Town to compensate 3.8 million francs of liquidated damages. The Administrative Court ruled that the contract still has binding force on both parties and they shall continue the contract.

A recent case is about the city government of Lyon financed the renovation of a church in Algeria. The focus of the controversy is that the plaintiff believes that the Lyon city government's funding of a church is in violation of the constitutional principle of separation of church and state, but the Administrative Court ruled that it belongs to the funding of cultural undertakings and thus avoided the constitutional principle. This case is also very interesting, the majority of the Lyon city government voted for the funding, and a small number of government officials who voted against filed the lawsuit. It is a lawsuit by a small number of officials in the city government who filed the lawsuit to the Administrative Court. Although the urban cooperation agreement is a contract, the dispute can still be resorted to the Administrative Court. But this rarely occurs. In order to continue the cooperation, the dispute should be resolved through negotiation, to reach an agreement, and to avoid future disputes.

Currently, regarding Beijing-Tianjin-Hebei region, the Yangtze River Delta, the Pearl River Delta, many people are calling for an institutional mechanism or a legal mechanism to resolve regional disputes. Though France has such a mechanism, it rarely uses it. Most disputes are resolved through consultation and negotiation. The settlement agreement is also an administrative contract. It must be legally binding, and should not be resolved by removing or lifting the duties of the parties or make what's illegal legal. To ensure a smooth implementation of the agreement, and to avoid disputes because of violating the agreement, the French law requires the regional executive heads to be involved in the signing and closing of city cooperation agreement. In civil law, responsibility will be held for not only breach of contract, but also liability fault during the conclusion of the contract. There will be such problems in administrative contracts as well, which requires the chief executive of the region to be involved in the conclusion of such a contract to supervise. The chief executive of the region can also coordinate the cooperation disputes between various cities.

3. The enlightenment of French collaborative cities

The Third Plenary Session of the 18th CPC Central Committee has put forward the issue of advancing the modernization of state governance system and governance capacity. This is a very important issue for our country and our reforms. After this proposal, the State Concil has launched, Guidance on the Reform of Central and Local Fiscal Responsibility and Expenditure Responsibility, which clearly defined the necessity of establishing boundaries of central and local financial responsibility and expenditure responsibility to promote modernization of national governance system and governance capacity. This is a very important document. The second item of the general requirements of the document mentioned that to mobilize and protect the initiatives of local officials, the central government should minimize its direct management of micro-affairs, and give full play to local governments' management of local affairs.

At the same time, Planning of Yangtze River Delta Urban Agglomeration was launched in this May, involving 26 cities. Our urban agglomeration construction comes from two initiatives: regional economic integration and urbanization, and is now an important part of the modernization of governance system and governance capability. There are a lot of similarities with French cities in terms of reform and urban cooperation. According to China's national situation, I am afraid that we cannot just copy the French model when it comes to urban collaboration. Through my observation I found that they are city autonomy, while we speak of the right of local autonomy, even with the State Concil's documents, we are far from city autonomy. In the case of city autonomy, the city system and the central system are separate but complementary to each other. We may not be able to meet this requirement, but there are still many common places. And in regards to the State Concil's document, in many countries it would be the constitutional document passed by the Parliament. Currently it is a guiding document of the State Concil. But I think there are still many places that we can learn from, such as the coordination agencies, cooperation agreements, dispute settlement mechanism etc..

Collaborative Governance Innovation for Disaster Resilience in Metropolitan Areas

Naim Kapucu

Professor and Director of the School of Public Administration
at the University of Central Florida

Almost none of the presentations today highlighted the very specific topic that is Collaborative Governance Innovation for Disaster Resilience in Metropolitan Areas. Almost every presenter, in their response to questions, or in their presentations, mentions the issue of safety in major cities. Unfortunately, most of the times, either because of lack of resources or lack of disasters, we forget to invest in collaborative governance of either man-made or natural disasters. Unless something happened, investors, citizens or individuals will not notice disasters. This is the highlight of my presentation, focusing on collaborative governance, innovation and disaster resilience as open government.

1. The meaning of collective governance and its application in the United States

The phrase collective governance is hard to define, but it is how we prepare citizens collectively as a whole community, if anything happens, they can at least respond to damages, on behalf of citizens, industry and the society at large. I will briefly highlight some important lessons learned in disaster relief in the United States which might be helpful to other countries or metropolitan areas.

Based on my research and the feedback from my friends in the group who have a lot of experience in disasters management at the US, the country has the best disaster management system in the world. In the US, Florida has the best disaster management system because of their rich experience. If you remember, we have a couple of hurricanes a few years ago. You didn't see a lot of human damage. Eight people unfortunately died. But the economic cost was more than 25 billion. Even if there is an alert hurricane expected, we know the track, but the damage can be devastating for the city. Most of the damage was in North Carolina.

2. The collaborative governance system for disaster resilience in the United States

I will highlight what do we mean by collaborative governance and network, and how they are implemented in response to disasters, and use some examples in the US, and some were based on key issues of disaster responses as well as changes of policy.

The quintessential metro governance involves governance of application of disaster management, coordination and collaboration of resources. At my university (University of Central Florida), we usually invite guests to present on disaster management and I asked them what the three most critical elements in disaster management are. They respond: coordination, coordination, coordination. So this is the key element of collaborative governance in response to disasters. There are several initiatives in the US to coordinate resources at the local, state and national level. And the best lessons I found is the treasure to see policy of framework in terms of response, recovery, prevention, mitigation and disaster preparedness. And each framework partners as a framework reference for local government. The officials have to coordinate resources. I will briefly provide you background for disaster responses framework and then the most relevant framework about disaster recovery which highlights the coordination of resources both in terms of recovery and in terms of capacity building.

The traditional disaster response/management cycle have five phases. We used to have four phases, but the fifth phase was added after "9.11". The prevention is more focused on man-made disasters, or terrorism disasters. And response, recovery, preparedness and mitigation are traditional perspectives.

I mentioned that Florida has the best disaster management system in the country. If there is no disaster, there are only a couple of people in the Emergency Operations Center (EOC) in Florida. Usually, there are five people, only three of them are experts on emergency management, others are either letter writers or secretaries. So imagine a metropolitan with a population of more than 2.5 million people is hit by a disaster, how five people can manage the disaster. Imagine Shanghai, there's 911 emergency line, but I'm not sure if you have EOC. I saw a presentation about the training session. They want to be innovative in response to disasters, but they depend too much on money from central government. The key aspect here is what people do if there is a disaster? Prepare, do exercises and understand where the resources are as well as identify who the people are and how much they know. There is a famous saying about disaster management is that when disaster happens, there is no time to exchange business card. You have to know the situation before anything happens.

This is a picture of four hurricanes took place in Florida 2004 (Fig.1). You can see the symbol of our university was at the middle of the hurricane. We had three hurricanes in less than four weeks. We have the Activated EOC of five members in the building, and there are about 180 people in the same building. Imagine those five people didn't know anything before the hurricanes or other types of disasters, there is no way that they will know their partners, their cultures, their understanding and their capacities. But this should be important coordination and cooperation among people, which is as important today as when there is a disaster.

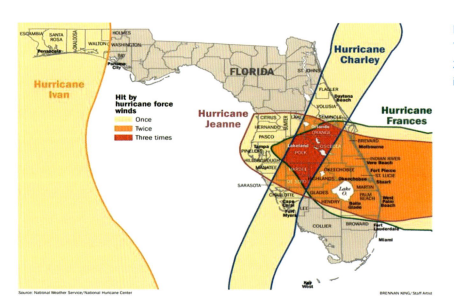

Fig.1
The paths of the 2004 hurricanes in Florida

In the history, substantial shift happened in the US, in terms of the policies, the framework, organizational structures and Emergency Operations Centers. The shift is more from upward perspective. In the US, for example, the key decision makers are counties and cities. And local governments are legal unit, counties are responsible for preparing for disasters and responding to disasters as well. So it's more bottom-up. The counties make a decision, then the states, and if the states think it is big enough and should be more involvement, and they involve the federal government. It is the congress decision that the country can mobilize billions of dollars in disaster recovery and response. If this procedure was not followed, there was only about several million dollars which is not quite enough to respond to any major disasters. But the key for bottom-up decision requires substantial government cooperation and collaboration on the states level, and mutual agreements among the local government.

3. Network governance for disaster resilience in the United States

I mentioned in my discovery there is a number of perspectives quite a treasure for me and I have been using network governance as a methodology to understand the disaster response. And they made some sense. Recently I did a study about 30-year publications in major journals to see the way they define network cooperation governance issues. I read about 1 800 articles, only 30% define what they mean by cooperation. If you don't define what network cooperation is, you can't define the relationship. Only 70 papers use the network governance. My emphasis is that it's a great form and I hope people can use network analysis. This is one of the response networks I have created with our engineers and architects (Fig.2). If disaster happens, we don't have this complicated demonstration because you may not have the person responsible in charge of emergency management. The citizens, counties might not be reachable in the case of a disaster. How do we mobilize the resources to communicate and reach a conclusion to make sure the citizens get the solution to respond to disasters? For example, in "9.11", it's not the common practice. The mayor reached directly to the president because the size of the disaster. The regular communication process was broken, the mayor was in constant communication with the president and the president will make quick decisions.

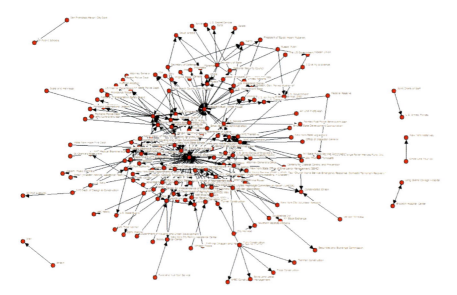

Fig.2
911 Response
network

There are factors included here based on my research and some of the researches of others'. The major development is that you can improve the whole community, citizens, NGO, and local government disaster response mechanism. One of the key information to establish a framework is to help build the network and collaboration based on certain functions. For the framework of disaster response, organizations are getting together to coordinate resources and communication, transportation and other aspects of disaster management. This gives me an opportunity to see the big picture in disaster response framework and recovery framework, it also gives me a perspective to evaluate why there is transportation and communication and whether there is any improvement to the present process. There are lots of room to do research as well as practice. There are all sorts of responsibilities in terms of what function is the organization identified as primary function. This is similar to organization chart and there is difference between the organization chart and the way people actually operate. Take an example of "9.11". There is an emphasis on what is formal and informal. I have done a research among more than 3 000 people in the US. And I asked them what is the critical element of collaboration, and 85% responded: trust, meaning that if you don't have prior relationship building, you won't be able to deliver coordination, cooperation and function successfully in response to disasters.

This is network governance and resilience (Fig.3). The focus was the metropolitan level community resilience, you can define community geographically, ethically or population based. There are certain elements at the organization capacity as organizations as well as government entities, and the citizen organizations. And what the research cares about is the community resilience. There are a lot of external factors in terms of money and other resources available. For the US federal system, there is the federal government at national level. And there are regional emergency management disaster response systems, state management, and each single organization have its different system. This is the reason to focus on regional level to increase coordination and cooperation as most disasters don't cage in one place. And when a hurricane hit the boundary cities and boundary counties, regional coordination is required. The new framework emphasizes on old communities, how you place non-profit organizations to make sure their part of the system and place them to help and sustain the resilience of communities. The way I use for network governance is element of coordination to make sure the resources are coordinated, information are shared in a timely manner so the response and cooperation are successful.

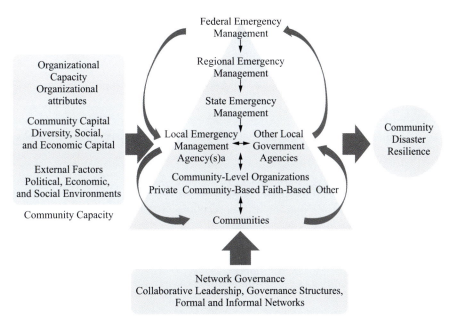

Fig.3
Network
governance &
resilience

Dialogue

Audience: I have a question for Prof. Ye, how about the security capability of French cities? Any good methods that we can learn from? And my second question is to Prof. Kapucu, what is the experience of US in terms of safeguarding the city safety and security? What's the most important thing especially from the respect of city management and governance? What should government officials learn about?

Lan Zhiyong: First question goes to Prof. Ye. Recently there have been a few terrorist attacks in France. Some people say that it is because their towns and cities are too small and once an emergency happened, it's not easy for the police to enter the city to make timely response. So, how did France solve this problem? Another question is for Prof. Kapucu. From your perspective, what has changed in the emergency management after the establishment of Department of Homeland Security (DHS) ?

Ye Bifeng: My study is mainly concerned with the following aspects: What are the legal forms of urban cooperation in France? Can we learn from them? When we legislate, is there something to learn? Your question about the ability of security, is more of a public management issue, I did not communicate with them on this subject. So I may not be able to give you a satisfactory answer. This time I visited two places. One is the Greater Paris area, the other is the Le Mans city alliance. I have not got into the specific details about security issues you mentioned like how did the police enter the town during an emergency. In regards to the city alliance, what I am most concerned about is the local autonomy. Why local autonomy? During the modernization of governance system and governance capacity, a very important issue is whether we can learn from the local autonomy of French cities. There were also no local autonomy in the past, after the reform they established city's complete autonomy. In China, our cities focus on cooperation with each other. I am afraid we have to have the appropriate autonomy to allow room for cooperation. If cross-regional issues are mainly decided by higher levels of government or the central government, then there are few room for cooperation among cities.

Naim Kapucu: First question was about safety measures. Is the US safe in terms of responding to terrorism or natural disasters? Of course, there are a lot of changes mainly after "9.11" and Hurricane Katrina and other disasters, and our organization structures and specific requirements change as well. But we can never say that we are 100% prepared for disasters. It's almost impossible. There are several initiatives in terms of meeting certain standards for preparation. There are anticipative institutions in the US that are very professional to give presentations to make sure counties and states are prepared. In the US, the Federal Center has an excellent education program and emergency management institutions. They do have regular training for firefighters and police and many emergency management individuals. In emergency management systems, they have to complete trainings to get promotions. The emergency management institutes also provide online courses of leadership development on communication, coordination, volunteer management. There are certain mechanism of training and education to make sure people are prepared. In Florida, we do have certain tax revenues go directly to disaster preparedness. We provide constant financial support to disaster preparedness. Usually, disasters provide visible opportunity for the decision makers and policy makers to invest on disasters issues.

The other question is about the major change of DHS, which was created to deal with "9.11". That was a big event. That was the second largest after creating the Department of Defense, the largest reform in the US government, involving about 22 bodies, regional organizations, substantial cultural changes and substantial policy differences. In DHS, there are two different cultures that are culture of people with gun and culture of people without gun. And it didn't work quite well. Most of the emphasis is on prevention of terrorism disasters.

After Hurricane Katrina, the government says we are pushing too much on the terrorism side, it's time to balance with focus on natural disasters as well. The major change after this is emphasis on framework of providing guidelines to local and state government instead of providing everything from federal government, so I think that is the major shift. The federal government provides guideline and framework to local government for them to develop on their own. These are the county and state's specific emergency management programs.

FORUM II

分论坛二

Urban Economic Transformation and Development

城市经济转型发展

主持人 · HOST
陈宪 · Chen Xian
上海交通大学安泰经济与管理学院教授
Professor of Antai College of Economics and Management
Shanghai Jiao Tong University

城市经济转型发展分论坛现场嘉宾聆听演讲

Guests are listening to the speeches attentively at the Urban Economic Transformation and Development Parallel Forum

上海交通大学安泰经济与管理学院教授陈宪主持平行分论坛二

Chen Xian，Professor of Antai College of Economics and Management of Shanghai Jiao Tong University，hosts the Parallel Forum II

伦敦大学学院巴特雷特规划教授吴缚龙在平行分论坛二上作专题演讲

Wu Fulong，Professor of Bartlett Planning at University College London，delivers a speech at the Parallel Forum II

上海交通大学安泰经济与管理学院教授罗守贵在平行分论坛二上作点评

Luo Shougui，Professor of Antai College of Economics and Management of Shanghai Jiao Tong University，comments on the Parallel Forum II

美国三一学院 Paul E.Raether 讲座教授陈向明在平行分论坛二上作专题演讲

Chen Xiangming，Distinguished Professor of Trinity College in
Hartford（Connecticut），delivers a speech at Parallel Forum II

复旦大学社会发展与公共政策学院教授任远在平行分论坛二上作点评

Ren Yuan，Professor of School of Social Development and Public
Policy of Fudan University，comments on the Parallel Forum II

深圳大学经济学院教授赵登峰在平行分论坛二上作专题演讲

Zhao Dengfeng，Professor of School of Economics of Shenzhen University，delivers a speech at the Parallel Forum II

深圳大学经济学院院长、教授陈勇在平行分论坛二上作点评

Chen Yong，Dean and Professor of School of Economics of Shenzhen University，comments on the Parallel Forum II

上海交通大学安泰经济与管理学院特聘教授陆铭在全球城市论坛平行分论坛二上作专题演讲

Lu Ming，Distinguished Professor of Antai College of Economics and Management of Shanghai Jiao Tong University，delivers a speech of the Parallel Forum II

上海城市创新经济研究中心首席研究员杨宏伟在平行分论坛二上作点评

Yang Hongwei，Chief Researcher of Shanghai Urban Innovation Economy Think-tank，comments on the Parallel Forum II

从巨型城市项目看未来城市治理：
基于伦敦和上海的比较

吴缚龙

伦敦大学学院巴特雷特规划教授

大家知道城市面临着很多挑战，要继续保持经济增长，要持续提供美好的城市生活，又要消除城市不同居民之间的不平等，同时还要保持良好的环境。未来的城市应该怎么治理？实际上，城市治理是城市创新、社会创新的一个试验田，主要问题是如何促进城市发展，谁来促进城市发展。这就是我们未来城市研究中很重要的一个议题。

1. 巨型城市项目兴起对城市治理的影响

简单回顾一下二战后英国城市发展的演化。20世纪90年代以前，英国的城市发展主要由政府主导进行城市改建，通过强制征收土地，清除贫民窟，实现现代化目标，但这种做法受到了来自"左"和"右"的批评。左派批评政府对贫民窟的清除，对居民冲击很大，打破了原有的社区。右派的批评是觉得政府干预过多，代替了社会的功能，同时增加政府的开支，所以引起了社会广泛的反对，从而使得一些城市开发项目停滞。

到了20世纪90年代，出现了一个新的动态，即所谓的新型巨型城市项目的兴起。这些新型项目基于所谓新自由主义的思想，充分强调市场机制，在原有的、老的、废弃的工业地和码头区进行城市建设，减少对原有居民的冲击，同时采取混合开发或公私联合开发的形式，但这种开发还是存在争议，就是谁在获益。90年代兴起的巨型项目，对城市治理造成很大的冲击。这些巨型项目的原意不单单是改善城市的居住环境，而是把城市作为一个经济实体，通过城市巨型项目来增加竞争力并取得收益。

比较一下战后英国的所谓巨型项目和90年代以来的巨型项目，可以看出，战后的那些老的城市巨型项目是以国家为主导的，而90年代以后，

分论坛二　FORUM II　　191

则是国家和私有企业共同主导的。它们的重点也不相同，以前的巨型项目更多的是提供基础设施、清洁的水以及便利等，而后面的项目则与经济发展相结合。从城市的景观上来说，以前比较单调，是郊区建新城的形式，现在则是综合发展。实际上，最大的挑战是，现在这些以私营为导向的大型项目开发模式是否带来了城市治理的变化。

最典型的大型项目就是伦敦的金丝雀码头（图1）。它是一个新金融区，由 SLN 进行总体设计，由 Olympia & York 这样大的开发公司来操办，建成了一个金融新城。再比如说巴黎的金融区；还有阿姆斯特丹南站，连通阿姆斯特丹的机场和市区，在这中间形成了金融新区。这样的新区不止一个，有可能会形成一系列，比如伦敦泰晤士河两岸的奥林匹克开发区等项目。这些巨型项目不单单是居住和产业的功能区，而是形成了包括金融、办公、商业、娱乐在内的综合开发。它们以产业转型、提高竞争力为目标，开发模式是市场导向、公私合作，特别是引用了新自由主义市场的思维。实际上，这种大型项目能够成功，需要政府的大力支持，特别是在交通基础设施上。伦敦金丝雀码头、千禧年地铁等就是在政府的大力支持下得到实施的。这些巨型项目往往强调整体设计、整体规划。但是，这些项目存在着开发的风险，往往是房地产开发的周期性风险。比如说，原有的开发商 Olympia & York，在开发的过程中破产。这些城市巨型项目对城市造成了很大的冲击，形成了很多高档公寓、办公楼、商贸综合体，改变了城市的形象，引起了城市周边地区的变化，还导致了城市治理的变化。

图1
伦敦金丝雀码头

对城市规划而言，巨型项目成为空间规划的对象，而不是综合的土地规划。这些巨型项目，因为它的特殊性——规模大、成本高，需要广泛的社会资源，故而可以从这些大型项目上看出城市发展的治理过程，城市发展过程中的规范、权力以及规划开发过程。通过大型项目来看未来城市的走向，学界对此有两个比较大的解释声音。

第一，新自由主义的解释，即市场的兴起和政府的退出。进一步有学者认为，比如 Eric Swyngedouw，他认为将来会出现一个后政治的社会，是由精英和技术人员按照技术的合理性来治理城市。城市的治理出现技术化，通过这种技术的处理将普通的公众排斥于城市的治理过程之外。而城市大型项目造成了用地与居住区的替换、公众参与的缺乏，标志着未来民主政治的衰落，将来传统的西方民主政治的过程就会慢慢消解，技术化的治理成为治理的主要方式。第二，就是对这种新自由主义解释的反思。他们认为新自由主义的解释未必是准确的。比如说，在英国伦敦的这种大型项目，实际上每一次的建设中间都存在着大量的社区动员，也存在着社区反抗和抗争，出现了居民公众参与和集体行动。这种解释是基于后工业化、后凯恩斯主义的背景，这种背景是不是适用于东方，或者说发展中国家、新兴经济体、转型经济体。大家认为，这样的解释未必是有效的。

2. 上海临港新城和伦敦老橡树地区开发治理的比较

我们能不能从中国的案例来理解中国城市的巨型项目开发，体现了什么样的未来城市治理模式呢？ 2015 年，我们得到了英国国家基金会的一项资助，用于研究未来城市治理。我们在伦敦选取了老橡树和皇家公园（Old Oak and Park Royal）地区，这是伦敦未来 20 年继金丝雀码头之后主要的一个开发项目。在上海，我们选取了临港新城，这主要是因为它的发展模式是集重工业、现代装备制造业和以居住为主的新城于一体。同时我们还做了自由廊道的研究，但在今天的报告里面，我不会详细介绍这个案例。

最近，我在上海做了一些访谈和了解。临港新城处于上海东南 70 公里的地方。洋山深水港的建设，意在通过港口促进城市发展，但是因为集装箱运输的特殊性——并不在陆地进行拆解，而是迅速转移到其他地方去，所以这个思路并没有得到完全实现，但是港城联动的思路在继续进行。由德国 GMB 公司按照英国花园城市的理念，总体设计了临港新城。

包括主城区，也就是滴水湖周围花园城市模式的地区，还有一个重装备物流区，另外还有一个主产业区和综合区，现在主要的开发是在主城区和重装备区进行。下一步，上海觉得临港是一个城市发展的机会，是上海捕捉新的产业转移的机会，是大力发展现代制造业，进行产业升级的机会。临港的很多土地是沿海围田出来，土地资源比较丰富，可以吸引大量重装备的企业。但临港的人口增长和其他地区如松江和嘉定新城相比，增长相对缓慢。

伦敦老橡树地区位于高铁 2 号线和跨伦敦铁路的交汇点，这个节点是非常重要的。老橡树地区有 6.5 平方公里，横跨了三个所谓的伦敦的区。它现在的状况是 72% 的土地由公共所持有，如国家铁路，还有一部分是由私营企业持有。伦敦的房价一直上涨，很难为那些关键岗位的从业人员提供可负担得起的住房。老橡树地区的开发，主要是为了解决伦敦的住房危机。伦敦未来目标是要提供 5 万套新房，以缓解这种压力，而老橡树地区计划提供 25 000 套。另外，跨伦敦的铁路建设需要筹措资金，在中国国内，利用土地捆绑来做基础设施建设开发，已经运用得比较娴熟，所以，这也是英国想要学习的地方。伦敦的老橡树地区，想通过沿线土地的开发，特别是站点的开发来获得资金，以支持基础设施的建设。从伦敦未来发展的一个俯瞰图可以看出跟英国传统的开发模式非常不同，是一个高度密集的开发模式。

从项目的目标来说，伦敦和上海是不同的。临港在上海成为国际大都市的过程中间提供产业用地，促进城市进一步产业升级，在国际新的劳动力分工中获得一席之地。而伦敦更多的是应对成为全球城市之后可负担得起住房的压力，解决老工业地区翻盖的问题，希望通过对这些地区的整形和更新，把伦敦建设成漂漂亮亮的城市。

从治理的结构来说（图 2），也就是从国家、市场、当地社区的视角来看，我们可以看到，在临港有非常强的领导，但是并不是一个均质的主体。市场的作用相对来说较小。如果看政府或者是国家的层面，临港其实是相当复杂的结构。临港地区管委会由两个管委会合并而成，当时两大开

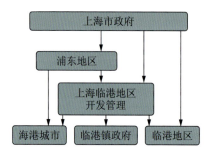

图 2
上海临港的治理结构

发公司之一的临港集团属于上海市所有，临港地区监管。而临港地区属于上海市浦东新区管，下面再管辖镇政府。

临港的开发主体是多元的，有多个国有开发公司。因为临港的开发比较缓慢，所以市政府推出了新的开发政策，就是希望浦东的四大开发公司挥师南下，各自承接一块临港功能地区的开发，这就是陆家嘴、金桥、张江和外高桥公司的开发。外高桥公司参与的开发相对比较弱，只是在临港的站点承接一些展览。

从参与开发的民营企业来看，有居住类的开发，比如说万科和宝龙；也有商业开发，宝龙集团开发了宝龙广场，还有大连的海昌开发了极地海洋世界。还有一些比较具体的，由政府跟民营企业所协商的开发，主要目的是让这些集团开发，形成人气，而不是单纯做房地产开发，所以我们把它们叫做"使命伙伴"（commission partner），因为它们带有一定的开发任务。从当地的社区来说，它有当地的居民，也有新临港人——外来的在临港工作的人员，也有外来的农民工、大学的学生等。

伦敦老橡树地区（图3），国家的角色是作为一个统筹规划的规划者，在市场中起到很大的作用。在市场上，有很大的私有土地开发者和土地所有者，在社区也形成了一些开发的社区集团、社区组织。伦敦的老橡树地区也做了一个开发集团。老橡树地区的开发集团直属于伦敦市，相当于是市属的开发集团。它有很强的功能，自己从事开发，同时从事规划管理，还可以审批规划。

图3
伦敦老橡树地区规划
架构

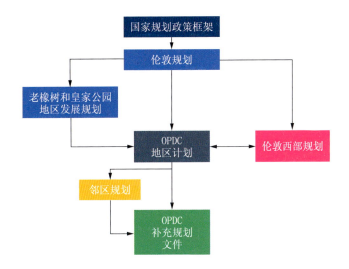

可以说，它是并行机构，在国家的规划开发体制下进行老橡树地区的规划和开发。它的地位在地方规划之上，可以替代地方规划，等于是一个

特区，在原来的地区规划上面做规划，这个规划比地方规划有更高的优先权。有一系列的空间规划文件，指导老橡树地区规划，包括伦敦规划。它的私有土地所有者有很大的势力，比如说那边有个做汽车买卖的公司，正好很幸运占有一大片土地，这些土地未来要进行开发。当然还有一些土地由国家铁路公司所有。还有一些其他的私有企业开发，像这个汽车开发的企业，就很强势进行它自己的规划。从社区来说，可以看出有很多不同类型的居民，包括少数民族、低收入的居民，在不同程度上，他们对未来的发展比较担忧。他们担心被排斥出去，包括一些小的工业企业，都有这样的担心。在这种情况下，市属的开发公司，反而是追求高密度开发。原因是我前面讲的，它要从大型的开发里面获得资金来支持伦敦的铁路开发建设。

这就是我对伦敦和上海临港地区的比较，可以发现，市政府和国家的体系的作用不同，在上海更多的是由国家所领导的，国家是一个领导者；而在伦敦，国家更多的是指导的作用。从国家市场开发和居民互动上来说，临港地区的社区是比较边缘化的，并不直接参与到规划当中，但他们也可以从规划中获益，主要通过拆迁获益，并不是说原有居民不能分享到开发的结果。比如说，在临港地区的开发过程中间，对原有居民进行拆迁，做了非常优惠的安置。某种意义上来说，上海通过对原有居民的优惠补偿来取得他们的支持。

随着临港地区的高速开发，也产生了一些环境问题。我们对居民访谈的结果是，他们不是反对拆迁，而是希望你尽量早点拆掉，好早点搬迁到其他的地方去。目前一些工业地区出现污染，他们更希望通过拆迁补偿到新的安置小区去，这样生活条件可以更好些。

在伦敦，有一个很明确的法定公众知情过程，公众参与的渠道比较明确。有一系列的规划咨询过程，同时居民的代表在开发公司（ODP）里面占有一席地位，这样使得居民公众可以进行高度参与。开发公司一定要和居民协商，不然很难开发。居民不仅仅是接受补偿，而且希望参与到预算当中去，进行实质性的参与。居民也对当地开发造成的包括噪音在内的环境困扰提出补偿的要求，如反对高铁2号的开发，如果要开发的话，就要进行补偿。这个原因是高铁项目在英国建设周期非常长，需要5年、10年或20年。你想想看，这一家人10年、20年在这样的工地环境上生活的话，肯定有很多不便和困难。如果我们比较一下临港和老橡树地区的公众参与，上海居民的一致性是通过高额补偿，使居民得到实际的好处来实现的，而老橡树地区则是通过地区的改善和对规划过程的参与实现的。

3. 未来城市治理的多元取向

从临港地区来看，未来城市治理是否就是一个所谓的新自由主义的走向呢？其实临港不完全是新自由主义发展的模式。临港有自己的开发使命，肩负着把上海提升到一个国际航运中心的责任，要把上海建设成具有全球竞争力的城市。特别是在现代制造业领域，它是由政府指挥的战略性项目，是由政府、国有企业所引导进行的。它的一些开发企业，像国有企业，担负着实现政府任务的使命，当然政府也不是叫它白白去做，它在做的过程中间也要获利，但是获利不单单是它的首要目标。临港的开发可能和中国其他城市也不同，并不是单纯的房地产开发，不是做土地的增值开发，然后出让土地获利，以便贡献地方土地财政，不单单是土地财政的模式。当然，有老师和同学可能有一些不同的看法。也许随着我们调查的深入，可以发现，实际上土地开发还是一个主要的模式。在这样的开发空间有一个很大的问题，这个问题就是政府如何主导开发，实现一个比较可持续的市场运行模式。这是当地很多开发企业面临的问题，如何能够维持它的运行模式。

临港开发是通过补偿来实现的，居民能够共享开发的好处，但是居民并没有直接参与到决策的过程当中。其中重要的一个问题就是我们缺少一个开发企业、开发机构和居民进行沟通交流的机制。虽然我们有一些展览，但这些多数属于公示，而不是实质性的参与。所以，事实上，临港提供了一个非常不同的治理模式。而就伦敦而言，它存在不同的社区群体，他们依法参加到城市建设的决策过程当中去，但是他们在多大程度上能够影响开发？在所谓的民主政治下，政府为了从土地中间产出资金来支持建设，而不得不对土地所有者让利，让土地所有者做他们想做的事，所以这个问题也出现在西方对未来民主政治的忧虑之中。

我说的这些案例，基本上是全球"北方"国家的案例。我觉得上海能够提供一些比较鲜活的案例，未来非常值得做进一步比较研究。

专家点评

罗守贵（上海交通大学安泰经济与管理学院教授）：吴老师的报告比较了上海临港和英国老橡树两个项目，给我们很多启发。因为大家看到老橡树有 6 平方公里，在西方国家是巨大的项目，但是从规模上来看，跟临港还是有巨大差异的。临港 311 平方公里，相当于三分之一的香港，超过了三分之二的新加坡，相当于澳门的 20 倍。我前期参加了这个项目论证，现在我们所看到的城市规划是德国专家做的。后来又扩充了产业基地等，早期没有考虑这么多。为什么当时考虑建设临港？中国大型项目开发的目标是多元的，往往复合了城市发展目标，复合了国家的开发战略。

当时，上海要建全球航运枢纽城市，这是参与国际竞争的需要。2000 年至 2001 年，上海集装箱吞吐量在全球排第三位。但是，上海市内已经不具备扩建深水港的条件了。因为长江口航道水深－11 米左右，不到－12 米。而第四代、第五代集装箱船的吃水深度需要－14 米到－15 米。经过反复论证，国家最终批准在洋山建设深水港。2002 年上海集装箱吞吐量在全球排第 6 位。2004 年洋山深水港口建好后，集装箱每年增长非常快，到 2010 年上海港的集装箱量已经到了全球第一位，把新加坡甩在后面了。因此，临港项目应运而生，这是一个大的系统，由港口、大桥和新城组成。

刚才吴老师讲的，比如说社区居民的参与不多，的确，在项目开发过程中让人民群体受益都是需要思考和关注的。以老橡树这个项目为例可以看出，从规划过程到公众的参与，均考虑了后续的发展与分享，这个值得学习。

全球城市中地方商街的多样性比较

陈向明

美国三一学院 Paul E. Raether 讲座教授

1. 地方商街比较研究的缘起

无论我们研究的是全球城市治理问题、经济发展问题，还是城市文化多样化问题，最终还是要回到人，就是我们这个城市中生活的群体。

然而，在全球城市研究中，这些最基层和最草根的尺度往往是我们所忽略的问题。我们总是从宏观看微观，从上往下看，关注结构因素。很少看人的行为、意识，以及他们所认同的东西。在日常生活中，很多在座的同学，你们最关注的往往是到学校周边的超市买食品是否方便。于是，我们选了这样的题目，选了6个全球城市，每一个城市选了两条街道，一共12条街道，从很微观的层面进行具体的比较研究，在每一个城市我们有一个小的团队进行实地调查、访谈以及运用其他各种各样的方法。

我们考虑为什么要研究地方商街这样的现象。这样小的空间、商店存在一种商业经济活动。我想举一个鲜明的观点，其实这样小的空间暗含的是一个有关社会活动、社会交往的研究。无论多么小的商店、咖啡店或者餐馆，都是我们日常生活、社区互动、人们交往之间的中心地。它们具有重要的意义。我们知道阿里巴巴、淘宝、京东以及大量的微商大大冲击了实体店，在我们研究的6个城市中，也发现很多这样的现象。

在这样的情况下，全球经济的一体化冲击了地区的实体经济，从而自下而上改变了社会经济商业之间的紧密关系。所以，我们将探讨这些商街如何变化，它们都变得一样了吗？什么使得它们趋同或有差异？随着时间空间推移的变化，商街会有怎样的复制、转换和再生的变化？

2. 地方商街的研究方法及其框架

第一点，全球地方商街研究的视角。我们选取了纽约和多伦多等 6 个城市。多伦多是一个全球化城市，纽约就不用说了。上海和东京代表东亚的两个全球城市，在欧洲我们选了阿姆斯特丹和柏林。我们已经开展了 3—4 年的调查，之后通过协作，还将对这个项目进行 5 年时间的研究。我想强调一下，商街这个小的空间，一般人会觉得没有特别大的意义、是习以为常的一个地方，而且我们经常使用这个空间。其实，买了一件小商品、喝了一杯咖啡、干一件小事，这其中暗含了很深层次的经济社会意义。此外，它还是一个公共场所，在这个领域大家相互交往，无论是生人、熟人，来自哪个地方，比如上海有很多农民工、流动人口，纽约有来自不同国家的人，50% 的多伦多居民生在国外，这其实是全球性的微观空间里面的一种展现。

第二点，全球化和地化的关系。全球化其实是一个一体化的过程，越来越趋同。在历史文化传承过程中，分散分割的局面很可能会出现很多的特性，我们怎么来识别全球化相关的共性以及表现在不同文化、地区上的个性。地方商街对我们研究全球或者本土的国内人口移动是个很好的视角。

第三点，全球地方商街研究的框架。很多西方国家的城市和上海的发展模式，都是由之前大拆大建逐步改变成密集型的发展模式。在这一城市转型过程中，商街的意义又是什么呢？下面我来简单分析一下我们的研究框架（图1），这里面看起来比较复杂，实际上并不复杂，我们可以看到有一个大三角和一个小三角，大三角指的是全球化动力最大、影响力量最强、渗透性最强的地方，影响到地方的商街。

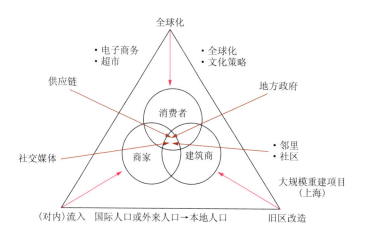

图 1
地方商街研究的框架

左下角是跨国或国内人口流动，在上海我们主要是指外来务工人员，在小商街这样的环境里面，精密度较高，他们竭力寻找生存的机会。右下角是指旧区改造，上海在6个城市比较当中有它的特点，重建规模比较大，纽约、多伦多两个城市只是重新改造城市中心，大家知道发达城市的发展是比较稳定和缓慢的。

我们研究的三个行动者，第一个是消费者，第二个是小商店里的店主或经营者，第三个是出租商铺的房东。上海很多人把自己的房子出租了，比如杨浦区工人社区的街道。我们选了这些个案，我强调每一个城市两条街道，老城区发展最早，很多居民被推到边缘。我们选了一个边缘区，一个中心区，中心区街道的商品价位较高。另外一条靠边缘主要生活着蓝领工人，研究这里不同类型的商店、不同的经营者和不同的移民背景，这些不同的因素对商店生存发展和更新取代所产生的影响。在东京，我们选了其中一条街道，纽约选的是布鲁克林的一条街道。这些小商街反映的是历史的持续性和变化性。很多商店之所以能够生存下来，因为它有一个历史上的延续，家庭一代一代传下来的小商店，能够持续几十年。随着全球化的渗入、移民的涌入、城市的更新，有些商店就会发生巨大的变化。

另外，我想讨论有关怀旧的一个问题。我们怎么看待文化遗产保护的问题？上海有个很明显的标志，老上海的东西，通过一种新的形式表现出来，然后和一些新的商业消费结合在一起，无论是高档的、中档的还是低档的。在澳大利亚，有个小伙子开了一家咖啡店，取的名字叫"公社"（Kommune），首字母C变成K，表现了一种政治上的怀旧，它的杯子都是老式的，有毛主席像的杯子，可以喝一杯咖啡，体会一下小咖啡店的情调，有历史往回走的感觉。

在全球化背景下，通过小的商街这样一种转换，我们发现一个地方就是一种文化情调、文化意识，可以跨越一个国界到另外一个地方展现。上海老的石库门，现在变成卖高档围巾的商店。中西的结合，很难说是中还是西，是两者之间一种混杂。石库门变成了意大利的餐馆，或是同时可以把美国的历史、美食展现出来的地方。

从我们举的例子可以看到，城市空间是一种制造和再造的过程，使不同的商界保持了共性，同时又看到了很多的聚集，带有文化色彩、历史背景的特性。

3. 地方商街中三个空间的理论思考

我们的理论构想包括三个空间：第一个是组织结构的空间；第二个是生活的空间，人在小的空间既可以工作又可以生活，如果住在二楼，一楼可以经营小咖啡店；第三，我们想象当中它的意义在什么地方？更大的意义在哪里？这样具体的分析框架，前面已经讲到了，我们要看外界因素和内在的因素的结合。至于小商店的供应链，不像大的连锁店，但实际上它们也有自己的供应，这个供应链可能很长，有一个地方全球经济联系的问题，同时刚才讲到地方政府的重要作用，对这些商街有哪些影响。政治上的对法律的制定、对规划当中的一些具体的管理如房屋执照的颁发，以及对其他各方面的管理起了很大的作用。我们的研究中有个扬州小伙子开美容店，给周围的老人剪头发，收费很低，这给上海应对老龄化加速提供了借鉴。又如，大众点评，它对消费方式的改变也起了一个很大的作用。政府有各种各样的机制影响小的商界，我们前面讲的有规划、税收、移民进入城市的管理问题。在上海还有其他问题，比如治安的问题，不允许小商贩在某些地方经营。还有政府的资金控制问题，我们现在物价这么高，很多商贩付不起这样的房租。

第二个是生活的空间，还有一个审美的问题。小商店怎么展示它的商品才能更好吸引顾客进来？卖的不是一个简单的东西，实际上是在卖品牌，卖一种文化和个人的意识，这对我们全球性城市带来很多文化多元的东西，还有社会交往的问题。以前上海退休的老人坐在街道上，但是田子坊拆迁以后，老人照样去。随着生活方式的变化，现代化使得传统的方式慢慢淡化，但是根基的东西不容易改变，新空间也给它带来不同的情调。

最后，我想讲的是想象的空间及其影响。以旅游为例，有些游客的网站，对餐饮的评价，对消费者和小商店的老板都有很大的影响。我简单介绍一下我们采用的几种不同方法。我们要了解一下 6 个城市 12 条街道人口变化的情况，搜集了每条街道 30 年的材料，上海历史较短，搜集了只有二十九年。此外我们还进行了行走的人数调查，我们每一个研究团队在这条街道上走来走去，从头走到尾。在田子坊，街道错综复杂，民星路有100 家商店，我们收集它的资料，有一个可比性，并进行了深入的访谈。我总结为 ABC，A 代表最简单的东西，比如最简单的画廊；B 代表特色，如精品店；C 是咖啡店。ABC 都是小商店代表性类型。老的街道首先因为有老的咖啡店，吸引了很多人不断搬进来，然后画廊、餐饮非常重要，喝咖啡不一定重要，在座的年轻人去星巴克的很多了。街道的改造现在越来越多地变成了这三者的结合，改变之后将出现什么情况？越来越多的文化多元。在纽约我们可以看得出来，90% 的洗衣店是移民在开。在上海，很大的流动人口经营这些小餐馆、各种各样的服务业，给我们的市民带来了很多生活上的方便，对提高市民的生活水平、提升全球城市文化资源是非常重要的。

专家点评

任　远（复旦大学社会发展与公共政策学院教授）：我很荣幸来评议陈向明教授的报告，最近10年来在这个方面我们一直在合作，我们看到最近陈向明教授关于地方商街的研究，从微观的视角看到上海发生的发展转型，在全球化力量下发生的改变。陈教授说到了不同商街的行动者、业主、创业者、地方居民，以及消费者如何受到全球化力量、资本力量的影响，谈到了地方政府规制和产权的作用，以及历史文化的积淀和核心文化的共同作用的印记。关于全球化地方的发展转型，我觉得这里面有非常多的可以挖掘的东西，比如说传统文化的保留和传承，地方产权制度和创新性产业的发展。这些都是全球城市鲜活成长的见证，是由上到下外部力量作用之下或者由下到上内部力量作用下的成长，它本身也受到人的活动的影响。这样的活动包括移民者、消费者，我们看到移民者进入城市之后，改变生活的价值，创造出不一样的城市。

这种全球生长是生机勃勃的，充满着生命力的。从地方商街的发展，它可能给我们一些新的启示。举个例子，我家小区边上的商街有非常多的房地产公司，而且一排排房地产公司甚至比餐饮都大，说明全球化资本力量在改变地方商街，地方商街功能可能就是有一种从地方商业、地方社会脱离的功能，过分强调了全球化力量之下，资本力量可能会脱离于地方社会这样的社会功能。这个可能就是全球商街发展中隐含着的一些威胁。

我们会发现在一些国际的消费者以及青年的创业者发展地方商街的过程中，把老人、贫困群体排挤出去了，有一些地方商街则在全球化商业过程中被整体排挤出去了。在全球化过程中，我们看到地方商街发展正在生机勃勃的同时，也需要注意到全球化可能对于地方商街的威胁。

深圳创新驱动经济升级的经验

赵登峰

深圳大学经济学院教授

1. 深圳在经济增速逐步收敛的同时成功实现了增长方式转变

2015 年深圳 GDP 的总量是 1.7 万亿元人民币，是上海的一半。深圳的人均 GDP 和年均 GDP 的增速，也在下滑。刚建特区的时候，深圳经济增速很快，起伏很大。这几年逐步下滑，到 10% 以下了。这是平均增速的方差（图 1），这个方差说明什么呢？近几年深圳经济增速虽是下滑的，但是比较平稳，起伏不大。与全国经济增速相比，深圳肯定比全国高一点，但是这个高的趋势越来越少，所以向全国平均水平回归。不仅深圳这样，北京、上海也是这样的，总量越大的城市，它回归的速度越快，北京、上海比深圳回归得更快。天津和重庆有点特殊，它们依然依赖于大规模投资的增长。深圳是一线城市里面投资率最小的城市。通过对京、沪、穗、深、津、渝等国内 10 个主要城市 GDP 及人均 GDP 增速变化情况的分析，我们得出以下两点结论：（1）各个城市 GDP 增速走势基本相似，总体呈下降趋势（2014 年下降到 10% 以下），经济总量越高的城市，增速

图 1
深圳市 GDP 平均增
速的方差

向全国均值回归的速度越快；（2）各市人均 GDP 差异比较大，说明各市发展质量参差不齐。

人均 GDP 是每年创造的财富，我把它折成每个月、每天、每小时，这是一个非常简约的劳动生产率的概念。深圳的人均 GDP 分母怎么算？深圳人口从来都是一个谜，常住人口 300 万，公安局登记的 110 万，但老百姓说有 2 500 万。深圳的面积仅有 1 954 平方公里，是一个非常小的城市，人口密度相当高。加之深圳年轻人和儿童人口很多，解决小学及初中就学问题成了深圳市政府最大的难题。

总的来说，35 年来深圳 GDP 增速逐步向全国平均水平收敛，但递减幅度逐渐减弱；人均 GDP 则长期保持全国领先，尤其 2010 年后深圳人均 GDP 增速稍快于其他城市，且领先优势呈扩大趋势，2014 年深圳人均 GDP 超过 2.4 万美元，进入成熟高收入城市经济体行列，这表明深圳在增速下降的同时，发展质量稳步提升。

2. 深圳产业转型升级与创新驱动增长的主要特点

深圳产业转型升级的成功实践主要得益于以下几点。（1）从农业社会变成现代社会，深圳实现了一个跨越。（2）抓住全球价值链和生产链重组的机遇。20 世纪 80 年代末 90 年代初，富士康在深圳建厂，从而使深圳在信息产业领域确立了在全球产业链和价值链当中的地位，被《经济学人》杂志誉为全球硬件的首都，硅谷的软件业也曾获得这个荣誉。从 PCT 国际专利 Top25 中的中国和美国比较来看（图 2），中国基本上集中在深圳，主要包括华为、中兴、腾讯、华星光电等。华为终端现在东莞注册，它的

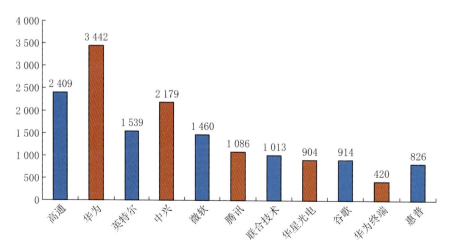

图 2
2014 年 PCT 国际专利申请 Top25 中美比较

总部华为全球控股公司在深圳的坂田基地。而微软、英特尔、联合技术和谷歌都是美国公司。高通前不久在深圳建立了研究所。苹果也到深圳建立了研发中心。富士康将大型制造厂搬到了山东、河南和四川，但是核心的研发中心仍留在深圳。其他的研发机构也集聚到深圳，这是一个典型的产业升级过程。

（3）人力资本的积累和科技创新，结构升级和增长方式转型。深圳市研发投入占 GDP 的比重超过 4%，接近于以色列的标准，超过全球 2.5% 的平均水平和我国 2% 的水平。北京是 6%，因为它有大研究所和大学。深圳没有这些，是以硬研究为主，主攻能够实现市场化的产品，这是深圳的特点。（4）深圳较好地发挥了市场和政府的作用，是全国少有的小政府，建立了比较完善的法治化市场体系，真正激励企业创新，实施产业分工政策。（5）不断提高产业要素生产率对经济的贡献。近 25 年来，深圳的全要素生产率总体呈上升趋势，且非常稳定（图 3）。2001 年高于全国水平，2012 年达到了 60%，接近发达国家水平，来自土地、劳动力和资本的贡献，为经济持续稳定增长提供了有力支撑，也成为深圳结构升级和转型成功的重要标志。

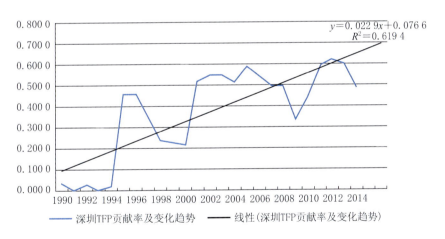

图 3
深圳全要素生产率贡献率及变化趋势

3. 创新是深圳实现可持续发展的动力之源

科技创新是引领深圳发展的第一驱动力。以科技创新为中心，以企业为主体的创新，依赖于基础科学的突破。高质量的增长表现为高新技术产品产值的增长，而拥有自主知识产权的高新技术产品产值的增长又是可持续的含金量最高的增长。自主知识产权无一不是来源于企业自身的研发努力，我们以大中企业 R&D 经费支出占主营业务的收入比重来代表企业自身的研发努力程度，那么，R&D 经费支出占主营业务的收入比重（以 SHAREr&d 表示）越高，拥有自主知识产权的高新技术产品产值占全部高新技术产品产值的比重（以 SHAREoutput 表示）就会越高。

回归测算可得如下预测方程：

$$SHAREoutput = 56.803\ 6 + 1.410\ 83\ SHAREr\&d\ (R^2 = 0.819\ 34)$$

其实华为现在跟高通的专利交换，高通在华为前面用了自主知识产权的 4G 技术，但基础专利方面还依赖于美国公司。图 4 和图 5 是深圳的专利申请量、授权量和高新技术产值的情况，R&D 经费的情况。

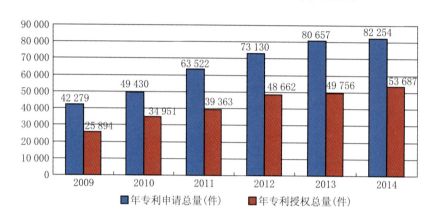

图 4
2009—2014 年深圳
专利申请量和授权量

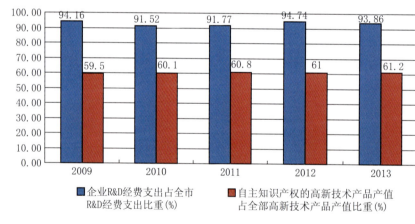

图 5
2009—2014 年深圳
高新技术产值情况

创新要素的汇聚和分工网络的演化，推动了深圳新产业新业态的迅速发展。放眼全球，深圳可能是仅有的集金融中心、科创中心和制造中心于一身的城市经济体。深圳有 350 家上市企业，200 多家在沪深两地上市，100 多家在海外上市。深圳制造业在通信设备、生物医药产业，包括一些高端制造业的前沿工业表现不俗。金融中心、科创中心、制造中心在美国的演化也是不一样的。像美国生物医药集中在波士顿、旧金山湾和圣地亚哥三个地区，而条件很好的新泽西、纽约、西雅图却失去了发展机会，重要原因是研究机构、医院、公司和风险投资机构并没有形成紧密的合作网络。因此，发展需要投资人、企业和研究机构的合力。三者在每个地方的主导不一样，一个要素主导了，另外两个要素就被吸引过去了。三个地方有三个地方的特色，波士顿的大学很发达，硅谷的创投很发达，圣地亚哥企业理念很发达，它们可以把风险投资和研究成果引过来。深圳是三个条件都具备的，这也要感谢深圳人自己敢闯，和上海差不多时间申请了证券交易所。

蔚然成风的创新氛围，孕育了深圳创新创业的蓬勃活力。人们来深圳追求公平，追求财富，追求自由，来了就是深圳人了。这是深圳文化，深圳没有任何地域歧视，深圳本地人也说普通话，深圳是移民城市。深圳具备较好的创新法制保障，相对公平、开放、透明的市场环境，比较健全的激励创新体制机制。深圳人敢闯，敢为人先，勇于冒尖，创新已经成为深圳的一种价值导向和生活方式，人人崇尚创新，人人希望创新，人人皆可创新的社会氛围在深圳蔚然成风。深圳汇聚了国内的追梦者和数以万计的国际创客，他们潮涨潮落般地自由来去，在深圳流动，在深圳沉淀，正是这千千万万的新移民，演化着深圳创业创新的城市性格，孕育着深圳创新发展的蓬勃活力。

4. 深圳市政府治理的几点启示

一是国家有一个大发展的好环境。由点到面实施对外开放政策，土地使用制度改革、价格改革等在深圳率先实施。在市场化、国际化、法治化方面，深圳做得也不错。

二是注重高效优质的公共产品供给。当然包括教育，尤其是要引进基础教育和高等教育。哈尔滨工业大学、北京大学、中山大学在深圳均有分校。

三是制定了合适的产业竞争和产业分工政策。深圳的产业政策是提供一个产业环境，深圳要扶持哪一家企业，不会扶持足够大，而是扶持一个相对应的企业来对抗它。比如，深圳要给华为订单，它一定也会给中兴。给光启，也会给其他一个相应的公司。所以，对于航空航天、机器人、未来产业，深圳也是有这样的规划。深圳市政府的作用是看得见的，但是非常有限。华大基因在北京发展不下去，去了杭州，最后到深圳来了，它拥有全球最强大的高通量基因测序仪的测序能力，全球第一。新疆的小米育种全部来自深圳的华大基因，这个小米有一些高热量的特点。不仅这些，像光启研究院是杜克大学的一个博士创办的。他是深圳中学毕业，在浙江大学上的本科，美国杜克大学读的研究生，拿到博士学位后，他想开发一种超材料，抹在飞机上，信号反射过去，雷达测不到，叫隐形材料。他想在国内实现产业化，第一次去了北京，北京副市长和他谈说给几百万元试试，他说几百万给我，我做不出来，做出来一定是骗子。又找到上海，上海说到我们国企部门，他觉得不能实现自己的梦想。回到深圳，准备打道回府了，回美国做普林斯顿大学教授去。深圳许勤市长是分管高科技的，知道这个消息马上叫他来谈，让专家组织了八轮论证，大家也都不知道他的东西是真是假，到底能不能行。深圳得出一个非共识创新，大家不能取得一致的意见，说试试看。第一轮是官方的资金扶持，让他以民营的研究机构进行企业化运作，后来起名光启。国家科技部前部长徐冠华来深圳考察，问他为什么起名光启，他说我特别崇拜明代天工开物的徐光启。现在，我们国家超材料研究中心也在深圳。广东省也计划扶持 1 800 万元。光启的专利生成很厉害，但是产业化还有待验证。

专家点评

　　陈　勇（深圳大学经济学院教授）：刚才赵老师把整个深圳的情况做了介绍，我再讲一些微观的。有人曾经问一个问题，为什么深圳出现了这么多伟大的企业，而上海没有出现。深圳伟大的企业有中兴、华为，金融业的平安集团、招商银行，还有腾讯。当时创始人想以 300 万卖掉腾讯，但是卖不掉，成就了现在这么巨大的企业，在香港上市市值 2 万亿港币。还有万科、比亚迪等很有国际影响的企业。

　　像赵老师讲的，深圳的一个特点就是小政府，深圳没有国有企业，在这些看起来不可能发展科技产业的环境下，恰巧深圳的科技产业得到很大发展。这是因为深圳是特区吗？最早一批经济特区有五个，但是最终只有深圳发展了，到底是什么原因？深圳的人口密度这么高，大家来自各个地方，到这里来就是想挣钱的，毕业的时候我导师叫我留在复旦，当时我如果留校读研究生每个月有 71 块钱，开始是 61 块钱，但是我到了深大工资是 200 多块钱。另外小政府有小政府的好处，很多大政府有自己的国有企业。钱往哪里放？自然都给了国有企业，小政府管不了那么多，让企业自己发展。

　　这些都是我零散的思考，深圳有些很好的企业，这是一个事实，只是现在还没有得出很好的原因去解释。另外，我最近在深圳创新投资集团挂职半年，刚刚结束。我在那边半年很有体会，那是一个政府控股企业，是中国 VC 行业最大的企业，管理的资金是 2 000 多亿人民币，完全是市场化操作。深圳政府给它 1 000 亿，佛山政府也让它管，此外还与全国各地政府建立了很多的基金。但是集团的整个运作，包括员工招聘，完全是市场化的。除了总裁跟董事长是组织部任命的，其他的员工都是通过市场化招聘来的。集团大概每年交给政府十个亿，其他的都按照市场化进行分配。我感觉深圳市场化根基的确比较深厚。

但是，深圳也有一些问题，税收太依赖于大的企业，大企业一旦走了，就会对深圳的税收产生很大的影响。有大量的企业，像华大基因，对深圳税收没有做出什么贡献。另外，还有巨无霸型的企业，像腾讯这些企业形成了自己的生态系统，你只要跟它竞争，就立即被收购，绝对不让你长大。这种情况下，政府如何去监管也有很大问题。一方面像腾讯这样的大型企业会越来越大，政府不敢反垄断，你不留我，到其他的地方，人家给我更好的待遇。这对竞争性行业产生了很大问题，在美国就会面临拆分。所以 BAT 可能是越做越大，百度相对弱一些，腾讯现在太强了，一般在香港上市公司的 PE 都是几倍，市值非常低，而腾讯可能是 40 来倍。全球发展比较中端的医疗器械生产企业迈瑞，它在美国上市，PE 也就 10 多倍。所以，我们对于产业政策，需要考虑怎样掌握这个平衡，哪怕是在深圳这个小政府的城市里，也遇到了垄断的问题。我提出的都是一些问题，供大家思考。

大城市的宜居和发展

陆　铭

上海交通大学安泰经济与管理学院特聘教授

今天我要谈谈城市的宜居和发展，特别是特大城市的宜居和发展问题。

1. 关于大城市宜居的理解

从理论上来说，对于大城市的宜居，跟小城市的宜居概念不太一样，我想提出以下三个方面。第一，大城市的宜居应体现对创业的构造和创新的推广。一个没有活力的城市是无从谈宜居的，特大城市宜居首先体现在其强大的活力和创新能力。另一个重要活力在于消费的多样性，城市经济借助于规模经济能实现消费的多样性，特别是服务消费的多样性。第二，大城市的宜居应体现交通的便捷。说到便捷便要强调路网、地铁网等方面，还有像香港中环的地上地下的连接通道。一个城市如果要建设路网、地铁网等基础设施，恰恰需要高密度的人口来支撑，如果没有高密度的人口，这些基础设施便无规模经济效应，那么在经济上也无法实现可持续发展。第三，大城市的宜居应体现环保。各大城市的环保不在于建大绿地、大公园。如今许多大城市里出现的公园往往是在工业化早期形成的，它们最大的价值不是绿地的价值，而是历史的价值。在出行方面，特大城市要强调绿色出行，这意味着高频率的地铁应用，自行车出行，甚至提倡步行；在公园方面，特大城市要注重"口袋公园"的建设，小而多；在绿化方面，特大城市要实现垂直绿化等立体绿化。

2. 关于大城市发展中的问题

首先来看城市规划方面的讨论。请大家明确这样一个概念，我们在讨论特大城市问题时，往往对"城市"概念的理解存在误区。例如，在东京和欧洲的很多城市里，"市"这个概念指的是一级公共服务和治理的管辖单位。但从经济意义上来说，其实是一个城市的概念，因为东京人完全可以住在新宿区或千代田区，但工作在东京。那么这个城市有多大呢？如果大家在图上关注东京的都市蔓延，会发现其直线距离有70公里，而且注意东京的地形，左边是山，右边是海，自然的边界导致了它的城市蔓延收缩。

其次来看城市基础设施。东京路网非常鲜明的特点就是街道特别密集，小马路多。欧美城市里很多老城市也是如此。比较密集的小马路，有毛细血管的作用，有疏解交通拥堵的作用。更重要的是，这么大密度的路网，使得街边比较易于行走。易于行走，人流就会增加，人流的增加也会增加商业和服务业的密度，进而减少附近居民生活的半径，减少生活半径会减少居民出行的需要，这是一个良性循环。接下来看十字路口的国际比较（图1）。这是世界银行所做的国际比较。前四个城市是东京和欧洲城市，每平方公里的交叉路口都在100以上，而东京已超过200，但在上海的浦东和北京的城北，每平方公里交叉路口的数量却只有东京的十分之一，这样的模式比较利于开车，而不利于街边的商业活力的形成，这会增加大家通勤的半径，反而不利于缓解拥堵。再看地铁方面，我们认为上海的地铁已经达到全球最长了，因为我们所用的地铁概念不同于其他国家。这个概念在其他国家被称为有轨交通，包括轻轨、轨道电车和城际铁路等，一起形成了这样的形态，它的密度和长度都远远超过了上海。据统计，东京的轨道交通在出行的占比超过80%，高峰期达到90%，所以它的地面交通拥堵大大得到了缓解。

再次来看公共管理方面的问题。从教育资源布局和人口布局的关系来

图 1
十字路口的国际比较

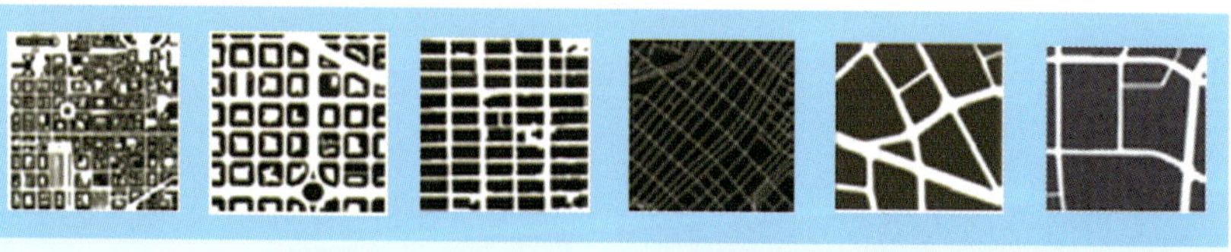

	都 灵	巴塞罗那	巴 黎	东京银座	上海浦东	北京城北
每平方公里交叉路口数量（个）	152	103	133	211	17	14
交叉路口之间的距离（米）	80	130	150	43	280	400

	区	"重点初中"	人口份额（2000）	人口份额（2010）	
中心城区	西　城	8	9.09%	6.34% ↓	28%
	东　城　72%	5	6.50%	4.69% ↓	
	海　淀	5	16.51%	16.73%	
	朝　阳	1	16.88%	18.08% ↑	
	石景山	1	3.60%	3.14%	
	丰　台	1	10.09%	10.77% ↑	
	其他边缘县	4	37.34%	40.26% ↑	
	总　数	25	100%	100%	

图 2
北京重点初中的分布

看，北京和上海这些城市有一个共同的特点，即优质的教育资源，中学或小学都集中在市中心。图 2 展示了北京重点初中的分布，三个中心城区的重点初中占 72%，而人口却只占 28%。这就形成了教育和居住地点的分离。在这样的情况下家长会如何应对呢？当然是开车送孩子上学。这种现象在通勤的研究里被称为是过度通勤，这样会增加交通的通勤量，那会引起怎样的交通变化呢？从北京交通的拥堵指数可以看到很多低谷区，凡是低谷的区域，都表示是在放寒暑假的时间段，因为这个时间段家长不需要送孩子上学。这种通勤实际上是由公共服务和居住之间的空间分离所导致的。

从居住地和就业地的关系来看，优质服务往往集中在市中心，上班地点也集中在市中心，而居住地往往在中心城周边。从第二次经济普查生活性服务业就业岗位的分布（图 3）来看，就业岗位主要集中在市中心。再

图 3
第二次经济普查上海市活性服务业就业岗位分布

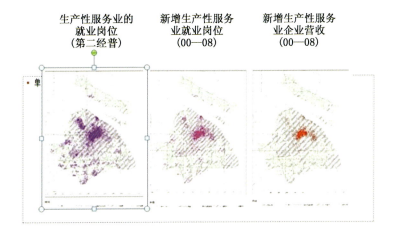

生产性服务业的就业岗位（第二经普）　新增生产性服务业就业岗位（00—08）　新增生产性服务业企业营收（00—08）

看增量也会发现，2000 年到 2008 年就业岗位的增量更加集中了，也就是营收更加集中了。服务业的特性会使它主要集中在市中心，而供给方会大量建楼，商贩的居住地又大量在郊区，这样就加强了城市里的"职住分离"。另外，我们用滴滴汽车的数据，显示早高峰打车下车的地方也是集中在市中心，因此不同数据验证了就业所在地还是在市中心。

从上海地铁卡的通勤（图 4）来看，可以非常清楚地看到高峰时期从郊区到中心城钟摆式的交通问题。

图 4
上海地铁卡通勤图

3. 关于大城市宜居和发展的建议

在城市里出现的很多问题，其实是供给方出了问题，供给方的问题还是需要通过供给方来解决。很多时候我们所抱怨的"城市病"，如公共服务的短缺，技术设施的短缺，是一个供给方和需求方的关系问题。如果抑制需求很有可能既损失经济增长，又损失效率，实际上还不一定是公平的，而增加供给既可以使经济发展和社会和谐，还可以有效管理、缓解和治理城市病。

理论上来说，市场和政府是互补关系。很多方面的问题都可以利用价格机制来调控，但我们往往没有充分地运用价格机制。尽管我们承认价格机制并不是完美的，而当市场上无法提供有效的价格机制时，政府的规划是非常重要的。但是规划一定要强调多种价值共生并存，市场和政府的结合一定要强调市场机制与政府的互补作用。

在实施规划和治理时，尽量针对行为本身，不要针对特定人群，尽量避免在一些工作政策中有这样的说法。我们处在发展的过程中，对实施这些政策的后果还没有很明确的认识。很多时候我们所制定的公共政策都是简单化的政策，却未能意识到我们简单化的做法对经济发展产生的负面影响。

随着城市的发展，必然会出现之前提到的一些问题，有高技能的人才进来，也会有低技能的人才进来。据我的研究，全世界范围都有这样的情况，越发达的一线城市，内部的收入差距就越大。道理很简单，因为最富的人进来了，为最富的人服务的人也进来了。那么，怎么来解决这个社会问题呢？通过公共服务的均等化，减少人们实际的福利差别。

专家点评

　　杨宏伟（上海城市创新经济研究中心首席研究员）：我想提一个自己一直在思考的问题，上海的挑战者究竟是谁？我之前对深圳做过研究，今天听了两位老师的演讲特别受启发，但我个人认为上海的挑战并不来自深圳，这是两个不同的城市。就像华为和招商银行是两个完全不同的企业，不是谁挑战谁的问题。大家对于深圳印象最深的就是它是中国最具活力的创新城市，这点是无人能出其右的。但是，上海的战略规划特别清楚。1992 年中共十四大报告已经把上海作为战略中心写进去了，经过将近 20 年的建设，已经基本上全部建成。现在上海要建的国际性的、全球性的中心至少有 10 个，除了经济、金融、贸易、航运中心，还有原来提过的亚洲医学中心、国际文化大都市，还有文化创意之都等。每个功能的实现都非常困难，上海能否同时支撑这么多的国际性中心建设，可能是上海接下来面临的最大挑战。我的建议是上海要进行反思，聚焦到最核心的功能上去。

Governing the Future City: Comparing Mega Urban Projects in London and Shanghai

Wu Fulong

Bartlett Professor of Planning at University College London

We have been well informed in the morning that cities nowadays are faced with many challenges. We should maintain a steady economic growth, provide better city life, fight against inequality and social desegregation and protect the environment at the same time. So how could we deal with the future city governance when confronted with so many challenges? There has been an immensely fierce inter-city competition for a long time. However, considering the political and economic diversification, urban governance is therefore a site for both urban and social innovations, which enables us to discover a new mode for future development. The central issue is how to and who should be delivering urban development. This is one of the most important issues concerning the future urban studies.

1. The impact of rising mega urban projects on urban governance

With a brief review on the history of British urban development, the state played a leading role in fulfilling modern public transportation and slum clearance before the 90's. It has long been criticized by both the left and the right. The left held the view that slum clearance would heavily impact the residents and disintegrate their original community. The right thought that over-inclusion of the state would replace the function of the society and increase the governmental expenditure, and as a result, the widespread opposition from the society may hinder the urban development projects.

In the 1990s, the so-called mega urban projects appeared as a new trend. They were based on Neoliberalism, laying emphasis on the market mechanism. The obsolete industrial lands on edge of cities and waterfront areas were used for urban construction to reduce the impact on the residents here. Meanwhile, these mega urban projects were characterized by new arrangements of public-private partnerships and mixed use of land. But such development pattern is quite controversial for it is still a question that who will be benefited. In fact, these mega urban projects have significantly influenced the city. They were not only intended for improving the urban living environment, but also establishing an economic entity to promote the competitiveness and gain profits.

By comparing the post-war urban projects with the mega urban projects since 1990s, we can see that the former is state-led while the latter is co-led by the state and the private corporations. Moreover, they attached emphasis to different aspects: the former laid more emphasis on infrastructures, cleaning and convenience while the latter is closely connected with economic development; and concerning the urban appearance the former is simply confined to construction of new town while the latter is more concerned with comprehensive development in all aspects. The biggest challenge for the mega urban projects is whether such a mode oriented towards the private-sector has brought about the so-called post-war political development.

The typical mega project, Canary Wharf in London (Fig.1), was operated by Olympia & York Company and designed by SION Company. There are some other similar financial new towns such as financial district of Paris, Amsterdam Zuid which connects the airport and downtown area. There is not only one such new district, but a group of mega projects, such as the Olympic Development Zone on the bank of Thames. These mega projects are not merely for living or industries. They form a large-scale comprehensive district for finance, office, business, entertainment and living. The development mode is characterized by its market orientation, public-private partnerships and especially the full application of the concept of market economy of Neoliberalism. In fact, the success of this mega project needs governmental support, especially in transportation infrastructures. Canary Wharf has actually been strongly supported by the government. These mega projects emphasize urban design and their overall planning. So there are usually some risks for them after the development cycle of real estates. Some property corporations may go bankrupt in the middle of development. In fact, these projects have brought about many impacts on the city. There formed a complex consisting of luxury residences, hotels, large office-towers and complexes and shopping malls. The projects produced spatial transformations through complex city and project management arrangements and structures and then changed urban governance.

Fig.1
London Canary
Wharf

Urban design is usually more concerned with mega projects and will not take the comprehensive land planning as the object of spatial planning. The particularity, large scale and high cost of these mega projects require the full mobilization of various social resources. Thus these mega urban projects will reflect the power, governance and planning in urban construction.

So what will be the trend of future urban governance? There are two major explanations within the academic circle.

The first one is the neoliberalism theory—greater market role while declining role of the state. Some scholars hold that there might be a post-politics society which will be governed by elites and professional groups. Urban governance will be superficial technical, excluding the wider public from urban governance. And replacement of residential areas caused by the projects will lead to little public participation. That will mark the decline of democratic politics, with traditional western democratic politics replaced by a highly technical mode of urban governance. The second is to reflect on neoliberalism theory among western countries. They believe that the explanation of neoliberalism theory might be inaccurate. For example, in London, there has been community resistance, even protests during the process of each mega construction project. The collective action can be seen in every mega project. The explanation is based on post-industrial and post-Keyness background. However, whether it works in the other countries like in the eastern countries or the developing countries remains uncertain. For instance, it makes no sense in the transitional economy.

2. The comparison between Shanghai Lingang and London Old Alley Area

Can we see what future governance mode is shown in the large-scale development of China's metropolis by making an analysis of some cases? In 2015, we received funding from the UK State Foundation for study of future urban governance. We selected Old Alley Area in London, which is the main development project for Canary Wharf in London for the next 20 years. In Shanghai, we chose Lingang New Town, which mainly for heavy industries and residence. We have also analyzed the case "Corridors of Freedom".

Shanghai Lingang is 70 km southeast of Shanghai's center city. Since the containers can't be operated on land, they are transferred to other area. Lingang has then gradually evolved into Lingang New Town because of the development concept of "One City, Nine Towns". It was designed by a German company and constructed according to the designing concept of garden city in Britain. The new town is divided into the following several parts: the main urban area, surrounded by Dripping Lake; a heavy equipment area and a logistics area; a main industrial area and a comprehensive area. And now the development of Lingang focuses on the urban area and the heavy equipment area. Lingang offers opportunities for both urban development and Shanghai's industrial transfer, and it also offers a chance to develop manufacturing industry and industrial upgrading. The area is abundant in land resources because a lot of land here comes from coastal enclosure. Thus it can attract a large number of heavy equipment corporations. Compared with other areas in Shanghai, the population growth here is at a relatively slower speed.

London's Old Alley Area is actually at the important intersection of High Speed Rail 2 and the Trans-London Railway. The Old Alley Area covers an area of 6.5 square kilometers across three London boroughs. 72% of the land is supported by the public. The National Railway is funded by private companies. The main problem London is facing is the housing crisis. The house price in London keeps rising and thus it is difficult for the common workers to afford the house. Therefore, London needs to build more than 50 000 new affordable homes per year to ease pressure. Half of them will be distributed to the old districts. In addition, the railway system across London needs funds. In China we bind the infrastructure construction with property development. London can learn from China. London's Old Oak Area acquires funds through establishing stations so as to support infrastructure. This is a glimpse of London's airscape. Old Oak is different from the British traditional development mode and a high-density one. The figure on the left is the typical British residential area and the present Old Oak Area will later develop into what is shown on the right figure.

So London and Shanghai differ from each other in their project objectives. Lingang offers industrial land for Shanghai, promoting its industrial upgrading and winning a place for new international labor force. While after becoming a global city, London has to tackle housing crisis and deal with reconstruction of the old industrial areas in order to revitalize post industrial London into a "shinier and newer" city.

In terms of the governance structure (Fig.2), Lingang New Town is composed of the following three parts: state, market and local community. The

Fig.2
Structure of
governance of
Lingang

market plays a relatively insignificant role here. But the structure of government is quite complicated. The district administrative committee is joint by two administrative committees. The two major development corporations belong to Shanghai Government, is only supervised by Lingang. Lingang New Town belongs to Pudong District, so it is governed by the local government of Pudong.

The main development body of Lingang is a highly diverse group composed of several state-owned development corporations. Considering its slow development, the municipal government launched a new policy, hoping that Big Four in Pudong could build a development zone in southern area which covers Lujiazui, Jinqiao, Zhangjiang and Gaoqiao. Gaoqiao is mainly responsible for undertaking some exhibitions.

As for the private corporations, there are developers like Vanke's Powerlong Square and Haichang's Polar Ocean World. At the same time, there are some specific development projects which are settled through the government's coordination with the private enterprises. The main purpose of these projects is not merely confined to property development, but to make these enterprises more popular. We call these corporations "commission partner" because they can fulfill the task of development. And as for the local community, it consists of local residents, new comers, company employees, migrant workers and university students and so on.

For Old Oak (Fig.3), the state plays a role as a planner in charge of coordinating and planning and plays a significant role in the market. There are

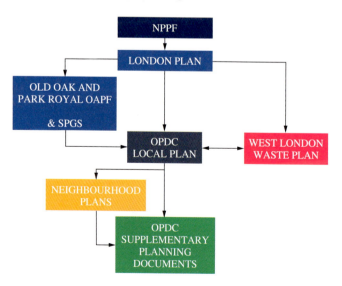

Fig.3
The Old Oak Area Planning

a large number of private land developers and landowners in the community, forming a number of development community groups and community organizations. Old Oak in London has its own developers and they belong to the London market alone, equal to a municipal development group. Its development group is not only engaged in development but also involved in urban planning.

Old Oak and Park Royal Development Corporation (OPDC) is such an organization carrying on the developments under the national planning and development system. At the same time it is above local planning and can be used as an alternative for local planning. It is like a community making planning on the basis of local planning. However, compared with local planning, it enjoys priority. There are a series of spatial planning documents including London plan. Its private landowners hold great influence. For instance, when a car company possesses a large piece of land which needs to be developed, it can make its own development plan.

As for the community, a large number of residents from various groups including ethnic minorities and low-income residents are concerned about their future development to different degrees. They are worried that they might be excluded one day. So are the small-scale industrial corporations. Under such a condition, the development corporations of municipal government are pursuing rapid development in order to, as I have mentioned just now, garner funds for construction of London railways.

Above all is my comparison between London and Shanghai Lingang Area. The municipal government and the state in the system in the two cities differ in their functions. The state acts as a primary driver in the urban development in Shanghai while in London the state acts the role of guidance.

In terms of Interaction between residents, state and developers in Lingang, local community in Lingang is relatively marginalized for it is not directly involved in planning. But it doesn't mean they can't share the benefits. They are mainly benefited through house demolition. For example, the middle part of Lingang Area could be demolished and the government will well relocate the residents and pay them gorgeous compensation. In a sense, Shanghai tries to win support by offering the residents favorable compensation.

With the rapid development of Lingang, a series of environmental problems arose. Residents we have interviewed told us that they were not opposed to demolition. Instead they hoped that it could be done as soon as possible so that they could move to other places. Since some industrial areas are heavily polluted now, the residents prefer a better relocation with better living conditions via the demolition compensation.

While in London, there is a broad range of mechanism for community participation including extensive public consultations from the OPDC and private developers. The representatives of the residents have a say in the affairs of development corporations and it ensures more participation of the public. The developers must consult the residents otherwise it is impossible for them to develop in that area. What the residents want is not only the compensation, but also substantial inclusion in decision-making of the budget. Besides, the residents have required compensations for noise and environmental problems caused by the development. And they strongly opposed the establishment of high-speed rail 2 unless they were paid with compensation. The reason is that this high speed railway construction project covers a long period in Britain, maybe 5, 10 or even 20 years. You can imagine that there will be much inconvenience and numerous difficulties for a family living in such environment. If we make a comparison of the public participation between Lingang and Old Oak, resident consensus is reached in Lingang through tangible benefit sharing like gorgeous compensation while resident consensus is achieved through promises of area improvement and inclusion into the planning process.

3. The pluralistic tendency for urban governance in the future

Is the future urban governance neoliberal governance in terms of Lingang? In fact, the development pattern of Lingang is not completely neoliberal. Lingang has its own development mission, to consolidate a hub of international transportation and create a "globally competitive" Shanghai. In modern fields, the state orchestrated strategic project is usually co-developed by the state and state-owned corporations. So the state-owned corporations are trusted with the mission of the state to fulfill the development. Certainly, the government will compensate for it. Meanwhile they will make profits from the development, but that is secondary objective. The development of Lingang is different from other areas. It goes beyond the property development which makes profits by selling the property. According to our research, the main method of development is actually land development. But it is a serious issue how the state should lead the development for a sustainable market operation. And how to maintain such an operation is the main problem most development corporations are facing.

Though resident consensus is reached through tangible benefit sharing in Lingang, the residents are not directly involved in decision-making because of the absence of formal mechanisms for them to communicate with the development corporations and organizations. Though the decision-making is put for public opinions, the residents are not substantially included in it. As for London, diverse community groups participated in decision-making of urban construction. But their influence on it is yet unknown. In spite of the democratic politics, in order to extract the planning gain, the state gives greater discretion to developers, the big landowners, and let them do whatever they want. That's one of the concerns of the western countries about their democratic politics.

All the examples that I have enlisted here are in the global scope. Shanghai can offer some more vivid cases and they are worth our further study.

Remark

Luo Shougui (Professor of Antai College of Economics and Management, Shanghai Jiao Tong University): Professor Wu has compared the two projects, Shanghai Lingang New Town and London Old Oak. It did enlighten us. The two projects differ in their scale. The Old Oak covers only 6 square kilometers, while Lingang covers 311 square kilometers, equaling one third of Hong Kong, more than 60% or 70% of Singapore, and 20 times as large as Macao. Indeed, I was included in the analysis of the project in the early stage. The urban planning shown in the picture is fulfilled by a German company. Later the project expanded to include the industry base. Why was it added to the project? The mega projects in China usually have multiple objectives, consistent with urban and national development.

During the research, we found that it was important for Shanghai to become an international shipping hub city with global competitiveness. From 2000 to 2001, the number of containers in Shanghai ranked in the third place of the world. However, Shanghai is not suitable for expanding the deepwater port any longer. The Yangtze River was badly silted up at its mouth. As a result, the water level rose at most to between 11 m and 12 m. However, the height of our fourth and fifth drafts need 14 m to 15 m, so here is not suitable for containers. Our state took it very seriously when we asked it for support because South Korea is to build a hub port in Busan, taking China as its hinterland.

Later in 2002, the number of containers in Shanghai ranked the 6th in the world. It increased rapidly every year after the establishment of the port in 2004 and then surpassed Singapore to be the first in 2010. This indicates that the project is actually a national strategy. The Lingang project builds a new town which connects the land with the bridge and expands from 100 square kilometers to 300 square kilometers. Consideration should be given to the funding of the project. This is very complicated, but Shanghai can find a way out. Balance of funds is not only within the project, but also outside the project. Just as Mr. Wu have mentioned in the speech, the development of state-owned corporations within the project, such as Shanghai Automobile City and building roads for cars, does not make any money in fact. However, developing a land nearby can make money. So it is difficult to balance the fund merely within the project.

But it also has some disadvantages, such as little participation of the residents. I knew that some of the indigenous rural residents in Lingang took the compensation and left after the project was completed. They just thought urban construction was none of their business. Thus there comes the issue of sustainability, including distribution of benefits. In the case I've mentioned, the residents were benefited while the state was not. Considering the planning, public participation and ensuing problems, we can learn from Old Oak.

Global Cities, Local Streets—Everyday Diversity from New York to Shanghai

Chen Xiangming

Paul E. Raether Distinguished Professor of Global Urban Studies and Sociology at Trinity College in Hartford，Connecticut

1. The origin of comparative study of local streets

No matter dealing with issues concerning global urban governance, economic development or urban cultural diversity, we will finally come to the topic of people, the group of those living in the city.

But this fundamental issue is usually ignored by us when we make the research on global cities. We always analyze an issue from the macro to micro level, from the bottom to the up or from the aspect of structure while pays little attention to what a person does and thinks and what he is concerned about his daily life. Most of you might be students of Shanghai Jiao Tong University and I think what you're most concerned might be whether it is convenient to buy food in the supermarkets. So we choose the topic and select altogether 12 commercial streets, two per city in the six cities around the world. We make our research from the micro aspect. There is a small team in each city doing investigations and interviews.

We have to think about why we have to study phenomena such as local streets, a small space where commercial activities take place. But I want to point out here is that the study of the local streets is actually study of social behaviors and social interactions. Small stores, coffee houses or small restaurants are all centers of our social interaction and communication in our daily life. They are of great importance. It is known to us that Alibaba, Taobao, Jingdong and a large number of online businesses have greatly impacted the physical business. It is also the case within the six cities we have chosen.

The economic globalization has had great impacts on the regional entity economy, changing the close relationship between the social economic businesses from bottom to up. So what we are going to explore is whether these are becoming the same, and what makes them the same or different. In addition, how will the commercial streets copy, transform and rebirth with the gradual change of time and space?

2. The research methods and recent findings of local streets

Among the six global cities, we have chosen Toronto and New York. Toronto is a very interesting city and also a global one. New York is a city you must be very familiar with. And we choose Shanghai and Tokyo, representing international cities in eastern Asia, and choose Amsterdam and Berlin in Europe. The project has last for 3 to 4 years and it will take another 5 years to do our research. Firstly I want to emphasize that such a small space like the commercial street usually means the place which is of little importance and one that we have been accustomed to and often utilize. But there are social and economic implications in purchasing a small item or drinking a cup of coffee. Besides, as a public place, people interact with each other here no matter they are strangers or not and where they come from. For instance, there are a lot of migrant workers and mobile population; there are people from various countries in New York; and 50% of residents in Toronto are born abroad. This is a manifestation of globalization in tiny space.

The second point is about globalization and localization. Globalization is a process of integration with differences becoming more and more alike. But during the development of history and culture, the fragmentation and separation will lead to localization. So how do we deal with the similarities and localities in different cultures and areas? I think the local commercial streets provide an excellent perspective for us to study global or local mobilization of population.

Thirdly, the study of local commercial streets all over the world will deepen our research. Cities like Shanghai and those in western countries have gradually adopted the intensive development pattern after demolition and reconstruction. What is the meaning of the commercial streets in the transformation of those cities? Let me make a simple analysis of this framework (Fig.1). It seems to be quite complicated, but actually not. Here we can see a bigger triangle and a smaller one. The bigger one means where is the greatest global impetus and the most powerful influence even on the local commercial streets.

Fig.1
Research framework of local commercial streets

In the left bottom, it is what we call transnational or internal population movement. We can see that in Shanghai migrant workers are trying to make a living by doing businesses in the small commercial streets. In the right bottom, what we can see is the reconstruction of old districts. Shanghai is distinguished from other cities in its large scale reconstruction. While New York and Toronto only reconstruct their city centers after demolition because, as we all know, developed cities develop more stably and slowly.

The three actors in our study are respectively the consumers, the small stores owners, and the house owners that rent the houses to the vendors. Many Shanghai house owners have rent their houses out, such as those Workers' Community in Yangpu District. We've intentionally selected two residential districts in each city. One is a marginalized district where most blue-collar workers live and the other is in the center of the city where the prices are usually higher. Thus we can see how various elements like different kinds of stores, different store entrepreneurs and migrants from different background, will influence the development and upgrading of those stores.

We have chosen two streets in Tokyo and Brooklyn District of New York respectively. The small commercial streets reflect the continuation and variation of history. Many of them can survive because of the continuation of history. The small stores were passed from generation to generation, some of which could last for decades. While some of them underwent a tremendous transformation influenced by globalization and immigrants and upgrading of the city. I will elaborate this later.

Besides, I want to talk something about nostalgia. How should we treat preservation of cultural heritage? Old Shanghai things, one distinctive characteristics of Shanghai, reappear in a new form via combination with some new ways of consumption of different levels. An Australian young guy opens a coffee house, named Kommune. This coffee house indeed reflects the political nostalgia. He replaces the "C" in commune with K. Commune is a word with strong political tint in Chinese. And the coffee cups are very quaint, with Chairman Mao's picture on it. You can have a cup of coffee, experiencing the atmosphere of the small coffee house. It is like travelling back to the past.

Owing to globalization, the culture in one area can transcend the national boundaries to be displayed other areas in the world through small business streets. As the landmark of Shanghai, the Old Shikumen is now converted to a store selling high-end women's scarves. It's hard to define whether it is east or west. It is in fact a combination of Chinese and Western culture. This is an Italian restaurant in Shikumen. And over there are restaurants displaying both American history and delicacies. People could come to enjoy the meal, and at the same time learn about the history.

According to these examples, urban space is continuingly constructed and reconstructed in which different business communities can maintain their own constant quality and different cultures with strong locality and historical background congregate.

3. The theoretical framework including three kinds of space

Now I would like to elaborate our theoretical framework which includes three kinds of space. The first is structured space. The second is about living space, where people can work as well as live. For example one could live on the second floor and open a coffee house on the ground floor at the same time. Besides, we should think about what is meaning of it. Well, the specific analytical framework has already been mentioned before. We should take both external and internal factors into consideration. The small stores have their own supply chains, which are quite different from the big chain stores. Their supply chains may be very long, and they reflect the relationship between local and global economy. We have already talked about the important role of local governments and how they influence these business streets. The laws and regulations also exert great influences on the administration of licenses of some houses. There is a young guy opening a beauty shop aiming at the elder people around with very low charge. In a sense, it helps to tackle the problems caused by increasing expansion of aging population in Shanghai. Additionally, it comes to the popular app Dazhong Holdings. Whenever we dine out, we can make a comparison between the restaurants on this app to decide which one to choose. And we can also comment on the restaurants or the coffee houses on it. It greatly changed the consumption history. The governmental mechanisms also have an effect on the small businesses, such as taxes, management of immigrants we have mentioned. And the vendors are prohibited in some places for security. The governments also hold great influences in financial control. Some small store entrepreneurs cannot afford the rent due to the high prices.

Besides, it is a matter of aesthetics in the living space for the small store entrepreneurs to display its goods to attract customers. What they are selling is the brand, the culture and their personal taste rather than a simple item. In this way, it contributes to cultural diversity and social interactions. The retired elder people used to sit in the street in Shanghai and they still went to Tianzifang after it broke down. Modernization alters our lifestyles and the tradition ones are fading away. But what is deep-rooted in our culture will last and new living space will add a new element to it.

Finally, I want to talk about the imagined space and its effects. Taking tourism as an example, the comments on those travelling websites have greatly affected both consumers and small store entrepreneurs. Let me briefly introduce our researching methods we employed. We had a general understanding of population change in the twelve streets of the six cities by collecting data of the recent 30 years (We only collected the recent 20 years' data of Shanghai for its short history). Moreover, our team walked on every street to collect data and materials as well as did interviews. The streets of Tianzifang are very complicated. There are totally 100 stores on Minxing Road. We collected information there and did in-depth interviews. Here I would like to conclude my opinions as ABC. What A stands for? A stands for the simplest thing, such as the simplest galleries; B stands for properties, such as boutiques; C stands for the coffee shop. They are all the places with the most representative small stores.

The old streets at first usually attract a lot of people to move in because of the old coffee houses. The art galleries and restaurants are very important. Coffee houses are not necessarily important, because more and more young people here tend to go to Starbucks. Therefore the combination of these three is more and more typical in street reconstruction. What would happen then? The culture would be more and more diverse. In New York, 90% of the laundries are opened by the immigrants. And in Shanghai the migrants are operating stores, restaurants and other service industries. For themselves, their lives is improved. At the same time, it makes our life more convenient. So the global urban cultural resources are of great significance.

Remark

Ren Yuan (Professor of School of Social Development and Public Policy of Fudan University): We have been cooperating in this area in the past 10 years. We've noticed that Professor Chen's report has presented us the transformation of Shanghai influenced by globalization from a micro-perspective. Professor Chen also talked about how different street merchants, owners, entrepreneurs, local residents and consumers were affected by globalization and global capital; he also mentioned the role of the local government in reorganizing and reallocating local property; besides he expounded the influence of history and culture. There are numerous issues worth our attention, such as preservation and inheritance of our traditional culture, the development of local property rights and innovative industries. All these mentioned above are marks of vibrant growth of the global cities, from the bottom to the top influenced by external forces and from the top to the bottom influenced by internal forces. Such a growth is also affected by activities of people like immigrants and consumers. We could see that immigrants have changed their own lives as well as renewed the city since they entered into cities.

The local business streets also give us some illumination. Today when I am walking on the surrounding of our community, I see a lot of real estate companies on each side of the street, which are larger than restaurants. It indicates that global capital is altering the local commercial streets. But the local commercial streets might separate itself from local business and local society. Overemphasis on global capital might lead to separation from the local society. This may be one of the hidden threats in the development of the global streets.

In addition, the development of local commercial streets also did harm to some people. For instance, the inclusion of international consumers and young entrepreneur might lead to exclusion of the group of old and poor residents from the process of development. And sometimes the whole local commercial streets might be excluded from global business. Therefore, we should not only pay heed to the growth of local commercial streets, but also to the threats it might bring us during the process of globalization.

Experiences and Enlightenments of Shenzhen Innovation-driven Transformation and Upgrading

Zhao Dengfeng

Professor of School of Economics of Shenzhen University

1. Shenzhen has successfully changed its way of growth with convergence in the face of slowing down of economic growth

Shenzhen's total amount of GDP is 1.7 trillion Yuan in 2015, which is half of Shanghai's GDP. The growth rate of per capita GDP and the average annual GDP in Shenzhen are also declining. When the special economic zone was first set up, Shenzhen's economy underwent a rapid growth. But it is gradually sliding over the past few years, below 10%. This is the average growth rate variance of Shenzhen's GDP (Fig.1). What does it mean? It means that in recent years, Shenzhen's economy slipped, but it is relatively stable. The fluctuation is not high. Compared to national economic growth rate, Shenzhen is higher, but this trend is less and less, and is returning to the national average level. Not only in Shenzhen, Beijing and Shanghai are the same case. The greater the total economy size of the city is, the faster it returns to average level. Beijing and Shanghai return faster than Shenzhen. Tianjin and Chongqing are a bit special, as they still rely on the growth of large-scale investment. Among the first-tier cities, Shenzhen has the smallest investment rate. Through analysis of the growth rate of GDP and per capita GDP of 10 domestic cities including Beijing, Shanghai, Guangzhou, Shenzhen, Tianjin, Chongqing and so on, we have drawn the following two conclusions: (1) GDP growth in various cities is basically a similar general downward trend (In 2014, the growth rate fell to 10% and less), the greater the total economy size of the city is, the faster it returns to average level. (2) The gap among cities is large, indicating the uneven development quality.

Fig.1
Average growth
rate variance of
Shenzhen's GDP

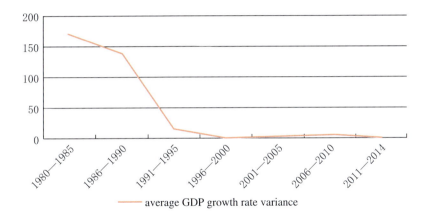

average GDP growth rate variance

Per capita GDP can be counted by month, day and hour, which is a very simple concept of labor productivity. How to count the denominator of per capita GDP in Shenzhen? Shenzhen's population has always been a mystery. The household population is 3 million. The living population registered in the Public Security Bureau is said to be 1.1 million. But people say there are 25 million. Shenzhen's land area is 1954 square kilometers, which is a very small city, and the population density is very high. Besides, Shenzhen has many young people and children, the schooling of primary and junior school students is the biggest problem faced by Shenzhen Municipal Government.

Generally speaking, in the past 35 years, GDP growth in Shenzhen slows down to the national average level, but the decline gradually weakens. Its per capita GDP goes ahead of the rest country in the long term. Especially after 2010, Shenzhen's per capita GDP grows faster than other cities. Besides, its leading advantage tends to expand. Its per capita GDP in 2014 exceeded over 24 000 US dollars, entering mature and high-income rank of urban economies. This shows that despite the growth decline, Shenzhen has been improving steadily its development quality.

2. Main features of Shenzhen's industrial transformation, upgrading and innovation-driven growth

Shenzhen owes its successful practice of industrial transformation and upgrading to the following points: (1) Shenzhen has achieved a leap-forward development by changing from agricultural society into modern society. (2)

Shenzhen has seized the opportunity of reorganizing global value chain and the production chain. In the late 80s and early 90s, Foxconn was set up in Shenzhen. Hence, in the field of information industry, Shenzhen established its position in the global industrial chain and the value chain. Besides, Shenzhen is hailed as the capital of global hardware by *the Economist*. The software industry in Silicon Valley also won this honor. By comparing China and the United States in the top 25 PCT international patent application in 2014 (Fig.2). China is basically concentrated in Shenzhen, like Huawei, ZTE, Tencent and CSOT (China Star Optoelectronic Technology). Huawei terminal is registered in Dongguan, Guangdong province. But its headquarters, the global holding company is in Bantian base, Shenzhen. Whereas Microsoft, Intel, Google and UTC are American companies. Qualcomm established a research institute not long ago in Shenzhen. Apple also set up a research institute in Shenzhen. Foxconn moved its large manufacturing factories to Shandong, Henan and Sichuan province, but the core R&D center is still in Shenzhen. In addition, the other R&D institutions also come to Shenzhen. This is a typical upgrading process.

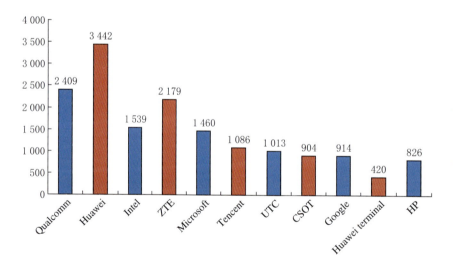

Fig.2
Comparison between China and the United States in the top 25 PCT International Patent Application in 2014

(3)Shenzhen attributes its success to the accumulation of human capital, innovation, structural upgrading and transformation of growth mode. In Shenzhen, R&D accounts for over 4% of GDP, close to Israel standard, surpassing the global average level of 2.5% and our national level of 2%. Beijing is 6%, as it has large research institutes and universities, but Shenzhen doesn't. Shenzhen focuses on hard research and marketable products. This is the characteristic of Shenzhen. (4) Shenzhen gives full play to market and the government. It has a small government, which is rare in China. The government improves the law-oriented market system, truly encourages business innovation and promote industrial division policies. (5) Shenzhen has been continuously improving contribution of industrial productivity to the economy. Shenzhen's total factor productivity in the past 25 years presents an upward trend, and it is very stable (Fig.3). In 2001, it is higher than the national level. In 2002, it reached 60%, which close to the level of developed countries. Contribution from the land, labor and capital strongly supports the stable economic growth and is also the important sign of successful industrial upgrading and transformation of growth in Shenzhen.

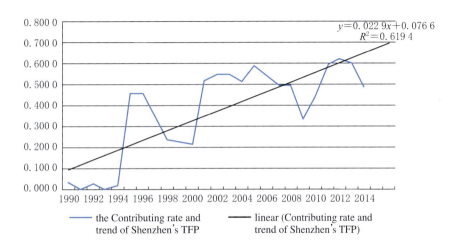

Fig.3 Contributing rate and trend of Shenzhen's TFP

3. Innovation is the origin of driving force in helping Shenzhen realize sustainable development

Scientific and technological innovation represents the first driving force steering Shenzhen's development. Innovation centered on science and technology and which enterprises function as key players in depends on the breakthrough in the basic science. High-quality growth is manifested by the growth of the value of high-technology products. Furthermore, the growth of the value of high-technology products with independent intellectual property is sustainable and has the highest value. In addition, independent intellectual property comes from the R&D efforts of enterprises. Here, we use the proportion of R&D in main business revenue of all sizes of firms to measure their R&D work. Therefore, the higher the R&D fund accounts for the main business revenue (it is displayed by SHARE R&D), the higher the value of high-technology products with independent intellectual property occupies in all high-technology products.

A prediction equation can be drawn from the regression measurement.

$$SHAREoutput = 56.803\ 6 + 1.410\ 83\ SHAREr\&d\ (R^2 = 0.819\ 34)$$

In fact, Huawei today exchanges patents with Qualcomm. Qualcomm adopts independent intellectual property rights in 4G ahead of Huawei, but its basic patent still depends on the American company. This is the amount of patent applications and licensing, value of high-tech industries and R&D fund (Fig.4 & Fig.5).

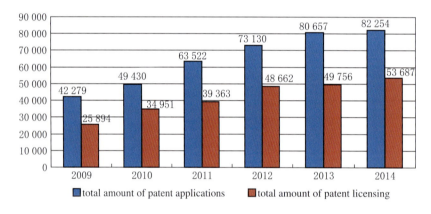

Fig.4
Amount of patent applications and licensing from 2009 to 2014

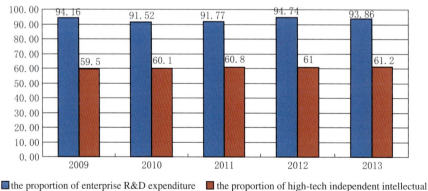

Fig.5
Value of Shenzhen's high-tech industries from 2009 to 2013

The convergence of innovative elements and evolution of division network promote the rapid development of new industries in Shenzhen. Around the globe, Shenzhen might be the only urban economy integrating financial, technological and manufacturing center. There are 350 public companies in Shenzhen, over 200 of them are listed in Shanghai and Shenzhen, and more than 100 companies are listed in overseas market. Shenzhen's manufacturing industry performs well in communications equipment, biotechnology, including some high-end manufacturing industry's leading edge manufacturing. Financial, technological and manufacturing center in the United States have different evolution, like biotechnology and medicine are concentrated in San Francisco, Boston and San Diego. But New Jersey, New York and Seattle lost development opportunities despite their good conditions. The major reason lied in the research institutes, hospitals, companies and venture capital institutes didn't form a close cooperation network. Development depends on the synergy of investors, enterprises and research institutes. Each place focuses on different attraction goal. If one place dominates one factor, the other two factors are also attracted. The three places have their local characteristics, Boston boasts wonderful universities, Silicon Valley's venture capital investment is quite developed, San Diego has very developed enterprise concept. They can introduce risk investments and research result. Shenzhen is equipped with three conditions, and it is due to that Shenzhen people are daring. They applied for the stock exchange almost at the same time with Shanghai.

Prevailing innovation atmosphere gives birth to the vitality of innovation and entrepreneurship. People come to pursuit fairness, wealth and freedom in Shenzhen. They become Shenzhen people after arrival. This is the culture of Shenzhen. There is no geographical discrimination. The local people also speak Mandarin. Shenzhen is an immigrant city. Therefore, Shenzhen is equipped with sound legal guarantee, relatively fair, open and transparent market environment and sound innovation-encouraging system. Shenzhen people are adventurous and daring to stand out. Innovation has become value orientation and lifestyle of Shenzhen. Everyone advocates innovation, wants to innovate and can innovate, which becomes a common practice in Shenzhen. Shenzhen gathers domestic dreamers and tens of thousands of creators. They come and go as free as the tide, move and root in Shenzhen. It is those millions of new immigrants who have evolved the city character of entrepreneurship and innovation and produced the vitality of innovative development in Shenzhen.

4. Some enlightenments of Shenzhen government governance

First, the country has a good development environment and carried out opening-up from a pilot area to a broader region. So, land use reform and price reform were first implemented in Shenzhen. Furthermore, Shenzhen does well in marketization, internationalization and legalization.

Second, Shenzhen focuses on efficient and high-quality public product supply, which includes education, especially basic education and higher education. We have had branches of Harbin Institute of Technology, Peking University and Sun Yat-sen University in Shenzhen.

Third, Shenzhen government formulated industrial policy concerning competition within the industry and labor division between industries. Shenzhen's industrial policy is to provide an industrial environment. Shenzhen will not support an enterprise too much, but support rivals against it. If Shenzhen places order to Huawei, it will also give orders to ZTE, or if it gives order to Kuang-chi, it will also give order to its competitors. As for the robot, aerospace and future industries, Shenzhen will implement the same policy. The role of the Shenzhen government is visible, but very limited. BGI couldn't go on in Beijing at first, it then moved to Hangzhou and finally came to Shenzhen, which has the world's strongest high-throughput gene sequencing ability. The breeding of Xinjiang's millet with high-calorie feature comes from BGI. Besides, Kuang-chi Research Institute was founded by a PHD graduated from Duke University. He graduated from Shenzhen High School, and took his undergraduate program in Zhejiang University. After taking the doctoral title, he wanted to achieve a kind of invisible metamaterial in China which can be spread on the plane, and radar can't detect the signal reflected by it. He first went to Beijing. The deputy mayor talked with him and planned to offer several million Yuan. He said that he couldn't make it with that amount of money. Then he turned to Shanghai and was asked to go to state-owned enterprise for trial, but he thought he couldn't realize his dream. He finally went back to Shenzhen and decided to return to America and work as the professor of Princeton. Xu Qin, deputy mayor of Shenzhen, who is in charge of high technology immediately asked him to discuss after knowing the news. Xu asked experts to do eight rounds of arguments, but no one knew what he said would be true or false or viable. So Shenzhen reached a non-consensus innovation, and had a try. The first round of official funds supported him to execute business-oriented operation in the name of private research institution. The institute name was later called Kuang-chi. Xu Guanhua, former minister of National Ministry of Science and Technology, visited Shenzhen and asked why it was called Kuang-chi? He said I worshiped Xu Kuang-chi, author of Heavenly Creations in the Ming Dynasty. Now, China National Research Institute of Metamaterial is also in Shenzhen. Science and Technology Department of Guangdong province says that Guangdong Province plans to support 18 million. The patent generation of Kuang-chi is very powerful, but the industrialization still needs further proof.

Remark

Chen Yong (Dean and Professor of School of Economics of Shenzhen University): Professor Zhao has introduced Shenzhen about its macro-situation and I would like to talk about some microaspects. Someone once asked a question: Why are there so many great enterprises in Shenzhen, whereas only few in Shanghai? Shenzhen has enterprises, like ZTE, Huawei, Ping An Group, China Merchants Bank as well as Tencent, which was once to be sold by its founders for three million yuan, but could not find any buyer, and now it has developed into a huge enterprise, with its listed market value of 2 trillion Hong Kong dollars. In addition, there are many companies with international impact, such as Vanke and BYD.

As Professor Zhao has said, one of the characteristics of Shenzhen is its small government, there is no state-owned enterprises in Shenzhen. Under these seemingly unfavorable circumstances to develop technology industry, Shenzhen's technology industry has developed rapidly. What is the reason? Is it because Shenzhen is a special economic zone? Among the first five special economic zones, only Shenzhen has developed into today's stage, what is the reason? Actually, Shenzhen has attracted a large number of people all over China, whose sole purpose is to make money. Upon my graduation, my instructor asked me to stay in Fudan University for further study. At that time, a postgraduate in Fudan can get 71 yuan each month, but I earned more than 200 yuan as a teacher in Shenzhen University. Moreover, small government has its own advantages. Many large governments have their own state-owned enterprises, and they will support the enterprises financially. But with a small government in Shenzhen, it will not interfere with the enterprises and let them develop on their own.

These are my thoughts. It is a fact that there are many great enterprises in Shenzhen, but presently there aren't any good explanations for it. In the last six months I have taken a temporary post in Shenzhen Capital Group, and I have deep feelings for that experience. It is a government-controlled enterprise, the largest in China's venture capital industry, with managing funds of over 200 billion yuan. Even though it is government-controlled enterprise which manages 100 billion yuan government funds of Shenzhen and has established funds with Foshan and other cities' governments all over China, its overall operation is fully market-oriented, including staff recruitment. In the whole group, only the president and the chairman of the board of directors are appointed by the Ministry of Organization, other employees are all recruited through market operations. I feel that market-orientation is deeply rooted in Shenzhen.

However, there are also some problems. The tax revenue of Shenzhen is too dependent on large enterprises like ZTE, Huawei, and Tencent. Once they are gone, it will have significant impacts on Shenzhen's tax. There are also a large number of enterprises which didn't make any contributions to Shenzhen's tax revenue, for example, BGI. Besides, there are jumbo enterprises, such as BAT and Tencent. They have developed their own ecosystems, as long as you compete with them, you will be immediately acquired, having no chance to develop. In this case, the government also has regulation problems. Large enterprises such as Tencent will become increasingly large, and the government, being afraid that the enterprises might move to other cities, would not dare to implement antitrust practices. This will be detrimental to competitive industries. Such enterprises would face the risk of being split in the United States, but it's totally different in China. So BAT may grow even bigger, Baidu might be in a relatively moderate state, but Tencent is now too strong. Generally companies listed in Hong Kong have low P/E ratio, for enterprises like China Construction Bank the ratio is three to four times, but for Tencent, the ratio is around 40 times. Mindray, a global mid-end medical device manufacturer, when listed in the United States, the P/E ratio was around 10 times. Now it has been delisted from the US, the shareholders divide their accumulated billions over the years as dividends, and then make investment and list in China. So there are many problems in our industrial policy, how to solve such problems as balancing development and carry out antitrust in Shenzhen with its small government remains a question. That's my comments, mainly raising questions for your deliberation.

The Livability and Development of Mega Cities

Lu Ming

Distinguished Professor of Antai College of Economics and

Management，Shanghai Jiao Tong University

Today, I am going to talk about the livability and development of cities, especially mega cities.

1. What is the livable mega cities

Theoretically, I would like to mention the following three aspects of livable mega cities, which are different from the concept of livability in small cities. The first feature of a livable mega city is the promotion of innovation and entrepreneurship, a city without vitality can never be counted as a livable city. So the first feature for mega cities to be livable should be their vitality and innovation. Another important aspect to show the vitality of cities is the diversity of consumption. With the scale economies of cities, diversity of consumption can be achieved in urban economy, particularly the diversity of consumer services. Secondly, a livable mega city should have a convenient transportation which mostly emphasizes the use of metro network, roads patterns and connecting path like Hongkong's central ring road which connects the ground and underground. A high-density of population is just needed if a city wants to build metro network or roads patterns. Without a high-density population, these infrastructures can never achieve their scales of economy, which doesn't contribute to the sustainable development of the economy. Thirdly, a livable mega city should emphasize environmental protection. Environmental protection in major cities lies not in their building of a large green space or large parks. Nowadays, the large parks seen in major cities were mostly built in the early

分论坛二　FORUM II　｜　249

stages of industrialization, and their greatest value lie not in the value of a green land but the value of being historical. Speaking of travel in mega cities, green travel should be promoted, which means the high frequency and large use of subway, bicycle, even on foot. As to park construction, small but greater number of Pocket Parks should be promoted. With regard to green coverage, vertical greening should be achieved in place of the construction of large-area parks.

2. The problems during the process of mega cities development

First of all, please take a look at the issue of city planning, here, I would like to clarify a point: nowadays, when we are talking about mega-city issues, we even have misunderstandings about this concept of "city" in most cases. If we look at the situation in Tokyo, and many cities in Europe, the concept of the "City" actually refers to the fact of the first level of jurisdiction units for public service and governance. But in the sense of economy, it's just a mega city, since it's normal for Tokyo citizens to live in Chiba, but work in Tokyo. Then how big exactly is the city? As you may see from the map, the city area of Tokyo has spread to this location, which is actually a straight-line distance of 70 km. And if we pay attention to the terrain of Tokyo, we'll find that the left side of the city is mountain area, and the right part is the sea, which means the natural boundaries of the city has led to its contraction of urban expanding.

Next, let us look at the condition of infrastructure.The road condition in Tokyo reveals a very distinctive feature: the street network is particularly dense and there are lots of small roads. Many old cities in Europe and America are also like that. Dense small roads could play the role of capillaries which is quite useful to ease traffic congestion. Also, such high density of the road network makes the streets easily accessible which will increase the density of human flow. Thus resulting in more prosperous commercial activities and service industries, thereby reducing the radius of the residents living nearby which may reduce their needs to travel, which forms a virtuous circle, therefore, the model of small roads helps to ease traffic congestion. Next, let's look at the international comparison of crossroads (Fig.1), which is done by the World Bank. The first four cities displayed here are Tokyo and some European cities, it's easy to see that the number of intersections each square kilometer exceeds 100 in these cities, and Tokyo has already reached 200. But in Pudong of Shanghai and the northern part of Beijing the number of intersection per square kilometer is only one-tenth of Tokyo. And such a model is more conducive for driving, but it is not beneficial to conduct commercial activities on the street, which will increase the radius of commuting, therefore not being conducive to alleviate traffic congestion. And as for the subway, we believe that Shanghai subway is the world's longest, however concept of subway we use here is broad, this concept actually is equivalent to rail traffic in other countries, including light rail, rail tram, and intercity rail. So, the density and length of all those altogether in other countries' cities will definitely exceed those in Shanghai. According to statistics, the rail traffic use in Tokyo has accounted for more than 80%, and it is 90% in peak hours. Therefore, its ground traffic congestion has been greatly eased.

Thirdly, let's look at the issue about public administration. From the relationship between education layout and population distribution, one may find cities like Beijing and Shanghai have a common feature. Many of our high-quality educational resources are concentrated in the middle of the city. Fig.2 shows the distribution of key junior high schools in Beijing, the three central districts have accounted for 72% of key junior high schools, while the population in these areas is only about 28%, which means the separation between

Fig.1
The international comparison of crossroads

	Turin	Barcelona	Paris	Tokyo Ginza	Shanghai Pudong	Beijing North
The number of crossroads per square kilometer	152	103	133	211	17	14
The distance between crossroads	80	130	150	43	280	400

educational area and residential area. What then will the parents do in such situation? Certainly they will drive their children to schools. This is known as excessive commuting in commuting studies which increases traffic commuting. And what kind of traffic change it will lead to? The traffic congestion index in Beijing has shown a lot of bottom points, which refers to the traffic condition in summer and winter holidays, when parents do not need to drive their children to school. It's all clear to see that such commute is actually caused by the separate spatial distribution between public services and the residential areas.

From the relationship between place of residence and employment. One will find quality service is often concentrated in the city center, so is work place, but residential area is often around the city center. And according to the service industry employment positions distribution during the second economic census in Shanghai (Fig.3), it reveals the majority of employment positions are in the city center. If we look at the increments, we will find the increased employment positions from 2 000 to 2008 are also centralized in the city center, so does the revenue. The characteristics of the service industry means it'll be mainly concentrated in the city center, and the suppliers will provide a large number of commercial buildings, but the residential areas for vendors are mainly located

Fig.2
The distribution of key junior high schools in Beijing

	District	"Key Junior High Schools"	Population Share (2000)	Population Share (2010)	
Central District	Xicheng District	8	9.09%	6.34% ↓	28%
	Dongcheng District 72%	5	6.50%	4.69% ↓	
	Haidian District	5	16.51%	16.73%	
	Chaoyang District	1	16.88%	18.08% ↑	
	Shijingshan District	1	3.60%	3.14%	
	Fengtai District	1	10.09%	10.77% ↑	
	Other Counties	4	37.34%	40.26% ↑	
	Total Number	25	100%	100%	

in the suburbs, thus strengthening the "separation between work place and residential areas" in cities. In addition, we have used Didi data to see the pickup and drop-off places during peak hours, and find out that the places are also concentrated in the city center, so different data have validated that the locations of employment are mainly in the city center.

Fig.3
The Service Industry Employment Positions Distribution during the Second Economic Census in Shanghai

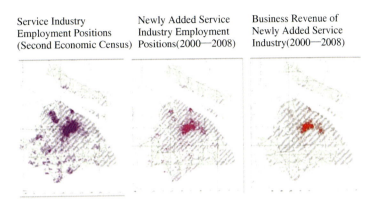

Service Industry Employment Positions (Second Economic Census)

Newly Added Service Industry Employment Positions(2000—2008)

Business Revenue of Newly Added Service Industry(2000—2008)

From the subway card commuting map (Fig.4), the pendulum-style traffic problems from the suburbs to the central city during peak period is clearly revealed.

Fig.4
Subway card commuting map in Shanghai

3. Suggestions for the livability and development of mega cities

Lots of the problems we now encounter in cities are, in fact, caused by problems from the supply side. And the problems from the supply side should surely be solved by the same side. The urban diseases, such as the shortage of public services or technical facilities, that complained by us often result from the unbalanced relationship between supply and demand. If we suppress demand, it is likely to result in the loss of both economic growth and efficiency which could be unfair. Whereas, an increased supply can not only promote economic development and social harmony, but it also can effectively mitigate and govern urban disease.

Theoretically, there is a complementary relationship between market and government. The price mechanism can be frequently used for many aspects, though we haven't yet taken it to full advantage. We admit that the price mechanism is not perfect, but when it is not effectively used in the market, it's vital that government planning should come into play. But government planning must emphasize multiple values, symbiosis and coexistence. The combination of the roles of both market and government must place emphasis on the complementary role of market mechanism and the government.

In addition, in terms of economic policy, during the process of its planning and implementation, try to target against the certain behavior in itself, rather than the specific groups, and try to avoid such terms directed to specific groups. We are in the process of development and have not yet been fully aware of the consequences of this policy. Our public policy tends to be simplified, but most of us are unaware of the negative impact of such simplified approach on economic development.

With the development of the city, some problems I've mentioned earlier will definitely emerge, more and more high-skilled talents will come in, so will the low-skilled talents. According to my research, it shows that such a situation happens all over the world, the income gap will be greater in the more developed first-tier cities. And the reason is very simple, because with the richest people entering the city, those who work for them will come along. Then how to deal with this social issue? Through the equalization of public services as well as bridging the welfare gap among different groups.

Remark

Yang Hongwei (Chief Researcher of Shanghai Urban Innovation Economy Think-Tank): I would like to start by a question which I have been thinking about for a long time, who is Shanghai's challenger? I have once made researches on the case of Shenzhen, and today the two experts' presentation inspired me deeply. But in my personal point of view, Shanghai's challenge does not come from Shenzhen. Shanghai and Shenzhen are two different cities. Just like Huawei and China Merchants Bank, they are two completely different enterprises. So there is no challenge in their relations. I think Shanghai's advantage lies in its clear strategy layout. Comparatively, when talking about Shenzhen, we are mostly impressed by its vitality and innovation, which has no rival in China. Report of the 14th National Congress of CPC in 1992 has put Shanghai as a strategic center, and after nearly 20 years of development, basically all the objectives have been completed. Shanghai is still moving on, with clear positioning. At present, there are at least 10 international global centers to be built in Shanghai. Shanghai is now developing into four international centers, namely, economic, financial, trade and shipping center. Besides, other objectives have been put forward, such as the Asian Medical Center, the international cultural metropolis, cultural and innovation capital. As far as I am concerned, each function is very difficult to achieve. The problem is that whether Shanghai could afford to serve so many international centers at the same time. This, I believe, is the biggest challenge that Shanghai faces in the years to come. My proposal is that Shanghai should focus on its core functions.

FORUM III

分论坛三

Innovations in Urban Transportation Governance and Management

城市交通治理创新

主持人·HOST
彭仲仁·Peng Zhongren
上海交通大学船舶海洋与建筑工程学院教授
Professor of School of Naval Architecture，Ocean and Civil Engineering，
Shanghai Jiao Tong University

城市交通治理创新分论坛现场嘉宾聆听演讲

Guests at the Innovations in Urban Transportation Governance and Management Parallel Forum are listening to the speeches attentively

上海交通大学船舶海洋与建筑工程学院彭仲仁教授主持平行分论坛三

Peng Zhongren，Professor of School of Naval Architecture，Ocean and Civil Engineering of Shanghai Jiao Tong University，hosts the Parallel Forum III

东南大学土木建筑交通学部主任王炜在平行分论坛三上作专题演讲

Wang Wei，Dean and Professor of the College of Civil，Construction and Transportation Engineering，Southeast University，delivers a speech at the Parallel Forum III

纽约大都会交通管理局副局长麦克·谢佛在平行分论坛三上作专题演讲

Michael Shiffer，Vice President of Metropolitan Transportation Authority in NYC，delivers a speech at the Parallel Forum III

新加坡土地交通管理局研究院院长雷德顺在平行分论坛三上作专题演讲

Looi Teik Soon，Dean of Land Transport Authority（LTA）Academy in Singapore，delivers a speech at the Parallel Forum III

同济大学交通运输工程学院陈小鸿教授在平行分论坛三上作点评

Chen Xiaohong，Professor of College of Transportation Engineering of Tongji University，Comments on the Parallel Forum III

北京工业大学建筑工程学院关宏志教授在平行分论坛三上作点评

Guan Hongzhi，Professor of College of Architecture and Civil Engineering of
Beijing University of Technology，comments on the Parallel Forum III

麻省理工学院城市研究与规划系教授约瑟夫·费雷拉在平行分论坛三上作专题演讲

Joseph Ferreira，Professor of Urban Studies and Planning Department at
MIT，delivers a speech at the Parallel Forum III

日本广岛大学教授张峻屹在平行分论坛三上作专题演讲

Zhang Junyi，Professor of Hiroshima University，delivers a speech
at the Parallel Forum III

同济大学建筑与城市规划学院教授潘海啸在平行分论坛三上作点评

Pan Haixiao，Professor of College of Architecture and Urban Planning
of Tongji University，comments on the Parallel Forum III

上海交通大学船舶海洋与建筑工程学院教授李朝阳在平行分论坛三上作点评

Li Chaoyang，Professor of School of Naval Architecture，Ocean and Civil Engineering of Shanghai Jiao Tong University，comments on the Parallel Forum III

城市交通拥堵的形成机理与缓堵策略

王 炜

东南大学土木建筑交通学部主任、教授

1. 中国城市交通大规模拥堵的成因

　　城际交通越来越快、城市交通越来越堵是当今中国交通的两大特点。中国城市交通为什么出现大规模的拥堵？我认为最重要的原因是交通需求与交通供给之间的一种失衡。众所周知，进入 21 世纪以来，快速城镇化使大城市居民的平均出行距离从 2 公里增长到 6 公里，从以前的骑自行车出行到现在乘车开车出行。中国城市交通正在经历从自行车主导的非机动化供需平衡向以机动车为主导的机动化供需平衡转变。我们举两个例子，北京 2015 年机动车增加到 430 万辆，南京 2015 年私家车增长 80 倍。这一阶段交通失衡的原因是机动化需求突然增长，而对应的交通供给却相对滞后，这最大限度激化了供需矛盾，即快速城镇化导致交通供需失衡，造成交通结构的转型。

　　我们需平稳度过转型期，因为交通结构转型一旦形成，很难逆转。问题的关键是，我们采取什么样的转变形式？当然，我们希望以自行车为主导的供需平衡向以公交为主导的供需平衡转变。如果这样，交通问题将比较容易解决。但是，如果要朝着私家车主导的供需平衡转变，当前的基础设施建设成本和将来的交通设施维护成本会非常大。更重要的是，过度的大型交通基础设施建设，把城市建成了"钢筋混凝土森林"，城市生态环境受到严重破坏。因此，在中国缓解交通拥堵，最好的方式就是建立公交主导的交通体系来实现供需平衡。

2. 缓解中国城市交通拥堵的三条技术主线

　　城市化与机动化的双重压力使得公交主导策略的实施难度非常大，那么怎么解决？缓解中国城市交通拥堵，要沿着三条技术主线走：第一，通过交通引导城市扩展，提高交通供给的有效性，提升运输能力，实现城市综合交通系统的供需平衡；第二，通过城市综合交通体系的系统协同，提升城市交通质量；第三，通过发展城市智能交通技术（ITS），重构城市交通理论体系、开发城市交通系统软件、搭建城市交通虚拟平台，提升城市综合交通系统的效能。下面详细介绍每条主线的内容：

第一个技术主线策略是城市交通系统的供需平衡。我们要从源头上缓解交通拥堵，需要解决三个问题。

一是城市空间、土地开发跟城市交通的协同问题。城市形态与土地利用开发决定了城市的交通需求总量与空间分布。城市形态不合理、土地开发无序，就会产生非理性的交通需求。中国长期以来城市交通规划跟城市总体规划是严重脱节的，交通设施建设是被动适应城市的开发，交通设施规模过大，综合功能低下，造成大量非理性的交通需求。

二是城市交通结构的优化与技术引导。在满足城市居民出行效率的前提下，形成城市低碳交通系统结构，打造公交主导的机动化模式。我们要通过公交畅通来吸引城市居民通勤出行向公共交通转移，为老百姓提供一个高品质的公交系统；引导居民理性购买私家车，以实现城市交通结构的优化。

中国城市交通结构非常丰富，不同的出行距离有不同的交通出行方式，比如短距离步行单车，中距离普通公交，长距离轨道交通，远距离私人汽车。在一个特定的城市，居民出行的距离曲线是一定的。我们就可以根据模型确定这个城市的最佳交通结构。图1是我们东南大学对50多个中国城市出行调查后，根据步行、自行车、小汽车、公交车、地铁出行的最佳比例绘制的。大城市应该建立以轨道交通为骨干，地面公交为主体，步行、自行车、小汽车等多种交通方式协调运转的绿色出行系统。

三是建立一个高品质的城市公共交通体系。要抓住两个核心：一方面，要构建一个多模式、多层次的公共交通网络系统（包括骨架网、主干

图1
不同交通方式的出行距离

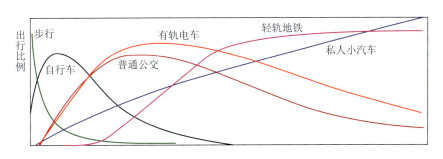

网、支撑网）；另一方面，要为解决城市公交系统快速通行问题提供技术保障。根据南京等城市主要公交线路延误情况的调查显示，2/3 的延误在交叉口，1/3 的延误在站点。由于造成公交线路车辆通行速度低的主要原因是交叉口延误，我们据此提出"公交主干线绿波通行技术"，通过路口时空资源优化利用及交通信号协同控制、公交车辆速度诱导，实现公交车辆绿波通行。这样可以大幅度提升公交车辆的通行效率，公交优先效果很好，社会车辆也不受影响。

第二个技术主线策略是城市综合交通体系的协同。我认为至少在以下三个方面需要进行思路的转变：

一是交通设施功能从土木工程向交通工程转变。我们交通基础设施总体数量不少，工程质量也很高，但是系统功能太弱。其根本原因是城市交通规划的缺失，导致交通供给的有效性不足。举一个典型的例子，2016 年 9 月 19 日，郑州市花 6.5 亿建成一座立交桥，通车首日就堵死，原因就在于这座立交桥跟周边交通网络没有形成很好的匹配，只强调土木工程，没有考察它的交通系统工程。

二是城市交通设施从越大越好到系统匹配转变。这 35 年我们都做大的交通工程，我们只重视大路（快速路、主干道）建设，不重视道路网络功能完善（次干道、支路密度不足，联通性差，交叉口通行能力低），道路网络整体功能与运行效率低。因此，应该对道路网络的等级进行合理配置，快速路、主干路、次干路、支路长度比例约为 1:2:3:6。

三是城市综合交通网络从条块分割到系统协同转变。当前城市交通很复杂，除了以前道路交通网络，更多的是轨道交通网络，例如地铁。但是这些网络长期以来都条块分割（图 2），没有形成一个系统，甚至相互之间是冲突的。因此，要研究以综合交通枢纽为核心，城市道路、轨道交通、

图 2
城市综合交通系统协同布局优化技术

地面公交、机场、高铁等互联互通的城市综合交通系统协同布局优化技术，实现主要交通方式之间无缝连接。所以我们强调首先是网络的协同，建设综合交通枢纽，关键是实现零距离换乘，然后是信息的协同，服务的协同，最终三位一体，提升整个城市综合交通网络的通行能力。

第三个技术主线策略是城市综合交通体系的效能提升。目前中国城市交通系统整体运行效率很低，交通系统脆弱，可靠性差。现在最好的解决办法是"城市智能交通技术（ITS）"，"互联网 + 交通"是智慧城市建设的核心之一。但是在实施"互联网 + 交通"的时候，我们存在巨大的技术瓶颈，ITS 实际上是 IT + TS，大数据解决了城市交通的监视问题（如交通监控中心），但还没有用大数据进行交通的科学规划、精准管控、优化诱导，而城市交通的解决方案仍然是基于传统的交通分析模型（如条件假设、理论推导、实验验证、工程应用的四阶段模型），二者严重脱节，缺乏科学手段。

一是要重构基于大数据的新一代城市交通理论体系。立足我国城市综合交通系统构成要素的基本特征，建立基于多源数据的交通行为成因机理解析理论，重构移动互联环境下的交通流模型，揭示全样本条件下的城市群综合交通系统供需平衡原理，形成基于大数据的新一代交通理论体系，为应用大数据技术实现城市群综合交通系统精明规划和精准管控提供精细化建模基础。

二是要为政府决策提供一个支撑平台。"城市虚拟交通系统决策支持平台"是实现城市交通系统规划建设、管理控制与运营服务智能化的基础。在可视量化测试平台中，规划局负责城市形态土地开发，交通局负责城市交通设施建设，交管局负责城市交通管理控制，发改委负责城市交通政策制定，各司其职，协同治理。

三是要开发城市综合交通体系的集成分析平台软件。城市综合交通系统的主体往往是复杂的超级大型网络，对交通系统的交通运行分析必须依托于大型平台软件。中国交通领域常用的交通分析大型平台软件都是国外引进的，例如美国 TransCAD、加拿大 EMME/4、德国 Vissim。但是照搬国外模式并不适合中国国情，我们要根据城市虚拟交通系统的建设要求，开发具有自主知识产权的交通分析系统平台软件。

芝加哥、温哥华和纽约的交通规划创新

麦克·谢佛

纽约大都会交通管理局副局长

很高兴向大家介绍芝加哥、纽约、温哥华的一些相关解决方案，这些都是我曾经工作过的城市。这三个城市跟上海在面积上大为不同，而且上海地铁的分布要比纽约大得多。上海的人口也比纽约多，纽约的人口是2 000 万，芝加哥大概是 1 000 万，温哥华大概 300 万。正因为人口上存在差距，所以我们解决交通问题的时候会有很大的不同，可能你已经在一个小城市工作多年，发现了一些可行的措施，但是换到大城市就完全是另外一回事。

1. 城市交通规划应关注的问题

我一开始是从事学术研究的，后来便投身实践。学术上，我们需要回答一些问题。比如，如何把创新政策和技术用于加强城市移动性。这是我提出的问题。我重点关注的是整个规划过程而非开车等具体实践，是规划性技术而不是交通技术。当然，我也会谈到交通技术中一些重要方面。

把系统化的规划程序应用于实践至关重要，但却不易实现。因为很多城市的规划程序都较复杂，即使我们竭尽所能来做，但实践有时却非常复杂，要真正施行系统化的规划程序还是有一定难度的。

对规划者来说，开发信息基础设施非常重要。刚才王教授做了一个精彩的信息基础设施应用时间表的陈述，非常震撼。这也是我 20 年来一直在努力追求的。我非常同意王教授刚才所讲的内容，因为系统式的规划确实非常重要。

当然，要真正开发人的能力，光有信息是远远不够的。在座的各位可以获得最好的信息、最好的工具，但是如果没有规划者的话，上述这些都是没有用的，所以我们需要优秀的人来做这些事情，这也是我在工作中一直努力追求的。

此外，创新技术应用也非常重要。一旦拥有了人力、信息以及规划，我们应随即将其投入工作，把创新技术运用到分析和讨论中，以此协助决策。因此我从学生时代便开始进行工作研究并运用了各种证明和概念。早在上世纪80年代，我们便就城市交通的数据可视化进行了实验。当时我们将电脑连接到影碟播放器再连接到电视进行实验。如果我们现在做实验的话，可以轻松地在电脑甚至智能手机上进行，但这在当时无法实现。

我还同麻省理工同事一起通过万维网找到了上述发现。我们和美国政府还有麻省理工的同事一起工作，在讨论像移动交通服务水平这样抽象的概念时，都不看具体数字，因为决策者想看到可视图像，想看到道路上来来往往的车辆。因此，多媒体工具就显得格外重要。类似的，我们在美国针对公共交通和承载量进行大量讨论，在加拿大我们则就未来的路线进行很多讨论。虽然这些都是区域性讨论，但实际上已达到全球水准。人们需要明白不同的模式，不同的操作环境都有哪些具体的操作特点。早在20世纪90年代，我们利用万维网就谈到了这个问题，这是些基础工作，是我离开学术投身实践时做的基础工作。我在芝加哥时，进度很慢，通常我当一段时间的教授，再做一段时间的从业者，然后再全身心地投入。其实我在芝加哥长大，我家里没有车，这在美国是十分罕见的，所以我对公共交通的重要性有特别的体会，这也是我工作的动力之一。重回自己熟悉的城市我深感荣幸，我想要带来改变。

2. 芝加哥交通规划的重点是"适应"

由于基础设施一直在改造，芝加哥交通规划的关键词是"适应"。近几年芝加哥的土地使用变化巨大，所带来的主要挑战就是由于公共交通投资不足，如何通过目标投资来增强辅助基础设施和交通基础设施的可靠性，以适应不断变化的交通模式。美国有很多老旧城市存在交通可靠性问题。目前已经大量投资，对传统的交通工具进行维护和修缮，这是关键所在。对于世界上其他地方是值得借鉴的经验。同时，保证持续性投资也很关键。我们已经落后美国其他地方了，所以我们现在正加倍努力迎头赶上。

芝加哥正在发生变化，你也会因消费者的习惯而受到蒙蔽，也会在那看到老旧的基础设施。目前，我们已解决大部分系统问题，同时也在继续解决剩下的问题。为了解决这些问题，我们会使用诸如数据以及地理空间信息技术之类的技术来协助人们分析讨论社区的未来。我们还运用多媒体工具。通常你坐在一个房间里，通过放置的摄像头，看到你所谈论的具体地点的情况，例如车站，视频可以跟踪列车，查看车站周围。我们在纽约、温哥华，以及我到过的地方，曾就此展开过对话。

与此同时，我们也会采用可视化书写工具。比方说像制图的媒体工具，对全身心投入规划过程十分重要。在本世纪初，芝加哥在智能汽车上是集大成者。从这个例子大家可以看到我们是如何运用数据来查看一天中某一条运输线的上下客情况。大家可以看到芝加哥一天的、夜间甚至是三个月间高峰时段的情况，而且数据时刻都在更新并上传到网站上，我们就此还和大学里的一些机构以及公共管理部门进行合作。

公交车也是类似的情况。了解有多少人乘坐公交车出行很重要。有2/3的芝加哥人坐公交车出行，也就是100万人坐公交车出行，50万人坐轨交出行。随后你会想用自动计数器来了解大家在哪里上车，在哪里下车，于是你便能看到各条道路上的上车情况以及道路使用情况。这一情况在温哥华也反复出现，之前我已经给各位展示过了。你也可以把这个应用在中国，应用于城市里的每一个站点，并且大家也已经看过同应用性相关的例子，这些例子都是21世纪初的。

3. 温哥华交通规划的重点是"平衡"

在温哥华，最重要的是平衡。中心城区的运力需求和郊区快速增长的人口之间存在矛盾，所以我们应该如何调节这种地区上的不平衡，如何去投资？是把重点放在中心城区，还是对郊区进行投资来促进发展？答案是平衡。我们在温哥华做的就是保持平衡。我们不仅有包括轮渡、火车、公交在内的公共交通，还有道路和轨交线。我们来看一个例子，这个例子仍旧是关于郊区，郊区的交通增长迅猛，数量众多。但是在城市中人们仍可以安心地在街区步行，愿意经常使用公交车，这就是平衡。我们再看一下数据。各位可以看到不同社区的人们所选择的交通方式，也能看到、感受到地区交通网络的样子。理解这个十分重要。与此同时，我们使用从基层得到的数据比如芝加哥的机动车模式进行分析。你在这里通过电子屏幕可以看到每个停靠站，人们什么时候上车，车什么时候到站，什么时候发车等。各位看到的一切都被转化成一张地图：绿色代表人们上车的站点，橘色代表下车站点，透明的代表公交车的平均负载因素。观察了多条线路之后，各位就会知道公交车是如何实现可视化，随后各位便能相应地改变公交车的运行模式。这就是普通乘客技术与地图和可视化相结合的简单例子。

将土地使用和交通连接起来也很重要。我们会听到其他演讲者谈论这个问题，如新加坡可能采取的措施、中国可能采取的措施等，也有教授在前面的发言中阐述过这个问题。一个优秀的设计对一个城市来说，从人行道到城市中的其他设施，都十分重要。

图1
芝加哥平衡交通示意图

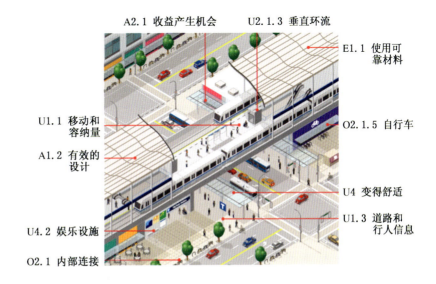

4. 纽约交通规划的重点是"网络"

我在纽约主要做铁路，铁路是一个重要的终端。其中的挑战是提高网络环境，通过服务基础设施和技术投资加强运力。我主要工作就是关注一些可以用到火车的新技术还有一些相当有竞争力的服务。从过去到现在，这些技术和服务就一直在解决各种挑战。恢复能力也很重要。纽约遭受过"桑迪"飓风袭击，但可惜的是我们的轮渡航线，列车运行线太长了，造成了巨大损失。所幸仍有一些能够切实改进和修复问题的措施。在规划中，我们主要关注以下三点：运营规划和分析、资本规划和编程以及长期规划。这些是我们用来进行表格分析的技术的例子。绿色代表列车性能很好，蓝色代表快速，红色表示糟糕。据此便能看出列车表中是否存在问题。我们通过数据可视化关注这些领域后可以改进列车表。此外，我们还会用技术来协助编写更加可靠的计划。比如用新的收费系统技术来改善人们与公共交通体系的互动。

这些技术目前发展良好。对纽约而言，因为它规模更大，所以需要花更多时间来使用技术，同时因为应用上的差距，所花费的时间也会更多。如图 2 所示，在资金规划中，半数的资金预算用于设备更新，另外 1/3 用于维护和修理。在各位考虑改善、提高资金预算和设备前，超过 80% 的资金预算都是用在维护和更新现有的设备。

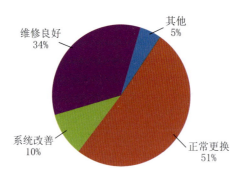

纽约中央车站是纽约市中心的代表，占有巨大空间。这里是纽约中央车站的内景：终点站的行人，拥有 100 年历史的地下两层终点站。我们使用各种技术对车站进行大量维修，让它能够更好地发挥功能和作用。此外，我们还用地理信息系统来更有效地了解车站的基础设施，从轨道到车站。在长期规划中，我们使用地理信息系统来协助规划新路线，比如这些新路线会穿越中央车站终点站台的地下，终点站台目前有两个隔间在施工。这些都会让 100 列火车受益，并且新的线路会改善曼哈顿和纽约其他地方的连接，我们就可以有多种方式进入曼哈顿。这些都是相关例子。

最后来总结一下今天所讲述的内容。在芝加哥我们改造辅助基础设施，通过目标投资来改善可靠性，适应变化的出行模式。在温哥华，实现城市和郊区的平衡至关重要，他们需要关注道路。在纽约，我们切实关注加强网络环境，通过服务基础设施和技术投资提高运力。在策略上，我们花大量时间关注土地使用的相互补充，从而提高通勤的服务质量，加大密度。我们改善维护和修理的情况，改善现存系统的适应力，持续进行这些方面的改善对一个疯狂增长的城市来说非常重要。同时，我们利用现有的一些交通基础设施来改良路线，相应地重新设计路线并全面利用投资来改善和其他公共交通系统的衔接，更好地扩大承载能力。同时，我们致力于改善公共交通的便捷性，因为在众多城市中人们需要有一个选择。我们希望他们选择公共交通来保持交通网络的平衡。

新加坡城市交通拥堵治理创新

雷德顺
新加坡土地交通管理局研究院院长

前面我们已经看到了纽约、芝加哥、温哥华的案例，现在回到亚洲，来看一下新加坡的具体案例。我想和各位分享我们在新加坡采取的行动，以及新加坡这座城市发生的变化。

1. 新加坡城市交通发展的历程及现状特征

前面王教授也介绍了中国国内的情况。在新加坡，我们会采取不同的策略和行动，图1所展示的就是已经采取的措施。

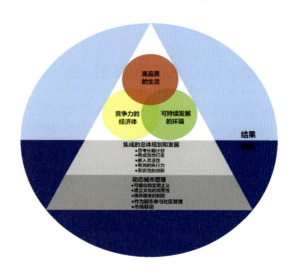

图1
新加坡城市交通方面
已采取的行动

新加坡1965年独立，在过去的50年间我们是如何发展的呢？新加坡本身是一个非常紧凑的城市国家，既是一个城市，也是一个国家。我们的人口很少，560万人口居住在720平方公里的土地上。如今12%的土地为道路，这对于一个紧凑的城市国家来说是很大的比重，此外还有15%的土地是住房用地。我们整个面积也很小，南北跨度不大，只有25公里，半个小时车程，从东到西一共49公里。1960—1965年，因交通需求量增长，新加坡出现了众多交通堵塞，而且巴士也不可靠。但现在，我们对交通进行了改造，将其转变为一个高效可持续的公共交通系统。

现在，新加坡人民正享受着一个全面的公共交通系统。该系统为人们提供更多选择，而且也更加实惠、可持续。请看这些数据。我们每天有100万人次乘坐出租车，还有340万人次选择轨道交通。以前有大约500万人次选择巴士出行，位居三种交通方式之首。由于轨道交通的发展，现在这一数字下降到430万，因此每天共有770万人次乘坐公共交通出行。现在来看一下道路。我们虽然使用道路，但是如图2所示，我们将其控制在一个中等的水平。道路网共计长9 200公里，高速路网共计长1 100公里，同时我们也控制机动车的数量，即把使用量控制在957 000辆这一合适数量。机动车、私家车的数量十分重要，我们也对其进行相应控制。

图2
适中的道路交通

接下来是巴士和轨道交通系统。巴士系统目前已达到广泛覆盖的规模。每天路上都有四个运营商。以前只有两个，现在有四个。两个新的运营商分别是"宝塔换乘"（Tower Transit）和"前进"（Go Ahead）。当前，四个运营商共有5 500辆巴士提供360余次服务，这比以往都要密集，我们高度重视他们的服务。比如，通过政府承包系统购买巴士，而且我们上个月便开始使用电脑换乘模式。就轨交系统来说，我们目前有两个运营商：SMRT列车和SBS列车，而不像中国香港只有一个。香港以前也是有两个运营商但是现在就只有一个。我们的运营商比香港多，而且它们在MRT和LRT线路上运营得很好。目前，我们拥有十余条轨交线，总长182公里，而且准备在2016年将轨交线的数量翻一番，以达到近50年来的峰值。所以还有很多工作要做。

2. 新加坡城市交通面临的挑战

图 3 是关于不同城市的巴士使用率，它体现了我们的观察和看法。各位可以看到，在巴士车队规模、巴士出行率以及运力上，我们处于高位。图 4 是轨交的情况。香港的轨交十分舒适，但是我们的轨交使用频率更高。巴士用得很好，你看一下巴士相对于私家车的使用量，与香港作比较，实际上我们利用率更高。从人均 GDP 的角度来看，我们私家车的平均使用率很低，但是我们仍旧有很多问题和挑战。

图 3
不同城市的巴士使用率

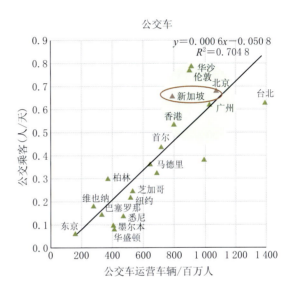

图 4
不同城市的轨交使用率

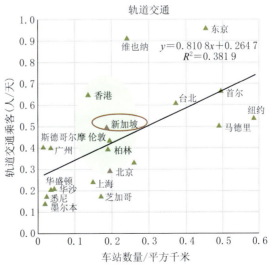

新加坡正在发展，面临着以下问题。一是人口增长。根据《人口白

皮书》，我们现在有 600 万人口，而且到 2030 年我们预计人口会达到 690
万，所以在这种情况下如何让交通更加完善呢？二是土地有限。已在前面
提到新加坡国土面积为 720 平方公里，其中 12% 为交通用地，15% 为住
房用地。那么为了满足 GDP 增长的需要，我们到底还需要多少土地？三
是通勤者的期望。通勤者的期望一直在变。新加坡在过去 50 年的发展中
进步很大，但是老年人口对交通的移动性有特殊的要求，所以我们设法将
这一移动性包含进系统。四是公共交通的可持续性。我们一直在不停地建
设公共交通系统，必须让系统实现可持续，必须使系统适应长远发展。这
同我们应该建设什么相关，后面我具体涉及。

3. 新加坡交通规划的主要做法

对新加坡来说，综合的土地规划发展是核心所在。自 1965 年取得独
立，新加坡的土地部门和其他发展部门之间就存在众多矛盾。部门之间确
实会互相角力竞争，但是我们应该在竞争的同时也要牢记各个部门应该携
手解决问题。

我们的规划跟其他城市类似。首先，我们先有一个长远的概念性规
划，每年都会将其细化。同时每十年就有一个新的概念性规划和建设规
划。各位可以重点关注一些组织机构。新加坡高度重视政府规划也特别依
赖政府规划，因为各部门随时都准备磋商，至少我们一起工作，一起规
划。当然我们也不会把土地和资产只分给一个部门。我们和很多机构合
作，如市重建局（URA）、土地交通局，还有裕廊集团（JTC）等。裕廊集
团已经建立了自己的城镇体系，这些机构应该有效地进行合作。

久而久之，我们就会有概念性规划、总体规划以及其他用于发展道路
和轨交的公共交通规划，同时还有长远规划和短期规划。为什么要在新加
坡这样一个紧凑的社会中进行长远的规划呢？理由很简单，我们要在高密
度中发挥最大的价值。这个想法很普通，但是在总体规划、法律行为以及
商业要求上却十分关键。我们要将土地使用最佳化，将价值发挥最大化的
同时也要加强系统的活力。更重要的是因为有了交通规划和城乡交通一
体化，我们才能根据规划来平衡车辆供给和出行需求，确保未来的交通
走廊。

现在快速解释一下这个例子。新康是新加坡的一个新镇，通过轻轨换
乘同新加坡市区连接起来的，这个轻轨换乘也是发展的一部分。这个换乘

系统中有一个换乘站，对新加坡人来说，这个换乘站巨大无比，可以实现家门口换乘坐轻轨。这个换乘系统非常新，以至于我们在想新加坡所有的换乘线都应该是这样的。那么我们该如何使土地使用最佳化呢？我们设有三条线，四合一出发站，以及一个换乘站，这就是我们想到使用土地的最佳方法。

做完总体规划之后，要进一步改进这个规划。早在2008年，我们就已经有了第一个概念性规划——土地交通概念性规划，也叫LTC规划。2013年，我们将这个概念性计划转变成了总体规划。如今我们已经超越了这个总体规划。这个总体规划分为三部分：更多的连接、更好的服务和充满活力的包容性社区。

我们希望传达三个关键指标。一个就是公共交通要承担高峰时期75%的交通；其次，85%的出行都要少于一个小时；最后，80%的家庭可以在10分钟内走到轨交站。于是我们有一个系统叫做"清淡用车"（Car-Lite），意思是减少用车。你也许没有车，但是如果你有车的话，那么你应该尽可能地少开车。"清淡用车"系统由四个部分组成："步行骑行"（Walk Cycle Ride）、公共交通、技术和电动及无人驾驶。我们希望通过专门设立自行车通道，鼓励人们步行，让这个系统在2030年变为现实。

不管是一般的城市还是高密度的城市，网络都十分普遍。我们创造了一个不错的轨交网络。虽然新加坡的轨交网络很好，但巴士服务也处于同等重要的位置。我们土地交通局做了很多工作，如改善连接、减少拥挤、提高可靠性，我们也实施像巴士振兴计划这样的政策来提高巴士服务，结果现在新增了1 000辆巴士。上个月，我们实现了从分配系统向巴士承包模式的转化。现在我们一共有三个标书在积极发标，包括五年的合同加上两年的扩展，此外还有九个标书正在谈判和运营。这一切都是从以前的操作模式向全新的巴士承包模式转变中的一部分，当然其中一些情况还有待进一步讨论。现在众多事物都发生了变化，整个框架变了，包括巴士承包模式以及轨交融资框架。整个系统都要可持续，这样我们才能自给自足，否则会给后代留下债务。

"步行骑行"是一个非常重要的运动。在这个运动中最基本就是要培育或者形成一个全新的移动文化。一个在众多要求中前进和发展的城市，需要这样的文化。我们有共享单车，连接了车站同住宅间的第一英里和最后一英里。我们在公交站周围建立了轨交系统和巴士系统，同时轨交系统协助连接最后一英里，连接了整个网络。甚至在设计的时候，我们也改变了一些概念，如谁用公共车辆进行换乘。我们从所有权和使用上入手，花了大力气来控制私家车。这种做法很常见，在新加坡到处都是类似的信息，不管是有关所有权的措施还是和使用权相关，不管是否与财政相关，这些信息都简单易读。

我们在机动车方面也取得了一些成果。我们发现新加坡机动车增长率从20世纪80年代的7%下降至0.25%。紧接着是定价。我们在定价系统上花了很多功夫。回顾过去，我们还控制了速度，速度有一个范围。如果超过一定值，那么价格就会减少。这就是目前已有的电子道路计价。根据现有的这些东西，各位可以看到中央商务区交通高峰时的汽车、人口、机动车和道路的增长情况。下一代的电子道路计价系统即将面世。

接下来是智能移动。新加坡在自动驾驶汽车领域的成就有目共睹。我们发展自动驾驶汽车的原因主要有三点。其一，固定班次的巴士服务。其二，将要发展的点对点的出行需求。此外还有运费和实用。明确了这些原因，整个做法便分成：一是必须减少汽车所有权需求；二是必须减少高峰时刻的道路拥堵；三是必须减少对人力的依赖。这就是我们依靠巴士，并保证每辆巴士都必须有足够的服务人员的原因。

两年前我们做了一个关于自主机动车的实验，如今我们把这个实验扩展到纬壹科技城。我们希望到2020年，能有一个试点部署自动驾驶的巴士服务，以及在潜在实验地点能有乡镇水平的共享自动驾驶汽车。现在共有两家公司参与自动驾驶汽车的紧急移动需求实验。第一家是德尔福汽车公司，第二家是努·托诺米（nuTonomy）公司。此外还有其他的自动驾驶汽车新兴企业如位于南洋理工大学的NAVYA和自动行者（Auto Rider）（EZ10）。

最后，我们希望能够设计一个绿色、紧凑、宜居的，而且交通非常方便、生产率很高的城市。

专家点评

陈小鸿（同济大学交通运输工程学院教授）：刚才三位演讲者给我们分享了很多信息，既有整体的解决方案，又有很多非常生动的案例，对于我们全球城市建设提供了很多的借鉴。今天这个论坛名称是"全球城市论坛"。实际上，上海新一轮的总体规划已经把上海的发展目标定为全球城市。在全球城市和城市治理方面，王教授已经讲到，对中国来讲，任何城市的发展和城市治理，第一个碰到的就是交通拥堵问题，这是我们最现实的问题。但是长远来讲，我们要实施绿色发展，实现可持续发展目标。王教授所提出的供需平衡、系统协同、效能提升等三个解决路径，其实为上海建设全球城市的路径，甚至对我们国家很多还是处于建设和治理双重解决路径的城市给出了一个大的框架。在这个大的框架里边，王教授给我们提出了很多需要研究的问题。

麦克·谢佛先生带来了纽约、芝加哥、温哥华三个城市的经验。其中，纽约是上海城市标杆之一。这三个城市的案例，都是在城市规模基本稳定，城市基础设施建设到了一定程度之后，如何做更好的、不同的、可执行的方案。如何让既有的设施来适应现在的变化，如何让城市的中心区和郊区获得更平衡的发展，以及在怎么样的建成地区仍然强化它的轨道网络，通过维护好我们已有的设施来获得更好的服务。尤其是给了我们很多技术上的案例，用大数据分析，特别是用可视化数据分析需求和活动，从而寻找到我们既有设施需要改善的重点，以及改善可能达到的效果。

雷先生提供了一个新加坡的案例，其实上海从新加坡学习很多，尤其在车辆拥有和使用管理，以及如何用公共交通让人的活动更加便捷上，新加坡给了上海非常多的启发。雷先生不仅仅介绍了新加坡既有的经验，也给我们讲述到 2030 年，现在已经能看到曙光的新技术，比如说自动驾驶技术，能让城市交通达到一个更好发展的可能性。雷教授也告诉我们，真正城市交通的解决方案，一定不仅仅是铁路的，也不仅仅是公交的，不仅仅是设施和线路的优化，它是综合的。刚才讲到一些新公交营运方案，对于城市如何治理和提高治理水平，都给出了很好的观点。

关宏志（北京工业大学建筑工程学院教授）：首先，王教授在演讲当中，非常深刻地揭示了多年的经验，揭示了中国城市拥堵的主要问题，也开出了一个比较系统的解决方案。刚才陈小鸿教授已经从三个角度做了总结。我们总体印象是，这个解决方案是一个非常系统的，要充分发挥政府职能的，有远景和战略意义的思路。在这个方案当中，我们应该思考的另外一个问题是，当城市已经不再是新建的城市时，我们面临的很多问题是在既有建设好的城市基础上，如何去解决和改善。所以说，这是我们中国学者，以及愿意帮助我们的世界学者们共同应该思考的问题。

其次，麦克·谢佛先生是从具体的点给出一些非常成功的案例。这些案例所描述的城市各有特点，有的是注重技术，有的是注重规划、战略。要是从系统角度来说，和王教授的总结有不谋而合之处。它给我们更多重要的、可参考的借鉴，就在于是已经付诸实践的。从中我们也看到美国学者，或者说美国的交通工程师在解决交通问题当中，与我们注重策略、注重战略相比，他们是更加注重技术。

第三位雷先生的演讲也非常有特色，其中有两个重点给我印象比较深刻。一个就是和我们中国一样，发挥政府在规划当中的主导作用。雷先生演讲的第二个重点是给出了我们未来的发展前景。实际上王教授讲到，中国政府已经在大力尝试引进最先进的技术来开发和推动，比如说无人驾驶技术的使用，相信这些技术以及国外同行的先进经验，会推动我们国家交通事业的发展，也将会推动我们城市交通问题的解决。

新加坡未来交通流动性的研究与创新

约瑟夫·费雷拉

麻省理工学院城市研究与规划系教授

我在新加坡参与了一个麻省理工学院的计划，想以此为背景讨论一下城市交通发展趋势和无人驾驶方面的前景，会结合一些现实问题进行分析，利用在新加坡工作遇到的一些例子，来观察和研究支撑未来交通流动性的城市规划、城市管理和城市信息基础设施。

我是一名建筑学的教授，我的职责是负责城市规划研究和企划。我们关注城市的可持续发展领域，而我自己感兴趣的领域是城市信息系统。为此，我们建立城市分析模型和信息基础设施服务。目前我居住在新加坡，同时也在位于新加坡麻省理工学院的研究和技术联盟中心工作，并作为麻省理工学院九个系之一的老师参与到这个未来城市交通流动跨学科研究小组中来。这个小组是由新加坡国立研究基金会和几个国际跨学科研究组织投资建立的，新加坡主要资助的是从化学到生物学的项目。这也是未来发展的走向。

1. 信息通信技术对城市交通的影响

城市中信息和通信技术的变化，明显大于其他地方。我们如何管理道路？交通互动的应用有点像我们开始看到的由信息通信技术在大都市地区部署人员和服务所引发的涟漪效应，就像一战之前的汽车工业。现在我想就城市信息基础设施提出一点建议。由于社会发展迅速，我们必须不断积累、解释和使用城市的相关知识，这些知识包括人们如何理解和适应新情况。我们专注于今天的拥堵问题，也在积极想出策略来缓解交通拥堵。但是，人们往往会在实施过程中改变想法。因为我们不确定这些技术驱动的流动性有多大，所以可能明天又会有新的拥堵问题需要处理，我们需要保持足够的领先。所以我们必须迅速学会观察、学习和适应，那么这些通过信息通信技术和基础设施改善所产生的趋势到底是什么？目前可见的一些趋势包括汽车共享、自动驾驶车辆和更好的结构化建设。

与此同时，我们看到城市化和全球化对人口密集程度、收入提高和教育进步的影响越来越大。但是，人们出行越来越多，汽车出行越来越频繁，汽车尾气排放量增加以及交通堵塞情况越来越严重，所以扭转这种趋势需要加强规划和监管。信息通信技术正在改变经济的土地利用。你可以看看网上购物、物流配送等信息通信技术应用，公司经过碎片化后分散在各个地方。由于经济发展需要各种经济活动又集中在城市的中心，那么我们应该如何分配交通，使得这些分散在城市各处的人们不需要经常性地穿越整个大城市来通勤？当下对这个问题的解决也有一些创新性的但仍旧处于设想初期的方案，例如对公司的交通出行实行补贴。那么这类补贴应当是政府出资还是分摊在公司头上呢？诸如此类等等。因此，流动性的新选项是主动摒弃传统保守的解决交通问题的方式，这使得有关部门不再陷入被动。我们有很多家庭有两个或两个以上的劳动力选择在其他地方工作，并且需要多程通勤。因此，解决这些问题需要我们具备清晰的目标与方向。

2. 无人驾驶的潜在影响

我要介绍一下无人驾驶。无人驾驶在美国是比较时髦的，在中国也是一个比较热的话题。我相信它蕴含很多投资机会，现在 3 000 美元就可以买到一辆谷歌无人驾驶车，高尔夫车（Golf Cart）是两万美元，上面安装的电子设备有助于解决"最后一公里"问题。关键是在政府政策范围内怎样开辟一条科技创新的路径，并加以规范？比如说，在道路交通方面，是否要批出专用道，并且让其他车辆的行驶也遵循这个思路？如何进行停车管理也是另外一个需要解决的问题。

此外，交通工具的所有权与实际使用权也是两码事。无人驾驶汽车面世后是否会造成一些负面影响？人们上了无人驾驶车就可以做其他事情，他们可能不在乎开多长时间，那样也许会增加很多不必要的交通量，这些情况我们都要加以预估。

我们现在看一下新加坡的情况，我的同事已经写了有关这方面的论文。分别看一下新加坡和美国的情况，先看新加坡，大约 8 000

或 9 000 辆中有 3 000 辆完全是自动驾驶，基本上这 3 000 辆无人驾驶可以满足以前 8 000 辆车的交通量。人们只需等 15 分钟就可以等到，这里面就蕴含着生产力提高的可能。现在出租车一半时间都是空跑，有了无人驾驶车，就可以很大程度上解决好这样一些问题。当然这还涉及交通模式的替代，还有占用的车道、停车等问题都要加以考虑。

我们看一些数字，由于没有时间逐个讲，只强调一些主要的。我们来识别不同的驾驶模式，一种是人力开的，一种是无人驾驶，还有一种是混合式的，即人工操作下的无人驾驶。关于这几种不同的类型，我们可以比较一下新加坡和美国的每公里行车成本和综合效率。通过计算，人力驾驶的成本，美国是 3 万美元，新加坡是 3.2 万美元，实际上新加坡这里面还包括了 5 000 多美元的驾照费。目前状况下虽然拥有了这项技术，但仍未出台相关的规定，如果政策加以完善，成本将可以降到 1.5 万美元，自动驾驶很快就会普及。

我们要看一下这样的技术出来之后，它会有什么样的后果。无人驾驶是否会依赖特定的行车道路？是否应该持续地推广无人驾驶和汽车共享？如果全部是公共交通，这对土地使用又有什么影响？对城市与郊区的重组有何种作用？未来的自动驾驶，一定有很多的专门市场。先发展专门市场，然后在总体市场上加以应用。比如说，道路清洁与货运可能是需要优先考虑的，这两类专门市场影响的范围较大。

此外，合理有效的管理对于向自动驾驶过渡是十分重要的，不然成本会过高。比如说要运输 60 个人（图 1），到底要多少车辆？你可以看一下私家车和 Uber，还有无人驾驶车，可能用的车辆数是一样的。

图 1
运输 60 人所需空间

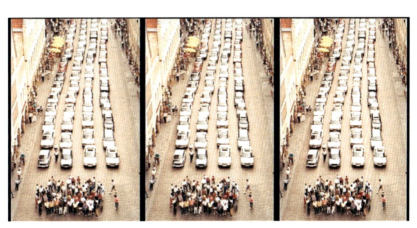

私家车　　　　　　　　　　Uber　　　　　　　　　无人驾驶车

3. 汽车共享的应用趋势

我们来看一下在新加坡做的范例。分析一段运程最开始的情况。在新加坡很多人乘坐巴士的目的地是赶往地铁站，因此人流量都往地铁站聚集，我用颜色标识出来的地方，都是每天人流量较大的站点。新加坡有交通卡，我们完全可以根据交通卡搜集这些信息。经过 31 站后，来到终点的乘客数从 15 000 减到了 1 700，由此可见巴士的承载效用是逐步递减的。

如果改善最前面一公里状况的话，也许最后的结果就会大不一样。例如，共享汽车就可以解决很大的问题。如果对于前一公里拼车实施优惠减免的政策，整个效率就会提高很多，不管对于控制风险和密度还是提高经济效益都是非常有益的。那么所产生的成本需要谁来承担？谁可以通过政策影响并解决市场问题，使公众从中受益呢？我想这个问题值得仔细研究。新加坡做了很多研究，包括对于无人驾驶的试验也做了不少。其他机构跟新加坡理工大学也在做合作研究，其中一个研究项目成果已得到推广。新加坡土地交通管理局也进行了这方面的试验，对油电混合车以及新能源车的性能进行比较，并提供了充电桩的支持。显然，我们需要应用更多的技术来进行更好的设计。技术更新换代很快，但是我们要抓住每种技术带来控制管理好需求的可能性，并且平衡好这种需求与公众利益之间的关系。以此来监测和规划下一步，这样才能意识到城市基础设施对于我们所做工作的重要性。

另外，交通是基础设施的一个部分，对于我们可能也会看到一些其他信息，比如说政府投入以及其他一些需要共享的电子数据。从日常的数据信息搜集处理中，我们才能了解到基础设施的管理以及城市的基本信息。城市数据也是一般的商品，涉及它的所有权，以及发布时间。还有一些详细的应用，像个人的定位追踪、全球定位系统（GPS）、谷歌通用数据标准（Google GTFS），通过这些应用的共享我们可以满足个人需求并且共建大数据分析，从而共同分享这些数据，以实现我们的目标。我们应综合性地整合这些信息，鼓励城市居民以更加智能化的方式出行，通过创新的规划和方式来解决问题，并进行以信息技术为基础的规划和管理。

日本城市交通问题治理创新

张峻屹

日本广岛大学教授

1. 引　言

20 世纪 60 年代至 70 年代，由于日本经济快速发展，东京、名古屋和大阪这三大城市的人口过分集中，日本曾经经历了交通堵塞、交通事故、空气污染等各种严重的交通问题。经过这样的经历，与其他国家相比，日本已经做出了巨大的努力并成功地解决了这些问题。交通事故死亡人数从 1970 年的 16 765 人降至 2016 年的 3 904 人。公共交通系统占东京 23 个区整体份额的 80% 左右，其中东京大都市区约占 50%。总体来看，交通系统的环境负荷自 21 世纪初以来已经有所下降。这些成功源于各种创新方法，大致可分为三类（见图 1）：系统、用户和技术方法。实际上，大多数最成功的创新方法是由私营部门发起的，得到了政府的大力支持。本文主要描述日本大城市（特别是上述三大都市）的创新。

图 1
日本城市交通问题治理创新的类型

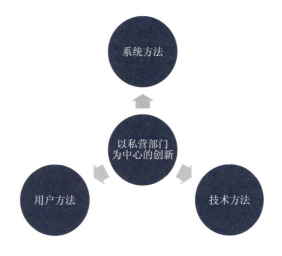

2. 系统方法：沿线开发 (EK)

以公共交通为导向的发展模式（TOD）这一著名概念是由几个美国建筑师在 20 世纪 90 年代提出的。然而，相似的概念及理论早在 20 世纪初期的日本就已存在了，叫做沿线开发（EK），比如：铁路地区发展。自 20 世纪 60 年代以来，私营铁路公司积极实施 EK。在那段时期，快速的城镇化和人口的过快增长致使中心城区的地价过高，以至于很多人，甚至是那些中产阶层人士（或白领）都买不起住房。尽管如此，大城市人口仍然过分集中，尤其在上述三大都市比较显著，原因在于越来越多的当地城市和农村人口迁入了大城市。为了应对密集型人口增长带来的巨大的住房需求，在陆路运输领域处于垄断地位的私营铁路公司，首先建造了延伸到郊区的铁路线，并沿线，特别是在周边车站，开发了住宅区和商业区。私营铁路公司的发展战略是通过采购铁路沿线的土地并建造住宅区，从而产生足够多的用户来维持铁路运营而获取利润。因此，沿线开发是由私营铁路公司发起的。但是，以公共交通为导向的开发是一种政府铁路运营商和城市开发商之间的共同发展模式。

3. 用户方法

我去过许多国家，包括美国、欧洲及亚洲的一些国家。我认为，日本的确拥有世界上最佳用户友好型公共交通系统。

（1）私营公司的关键作用。日本的公共交通系统主要由私人公司经营，中央和 / 或地方政府有一些补贴。然而，这个数额远低于其他发达国家。因此，私营企业必须在旅行之前 / 之中 / 之后进行各种努力以满足用户的需求。日本的服务业，包括公共交通服务业，往往强调服务必须符合用户的期望，超过用户期望的服务被认为是最好的服务。这样的思想使得日本的公共交通系统清洁、可靠、安全，经常非常准时和舒适。火车 / 巴士指挥和地勤人员训练有素，非常友好。

（2）用户友好的可达性。为了与小汽车交通竞争，日本大城市的公共交通系统要尽可能地覆盖城市空间的不同部分。铁路公司在政府补贴非常有限的情况下，大力拓展交通网络。最终，建立了广泛的公共交通网络。由于运输网络的广泛，用户需要在出发前搜索旅行信息，这些信息可通过各种离线和在线媒体都可获得。因此，保证了用户友好的可达性。

（3）可靠的守时性。作为对用户的严肃承诺，日本的公共交通系统是以公众可获得的时间表为基础良好运行的。为了履行这一承诺，私营公司即使在紧急情况下（例如事故）也充分利用现有的资源和技术。因此，东京的火车运行是世界上最准时的。

（4）跨公司共享经营。令人惊讶的是，日本的铁路和地铁系统已经成功地在不同公司间引用了相互直接运营模式。这种相互运营允许不同公司的火车分享轨道，即一家公司的火车可以直接在另一家公司的轨道上运行。2013 年，东京地铁在自家轨道的运行里程为 18 009.9 万公里，其他公司的火车在东京铁轨的运行里程为 10 455.4 万公里。相比之下，东京地铁则使用其他公司的线路运行火车的里程为 10 486.6 万公里。根据车辆运行里程相互抵消作为共享运营成本的基础，如车辆和铁路线的使用可相互抵消。私营企业以一种非常复杂的方式为确保准点运营进行信息共享，并为之付出了巨大的努力，如安装合作伙伴公司的信息显示，为不同公司建立协调运营系统等。

（5）共享交通 IC 卡。据日本土地、基础设施、交通运输和旅游部称，铁路系统交通 IC 卡已被广泛引用。特别是跨公司、跨地区的共享已得到了积极推进。自 2015 年以来，近 80 家公司推出的 IC 卡类型超过 25 种，已售出 8 700 多万张卡，可用于 5 000 多个车站。20 多种类型的 IC 卡可以在全国各地相互使用。

4. 技术方法

日本引进了各种先进技术来支持它的交通发展。这里主要讲述智能交通系统（ITS）、电动汽车（EV）、插电式混合动力车（PHV）和自动驾驶车（AV）。

（1）日本智能交通系统。日本是全世界智能交通系统发展方面的领先国家。日本的智能交通系统是根据九个发展领域组成的综合计划而发展的，包括：导航系统的进展；电子收费系统（ETC）；安全驾驶辅助；优化交通管理；提高道路管理效率；支持公共交通；提高商用车业务效率；支持行人；支持应急车辆运行。日本的智能交通系统架构包括 21 个用户服务和 172 个用户子服务。涉及四个由内阁办公室管理的部委，包括国土交通部（MLIT）、国家警察局（NPA）、内政部（MIC）和经济产业省（METI）。此外，智能交通系统标准化委员会和日本智能交通系统是两个外部支持组织。日本的智能交通系统旨在改善交通安全，提高运输效率，减轻环境负荷，提高交通系统的便利性，区域振兴，提高基础设施建设和标准化。日本的智能交通系统已经通过三个阶段有序地部署。第一阶段是促进实际应用；第二阶段是促进智能交通系统的传播，加快回报社会效益；第三阶段是在每个阶段的重要时刻回应社会问题。日本分别在1995年（横滨）、2004年（名古屋）和2013年（东京）举办了智能交通系统世界大会。

（2）日本电动汽车、插电式混合动力车。由经济产业省（METI）发起的电动汽车、插电式混合动力车城镇计划已将日本的电动汽车、插电式混合动力车作为一体化发展部署。根据这一举措，市政当局和本地企业基于以下四个基本目标相互合作：创建电动汽车、插电式混合动力车的初始需求；建设充电设施；电动汽车、插电式混合动力车的广泛使用；评估方案的效果及改进措施。这个方案选择了18个县，这是制定总体规划和行动计划所需的。图2显示了日本电动汽车、插电式混合动力车和充电器的增长情况。

图 2
日本电动汽车、插电式混合动力车以及充电器的增长

（3）日本的自动驾驶车。日产汽车公司于2016年8月24日发布了一款新型的SERENA车，这是一款小型的货车，配备Pro PILOT技术，是一种专门在单车道高速公路使用的革命性自动驾驶技术。Pro PILOT技术使日本汽车制造商的自动驾驶成为第一。在发布后大约一个月内，日产收到SERENA的20 784份订单（约为每月目标的2.5倍），其中70%配备了Pro PILOT技术。配备Pro PILOT技术只需不到20万日元。由于这种发展

是私营公司发起的，日本政府就国际标准、意外事故赔偿规则，发展和推广自动驾驶车(AV)技术，运用自动驾驶车技术等方面，积极提升了自动驾驶车(AV)的发展。实际上，日本的几家保险公司已经开始免费提供自动驾驶技术的保险，包括东京海上日动火灾保险有限公司和日本兴亚保险公司。日本政府已经开始了最后一公里运输服务（全国四个站点）的社会实验以及人口稀少地区（全国十个站点）的运输服务。此外，在2020年东京奥运会的那一年，日本计划在选定的路段上运行数千辆无司机自动驾驶出租车。

5. 对中国的启示

与过去的快速经济增长期不同，日本现在面临着人口老龄化和低出生率的问题。以前的成功案例可能不适用于这种新情况。同时，如何缓解东京人口过度集中造成的各种问题仍然是国家重要的政策问题，交通拥堵、交通事故、空气污染问题也仍然存在。以前解决这些问题的方法主要是以数量为导向，相比之下，目前和未来的解决方案主要是以质量为导向。为了应对决策制定环境的这种变化，各部门间（政府内外）的合作应该发挥重要作用，然而，日本的相关决策的制定长期以来都受到不同部门之间不良合作的困扰。大规模建设交通基础设施已成为历史，交通基础设施的维护和更新反而变得越来越重要。新措施主要依赖新技术的发展，但是新技术有时会导致新问题的出现（例如节能技术的反弹效应）。要解决这些问题，公众参与是一项有必要且有用的措施，但这有时候太费时了。考虑到以上诸多问题，我们有必要根据适应中国城市的实际情况，有选择性地借鉴日本的成功案例。

由于政府干预措施相对薄弱，日本的成功经验主要依靠的是私营部门的努力。特别是私营铁路和有轨电车公司，以市场竞争为出发点，提供了优质交通基础设施和服务，即使在政府有限的补贴下也是如此。日本私营企业的成功经验对于解决中国的交通问题无疑是有用的。中国应该就交通发展方面为私营部门提供更多的商业空间和权力。

在中国，越来越多的人迁入北京、上海、广州、深圳等大城市。20世纪60年代至70年代期间，日本也出现了类似的迁移模式。长期以来尽管采取了各种应对策略，然而，情况还是没有得到改善。最近，安倍内阁领导下的日本中央政府刚刚决定制定更有力的政策，鼓励人们搬到当地的城乡农村地区，但效果并不如预期的那么显著。人口长期被视为交通规划的一项考量因素，但是，交通发展可能会影响人口分布这一现象是容易被忽视的。因此，通过包括交通政策在内的各种公共政策，控制人口过度集中及其在城市内外的空间分布是重要的。

东京大都市区环路建设的延误，一定程度上促成了公共交通系统的成功发展。限制道路能力绝对有助于鼓励更多的人使用公共交通系统。因此，尽早建设公共交通基础设施比建设主要道路更为重要。

旅行需求的增长往往快于供应。毫无疑问，建设必要的交通基础设施需要迅速采取行动，充分利用各项资金。然而，从日本的经验中学到的另一个重要的教训是，应对旅行需求比供应基础设施更为重要。这是因为新的基础设施供应往往会引发新的旅游需求。因此，基础设施供应一直落后于旅游需求的增长。实际上，日本的系统性的停车政策（即一种汽车交通需求管理）有助于解决各种交通问题。关于公共交通运营的各种有效、便捷的信息系统对吸引汽车用户是有用的。旅行需求需要更好的管理。

最后，交通运输发展涉及各方面，因此共识建设变得重要。有必要基于科学评估来说服大多数人，花更多的时间来实施政策。尽管这样做确实是耗时的，但这有助于促进交通可持续发展。换句话说，我们的城市需要的是一个适度的发展，而不是一个过快的发展。只有这样我们才能做得更好！

专家点评

潘海啸（同济大学建筑与城市规划学院教授）：首先，第一位报告人涉及的概念已经在世界上被大多数人所接受。其次，我们要看到未来城市的发展受很多因素影响。未来社会经济发展变化有几个方面。

第一，像上海这样的大城市，人口老龄化、少子化后交通要求可能会发生变化。第二，现代技术的发展会给土地使用和交通关系带来很大的变化。在此背景下，我们必须思考能不能通过运用新的技术使人们在城市里生活得更方便。这个技术是为人们的生活解决问题的，但有时候并不是技术本身的问题。在解决交通问题的时候，很多城市都引进了一种停车诱导系统，但我也从来没有看到过它的效果。然而，南京有报道，有个地方原本停车很混乱，后来调整了停车费，警察也加强管理，从此就出现了很多空车位。这说明有时价格政策和管理手段是解决交通问题更为有效的办法，因此我们要将两者结合起来。

另外，报告人讲到，信息基础设施作为公共物品来考虑，是城市治理非常大的短板。对于未来城市发展，如果没有信息提供给研究人员参考，很难将这个城市管理得井然有序，因为你必须做全面深入的分析。然而，我们会发现这些信息放在不同的部门和不同的单位，从来不共享。这样治理就很难提高。因此，数据共享是非常重要的。

张教授告诉我们日本很多成功的经验，我们同作为亚洲城市，也都是高密度的城市，为什么会有这么大的差别？日本有着非常好的经验，其轨道交通非常分割，各种各样的公司在同一个站上运行，如果没有相互协调，或者以人为本，那么一切就要混乱。在中国，一个城市有三个火车站，以前是难以想象的，现在已经通过技术把它协调起来。

李朝阳（上海交通大学船舶海洋与建筑工程学院教授）：当前我们国

家发展的理念是"创新、协调、绿色、开放、共享",这也是两位教授演讲中重要的核心价值观和取向。

第一位教授研究先进的技术怎么样应用于新加坡。有几点值得在座的各位在今后工作研究中注意。第一点,他讲到现在的交通发展的潮流,一般都能看到新的技术、新的需求。但是,现在碰到的问题是价值取向问题,在发展过程中我们要有什么样的交通价值观?要有什么样的交通文化?这是值得我们思考的。关教授专门研究交通文化,当代人比较容易现代化,但是我们价值观要扭转要现代化,我感觉还有很多工作要做。第二点,报告讲到很多新的技术,像无人驾驶汽车。在中国,交通系统实际上越来越复杂,不像日本交通越来越简单。我们有电瓶车、自行车及其他类别的车。这种情况下怎么让这种无人驾驶车在中国马路上跑起来?还有要建信息基础设施,中国在研究过程中还发现一个情况,就是好不容易做了检测流量数据,道路一改造把这些成果毁掉了,这和国外也是不一样的。另外,他讲到新加坡公交换乘很便利。我们中国公交站一般离路口80米,距离很远,而且公交站往往很难识别,但是新加坡的相隔公交站一般不超过300米,每一个站有一个代码,告诉你几点几分会到。

第二位教授讲到日本的交通问题,这些问题我们国家正在发生,但是这些问题日本现在应该来讲都解决了。他讲了三个技术的创新,要建轨道城市,铁路上的城市。但是现在又碰到我们城市里面高峰时间上不了地铁的问题,我们都在限流,这怎么办?把所有铁路系统拿出来,和日本一个公司、一个系统来比,这个是没有可比性的。所以说我们是世界第一的说法是比较荒谬的。我们服务的品质要达到第一,还有很多工作要做。我们从地铁站出来怎么换乘,方式五花八门,但是在新加坡很简单,出来以后坐公交,不坐公交就走路。

The Formation Mechanism of Urban Traffic Congestion and the Mitigation Strategy

Wang Wei

Dean and Professor of the College of Civil, Construction and Transportation Engineering, Southeast University

1. The reasons behind the traffic congestion in China's mega-cities

Nowadays, there are two major characteristics of transportation in China: the faster transportation between cities while the more crowded transportation within cities. What caused the current situation of traffic congestion inside cites? For my part, the most important reason lies in the imbalance between the demand and the supply of transportation. In the 21th century, the scale of cities is becoming larger and larger. As we all know, people used to ride bicycles when they went out while today people turn to cars and buses, due to the average trip distance has increased from 2km to 6km because of rapid urbanization. And this leads to the change of traffic structure in cities, namely motor-driven pattern. Let's see two examples. In 2015, the number of motor vehicles raised to 4.3 million in Beijing and in the same year, private cars increased 80 times in Nanjing. The demand for motor vehicles skyrockets but the relative supply of transportation lags behind comparatively, which makes the conflict between demand and supply get worse. What caused the imbalance of transportation during this period? That is rapid urbanization, and we call this phenomenon "the transformation period of traffic structure".

What we need is to get through this transformative period steadily. Once the transformation format is settled, it is almost irreversible. The problem lies in which kind of transformation pattern that we should adopt. Of course, we hope that the transformation direction transforms from bikes to public vehicles. If so, traffic problems would not be a big issue. However, if the transformation goes from bikes to private cars, the infrastructure construction in the current moment and the maintenance of traffic facilities in the future will cost a lot. Moreover, too much traffic construction will turn our cities into a "concrete forest" and cause serious damages to the ecological environment of our cities. In light of this, the best way to solve the traffic congestion issue is to construct the public transport-dominant system, realizing the balance between demand and supply.

2. Three main strategies to alleviate urban traffic congestion in China

The rapid urbanization and the motor-driven transport fact make it more difficult to implement the public transport-dominant system. Therefore, here are three main lines that we need to pay attention to in order to better and faster solve this problem.

First of all, it is necessary to improve the effectiveness of traffic supply and the capacity of transportation, achieving an integrated, well-balanced city transportation system. Secondly, we need to improve the inner coordination and connection of transportation system. The third one is to improve the traffic reliability by developing "Intelligent Transportation Systems" technology. I will introduce each aspect in details in the following part.

(1) The first strategy is to achieve the balance between traffic demand and supply.

We need to solve the traffic congestion problem from its origin, and there are three aspects that need much attention.

First, it is about the cooperation and harmony among urban space, land utilization and urban transportation. In China, the urban transportation planning is disjointed with over-all urban planning, which means our transportation infrastructure is always passive to adapt to the development of the city: traffic facility size is too large whereas comprehensive function is low, therefore causing a lot of irrational traffic demand. The urban form and land exploration decide the transportation demand and spatial traffic distribution in the city. So we need to keep the pace of the urban traffic planning with the over-all urban planning.

Second, we need to optimize the urban traffic structure and strengthen technical guidance. We are trying to implement the public transportation-dominant pattern of motorization, making mass transit more efficient and smooth to attract more residents, and guiding our citizens to purchase private cars rationally, as well as providing a high-quality mass transit system for everybody. Only in this way can we realize the optimization of traffic system.

The urban transport structure in China is very complex. Different trip distance has different ways of travel (Fig.1). For example, people would like to walk or bicycle for a short distance, take a bus or tram for middle distance, and choose railway transportation for long distance and private cars for further distance. The travel distance in a certain city is comparatively settled. We can try to get the best traffic system for the city. Based on a survey of transportation ways in fifty cities in China, our university put forward "the green travel system", which is characterized by giving priority to railway transportation, emphasizing ground public transportation and integrating means of walking, bicycles and private cars as well.

Fig.1
Different
transportation
method for
different trip
distance

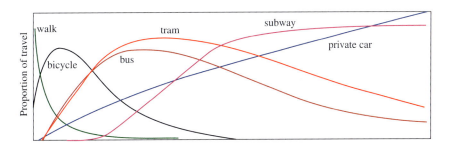

Third, we need to seize on two cores to develop a high-quality urban traffic system. On the one hand, we want to build a city with multi-modal, multi-level public traffic network system (skeleton network, backbone network and supporting network); On the other hand, we want to provide technical support to solve the problem of urban bus rapid transit system. According to a survey conducted in Nanjing, Los Angles, 2/3 of traffic congestion or delay happen at road intersections, 1/3 of them occur at bus stations. Therefore, the main reason of low speed bus lines lies in the delay at road intersections. We come up with this concept "Green Wave Technology for Main Traffic Line", which gives Bus Rapid Transit priority and greatly enhances the efficiency of public transport vehicles without affecting the social vehicles.

(2) The second strategy is to achieve excellent inner coordination and connection of urban integrated public transport system.

I think we should focus on three points:

Firstly, the traffic facilities and functions should shift from civil engineering to the traffic engineering. The scale of our transportation infrastructure is large, and the quality is also very good. However, the whole transportation system function is too weak. The main reason is the lack of urban traffic planning, which leads to the inefficiency of traffic supply. Take this case as an example. On 19th Sept. 2016, an overpass which costs Zhengzhou city 6.5 hundred million RMB was completed. However the traffic was blocked on the first day when it opened because the intersection with the surrounding traffic network was not in a good match. Our emphasis was only on civil engineering, neglecting the transportation systematic engineering construction.

Secondly, urban transport facilities need to transform from bigger, better to more systematic, connected. In the past 35 years, we have always been doing big traffic engineering, only building fast trunk roads and wide roads without the improvement of road network function. The secondary main roads and branch ways lack density, the connectivity of transportation is poor, the intersection traffic capacity is low, and road network as a whole is inefficient. Therefore, we should be rational in planning the allocation of road network level: the ratio of expressway, main road, secondary main road and branch way ought to be 1:2:3:6.

Thirdly, urban transportation network needs to shift from fragmentation to the system synergy. The current urban traffic network is complex. Besides the former road traffic network, more railway network appears, such as subways. However, these networks have long been fragmented. It does not form a system (Fig.2), even they are in conflicts. This problem must be solved. We designed a layout which has a comprehensive transport hub as the core, with the integration of city roads, railway traffic, bus transportation, airport and high-speed rail, together realizing a seamless connection between these main traffic means. The key point is to achieve zero-distance transfer, then comes to the system synergy of network, information and service. Our ultimate goal is to fully combine these three aspects to enhance the urban transportation network comprehensively.

Fig.2
Collaborative
transportation
system

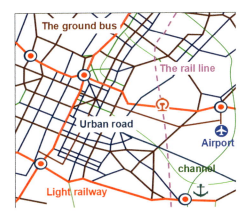

(3) The third strategy is to improve the efficiency of urban comprehensive transportation system.

At present, China's overall urban transportation system efficiency is low; the traffic system is fragile and has poor reliability. Now the best way is to take the urban intelligent transportation technology, called ITS, which is a combination of Internet and Transportation. ITS is one of the core technology in urban traffic system. But we also find that when we implement this technology, we have huge technical bottlenecks. ITS actually is IT + TS, big data has solved the problem of monitoring the urban traffic (such as Traffic Management Center), but it does not provide solutions on how to do scientific planning, induced precision and control optimization. We can see the whole city traffic conditions in the office on the screen, but the core of transportation technology that we use is still outdated and disjoint. To change this situation, we need to work hard from three aspects.

The first is to rebuild the urban traffic system based on the theory of big data. Our current theory system does not support such a comprehensive transportation network construction. Focusing on the basic character of our urban integrated transport system and the theory of formation mechanism of human error, we need to reconstruct traffic flow model in the mobile Internet environment, and reveal the principles of urban transport system supply and demand balance in the whole sample, forming the new generation of transportation theory system, in order to provide basis for precise modeling of integrated transport system smart planning and precise control.

Second, we need to provide a support platform for the government decisions. "Urban Virtual Transport System Decision Support Platform" is such a platform where different departments of the government have chances to share information and manage the traffic issues together. We should have a virtual platform, on which we can carry out the urban development policy, the policy of traffic control and traffic management policy.

Third, we must develop the urban comprehensive transportation system with the integrated analysis platform software. The traditional software introduced from foreign countries (the United States, Canada and Germany) are not suitable for China's national condition; we need to develop our own traffic analysis platform software according to the requirements of the virtual city traffic system construction.

Finally, the fundamental reason of urban traffic jams is the imbalance between supply and demand caused by urbanization, and the only one method to solve it is to implement the smooth bus transportation. And there are three principles: specification of profit, sincere security, as well as science and technology innovation.

Transport Planning Innovations in Chicago, Vancouver and New York

Michael J. Shiffer

Vice President of Metropolitan Transportation Authority

I'd like to share some experiences that I had in Chicago, New York and Vancouver. The three cities are very different in size from Shanghai, and the metro area in Shanghai is much larger than that of New York. Also Shanghai has a larger population than New York. New York has a population of about 20 million, Chicago 10 million, and Vancouver about 3 million. These are different scales, and because of these different scales, different solutions occur. You may work in a smaller city for many years and find some applicable solutions, but it would be a different story in a larger city.

1. The issues of urban transport planning that we need to pay attention to

I naturally started as an academics, and now I am a practitioner. Academically, we need to answer some questions, such as how to apply innovative policies and technologies in enhancing urban mobility (transportation). That is my question and I would focus primarily on the planning process rather than on actually running the trains. My focus is on planning technologies rather than transport technologies. In this field, there are some important aspects as well that I would talk about.

It is very important to apply a systematic planning process in practice, but it is not easy to achieve that because sometimes the planning process is a little bit complex in many cities. Trying as best as you can to facilitate the society is vital, but sometimes the practical world is a very complex place. So it is difficult to implement such a systematic planning process.

It is also very important for planners to develop the information infrastructure. Prof. Wang Wei did a presentation previously on wonderful time-set application of information infrastructure, which is something wonderful that I have been trying to achieve for over 20 years. I agree with Prof. Wang because that is really an important thing to achieve for planning.

It is of course beyond the information to really develop human capabilities. All of us here today can have the best information, the best tools, but without proper planners, the tools could not have been helpful. We really need good people, and that is one of the things that I tried to work towards in all my professional work.

Also, the application of innovative technique is important. Once we have possessed the human resources, information and planning, we can put them into work to assist decision-making by applying innovative technologies to analysis and discussion. Therefore I started in my work and studies when I was a student, and I applied different proofs and concepts. For data visualization in urban transports, we experimented that back in the 1980s with a computer linked to a video disc player, and then to a television. If we do that now, it is very simple to be realized merely on the computers and even on smart phones, but we did not have that back in the years.

I also worked to find the above ideas through the worldwide web with my colleagues at MIT. When we were working with colleagues in government and MIT in the United States; and talking about abstract concepts like portable traffic level of service, we do not look at numbers because decision-makers want to see visual images, see cars on the road, appearing or disappearing. Therefore multi-media tools would be particularly important. Likewise, we have a lot of discussions on public transports and carrying capacity in the United States, and we discussed future routes a lot in Canada. It is often a regional discussion but it is at the globalized level. People need to understand what the operating characteristics of different modes and different operating environments are. We talked about that back in the 1990s with a guide on the worldwide web. That is some of the ground work, the early ground work for what I did, and then I moved out of academic and into practice. In Chicago, I moved very slowly—I was a professor for a part of time and a practitioner for a part of time; then I seized in. I grew up in Chicago, actually in a family that did not have automobiles. That is quite rare in the United States, and because of that, I had a very special appreciation for the importance of public transportation which becomes a part of my passions. With a great honor to go back to the city where I live in, I try to make a difference.

2. Chicago's transport planning is "adapt"

In Chicago, the key word of its transport planning is "adapt", because its infrastructure has always been under reconstruction. The land use in Chicago is changing in recent years dramatically. The key challenge is how you adapt in assisting infrastructure, transportation infrastructure, through targeted investment to improve reliability and accommodate changing traffic patterns. The reliability was very problematic in a lot of old cities in the United States, because there lacked investment in public transportation. Now we have invested a lot of money to bring it to a good status and a good repair. It is the very key. It is an important lesson applicable to other parts of the world, and making the investment continue is very critical at the same time. We were lagged behind for a while in the United States, and we are now trying to work harder to catch up to that.

Things are changed in Chicago and turn to blind you in terms of customers' habits: you see some old infrastructures there. Much of the system has been resolved and continued into being resolved. To do that, you use technologies, such as data and spatial geographic information technology, to help support how people talk about the future of their community, and how they analyze that. We also use multi-media tools. You are often in a room, focusing on the specific site, and you can see what you are talking about through the camera you placed. For example the station. The video can trace the trains and look around the station. We have talked about it in New York, and we have such conversations in Vancouver, in everywhere I have been.

We also use visual writer tools, such as sphere media, which are very important to seize into the planning process. Chicago was a "Doctor" of smart cars back to the early 2000s. Here you can see in the examples of how we would use that data to look at the boarding on a right transporting line over the course of a day. You can see the peak and the rush hours in the evening, or over a course of three-month period, and this is updated constantly on the internet in Chicago. We work on it also through partnership with authorities in universities and the public authorities.

It is similar to buses. It is very important to know how many people are on the buses. In Chicago, two-thirds of public transport ridership is on the buses, that is, one million trips on the bus, half a million on the train. Then you want to know where people get on and where they get off by using an automatic passenger counter. So you can see boarding and routes utilization over the courses of routes. This is the same thing that was repeated in Vancouver. I have shown you at that moment. Then you could apply that here, in China, to every stop in the city, and you have seen examples of that applicability which were in the early 2000s.

3. Vancouver's transport planning is "balance"

The key in Vancouver is "balance". There is a tension between the capacity needs of the central city with a very rapidly growing suburban area, and so how do you balance the regional tension and investment? Whether to put emphasis on the central core or invest more in the suburbs in order to promote development? The answer for these questions is to balance. That is what we did in Vancouver. We have not only public transports, including ferries, trains and buses, but also roads, subways in that kind of ways. Here you see an example. Traffic in suburbs is growing rapidly, yet in the city you feel secured to walk around the blocks and willing to get on highly-used bus, in this way you have the balance like that. There we look at the data again, and you can see what the travel pattern of people from different community was, and what the look and feeling of the regional transportation network were, which is important to understand. We use data gathered from the bottoms. For example, the automatic patterns in Chicago. You can see specific stops here on the screen and see the boarding, arriving, and departing. All that you can learn are visualized on a map—the green bars represent where people get on the bus; the orange bars represent where they get off the bus, and the clear bar is the average load factor on the bus. Over the course of several routes, you have an idea about how the buses are visualized, and you can then change your travel pattern of the bus accordingly. That is a simple lesson given on ordinary passengers counter technology with a map and visualization.

It is also very important to link land use with transport. We will hear more of that from many other speakers here. Some speakers have previously mentioned things that have been done in Singapore and here. A good design is very important all the ways from the pedestrians to the cities.

Fig.1
Balanced
transportation
pattern in
Chicago

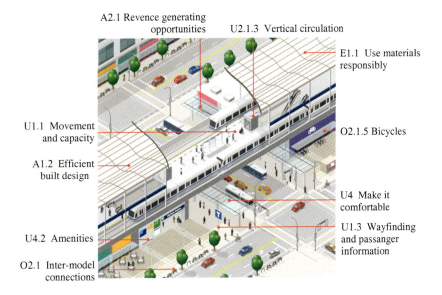

4. New York's transport planning is "network"

The area that I focus on is the railway in New York which serves as some essential terminal. The challenge is to strengthen the condition of the network and then enhance capacity through services, infrastructures, and technology investments. I basically focus on several types of railway technologies and also several competing services here, and they tackle challenges from the past. Resilience is very important. We had hurricanes "Sandy" in New York, but unfortunately, boat and train lines were so long that there were a lot of damages, and there were some requirements which really work to improve that and fix that. In planning, we focus on three areas—operation planning and analysis, capital planning and programming, and long-range planning. Here are some examples of technologies that we used for schedule analysis to look at how trains perform with green for good; blue for very fast and red for bad. You can see whether there are problems in the schedule, and focus on those areas using data visualization to improve the schedule of the train. Also we use technology again to help us to write a more reliable schedule. For example, we use new fare payment system technology to improve the ways that people interact with the public transport system.

This is growing right now, and it will take longer time in New York because New York has a much larger system, and due to a scale of application to there, it also takes longer. On capital planning (Fig.2), we spent half of our capital budget on replacements, another third on the state of good repair, so more than 80 percent was used to just keep the system working before you think about improvement and expansion.

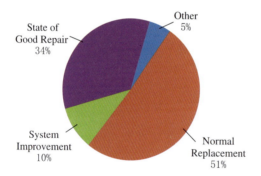

State of
Good Repair
34%

Other
5%

System
Improvement
10%

Normal
Replacement
51%

Fig.2
Components of
capital budget

Grand Central Terminal is a showcase in the center of New York with a grand space. This is what it looks like. This is the terminal crowds, and that is underground, 100-year-old terminal which is double decked. It needs serious improvement to keep that going effectively, which is supported by technologies. We also have a geographic information system as well to understand the infrastructure effectively, everything from the track to the stations. In terms of long-range planning, we use GIS to help plan new routes, like these new routes going deep under the Grand Central Terminal where there are two large cabins in built right now. That will help 100 railway trains, and finally new routes would better improve access to Manhattan and to other parts of New York so that we have multiple ways to get in. Here are some examples.

To summarize, in Chicago, we adapt in assisting infrastructure, improve reliability through targeted investment and accommodate changing travel patterns. For Vancouver where balance is essential in the city and the suburban areas, they need to develop roads and focus on roads. In New York, we really focus on strengthening the condition of the network and enhancing capacity through services, infrastructures and technology investments. In terms of strategies, we spend much time focusing on supporting complementary land use with high quality and frequent transit service. We improve the state of good repair, the resilience in the existing system, which is very important to continue to do for a wild growing city. We leverage the existing transport infrastructure to improve the routes, reroute trains accordingly and take full advantage of investments that we had, and we improve connections to other public transports system. At the same time, we work to improve the convenience of public transports because people in many cities have a choice. We want them to choose public transports to keep a balanced network.

Singapore's Urban Transport Policy: A Comprehensive Urban Solution

Looi Teik Soon

Dean of LTA Academy Land Transport Authority, Singapore

Previously, we have seen cases in New York, Chicago, and Vancouver. Now we are coming back to Asia. Here I would like to share with you what we have done in Singapore in order to bring further the work and what had happened to that city.

1. The development process and present characteristics of urban transport in Singapore

Prof. Wang has shown the situation in China. In Singapore, different strategies and actions are implemented, and I will show you what we have done (Fig.1).

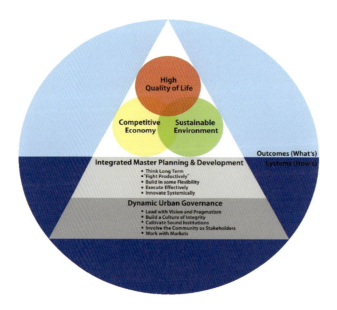

Fig.1
Different strategies implemented in Singapore

Singapore gained its independence in 1965. So how do we fare in just fifty years? Singapore is actually a compacted "city-state", not only a city but also a state. Our population is very small which is about 5.6 million, not reaching 10 million, living in an area of 720 square kilometers. Today we have 12 percent of land used for the road which is quite ubiquitous in a compact city, while housing accounts for 15 percent. The area covers 25 kilometers from north to south, which is not very far that you can cover it in half an hour, and 49 kilometers from east to west. From 1960 to 1965, there were a lot of traffic congestion, resulting from the rising travel demand and unreliable buses, but now we have changed it to a very efficient and sustainable public transport system.

Today the public or the people in Singapore enjoy a full public transport system that offers more choices, affordable and sustainable. Please look at these figures. Taxi trip is one million, and 3.4 million are on the rail track came to join. Bus trips used to be about 5 million ranking at the top of three, and it now has reduced to 4.3 million because of rail trips. Every day you can see there are 7.7 million ridership on the public transportation. Let us look at the roads. We still use roads but we keep them to a modest scale (Fig.2). The road network is 9 200 lane-km, the expressway network 1 100 lane-km, and the vehicle population is something that we control its capacity, that is, 957 000 a day in the appropriate usage. The private car population in this section is very important, and we will get it controlled.

Fig.2
Modest road transport

Next is about the bus and rail systems. The size of the bus system is concentrated at a comprehensive coverage. There are four operators today. It used to be two, but now there are four. The two new ones are Tower Transit and Go Ahead. Today we have 5500 GICT buses and 360 services, which are quite denser than usual. Their services are highly evaluated. For example, we buy buses via government contracting system, and we moved on to the computer transit model just last month. On the train side, unlike Hong Kong of China where there is only one operator, we have two operators—SMRT Trains and SBS Trains. There used to be two in Hong Kong, but now there is one. We have more operators than Hong Kong, and they work well on MRT and LRT lines. There are over 10 train lines in our city with a total length of 182 km, and we intend to double it in 2016, in our fifty years' height, so we have a lot of work to move on.

2. The urban transport in Singapore is faced with challenges

In terms of the bus (Fig.3), you can see that they are among the high brick on bus fleet, bus ridership and capacity. On the train (Fig.4), it is quite comfortable in Hong Kong, but we use it at a higher rate. The average usage of the private car is very low in terms of GDP per capita, but we do have challenges, too.

Singapore is developing, so what kind of problems do we have? Firstly, our population is growing. It is about 6.0 million today according to Population White Paper, and the capacity is expected to be 6.9 million in 2030. So how can we better transportation under such circumstance? The second is called limited land. I have talked about the topic previously that our area is 720

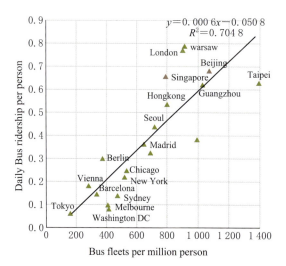

Fig.3
The usage of bus
in different cities

Fig.4
The usage of rail
in different cities

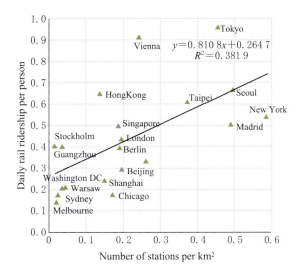

square kilometers; 12% is spent on transportation and 15% on housing. So how much more land in particular is needed to meet the demand of GDP? This is a challenge. Every day we are in need of food and housing. How can we meet the competing demand? Thirdly, commuter expectations are changing. Singapore has progressed over the fifty years and the aging people living there have special demand for mobility. So how should we combine the mobility with our system? In terms of the public transport sustainability, we have always been building public transportation, and ultimately you must make it sustainable and fit the long-term development. That is about what we would construct, and it will be discussed later.

3. The main practices of transport planning in Singapore

Integrated landing planning and development is the very core to Singapore. Since the state won its independence in 1965, there have been a lot of controversies between the land authority and other development authorities. We do fight against each other, but we should also keep in our competitive mind that we need to work together to solve the problems.

This is how we plan, which is similar to any other cities. First, we started from a concept plan in the long term and detail it year after year, and every ten years there comes a new concept plan, a new constructional plan. Please pay attention to a few organizations. Singapore is very concentrated on government planning, relying on them very much, simply because we are ready to talk, at least we work together and plan together. Certainly we would not allocate the land and property to only one. We work with organizations like URA (Urban Redevelopment Authority), Land Transport Authority, and JTC. JTC has built its town-and-city system. These authorities should all work together effectively.

Gradually, we have concept plans, master plans, and plans to develop our own public transport plans, majorly the road and rail plans. There are also the long-range planning and short-range planning. Why do we do long-range planning in such a compact society of Singapore? The reason is very simple: value capture promote high density. This is something quite common but very important in society in terms of master plans, legal acts and business requirements because we optimize land-taking, maximize the capture itself in terms of value and enhance system viability. More importantly, due to the transport planning and integration of transport and towns, we are able to balance vehicles supply and travel needs according to the plans, and thus safeguard the future transport corridors.

Here is an example which would be gone through quickly. Sengkang is a new town in the city where there is a light rail transit that connects to the city and contributes to the development as a part. For those in Singapore, it is going to be a giant interchange, enabling you to get on the light rail from the house. This is something quite new that we think of all the lines having interchanges in Singapore should be like this; then how should we optimize the land-use by taking up together? We have three lines, 4-in-1 deports, and one interchange. That is the very method that we think of to use to optimize the land-use.

We have had a master plan, and then we have to modify that plan. Back to 2008, we have produced the first concept plan, the Land Transport Concept Plan, or the LTC Plan. In 2013, we changed the plan to a master plan. Today, we are much beyond that master plan. There are three sections in the master plan: more connections, better service and livable inclusive community.

There are three key KPIs that we want to deliver. The first is that 75% of all journeys in peak hours should be undertaken on public transport; and then 85% should be completed in less than one hour. Last, 8 in 10 households should walk to a train station within 10 minutes. Therefore, we have a system called car-lite which means using car less. You may not have a car, but if you have a car, you should use it as little as possible. The system consists of "Walk, Cycle, Ride", public transport, technology and electric and driverless, which will be realized by setting specialized area for bicycle and encouraging people to walk in 2030.

Network is ubiquitous in a lot of cities, whether they are natural or highly-dense. We created a good network of rail lines. Even though the rail network in a city is in a good place, the bus service is equally important. We improve connectivity, reduce crowding and increase reliability. I have done a lot on this and on our policy in LTA: we did the Bus Boost Program, and there are 1000 more buses as a result. Last month, we have completed shifts from the allocated system to bus contracted model. Now we have 3 packages competitively tendered out, including 5-year contracts and option for 2-year extension, and 9 packages which are negotiated and operated by incumbents. This is in the transition from the historical operation to a new bus contracting model, and we are told that some of them should be discussed further. A lot of things have changed now: the frameworks have changed—the bus contracting model as well as new rail financing framework. System must be sustainable so that we can pay it by ourselves; otherwise the debts would go to our descendants.

"Walk Cycle Ride" (WCR) is an essential movement. In this movement, it is basically to nurture or shape a new mobility culture. As a city that moves and develops in such a flying demand, it needs such a culture. There is bicycle sharing and bridging the first and last mile from the station to home. We have railway systems and bus systems built around the bus stops, and the railway systems help to bridge the last mile and connect the network. Even in the way we design it, we change the concept like who use the public cars to transit. We have done a lot on restraining private cars in terms of ownership and usage. It is quite common and such messages are very popular in Singapore and easy to read in terms of ownership measures and usage measures, either monetary or non-monetary.

We also perform well in terms of vehicle. We have reviewed that the vehicle growth rate dropped from 7% in 1980s to 0.25%. Then it comes low pricing. We have done a lot on low pricing system. In a review, we control the speed. The speed has a range. If the speed goes up more than that, the price would decrease. This is the established ERP. Based on the things here, you can see that there is car growth, population growth, vehicle growth and road growth in terms of the peak traffic in CBD. The next ERP system is coming up.

Next one is smart mobility. Singapore is doing on Autonomous Vehicle (AV) and has acknowledged the successes of this system. There are four reasons that we are going to talk about: First, we have scheduled bus services. Second, point-to-point mobility-on-demand is where we are going to move on. Freight and utility are the rest. Having these three areas identified, the solutions emerge: 1) we must reduce demand for car ownership; 2) the road congestion during peak hours has to be reduced; 3) the manpower reliance should be reduced at the same time. That is why we rely on bus and guarantee that each bus should have sufficient service staff.

We launched an experiment on AV two years ago, and now we have expanded the experiment in one-north. We hope that in 2020 we can have a pilot deployment and service of AV buses and shared AVs at town-scale level at potential test sites. We have two companies for the AV mobility-on-demand trials. The first on is DELPHI, and the other is nuTonomy. There are other AV initiatives like NAVYA at Nanyang Technology University, and Auto Rider (EZ10).

Ultimately, it is this kind of city that we want to design: green, compact, livable with convenient public transportation and productivity.

Remark

Chen Xiaohong (Professor of College of Transportation Engineering of Tongji University): These three speakers brought us so rich information, which not only provided us with an overall solution, but also with many vivid cases to help us achieve the goal of the global urban traffic management. We named our forum of "Global Cities Forum". Actually a new round of overall planning in Shanghai has set the goal of entire development of Shanghai as a global city. Actually for the management of the global cities, as in Professor Wang's speech, the first problem is the traffic jams, which is the real problem. But in the long run, how do we have a green development and achieve the sustainable development are also important. Professor Wang put forward the balance between supply and demand, system coordination, and the improvement of effectiveness, which provided an overall planning not only for Shanghai urban traffic management but other cities in China. Actually in the overall planning, Professor Wang gave us a lot of insights.

Mr. Michael Schiffer gave us the experience of traffic management from three cities: New York, Chicago and Vancouver. New York is one of the benchmark cities for Shanghai. Vancouver is the earliest origin place. Mr. Michael Schiffer gave us the cases in these three cities and the better, different and possible plans when our urban construction is in a stable condition. He gave us some effective solutions on how to use our current infrastructure to adapt the changes, how to get the balanced development between the downtown part and suburb and how to strengthen the railway network to provide a better service. Especially some cases in technology are very useful for us to analyze based on the big data to achieve the possible effectiveness.

Mr. Lei gave us a case in Singapore. In fact, Shanghai learned a lot from Singapore especially in the ownership and management of vehicles and ways to improve the convenience of vehicles. Mr. Lei not only introduced the existing experience of Singapore, also let us foresee the possibility in 2030, which can be achieved by the new technology, such as the automatic driving technology. Professor Lei also told us that the real solution to urban transportation is not just through railway or bus, but it must be comprehensive. He talked about some new bus operation plans, which are very helpful for how to manage a city and how to improve the level of management.

Guan Hongzhi (Professor of College of Architecture and Civil Engineering of Beijing University of Technology): Firstly, Professor Wang made a very profound and systematic solution to the traffic management in China based on his rich experiences. He pointed from three aspects just as Professor Chen Xiaohong mentioned. I think the solution is very systematic, which asks for the good functions of our government. That will be a long-term and promising solution to our traffic problems. In this solution, we should think about another question. Since our cities are not new anymore and we have faced many problems based on the current city infrastructure, how to manage and how to improve remained to be thought again. So it is the question that our domestic scholars and some foreign scholars who are willing to help us should rethink.

Second it is about Mr. Michael Schiffer. If we say that Professor Wang made a systematic solution to traffic problems, then we can say that Mr. Michael Schiffer gives us some very successful and specific cases. In these cases, different cities have different key points, on technology or on overall planning. From the perspective of system, Mr. Michael Schiffer's speech agrees with Professor Wang's. He gives us more experiences to refer to. From his experiences, we can see that American Traffic engineers put more emphasis on technology and we highlight planning much more.

Mr. Lei's speech is also very distinctive, and two points impressed me deeply. One is the function of government in the management of traffic, which is the same with our country. This aspect is very special. And the other is that he mapped out a blueprint for us in the future. Actually, Professor Wang mentioned that our country is trying to introduce the most advanced technology, such as the AV technology. And we believe these technology and our rich experiences will promote our traffic construction in the future and help to handle the traffic problems.

Future Mobility Research and Innovation in Singapore

Joseph Ferreira

Professor of Massachusetts Institute of Technology

I am involved in a MIT program in Singapore. At the beginning, with this background, I would like to give you a brief introduction to the trends of urban transportation and driverless vehicle by referring to some of the real problems and analyzing the examples from my work in Singapore to make some observations and insight on urban planning and management and the urban information infrastructure to support the future mobility.

I am an Architecture Planning professor focusing on urban studies and planning. We are concerned about sustainable development of the metropolitan areas and my own area of interest is urban information systems. Therefore, we established the urban analytical serving modeling and information infrastructure service. Now, I am residing in Singapore and working at Singapore-MIT Alliance for Research and Technology. As one of nine MIT professors, I am involved in this future urban mobility interdisciplinary research group funded by the National Research Foundation of Singapore and some of international interdisciplinary research groups. Singapore has chosen to sponsor from chemistry to biology as the future development direction.

1. The information communication technology (ICT) effect on the urban transport

Overall, the information and communication technology has obviously bigger changes in the city than other places. How can we manage the pathway? I will talk about some examples of the best use of transportation interaction, as we begin to see ripple effects of ICT on how we deploy people and services in the metropolitan area, just like the automobile industry before World War I. Now I want to give some suggestions on urban information infrastructures. We should accumulate, interpret and use the city-related knowledge about how people can understand and adapt the new situation. We focus on current congestion and give strategies to alleviate the congestion, but people often change their minds in practice. Therefore, we may have to deal with new congestion problems, which mean that we need to take the leading position because we are not sure about the mobility driven by these technologies. We have to promptly acquire the abilities to observe, learn and adapt. So what are the trends of improvement by ICT and infrastructure? There are currently visible trends, including car sharing, autonomous vehicles and construction with better structural mechanics.

At the same time, we may realize more and more effects of urbanization and globalization on population density, income improvement and education. However, more travelling, more vehicles, more emission and more congestion also happened. Considerable effort on planning and regulation are required to change this trend. Now let's have a look. ICT is changing the economic land utilization. In the case of telecommunication such as online shopping, delivery and logistics, fragmentized firms are scattered in different places but the economic activities have to stay in metropolitan central areas. So how can we plan the population distribution so that people do not have to travel through the whole city? We have some innovative but still blurring planning, for example, subsidies for transportation. But should it be supported by government or company? New options for mobility mean that the old way of transportation no longer suits, which makes the related departments into a dominant position. We have many families having two or more workers who choose to work in other places and take more commuting time, so we need to have clear vision and directions.

2. The potential impact of driverless vehicles

I would like to introduce the driverless vehicles. Driverless vehicles are in style in the United States and also a hot topic in China. I believe it has a lot of investment opportunities. Nowadays, $ 3 000 can buy a Google driverless car and $ 20 000 for a Golf Cart. It has electronic equipment that can help solve the problem of "last mile." The key is to find a scientific and technological innovation path under the regulation of government. For example, on the road traffic, do we need to set special lanes and make other cars follow this design? In addition, how to manage the parking is another problem that we should think about it.

Also, the ownership and use of vehicles are different. If the driverless vehicles come out, will there be negative impact? Since people can do other things on the driverless car, they may not care about the time, so the traffic volume may increase. We have to estimate all of it.

Let's take a look at the situation in Singapore. My colleagues have already written the papers about it. Let's look at the situation in Singapore and the United States. For Singapore first, I know 3 000 out of 8 000, maybe 9 000 in the future are fully automatic driving vehicles which basically can meet the need of previous 8 000 vehicles traffic. People only have to wait 15 minutes, which contains the possibility of increasing productivity. Besides, the taxi is running without clients for half of the time. With driverless vehicles, this problem can be solved to large extent. But the problems concerning placement of traffic patterns, as well as lanes distribution and parking, should also be considered.

Now look at some of these figures. Having no time to mention one by one here, I only emphasize some of the majors. My colleagues have classified different driving models, manned, driverless, and a combination, namely the driverless under people's control. For different types, we can compare the cost per kilometer spent and overall mobility in Singapore and the United States. After calculation, the annual cost of manned driving is 30 000 dollars in the United States, 32 000 dollars in Singapore, which actually includes more than 5 000 US dollars license fee. In current situation, despite technology, we still do not have related regulations issued. If regulations are complete, the cost can be cut down to 15 000 dollars, and driverless vehicles will be well-spread.

We also have to know how it works after this technology come out. Does it need special lanes? Should we keep promoting this model or car sharing? For our entire public transportation, what kind of impact will it have on land use? What happens to the decomposition of cities and suburbs? The future for automatic driving must have a lot of special markets. We can develop special market first, and then put it into the overall market. For instance, it may be firstly used in road cleaning or freight, which has wider impact.

In addition, it is very important to make a good transition to automatic driving; otherwise the cost may be too high. For example, if we have 60 people to transport (Fig.1), how many vehicles do you need? You can look at private cars and Uber, as well as driverless vehicles. The number of these cars may be the same.

Fig.1
Space required to transport 60 people

3. The application potential for Car Sharing

For example in Singapore. At the beginning of commuting, a lot of people in Singapore take bus to the subway station, and then transfer to the subway. People are gathered by buses on these stations, the places which I used colors to identify are the subway stations with large number of people every day. We collect this information from the traffic cards which Singapore people use. The number of 15 000 people is reduced to 1 700 after 31 stations. The efficiency of buses is decreasing.

If we improve the situation for the first a kilometer, the result will be different. We can also share cars to solve the problem. If someone who shares cars for the first mile can get benefits from government, the efficiency will be greatly improved, including risk and density control or economic benefits improvement. Who will pay for the cost? Who is in such a position to solve market problem with policies and give people great benefits? I think we need to do a research. Here are some examples of what we have done in Singapore.

As we can see, Singapore has done a lot of researches, including the driverless vehicles. Other organizations, such as Singapore Institute of Technology are also doing cooperative research. One of their researches, using the driverless vehicles on public road, has been promoted. Singapore Land and Transportation Administration also has its own projects to compare hybrid cars with completely new energy vehicles which are supported by many charging rod. Obviously, we can design better only with more improved technologies. I know that technology is quickly updated, but we also have to seize every possibility that technology brings to us to control and manage the demand. At the same time, we need to make a good balance between public welfare and demand. In order to monitor and plan the next step, we shall know the importance of urban infrastructure for the work we do.

In addition, our traffic is a part of infrastructure. We may also see some other information, such as the investment from the government and other shared electronic information. Only from the daily data collection can we know the basic information of infrastructure management and the city. The city data can be considered as the general commodity, for example, the ownership and release time. More detailed applications such as personal tracking, GPS and Google GTFS can be used to share our needs, and finally a large data analysis system will be established to share these data and achieve our goal. We must integrate this information in a comprehensive way, encourage urban residents to travel in a more intelligent way, solve problems by innovative planning and methods, and plan and manage based on information technology.

Japan's Innovations in Managing Urban Transportation Problems

Zhang Junyi

Professor of Hiroshima University

1. Introduction

Japan had experienced various terrible transportation issues (traffic congestion, traffic accidents, air pollution, etc.), especially during 1960s—1970s when economic growth was very rapid and over-concentration of population was very serious in the three super-metropolis of Japan: Tokyo, Nagoya and Osaka. After such experience, the Japanese society has made tremendous efforts to tackle these issues successfully, in comparison to other countries. Traffic fatalities were reduced from 16 765 deaths in 1970 to 3 904 deaths in 2016. Public transport systems occupy about 80% of the whole share in the 23 wards of Tokyo and about 50% in the Tokyo Metropolitan Area. Environmental loads from transportation systems, as a whole, have declined since the beginning of the 21 century. Various innovations have contributed to such a success, which

Fig. 1

Types of Japan's innovations in managing urban transportation problems

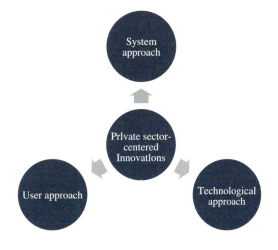

can be roughly categorized into three types (see Fig. 1): system, user, and technological approaches. Actually, most of the most successful innovations are initiated by the private sector and well supported by the government. Here, innovations in the large cities (especially the above three super-metropolis) in Japan are mainly described.

2. System approach: *Ensen Kaihatsu* (EK)

The famous concept of the transit-oriented development (TOD) was proposed by several American architects in 1990s. However, similar concepts and practices already existed in the early 1900s in Japan, called *Ensen Kaihatsu* (EK), i.e., railway area developments. EK has been actively practiced by private railway companies since 1960s. During that period, rapid urbanization and population growth had led the land price in central urban areas to be too high to be afforded by many people, even for those middle-class people (or white-collar workers). Nevertheless, over-concentration of population in large cities, especially in the three super-metropolis was remarkable in the sense that more and more people from local cities and rural areas had migrated into the large cities. To respond to concentrated population growth with considerably high housing needs, private railway companies, which were in a monopoly position in the field of land transport, first constructed rail lines stretched out to suburbs and developed residential areas and commercial areas along the lines, especially surrounding stations. As the development strategy, private railway companies secure profits by purchasing lands along railway lines and building residential areas, from which a sufficient number of users for railway operation can be generated. Thus, EK was initiated by private railway companies. However, TOD is a kind of joint development between a government-run railway operator and an urban developer.

3. User approach

The author has visited many countries, especially in USA, Europe, and Asia. His personal experience has evidenced that Japan surely has the most user-friendly public transportation systems in the world.

(1) Critical roles of private companies. The public transportation systems in Japan are mainly operated by private companies. There are some subsidies from central and/or local governments; however, the amount is much lower than that in other developed countries. Therefore, private companies have to make various efforts to meet users' needs before/during/after travel by themselves. In the service sector of Japan, including the public transportation service sector, it is often emphasized that services must meet users' expectations, and services exceeding users' expectations are regarded as the best. Such mindsets have made the Japanese public transportation systems clean, reliable, safe, and often very punctual and comfortable. Train/bus conductors and ground staff are well trained and very friendly.

(2) User-friendly accessibility. To compete with car traffic, public transportation systems in the Japanese large cities need to cover different parts of urban spaces as much as possible. Railway companies have made various efforts to expand their networks under the constraint of very limited subsidies from government. As a result, extensive public transportation networks have been established. Because of extensive transit networks, users need to search travel information before departure. Such information is well available via various offline and online media. Thus, user-friendly accessibility is guaranteed.

(3) Reliable punctuality. The Japanese public transportation systems are well operated based on timetables available to the public, as a serious promise to users. To keep such a promise, private companies make full use of available resources and technologies, even in case of emergency (e.g., accidents). As a result, for example, it is said that train operation in Tokyo is the most punctual in the world.

(4) Mutual direct operation across companies. Surprisingly, Japan's railway and subway systems have successfully introduced mutual direct operation across different companies. Such mutual operation allows trains from different companies to share the tracks, i.e., a train from one company can directly run on the track of another company. In 2013, Tokyo Metro's operation kilometers using its own lines were 180 099 000 km, while the trains from other companies used its lines to travel for 104 554 000 km. In contrast, Tokyo Metro used other

companies' lines to run its trains for 104 866 000 km. Cancel-out based on vehicle kilometers operated is the basis for sharing mutual operation costs, such as use of vehicles and lines. Private companies have made efforts of information sharing for punctual operation in a very complicated way, such as installation of information displays of partner companies, establishment of coordinated operation systems for different companies, and so on.

(5) Mutual use of transport IC cards. According to Ministry of Land, Infrastructure, Transport and Tourism, transport IC cards in railway systems have been widely introduced. Especially, mutual use between companies and across regions has been actively promoted. Since 2015, nearly 80 companies have introduced more than 25 types of IC cards. More than 87 million cards have been sold, which can be used at more than 5 000 stations. More than 20 types of IC cards can be mutually used across the whole country.

4. Technological approach

Various advanced technologies have been introduced to support transportation development in Japan. Here, intelligent transport systems (ITS), electric vehicles (EV), plugged-in hybrid vehicles (PHV), and autonomous vehicles (AV) are focused on.

(1) ITS in Japan. Japan has been a leading country in the development of ITS in the world. ITS in Japan has been developed based on a comprehensive plan consisting of nine development areas. They include, advances in navigation systems, electronic toll collection (ETC) systems, assistance for safe driving, optimization of traffic management, increasing efficiency in road management, support for public transport, increasing efficiency of commercial vehicle operations, support for pedestrians, and support for emergency vehicle operations. The ITS system architecture in Japan includes 21 user services and 172 user sub-services. Four ministries have been involved, including Ministry of Land, Infrastructure, Transport and Tourism (MLIT), National Police Agency (NPA), Ministry of Internal Affairs and Communications (MIC), and Ministry of Economy, Trade and Industry (METI), under the administration of the Cabinet Office. In addition, ITS Standardization Committee and ITS Japan are two

external supporting organizations. ITS in Japan has aimed at improving traffic safety, enhancing transportation efficiency, mitigating environmental loads, enhancing the convenience of transportation systems, regional revitalization, and infrastructure improvements and standardization. ITS in Japan has been deployed via three stages in a well-organized way. The first stage is to promote practical applications. The second is to promote the diffusion of ITS and to speed up returning benefits to the society. The third is to respond to social issues. At important timing of each stage, Japan held ITS World Congress in 1995 (Yokohama), 2004 (Nagoya), and 2013 (Tokyo), respectively.

Fig. 2
Growth of EV/
PHEV and
chargers in Japan

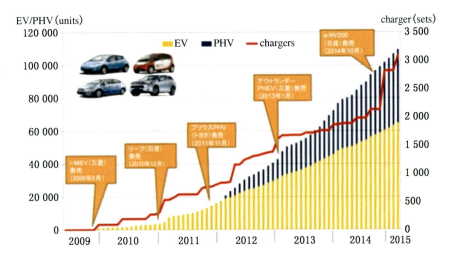

(2) EV/PHV in Japan. EV/PHV in Japan has been deployed as an integrated development through the scheme of EV/PHV towns, initiated by the Ministry of Economy, Trade and Industry (METI). Under this initiative, municipalities and local firms collaborate with each other based on four basic objectives: to create initial demand of EV/PHV, to construct charging infrastructure, to enlightenment the diffusion of EV/PHV, and to evaluate the effects of the scheme and to improve it. This scheme selected 18 prefectures, which are required to make a master plan and an action plan. Fig. 2 shows the growth of EV/PHEV and chargers in Japan.

(3) Autonomous Vehicles in Japan. On August 24, 2016, Nissan Motor Company released a new type of SERENA, a small Van, equipped with ProPILOT technology, which is a revolutionary autonomous drive technology designed for highway use in single-lane traffic. ProPILOT technology makes

autonomous drive first for Japanese automakers. Within just about a month after the release, Nissan received 20 784 orders (about 2.5 times higher than the monthly goal) of SERENA, among which 70% are equipped with ProPILOT technology. Adding ProPILOT technology as an option just costs less than 200 000 Yen. Because of such developments initiated by private companies, the Japanese government has actively promoted the development of autonomous vehicles (AV) in terms of international standards and the compensation rules in case of accidents, development of AV technologies and diffusion strategies, and social implementations for putting AV into practice. Actually, several insurance companies in Japan have started to cover insurances for AV technologies, free of charge, including Tokio Marine & Nichido Fire Insurance Co. Ltd. and Sompo Japan Nipponkoa Insurance Inc. The Japanese government already started social experiments for last-mile transport services (four sites across the whole country) and transport services in depopulated areas (ten sites across the whole country). Furthermore, in the year of the 2020 Tokyo Olympics, thousands of driverless robot taxis are planned to run on selected road sections.

5. Enlightenment to China

Different from the rapid economic growth period of the past, Japan is now confronted with the aging population and the low birth rate. Previous successful stories may not be applicable to such new situations. Meanwhile, how to mitigate the various issues caused by over-concentration of population in Tokyo is still an important national policy issue, and issues of traffic congestion, traffic accidents, and air pollution remain as well. Previous solutions to these issues were mainly quantity-oriented. In contrast, current and future solutions are mainly quality-oriented. To respond to such changes in policymaking environment, collaboration across sectors (both within and outside government) should have played an important role; however, relevant policymaking in Japan has long suffered from bad collaboration across sectors. Massive construction of transportation infrastructures has become a history. Instead, maintenance and refreshments of transportation infrastructures have become more and more important. New measures have heavily relied on the development of new technologies. Unfortunately, new technologies sometime lead to the occurrence of new issues (e.g., rebound effects of energy-saving technologies). To tackle such issues, public involvement is a useful and necessary measure, but sometimes it is too time-consuming. Considering the above matters, it is necessary to introduce the successful stories of Japan by adapting to actual situations in Chinese cities in a selective way.

Due to relatively weak interventions from government, Japan's successes have heavily counted on efforts from the private sector. In particular, private railway and streetcar companies have shown their abilities in providing high-quality transportation infrastructures and services based on market-based competition, even under the limited subsidies from government. Expertise of the Japanese private companies will be surely useful to resolve the transportation issues in China. China should give more business spaces and authorities to the private sector in transportation development.

In China, more and more people have migrated into large cities, including Beijing, Shanghai, Guangzhou, and Shenzhen. Similar migration patterns have been observed in Japan since 1960s—1970s. Various countermeasures have been taken over a long period; however, situations have not been improved. Recently, the Japanese central government under the Abe Cabinet has just decided to make more powerful policies encouraging people to move to local cities and rural areas. Unfortunately, effects are not that obvious as expected. Population has been long treated as an input to transportation planning. However, it has been neglected that transportation development may affect the population distribution. Control of population over-concentration and its spatial distribution within and across cities via various public policies, including transport policies, is important.

Delays in ring road construction in Tokyo Metropolitan Area have led to successful development of public transportation systems, to some extent. Limiting road capacity is definitely useful to encourage more people to use public transportation systems. Thus, earlier development of public transportation infrastructures is more important than major road construction.

Travel demand often grows faster than supply. There is no doubt that construction of necessary transportation infrastructure needs quick actions by making full use of various capitals. However, one more important lesson that should be learnt from the Japan's experience is that travel demand management is more important than infrastructure supply. This is because new infrastructure supply often induces new travel demand. As a result, infrastructure supply has been always behind the growth of travel demand. Actually, systematic parking policies (i.e., a type of car traffic demand management) in Japan have contributed to resolve various traffic issues. Various effective and convenient information systems about public transportation operation have been useful to attract car users. Travel demand requires better management.

Finally, there are various stakeholders involved in transportation development. Therefore, consensus building becomes important. It is important to take more time to put policies into practice by convincing the majority of people based on scientific evaluations. This is helpful to promote sustainable transportation development, even though it is surely time-consuming. In other words, what our cities need is a modest development, rather than a too rapid one. Only in this way can we do a good job!

Remark

Pan Haixiao (Professor of College of Architecture and Urban Planning of Tongji University): The first speaker has a very good topic concerning future cities which has been well recognized by many people. Besides that, we need to find out those factors influencing economic and social development of future cities.

First of all, the requirements of future transportation will not be the same as current situation in mega-cities like Shanghai as the population is composed of fewer children for mega-cities. Secondly, with the development of technology, the relationship between land use and transportation will experience a tremendous change. Under such circumstances, we must reconsider how to apply these new technologies to improve the efficiency of our urban lives. However, it is not simply the matter of technology. I remember that many cities have introduced the technology of parking guidance system in order to solve the traffic problems, which is not as effective as we have expected. As a contrast, raising the parking fees can effectively solve the traffic disorder. This example shows that the price policy and management are also effective methods to deal with traffic problems.

The speech also mentioned that the information about infrastructures, considered as a kind of public goods, has been viewed as a short-board of our urban governance. In order to build future cities, researchers are in need of adequate information to make an overall analysis. If we only confine those valuable data in our closets, it is hard to improve the level of urban governance.

Professor Zhang has shared with us the successful example of Japan. Japan is doing very well in making use of the most modern technologies to improve the standard of living. Japan's metro transport is separated, and all kinds of companies are able to operate in a collaborative way. When it comes to China, it often happens that there are more than three railway stations in the same city, so it is difficult to use technology to combine the three of them.

Li Chaoyang (Professor of School of Naval Architecture, Ocean and Civil Engineering of Shanghai Jiao Tong University): The current concept of national development is to focus on "creation, coordination, green, openness and sharing", which is also the core value in the speech of our two professors here.

The first professor made a thorough study on how to apply the advanced technology to Singapore. There are several points ought to be paid attention to: for the first point, he talked about the current trend of transportation development. We are quite familiar with the new technologies and new trends in this development. However, what we now are confronted with is the value tendency of our transportation development. Our Professor Guan has specifically studied the transport culture. The most difficult part is to transform modern people's values rather than simply achieve modernization, which I think it still has a long way to go. He also talked about a lot of new technologies, such as driverless vehicles. Unlike Japan, the system of our Chinese transportation is becoming more and more complex. Actually, our traffic is mixed with battery cars, bicycles and various types of cars. On this occasion, it is difficult for those driverless vehicles to drive on the roads. Besides that, we also need to perfect information of infrastructure facilities. However, scarcely have we obtained the data of test flow when these data have has been destroyed by the road reconstruction in China. The third point is about the public transport transfer in Singapore. Why people can get to the bus station easily there while we cannot in China? In China, the bus station is usually 80 meters away from the intersection, quite a long way. Also it is hard to identify our bus station. However, in Singapore, the situation is quite different. But in Singapore, the distance between bus stations is less than 300 meters, and each bus station can report the arriving time of the bus.

The second Professor talked about Japan's transportation problems.

These problems also exist in our country, but these issues in Japan had been resolved already. There are three technological innovations which we can learn from. We need to build a metro city, railway city. But now we are faced with overpopulation during the peak hours in our mega-cities. We cannot take our whole metro system to compare with a company's system in Japan because there are too many people who need to take subways. In addition, the quality of our service needs improvement. When people come out from the subway station, they may feel confused about how to transfer because there are many kinds of choices. However, you can either walk or take a bus in Singapore.

FORUM IV

分论坛四

Urban Eco-Governance & Innovation
城市生态治理创新

主持人·HOST
诸大建·Zhu Dajian
同济大学经济与管理学院教授、可持续发展研究中心主任
Professor of School of Economics & Management and Director of
Sustainable Development Research Center of Tongji University

车生泉·Che Shengquan
上海交通大学农业与生物学院副院长、教授
Professor and Vice Dean of School of Agriculture and Biology of
Shanghai Jiao Tong University

城市生态治理创新分论坛现场嘉宾聆听演讲

Guests at the Urban Eco-Governance & Innovation Forum are listening to the speeches attentively

同济大学经济与管理学院教授诸大建主持平行分论坛四

Zhu Dajian，Professor of School of Economics & Management of Tongji University，hosts the Parallel Forum IV

世界银行环境与自然资源局首席环境专家高柏林在平行分论坛四上作专题演讲

Garo Batmanian，Leading Environment Specialist of Environment and Natural Resources Administration of World Bank，delivers a speech at the Parallel Forum IV

德国弗朗霍夫研究所副所长冈纳·格论教授在平行分论坛四上作专题演讲

Gunnar Gruen，Professor and vice director of Fraunhofer Institute in Germany，delivers a speech at the Parallel Forum IV

上海交通大学农业与生物学院副院长车生泉教授在平行分论坛四上作专题演讲

Che Shengquan，Professor and Vice Dean of School of Agriculture and Biology of Shanghai Jiao Tong University，delivers a speech at the Parallel Forum IV

剑桥大学发展研究中心副主任沙拉亚·费莎教授在平行分论坛四上作专题演讲

Shailaja Fennell，Professor and Deputy Director of Center of Development Studies at University of Cambridge，delivers a speech at the Parallel Forum IV

中国城市发展研究院名誉院长李兵弟教授在平行分论坛四上作点评

Li Bingdi，Professor and Honorary Dean of China Urban Development Institute，comments on the Parallel Forum IV

上海交通大学农业与生物学院副院长车生泉教授主持平行分论坛四

Che Shengquan，Professor and Vice Dean of School of Agriculture and Biology of Shanghai Jiao Tong University，hosts the Parallel Forum IV

同济大学经济与管理学院教授诸大建在平行分论坛四上作专题演讲

Zhu Dajian，Professor of School of Economics & Management of Tongji University，delivers a speech at the Parallel Forum IV

以色列耶路撒冷希伯来大学教授阿里扎·弗莱舍在平行分论坛四上作专题演讲

Aliza Fleischer，Professor of Hebrew University of Jerusalem，delivers a speech at the Parallel Forum IV

上海交通大学环境科学与工程学院院长耿涌教授在平行分论坛四上作专题演讲

Geng Yong，Professor and Dean of School of Environmental Science and Engineering of Shanghai Jiao Tong University，delivers a speech at the Parallel Forum IV

世界银行社会、城市、农村和灾害风险管理全球实践发展局首席城市专家梅柏杰在平行分论坛四上作专题演讲

Barjor Mehta，Leading Urban Specialist of Social，Rural，Urban & Resilience Global Practice of World Bank，delivers a speech at the Parallel Forum IV

华东师范大学地理科学院教授蔡永立在平行分论坛四上作点评

Cai Yongli，Professor of School of Geographic Sciences of East
China Normal University，comments on the Parallel Forum IV

城市公共产品管理不能只靠规划

高柏林
世界银行环境与自然资源局首席环境专家

尽管我们的城市规划者将会对我的演讲发表评论，但我的演讲内容并不局限于城市规划。本报告是基于这样一个理念：如果超过了承受极限，城市对公共物品就无法实现很好的管理。这是中国空气质量和水质量管理出现的典型问题，仅仅通过城市内部的规划无法解决空气与水质问题。本报告主要围绕这些城市治理方面出现的问题进行探讨。

1. 空气质量管理的困境与对策

2015 年中国的雾霾非常严重，主要原因就是 PM2.5，这些颗粒能够移动到 500 公里以外的地方。所以，尽管北京正在把工厂转移到河北，实际上这不会有什么作用。因为北京处于河北的逆风向，云团仍然能够移动并将雾霾带回北京。

2015 年 12 月有一个重大事件，在某个时间点，上海和河北有同等程度的雾霾。图 1 是按照不同的污染物所界定的空气质量，包括二氧化硫、黑炭以及 PM2.5 等等。很多人不知道几乎有一半的 PM2.5 是由化学品的排

图 1
不同污染物所界定的
空气质量

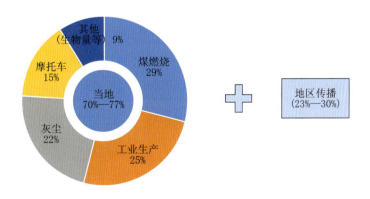

放引起的，这些化学品的次级化合物构成了 PM2.5 中的很多颗粒物。直到 2015 年中国才开始关注这些农业化学品，包括化肥中的氨肥。中国实际使用了比理论所需多 30% 的化肥量，这些化肥与其他化学品结合，就成了构成 PM2.5 的主要来源。所以，一座城市是无法解决这些普遍性问题的。

本报告引入了一个新概念：分气岭。分气岭与陆地上的分水岭是同样的概念。例如，新加坡是印度尼西亚分气岭的一部分，所以如果新加坡有污染物，印度尼西亚也会受到影响。下面给出一个亚洲范围内最有说服力的例子，这就是河北省石家庄市。虽然石家庄一直在向绿色城市努力，但它现在还不是绿色城市。作为河北的省会城市，石家庄市 23%—30% 的污染物来自本市以外的地方。所以哪怕石家庄将本市污染物减少一半，仍会有 30% 的污染物从外部进来。因此，解决方法很简单，亚洲城市应该建立联合机制从而防止空气进一步污染，并从城市层面进一步提高效果和降低相关成本。从这个角度来说，我们不能忽视农业，也要总体控制上游的空气情况。中国已经有了三个区域性规划，包括长三角、珠三角以及京津冀地区。我们在制定城市规划的时候就要将这些区域规划考虑进去，更好地通过协调判断需要关闭多少工厂，否则就会在不同城市之间造成分配不均。有时即使在河北没有产能，内蒙古却仍有可能有，这依然会造成空气污染。

2. 水资源管理的问题与对策

接下来是水资源。中国人均可用水资源占有量仅为世界平均水平的 25%，中国水资源总量有限，并有 65%—70% 的水用于农业，因为中国有大量水稻和其他农作物需要灌溉。这在以前没有任何问题，但现在随着城镇化的发展，城市对水资源的需求也在与日俱增。无论城市规划在水资源的回收利用等方面多么高效，中国仍然没有足够的水资源。这是第一个问题。

第二个问题是，中国使用的水其实已经被污染了。这在我的祖国巴西和其他国家很常见。比如，我们住在上海的河道附近，我们得到的水源可能就已经有了污染物，这时候我们还要花大量资金处理水质，确保它能够作为生活用水。因此，仅仅通过城市内部的优化，是无法解决水质问题并满足市民需求的。

城市在发展，并不是所有城市都和上海一样。比如北京和其他城市，它们既不靠近河道，内部也没有大型河流。这样的例子还有很多，最知名的是纽约，它让提供环境服务的人获得报酬，并由从环境服务中受益的人支付这一部分费用。这种机制如果在北京实施，就需要支付报酬给上游居民，让他们负责确保上游水质。这是比较有效的，道理很简单，上游居民能使用土地并且也能够获得好处。

接下来，我们看几个来自巴西的案例，图 2 是其中一个。图 2 中是巴西南部一条比较小的河流，也许没有纽约案例中的那么大，这个城市总体来说有点像中国的北戴河，人口在 15 万左右。这里有一个水务公司和不是很大的水源地，上游有许多养猪场，所以水质多多少少受到了污染。有相关人员来到这里为当地农民提供解决方案，就是投资 800 万美元打造新的分水岭，并且每年每公顷还需要花费 1.25 亿美元。

图 2
巴西水资源项目

3. 城市公共产品供给需要协同治理

最后要强调的是，有时城市是无法充分管理公共物品的，尤其是空气质量和水资源，以及其他一些超过了城市极限的事项。所以，同一分气岭和分水岭内的城市应该联合制订计划，并在不同的城市之间进行合理的责任分配，否则就会造成各城市负担不平衡。这能帮助我们提高效果、降低成本。同时，我们也需要政府和市场合力执行具体行动。在有了一个区域性的规划来管理水资源、控制空气污染之后，我们可以再在城市层面进行对汽油的改造。但需要注意的是，城市层面的规划只是区域层面战略的一部分，如果我们只是闭门造车进行城市规划，最后不但无法管理城市，而且成本非常高。在中国，正如我的祖国巴西一样，可以从政府法规出发，将政府监管和市场机制结合起来，出台一套与巴西《环境服务倡议》类似的法规。

可持续城市生命周期的能源管理

冈纳·格论

德国弗朗霍夫研究所副所长、教授

　　城市需要能源，且对能源的需求会随着生命周期而改变。如图 1 所示，到 2050 年，世界上将有 50% 的人口生活在城市，而目前世界上已经有将近一半的人口生活在城市中。城镇化的话题在欧亚都变得越来越重要，虽然在欧洲人口城镇化的增速不像在亚洲这么快，但我们仍要应对这个挑战。

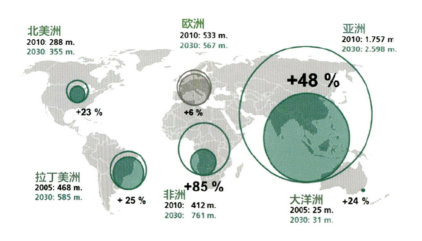

图 1
城市人口增长

1. 城市系统中的能源管理

　　当我们观察城市的各个系统时，会发现有不同的促进因素值得关注，这些因素能够进一步推动城市发展。第一是打造绿色有吸引力的城市环境，吸引人才与城市构建情感纽带。另外，我们需要建设绿色产业园为那些需要能源的人创造价值。

　　在过去的一年中，我们有更多的可再生能源可供使用。同时，有不同的尺度层面可供参考。首先是跨能源类别的能源管理。其次是在区域尺度层面，尤其是供热和供冷方面，我们也在考虑是否能更好地进行制热制冷系统的能源管理，并在不同的时间使用。接下来是在建筑尺度层面。我们都知道从电到热的能量转换，因此我们希望可以对可再生能源进行优化整合，从而获得更多供热。接下来我们可以看到如何在社区尺度层面进行能源结构的调整。因为我们现在有着极大的能源需求，更需要提高能源使用效率，同时对可再生能源在社区层面的制冷制热进行有效管理。德国经常有这样的处理方式。如果你想知道如何进行能源优化，你必须同时看使用能源的目的是什么，从而根据不同时段、不同能源种类、不同制冷制热系统来选择。例如，在超市供应供热负荷是因为大量冷藏食品带来的加热需求。

2. 城市运行中的能源管理

住宅楼宇中也需要供热系统，问题在于，是否能够优化其他资源转化为能量？这同样适用于溜冰场，那里有高制冷和高制热需求。在德国，我们经常做的就是高效使用可再生能源。举个例子，德国南部的一个城市有极大的汽车使用比例，在这个例子中，我们可以看到一个城市如何通过吸引能源供应公司以及服务建设单位的参与来改善城市层面的能源使用效率。首先需要有公共机构的参与。要在学校里推广这些节能计划，教育是很重要的一点，在学校里，节能的概念已经被写入了课程大纲，因此孩子们从一开始就能有节能的意识。除此之外，我们也对公司员工进行相关培训。其次是能源效率提升的问题。我们通过改善区域层面的能量供应系统来有效满足供热需求，同时使用了智能测量系统，帮助我们更高效地使用能源。关于可再生能源，我们的城市实际上安装了光伏设备，但并不是所有房屋都适用。同时还在城市之外建设了生物质发电厂，并发展了一个配套的概念来宣传城市所做的节能工作。我们还需要指标和测量方法来证明所做的这些措施是有效的。在德国我们经常讨论一次能源：说到能源的效率，现在使用了多少一次能源？我们的目标是降低一次能源的使用。有一个项目是 2000 年 4 月启动的，旨在降低一次能源使用，并有幸取得了卓越的成效。到 2020 年，我们希望工业区一次能源的需求降低 20%，同时提高汽车领域需求。这是我们在过去的项目部署中所取得的成果。

另一个例子是德国北部的一个城市，这个城市目前正将所有的能源来源都替换为可再生能源。他们希望提升整个系统的能源使用效率，同时使可再生能源的规模达到最大化。另外，他们也希望在生产、分配以及储存方面进一步应用智能化技术并最大化其参与程度，否则很难有效管理整个系统。图 2 展示的是二氧化碳的排放。相比较上世纪 90 年代，我们制定了一直延续到 2020 年的降低二氧化碳排放的战略，收效显著。但这之后，降低二氧化碳排放就变得更具挑战性了。我们不单在楼宇层面，或者区域层面，也需要在城市层面看节能。所以我们与国际能源署的其他同事合作，做了一个区域层面的工具，叫做"能源概念咨询"，其目标是将这些造楼的人纳入决策方，让他们无论是在市政层面，还是在地方政策的制定层面都能够参与进来。这个工具使用简单，指导详尽，即使是外行也能知道能源的潜力所在。

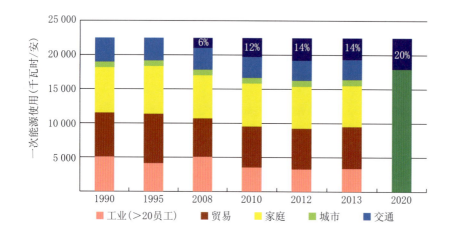

图 2
一次能源使用的发展

3. 城市更新中的能源管理

还有一个例子是德国南部的另一个城市。这个城市的居住区需要进行翻新。我们对这个地区的区域性供热资源与技术进行了相应的改善，包括住房、产业、超市、医院等。你可以把它们与不同的能源供应系统连接起来，并获知之前在这里使用了多少能源，改善之后又是如何，你可以获得翻新项目之前和翻新项目之后的信息，从而知道你使用了多少能源和初级能源。我们通过能源连接系统来进行计算，这是能源顾问在这个项目开展之前给我们的建议，一个很好的建议，它能够预测改造前和改造后的成效，以及我们是否能获得一个非常成功的能效系统。从能源使用分布图上可以看出，在翻新项目之后，初级能源的使用下降了约25%。

　　总而言之，我们必须关注能源使用效率，因为我们的城市在发展，能量能源需求增加了，因此能效就更为重要，节能问题必须与能效的提高同步推进。因此，可再生更新能源必须与能效提升共同部署，才能与我们的需求同步。同时，我们要把所有的子系统结合起来。这将是我们对未来趋势的一个展望。

生态城市与城市生态发展指数

车生泉

上海交通大学农业与生物学院副院长、教授

本报告共有四方面的内容，一是生态城市的现状，二是城市生态指标，三是中国城市生态指标体系及规划目标，最后是城市生态的发展指数。表 1 是一个生态城市的指标体系研究所列出的国际上一些代表性的生态城市，包括美洲、欧洲，还有亚洲，它们在不同气候条件下的生态系统中发展得相当好。

城　市	所在国	所在洲
温哥华	加拿大	北美洲
伯克利	美国	北美洲
波特兰	美国	北美洲
凤凰城	美国	北美洲
巴尔的摩	美国	北美洲
库里提巴	巴西	南美洲
哥本哈根	丹麦	欧洲
埃尔兰根	德国	欧洲
弗莱堡	德国	欧洲
马尔默	瑞典	欧洲
斯德哥尔摩	瑞典	欧洲
怀阿拉	澳大利亚	大洋洲
阿德莱德	澳大利亚	大洋洲
北九州	日本	亚洲
新加坡	新加坡	亚洲

表 1
国际生态城市代表

策略	温哥华	伯克利	波特兰	凤凰城	巴尔的摩	库里提巴	哥本哈根	埃尔兰根	弗莱堡	马尔默	斯德哥尔摩	怀阿拉	阿德莱德
土地使用和城市结构调整		✓	✓			✓	✓				✓		
交通最优化	✓	✓	✓	✓		✓	✓				✓		
生态保护和重建	✓	✓		✓							✓	✓	
城市绿地和开放空间	✓		✓	✓			✓				✓		✓
改善市政设施	✓	✓		✓	✓	✓		✓			✓		✓
能源和资源	✓	✓				✓	✓	✓					
生态经济	✓	✓											
生态城市管理体制			✓	✓									
生态文化	✓	✓	✓	✓		✓					✓	✓	
生态立法		✓											
生态示范社区											✓	✓	

表2
国际生态城市采用的策略

1. 中国生态城市的现状特征

表3是我们对中国城市的调研情况，我们总共搜集了300多个城市的资料。中国城市生态建设是从20世纪80年代开始的，直到现在，中国还在做一些生态城镇的尝试。我们调研的指标目前包括45个一级指标，其中有绿地状况、水质、城市能源消耗、单位GDP能耗以及社会文化要素。我们想通过这样的总结来看中国城市生态发展状况。同时，就中国的绿地

表3
中国生态城市

生态城	所在地区	所在省份
中新生态城	华北	天津
曹妃甸生态城	华北	河北
中瑞无锡生态城	华东	江苏
崇明岛国际生态城	华东	上海
中法武汉生态城	华中	湖北
深圳生态城	华南	广东

指　　　　标	平均值
建成区绿地率（%）	33.3
建成区绿化覆盖率（%）	37.5
城市人均绿地面积（平方米）	31.3
城市人均公园面积（平方米）	13.76
超过 10 公顷的城市公园 / 百万人口	0.26
受保护面积占城市市域面积比例（%）	10
城市道路绿化渗透率（%）	97.32
城市道路绿化达标率（%）	77.5
规划区生态空间比例（%）	40
年径流总量控制率（%）	40
地下水超采率（%）	1.07
公园绿地 500 米服务半径覆盖率（%）	77.68
大于 10 公顷的城市公园的完整性	—
城市绿色廊道密度（1 千米 / 平方千米）	—
至少连接 2 个带状公园的连接度比例	—
市域水域湿地面积净损失率（%）	1.5
本地木本植物指数	84.89
城市建成区野生动物比例（%）	0.4
自然水岸线率（%）	80.94
生物多样性综合指数（%）	0.4
生物入侵程度（%）	0.523
著名古树保护率（%）	96.91
空气质量优于二级标准天数所占比例（%）	82.96
城市热岛效应（℃）	0.91
水环境质量达标率（%）	86.10
饮用水源水质优于三级标准比例（%）	97.00
单位 GDP 碳排放密度 (t/y)	62.54
环境噪声达标率覆盖区比例（%）	90
城市污水处率（%）	89.27
生活垃圾无害化处理率（%）	96.40
车辆排放达标率（%）	80
人均生活垃圾（千克 / 天）	1.2
受损土地和荒地修复率（%）	70.76

表 4
调研的主要指标及现
状值

表5
建成区绿地率年度
变化（2009—2013
年）

	2009	2010	2011	2012	2013	平均增长率（%）
全国平均（%）	34.17	34.47	35.27	35.72	35.78	1.16
增长率（%）	—	0.88	2.32	1.28	0.17	
东部地区（%）	36.63	36.41	37.62	38.01	38.25	1.10
中部地区（%）	33.32	33.81	34.29	34.58	34.68	1.01
西北地区（%）	30.87	31.76	32.64	33.58	33.42	2.01
东北地区（%）	31.59	33.15	33.97	34.02	33.65	1.62

而言，我们的土地需要在承载它的同时容纳不同规模的人口。举个例子，大型城市绿地面积有所上升，但在中型城市却下降了，这是城市发展的特点。

从城市生态系统的指标来说，联合国、欧盟及英国的大学都有不同指标指示城市生态发展水平，基本有四大类：可持续发展状况、环境管理水平、生态的系统性、人类的福利。这些指标基本可以被总结为政策型、实践型和理论型。当然，这些指数来自我们对不同城市的定位，比如可持续城市、宜居城市、花园城市、绿色城市、低碳城市、生态城市等等。如果我们再分的话，可以把全世界所有的指标归纳为 15 大类（表 6），使用率比较高的是政策管理、水质以及空气质量。

表6
生态城市的各项指标
及出现频率

指标	频率	指标	频率
策略管理	17%	水质量	15%
数量和规模	11%	空气质量	9%
结构和布局	8%	生态服务功能	8%
废物处理	7%	制度改善	6%
资源和能源消耗	6%	公众参与	3%
生物多样性	3%	应用和新技术	3%
荒地处理	2%	噪音污染	1%
土壤质量	1%		

2. 生态城市指标的构成

在中国，如果将现在和过去的城市生态系统进行比较，我们需要这些指标作为基础支撑。我们把指标的构成分成三类，分别是自然、社会、生态。城市可以有一个完整的有机系统，其中生态压力不能超过上限。

图1是指标的构成。考虑到城市生态的保护与生态系统的建设，我们把它分为一级指标和二级指标。比如在生态空间的结构方面，我们关注绿地和人均的绿地率；在环境指标方面，我们关注水、空气、土壤的状况。第三个是生物多样性的保护，这与自然保护地密切相关，包括生态空间方面。从资源和能源效率的角度，我们都有不同的指标来界定它。在中国，我们有关于生态园林城市和生态城市的生态发展指标。我们希望这些指标对政府的工作能有帮助。这是我们对城市生态体系建设过程提出的指标。

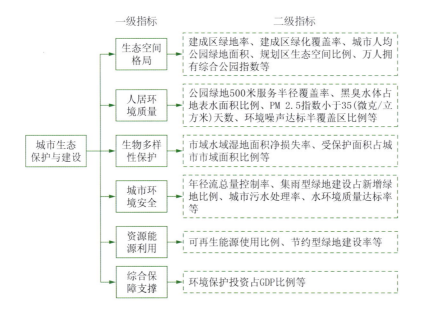

图1
生态城市指标构成

3. 城市生态发展指数展望

我们也想有一个城市生态的发展指数，指示目前城市生态的发展状态以及预测未来城市发展的目标。我们把指标分成四个部分：生态资源、生态环境、生态政策以及生态行为。生态压力是源于人类行为，所以人们需要谨慎行事，这也是生态系统的一个重要维度。

在生态资源方面，我们有绿地占城市比例、保护率。在生态环境方面，我们希望聚焦水质、空气质量以及受损的土地。生态行为包括很多，比如 GDP。当提及绿色垃圾、低碳交通时，我们希望能够有一些指标来评估和引导生态城市的发展。

可持续发展城市研究框架：公共政策和公共产品提供的不同关系之影响

沙拉亚·费莎

剑桥大学发展研究中心副主任、教授

1. 城市公共政策的挑战

本报告的内容是不同的公共政策的框架，并会特别强调PPP，即公私合作伙伴关系。除了水资源、空气质量，也包括一些软性因素，包括卫生和教育。上海有2 000多万人口，还有500多万外来人口，如何从软性的维度找到一些解决方案来应对这些挑战是很重要的。我们也希望其他发展中国家能从中得到启示。毫无疑问，在本次全球城市论坛上无需过多强调城市和可持续发展的重要性。另外，我想强调的是可持续发展相关的一些目标。从学界角度看，我们确实需要和城市政府以及其他企业利益相关方合作，更好地了解城市如何成为包容性的城市。这是每个人所面临的挑战，无论是从数据、研究，还是政策方面，都是一种挑战。

2. 城市内部的不平等

城市总体是非常强大的空间和场所，但也有一些不平等的情况。在城市里，贫富分化和不平等也是明显的。从这些图表中可以看到（图1、图2），如果世界继续发展，中国、印度、巴西以及墨西哥、巴基斯坦、孟加拉国等国家面临的挑战，是如何为大量新城市居住者提供居所。其中有很多年轻人，特别是在东南亚和非洲地区。如果他们要想进入城市生活，他们的挑战就是技能建设。国际调查表明，从农村进入城市，如何找到就业机会是比较有挑战性的。中国对劳动力的教育程度是排在第一位的，但是在上海市内顶尖学校和垫底学校的教育也有一些差别。我们要关注城市及其包容性，并逆转在亚洲看到的一些不平等现象。亚洲在发展着，特别是中国和印度有明显的增速，但是这种不平等以同样的速度在发展着。

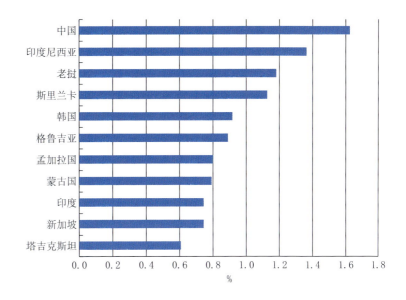

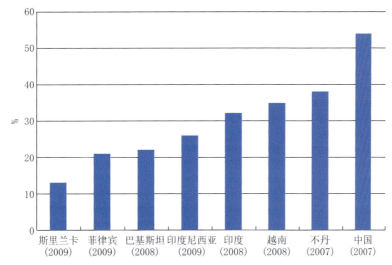

　　我们可以看到，不公平的现象主要集中在金字塔顶部和底部的 1%。此时，我们可以利用教育帮助缩小这种分化和鸿沟。在最后的结果实现平等是很困难的，但是我们至少要有享受平等的机会。再来分析金字塔前 20% 和底部 20% 相关的分层。在过去 20 年，很多国家，包括中国，这两部分都有明显的激增。如果根据不平等性进行划分，就会发现城乡之间的鸿沟是很明显的。

3. 城市公共产品提供的创新举措

城市虽然有社会服务，但贫困现象也更明显。因为很多穷人进入城市享受这些服务，城市的不平等性也超过了它们所在国家的不平等水平。图3是公共物品的供给，这是非常重要的，因为它满足了公共需求。它也有一些外部性，就像水和空气一样给家庭提供更好的健康。我们的挑战在于，虽然质量和数量彼此互补，但有时候未必总是能够协同发挥作用。政府会提供公共卫生和公共教育服务，但问题是国家公共部门是否能够持续保证它的质量，特别是考虑不同收入水平的居民。例如，进入城市的农民

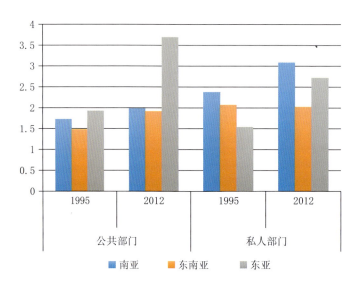

图3
公共和私营部门卫生
支出占 GDP 的百分比

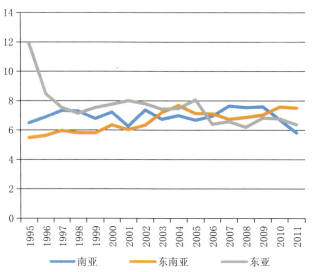

图4
公共部门卫生支出占
总公共支出

工的教育起点较低，也因此导致了收入不均。图 4 是公共部门和私营部门在这段时间的支出，东南亚、东亚、南亚地区在这段时间的私营部门支出都有明显增长，而公共部门支出都是持平状态。

教育和卫生方面都需要引入新的合作伙伴。那么 PPP 到底是什么呢？之前有交通运输具体的例子，其实我们也可以让公共部门和私营部门签订契约，英国和欧洲就已经有了相关合约。除此之外，政府还可以向市场销售一些产品和服务。所以我们可以思考一下，在卫生和教育领域如何找到新的方法帮助思维拓展。目前，PPP 关注的不仅仅是利润，还有其他一些诉求。

最后，我认为制度性的学习并不能由政府垄断。我们今天看到电视节目中有很多非政府组织在农村地区提供诊断的服务。因此，像上海这样的国际大都市，可以在这方面做得更好。在中国曾经有一个心脏病慈善基金会，照顾中国老龄化人口。今天的中国更需要这样的服务。所以亚洲 PPP 计划更需要全面的思考，从本地样本和案例中寻找更好的提供教育和医疗的方式，让我们的城市更具包容性。

专家点评

李兵弟（中国城市发展研究院名誉院长、教授）：高柏林先生提出了一个跨域的概念，他特别强调了环境的补偿机制。冈纳·格论先生给我们提供了协同发展的理念，他已经从单一的建筑扩展到整个城市，并且举出了关于社区能源管理的例子，强调了能效，而且用可更新的能源代替一次能源。车教授从更加宏观的视野展示了对全国350多个城市调研之后提出的生态城市的理念及城市生态发展指数。最后是沙拉亚·费莎女士，给我们解析了关于PPP模式，以及不同阶层之间的融合发展问题。这几位的报告集中起来有这样的启示。

第一，中国的生态城市建设理念已经融入了全球生态化的可持续发展理念之中。

第二，讲生态必须用生态最基本的理念，其实就是协同、共生、共享、共管、共治，就是要关注整个社会不同行业不同部门，使用不同的能源、水资源的时候，都要有一个共生共存理念。同时要实现一种共治，这种目标协同、指标协同和行动协同是我们下一步更需要落实的。而沙拉亚·费莎女士告诉我们还要关注最底层的老百姓。

第三，我们今天讨论协同治理共享发展，上海作为一个具有全球性影响的世界性城市，它的生态城市建设责任更重，需要更多的国际合作，也需要引进更多的先进理念，更多的政府、市场、老百姓共同行动。因此，生态城市的建设，是政府的责任，也是所有市民的责任，是社会的共识，更是大家共同的追求。

互动对话

提问者：请问车教授，您说的五个指标的依据是什么？

车生泉：城市的生态其实分三个层面，一个是生态源头的减量，第二个是中间的控制，第三个是末端修复。这三个方面，都包含了自然生态、社会生态、经济生态，还有文化的生态。从这几个方面来说，第一部分就是自然资源的状况。人类所有的活动过程产生的代谢物如果超过了一个城市的自然条件的能力，这个城市的平衡就被打破了。第二个部分是环境的状况。第三个我们要强调管理层面，就是政策、机制、鼓励性的措施。第四个就是生态行为，这一块超出了我的研究范围。这个指标和常规的城市生态或者生态城市评估的指标是不一样的。我们希望把它减量化，变成一种政府的管理或者城市发展状态的一种反应。我们也在互相探讨。

提问者：我想就风向问题请教一下高柏林先生，风的边界怎么能够清晰地界定？

高柏林：我们有两个概念，恒风及其平均速度。这取决于云的大小，虽然它并不稳定，但它不可能从北京跑到广西去，所以这可以看做是一个恒定的常量。因为山水等地理元素，我们并不能在地图上明确标示。但如果实际操作，我们仍可以获得一个大致的中心位置。比如你可以在北京建立一个中心，那么我们就可以得知在北京这个中心地区以外的恒风是什么样的，以上海为中心也是如此。所以分气岭这些点是固定清晰的。如果它的中心地区在北京以西 250 公里的石家庄，风可能会一路吹到山西去。但如果在北京，这个风会停在山西和陕西之间的山林。从这个例子中可以看到，做规划时，我们要考虑行政单位的边界。分气岭的划分独立于行政区划的边界，所以当我们做城市规划时，脑中要有行政区划的概念。总的来说，我强调两个因素，一个是恒风，一个是行政区划。

提问者：我想请教一下沙拉亚·费莎女士，PPP 引入教育系统是一个很好的建议，但是它同投资于基础设施不一样的是教育很难看到它的产出。那么 PPP 引入教育系统的最后一种模式，就是慈善，它的产出怎么去度量？

沙拉亚·费莎：我们总是有办法能够看到产出，比如说花多少年接受教育才能改善收入水平。在上世纪五六十年代，如果 18 岁接受中等教育毕业，你就可以有一份不错的收入。在过去的 20 年，同等收入要求求职者有大学文凭。在未来 20 年也许需要硕士文凭才可以获得工作。因此，教育投资的年份与收入回报之间存在一种关系，这种关系取决于公民的支付能力。考虑这一点，个人和社会的收益都是很大的。比如道路方面，路况良好的道路会让每个人获益，因为交通事故减少了，同时我们也可以高速行驶。同样地，如果教育机构的水平提高了，我们的学习时间就可以减少，这对我们和社会来说都是一个很好的收益。过去我们只有一个教育提供者，就是公共机构。但是现在我们有不同的专业化教育机构提供专业化教育，所以需要判断不同教育提供方所带来的产出和收益。因此，我们需要一个综合了学术、城市治理、文明社会的指标系统，判断哪些指标是我们所需要提高的。这也同样适用于医疗领域。

可持续性城市的绩效评估与分类
——从弱可持续性到强可持续性

诸大建

同济大学经济与管理学院教授

有一个问题大家经常听到的，但不一定实际思考。大家经常评论某城市可持续发展的排名，而且我们也经常看到无论是国际上或者中国，经常有可持续城市的排行榜。这种排行榜我们应不应该相信呢？最近有一个像麦肯锡那样很有名的欧洲公司做了一个中国、外国可持续城市的排行榜，上海、北京在中国名列第一、第二。这个排行榜里可持续发展评估有三个子系统，一个是经济系统，一个是社会系统，一个是环境系统。上海的经济系统排名是最前面的，但是环境系统是排在倒数几名，却仍然位列第一。这样一个可持续排行榜可信吗？本报告将讨论一个理论问题，来解释为什么这样排名不行，其中把这种排行榜叫做弱可持续发展，并提出一个新的强可持续发展。

1. 传统指标和排行榜的不足

图1是对可持续发展指标的分类，上面是经济系统，左边是环境系统，右边是社会系统。基本思路是把可持续分解成三个子目标，经济子目标、社会子目标和环境子目标。然后对经济子目标再进行分解，把有量纲的指标一层层无量纲化，最后一层层归到上面。社会子目标也是一样，有贫富差距、不公平等，然后把量纲去掉。环境也是一样，能耗、土地消耗，一层层保证。经济、社会、环境三个指数就出来了，无非是指标里的权重有差异。这个方法也决定了，无论我们的技巧再怎么高，到最后的结果，我们都不敢相信。

之前说到的排行榜里有一个深层的理论问题，它认为弱环境指数可以被高经济指数对冲。对冲的含义就是可以替代，这是经济学里的一个理论

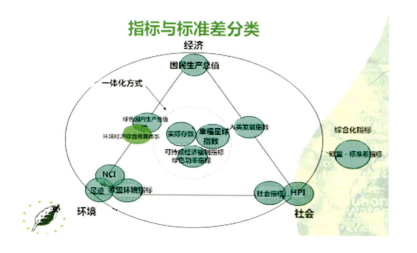

图 1
可持续发展指标分类

问题。如果我们认为可以替代，那么就算环境指标是零都没关系。只要经济、社会指标都是一百分就可以。再举个例子，招博士生的时候，有两种算法，一种是算总的分数，但是如果他外语只有二十几分，我们还会招吗？因此，另一种算法，我们认为还需要子目标，子目标有一个门槛值。那些排行榜的问题就是对深层的理论思考严重不足。

2. 强可持续发展指标体系

什么是可持续发展？发展是经济社会有增量的往上走，可持续是资源环境要有一定的门槛，不能突破。如果要用指标表达这两个内涵，就必须有两个门槛。图 2 是欧洲人经常用的，经济社会都往上走，但是资源环境的消耗往下走，有一个指标脱钩了。就如同之前做过的分析，我们应该用什么样的方法来决定是否录用一个博士生？加总的分数还是单科的分数？回到可持续发展的话题，尽管可持续已经讲了 20 年，但是这个理论还是有问题。

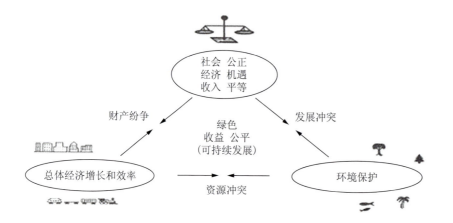

图 2
可持续发展指标框架

本报告设计了一个指标，有幸被 UNDP 认为是可持续的。一个好的城市有两个半球（图 3），上面这个包括人均 GDP、HDRA、幸福指数，都是往上发展的；下面这个指标是生态环境，这个指标消耗越少越好。两个维度应该分开考虑。这里有一张简单的图，包括了教育、期望寿命、人均 GDP，每一个指标都有它的上限，比如现在 80% 是可以接受的。与之相似，我可以再设计一个生态成本的指标，也就是下半球，包括了人均资源的消耗。真正的可持续，应该是在 II 这个象限里（图 4）。北京、上海属于 III，资源环境消耗很高，不是可持续的。如果用经济高对冲环境高，最后总数是可持续的，这是非常荒唐的。反过来，西部虽然强调生态文明、绿色发展，实际它也是不可持续的，因为发展不够。所以今天讲绿色发展，要清楚到底是只讲一个维度还是讲可持续的两个维度。

图 3
两个半球评价体系

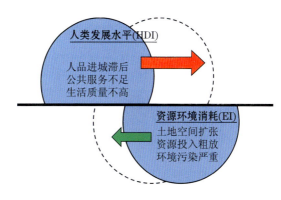

图 4
中国城市的人类发展—生态消耗象限图

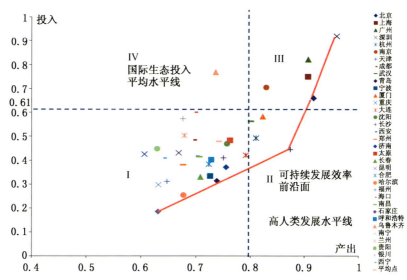

图 4 是中国城市的图，这个人类发展指数达到 0.8，这是非常高的，因此我们在发展方面很成功。生态方面，高于 0.61 的生态足迹指数是资

源环境不可持续的，这又是一个门槛。在这个图里，环境曲线是爬坡的阶段。左边的发展不够，右边北上广发展不错，但生态环境消耗高高在上。真正的目标是在象限 II。做定量分析的时候，套公式是远远不够的，思想比公式更重要。

3. 可持续发展的实现路径

实际上，不同的城市有不同的可持续发展路径，II 是目标象限，III 是发展，但是不包括生态，I 是有生态没有发展，IV 是既没有生态又没有发展。图 5 中的模式 B 是发展中国家的模式。中国可以选择跨越式发展，即模式 C，平着走过来，不要上去再下来。我们通常从 A 走到 B，然后降到 C，有没有一个可以减少成本的途径呢？当然这是两个方面的，定量表达以后，就有三种。举个例子，对上海、北京、广州都很适用，就是身体没长胖的时候要发育，不是长胖了以后再减肥；每个人都有两个阶段，年轻的时候要长个子，但是到 40 岁的时候要瘦身。所以可持续发展就像打麻将，第一阶段是摸麻将，要摸到 13 个牌，叫增量。如果摸了超过 13 个牌，那就犯规了，这个叫存量，也就是红线。现在要思考红线里面中国有没有本事发展，保持 13 张牌不变，拿出一个摸进一个，13 个总量不变，但是清一色就胡了。

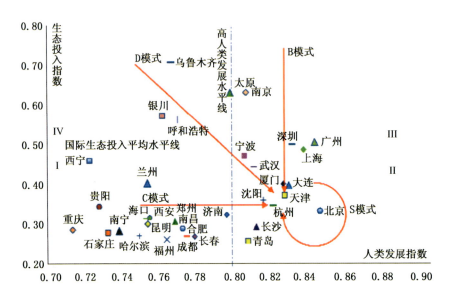

图 5
不同类型城市的不同
改进路径

城郊和乡村地区的农业旅游业
——经济与环境议题的融合

阿里扎·弗莱舍

以色列耶路撒冷希伯来大学教授

1. 农业旅游业的特征

本报告将探讨城郊地区和农村地区旅游业的发展。发展农业旅游业对城市和农村都有好处。农业旅游业包括自己采摘果实和蔬菜、农家乐、参观农场、游客中心、休闲娱乐以及一些户外活动等等。一些小农场及小型乡村企业开始参与其中，有些基于比较活跃的农场开展旅游活动，有些企业是在农村地区借助当地优美的环境发展旅游业。

农业旅游业一般是在城郊和乡村地区，也可能在城市外围，或者离这个城市更远的一些农村地区，并主要给来自城市的游客提供服务。例如，游客在市中心看不到足够的绿色空间，这时候城郊地区就成了市民的游乐场所。农业旅游业不仅使城市居民受益，也同样使城郊以及农村居民获益。农业旅游业以农村环境、农场、社区以及传统社会文化为基础，它是开放的空间，你可以零距离接触大自然、文化遗产、传统社会，感受人文气息。不仅仅基于大自然的绿色空间，也以传统社会和传统文化为基础，增加人与人之间的交流。做旅游业的企业都是小规模企业，其营业创收很高比例反馈于当地社区。

2. 农业旅游业的经济流程和影响

本报告的内容是描述促进农业旅游业发展的经济流程。我们在很多国家和区域都观察到这样的发展，它更多的是自然经济发展的产物。昨天我在上海郊区参观了一个农业旅游景点，它展现了农业旅游业在城郊的作用，也引发了我们对于农业旅游业在农村发展中所起的作用的思考。本报告也会介绍一个以色列农业旅游业发展的案例。

为什么农业旅游业在全世界如雨后春笋般地出现？这是因为城市化进程加快，大量人口从农村流向城市，在欧洲、北美，印度和中国以及其他地区都有这样的城市化。而那些仍然留在郊区和农村地区的农民在寻找除了农作以外的其他收入途径。这些农民发现农业旅游业是一个很好的替代方案，因为农业旅游业就是以农场和周围的环境为基础发展的。另外它可以满足城市居民以及附近居民的需求。我们会看到一些自下而上的发展案例，由地方或者农民自身发起的农业旅游业，在另一些国家则是自上而下，政府是发起者，会提供很多补贴和支持以促进农业旅游业的发展。

为什么农业旅游业能够帮助农村及城郊地区发展呢？因为它能够让城乡社会同时受益，能够让农村地区的失业者及社区获得额外收入，并且为城市及附近居民提供离他们自己家不远的休闲娱乐机会。比如说上海的居民对城市的钢筋水泥和空气污染厌烦了，他们可以开一两个小时的车去这些开放的绿色空间，徜徉其中，享受这个环境。还因为农业旅游业依靠的是现有的当地生产要素、农村和社区设施，不需要增添基础设施，可以和农业与自然结合起来，还能够保护环境，保护本地文化遗产和文化资源，它对农村地区的发展也是有好处的。另外，它也能够服务附近的一些城市居民。因此，发展这样的农业旅游业是双赢的。

为什么旅游业及农业旅游企业能得到很多补贴？例如，2007 年到 2013 年间，欧盟拨款 60 亿欧元支持旅游业以及农业旅游业。除了帮助农村发展以外，他们这么做也是为了支持农业旅游业。市场是很不完美的，所以还是需要有政府的补贴和支持。农业旅游业已经实现了一些国家层面的目标，比如从农村移居到城市的人口减少了。这对整个社会来说也是好事。还有就是外部性因素和公共产品。所有这些开阔美丽的景色和环境都是由农民来保护的，但他们并没有为此获得报酬，因此他们是需要津贴的。我们可以看到很少有农民会去银行，银行对他们也一无所知，即便农民们从事着正当行业，也无法从银行获得贷款，因此政府有不同形式的支持和补贴。欧洲、以色列、日本政府都在这方面投入大量资金，据说中国政府也在这么做。

3. 以色列农业旅游业市场案例分析

接下来分享一个关于以色列农业旅游业市场的案例分析。我们的研究目的是分析和模拟农业旅游景点的市场，比如自摘自采、观光农场以及其他的一些各式各样被逐渐纳入旅游业的活动。我们希望通过这个研究来回答下面的这些问题：在以色列，那些景点和农业的联系是什么？把农业旅游建在活跃的农场很重要吗？还是说农业旅游业应该仅包括自然开阔的环境？直接补贴和间接补贴，哪种更有效？

我们用了所有的测量方法，包括测量经济福利的、估算利润的等等，还比较和模拟不同的场景来寻求问题的答案。这个模型也同样适用于研究其他地区。以色列是个小国家，只有 800 万人口。我们有 200 多个不同类型的群体，囊括了各种各样的农业旅游景区。事实上，所有的景区都会得到农业局的支持，都获得了一些补贴。

为了模拟整个市场，我们做了一个理论模型和一个实证模型，然后利用工具估算参数。我们把农业旅游业市场看做寡头垄断的差异化商品市场，都是不同商品，每一个市场也都是不一样的。一个是旅游中心，另一个是草莓摘采中心。为了用模型和实证估计它，我们不能用常规的完全竞争市场，因为不同的景区其特征也不同。

消费者方面，我们可以用这个模型来看他们的效用。每个消费者通过选择不同的农业旅游景区来使效用最大化。这里的特性，可以是价格或其他任何东西，由此可以看出是哪个景区。再来看一下这个函数，是有关生产者的，生产者将利润最大化，也是一个特性。

第 i 个消费者从 j 公司获得的效用

$$u_{ij} = x_j\beta - \alpha p_j + \zeta_j + \xi_{ir} + (1 - \sigma)\,\varepsilon_{ij},$$

其中，x_j 为公司特征向量，p_j 为价格，$\zeta_j + \xi_{ir} + (1 - \sigma)\,\varepsilon_{ij}$ 为未观察到的公司特征附加效用，ζ 为公司特有的特征，ξ 为消费者和区域特有特征，σ 为嵌套 logit 参数，ε_{ij} 服从独立同分布，$\mathrm{E}\,(\varepsilon_{ij}) = 0$，为公司和消费者特有的特征。

当且仅当满足如下条件，消费者 i 会选择公司 j：

$$u_{ij}^* \geqslant u_{ik}\,\forall\, k \neq j.$$

垄断寡头的利润函数

$$\max_{pj}\,\pi_j = p_j q_j\,(p_1,\,\cdots,\,p_L) - c\,(z_j,\,q_j)$$

Z_j 为公司特征向量

F.O.C

$$q_j + \left(p_j - \frac{dc\,(z,\,q_j)}{dq_j}\right)\frac{dq_j}{dp_j} = 0$$

还有一个关于需求和价格的实证方程。我们对所有的参数，β、σ、α，进行估计，然后就可以在计算机中运行它们。我们可以看出企业或旅游景点基于真正的活跃农场或开阔的自然环境哪一个更好。如果建在活跃农场上，那么它在需求、供应、边际成本价格方面是有劣势的。

公司 j 的总需求：

$$\text{in}\left(\frac{p_j q_j}{\beta - \sum_{i=1}^{j} q_j p_j}\right) = x_j \beta - \alpha \text{in } p_j + \sigma \text{in}\left(\frac{p_j q_j}{\sum_{jctig} p_j q_j}\right) + \xi_j$$

公司 j 的定价方程：

$$\text{in}(p_j) = W_j \gamma - \text{in}\left(\frac{\alpha[1 - \sigma S_{j/g} - (1-\sigma)S_j]}{\alpha[1 - \sigma S_{j/g} - (1-\sigma)S_j] + 1 - \sigma}\right) + \omega_j$$

该系统方程的解将会产生每个公司的价格和市场份额、利润、消费者剩余和总福利。

	系　数	标准误差	弹　性
需求（市场份额）			
常量	-8.719 4***	1.577 3	
基于农村的活动	2.825 1***	0.659 5	0.54
游客中心	0.706 1***	0.236 6	0.57
农业产品销售	0.963 4***	0.368 6	0.97
食品销售	1.168 2***	0.261 4	1.18
引导行为	-0.563 4**	0.247 2	-0.47
投资规模	0.000 3	0.000 7	0.03
准入	0.631 7***	0.217 2	3.58
上加利利	0.657 4***	0.263 4	0.23
定价（边际成本）			
常量	3.581 0***	0.518 1	
基于农村的活动	1.295 6***	0.180 3	0.001
游客中心	0.327 2***	0.117 2	0.01
农业产品销售	0.475 3***	0.143 2	0.01
食品销售	0.348 0***	0.129 2	0.004
引导行为	0.064 2	0.127 4	0.000 6
投资规模	-0.000 5*	0.000 3	-0.001 6
准入	-0.027 0	0.136 0	-0.003
行为规模	-0.016 1***	0.005 6	-0.000 2
α	0.837 3**	0.374 8	2.21
σ	0.351 3***	0.129 7	

表1
市场模型的 GMM
估计

注：*、**、*** 分别表示该系数在 10%、5% 和 1% 水平显著。

如果通过参数得不到答案，就只能模拟所有场景。第一个模拟场景是建在活跃农场的景区，这不同于目前很多以自然环境为基础的场景。第二个模拟是比较了两种不同的支持方案。这是我们比较的结果。一个是目前的福利水平，另一个是对于实际发生状况的模拟。如果我们把所有的农业旅游业景点都建在活跃农场，会发生什么样的变化呢？我们会失去约58%的福利水平。这意味着，就以色列这个案例来说，农业旅游业在农村地区，在大自然这样的环境下比建在农场能够得到更好的发展，因为人们对这些地区的需求是处于增长状态的。

就支持而言，一个是对基础设施方面的支持，另一个是直接给农民资金或补贴。我们发现就福利来说比较好的是对基础设施的间接支持。在其他案例中，我们可以选择不同的特性，分析不同国家或地区感兴趣的问题。就上海的情况来看，可以考察它是不是属于某种农业旅游业组织，或者它到底能不能带来经济效益，以及如何改善福利。

	现　　状	所有景点建在活跃农场（%）	基础设施改进——区域层面（%）	资金支持——个人层面（%）
所有游客人数	2 344 350	-22.71	3.48	2.12
消费者剩余（百万美元）	35.5	-60.17	2.70	1.55
生产者剩余（百万美元）	17.2	-54.96	3.32	1.40
福利（百万美元）	52.7	-58.47	2.90	1.50

表2
模拟结果的比较

最后，有如下几点结论：（1）农场景点基于活跃农场更具成本效益；（2）游客非常喜欢游客中心以及基于农村大自然的各种活动；（3）在模拟中，所有景点都基于活跃农场的情况下福利有所下降；（4）直接支持优于间接支持。

城市碳排放研究

耿　涌

上海交通大学环境科学与工程学院院长、教授

本报告是关于温室气体排放的问题。我自己曾经从事过这方面的工作，主要职责是评估如生态产业园区等区域，以及如何使用创新方法帮助减少温室气体的排放。基于这段经历，我也进行了一些与温室气体减排有关的研究。

1. 目前及未来的城市化发展趋势

到 2050 年，全球的城市人口预计会增长到 25 亿到 30 亿，大约占世界总人口的 64% 到 69%。同时由于经济活动的急剧增加，城市地区也能够带来更大的 GDP 产出。这也就意味着城市成了温室气体排放的主要来源。目前城市占全球二氧化碳排放的 71%—76%，以及全球能源使用的 67%—76%。但是城市化并不等于排放增长，我们需要使用创新手段，引导创新行为，从而减少城市的二氧化碳排放。

2. 城市碳排放的计算和影响因素

如何计算城市的二氧化碳排放，主要有三种测量方法：一是和第一级的方法很相似，直接以地域或以生产为基础来计算；第二个方法是土地再加上供应链的计算法，与购买力和碳排放相关；第三个方法更重要，是以消费为基础的计算方法，就是使用者付费原则，因为我们要知道重要的排放有哪些。如果真的要降低二氧化碳排放的话，我们需要把排放的责任分摊到最终的用户那里。为了制定解决问题的政策，我们要考虑是哪些主要驱动因素导致了温室气体的排放。目前一些研究发现，人们的收入、人口

的增长，还有城市形态、地势位置以及经济结构都会影响到城市温室气体的排放。另外很有趣的一点是人均能源使用和碳排放之间的关系。在发达国家，城市人均二氧化碳的排放要低于国家的平均值。但在发展中国家，情况就不一样了，城市的人均温室气体排放要高于国家平均值。这是由于城乡之间的差异、收入不同、经济地位的不同所导致的。

以上是导致城市温室气体排放的主要因素，但是它们的影响是不同的。如果看温室气体排放的影响，经济、地理、收入、城市基础设施是影响比较高的因素。但在制定政策的过程中，我们更容易关注那些低水平的影响要素。这就会产生一种矛盾，也就是说不同的利益相关方相互之间要进行沟通，在制定减缓政策之前，确保所有人的关切点都会被考虑到。另外一个关键要素是基础设施，因为当衡量一个城市碳排放的时候，基础设施会导致很多的二氧化碳排放。导致温室气体的一些关键驱动要素包括建筑、土地的使用和运营、终止使用的基础设施等。发达国家基础设施导致的人均二氧化碳排放量要比发展中国家高 5 倍。主要是因为发展中国家没有成熟的基础设施，比如说他们不能够提供足够的水给他们的居民，这个被我们称为能源和排放通路的一个锁定效应，还有生活习惯和消费模式的锁定效应。这些问题决策者都应该要解决。

从各国的城市形态来看，不同的城市对于城市形态有不同的设计，我们还要考虑到比如密度、土地混合使用、关联性以及可达性等因素。这些因素也说明不同的城市形态具有不同的温室气体排放情况。比如美国的亚特兰大，其人口和西班牙的巴塞罗那一样多，但城市面积却比巴塞罗那大 32 倍。这就意味着在亚特兰大，大多数的人居住在独立的房屋，他们要开车到工作的地方，这就会导致更高的碳排放。而巴塞罗那人口密度更高，人们一般住在公寓里。因此他们就有能力直接使用这个分配系统。同时因为城市面积更小，人们在城市内部的迁移也更容易。

从减缓城市气候变化方面来看，在发展比较成熟的城市，要考虑上述的那些因素。但是在次发达国家，我们要考虑如何构造城市化过程中基础设施的环境，让其朝着可持续低碳的方向发展。还要考虑一些因素如机制安排、多层政府管理、空间布局、足够的现金流和激励措施，比如在中国即将会有一个国家碳排放标准的政策，我们提供足够多的财政支持，减少不良行为，同时提供专业人员，考虑如何改变我们的行为，或者说改变我们的生产模式，来降低二氧化碳的排放。同时还有一个概念叫伴随效益，这是一个比较新的概念，就是说如果有成熟的低碳政策，或许也能有效减少空气污染物。反之亦然，如果有很好的控制空气污染物的政策，则会使碳排放全面降低。

3. 城市碳排放研究的部分案例

下面分享一些我的研究成果。这是对中国一些特大城市的研究，因为城市功能不同，整个城市的碳排放表现也有很大不同。北京和上海都是超级城市，从政治上来讲，它们要比别的城市级别高；而天津和重庆是工业城市，则发展出不同的经济形态。图1中红色区域代表购买的电力，对北京和上海来说，因为它们有更好的政策，比如说北京2008年举办了奥运会，上海2010年举办了世博会，所以中央政府允许它们购买电力，这样它们就可以关闭自己的燃煤发电厂。而天津和重庆是传统的工业城市，不能像北京和上海那样购买电力，所以必须依靠自己的燃煤发电厂，可以看到它们购买的电力非常有限。工业中心的碳排放还在增加，而北京和上海的碳排放都降低了。图里的棕色区域是来自交通领域的二氧化碳排放。随着很多中国家庭变得富有，私家车数量增长，这会导致交通领域碳排放的增长。我们还需要知道哪些因素会减少超大型城市的碳排放。我们发现经济规模是导致温室气体排放的一个重要因素。很多人来到大城市，想在那

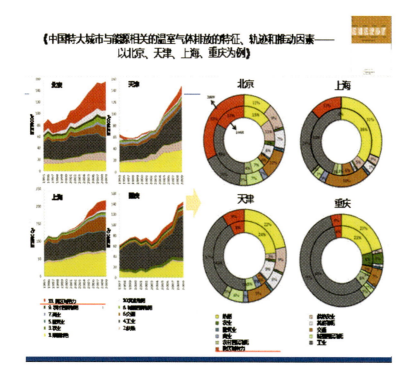

图1
中国大型城市能源相关温室气体排放的特征轨迹和驱动力

里获得就业机会。这些城市的政府也希望发展一些新的产能建设，因此大城市里出现了很多产业园区，这也是导致二氧化碳排放增长的一个重要因素。当然，科技进步会起到作用，可以抵消二氧化碳的排放，但这是不够的。所以在中国要考虑的是如何改善整体的情况，而不仅仅是降低排放的密度。而且由于经济发展速度很快，只注重降低排放密度是不够的。

另外一个关键的研究领域是如何在城市层面计算温室气体排放的整体情况。在一个城市之内，有很多交通工具，比如飞机、火车、汽车等等，这就导致计算困难。比如，从苏州开车到上海，我可以在苏州加油，也可能在上海加油，那我的二氧化碳排放该归哪个城市呢？从表面来看，这个碳排放应该归苏州，而不是归上海。所以这种情况带来很多不确定性。这项研究就针对这些不确定区域，制定一些规则来计算碳排放的归属问题，给决策者提供一种策略。

与之相似，人的行为也起着关键作用。图2是对家庭消费模式的研究。在这项研究中我们使用了一个模型，试图量化人类行为的影响。"衣食住行"，即我们需要食物、衣服、住房、出行等是日常生活中很重要的方面。但是，需要理解哪一方面是最关键的，这样才能把资源集中在这个方面。我们得出结论，人们的交通和住房会导致更高的排放。所以要着力推动绿色环保交通设施，鼓励人们多乘公共交通，而不是让每个人都去开私家车。绿色建筑的推广应用也是非常重要的，让人们能够享受一些高能效的材料技术和建筑技术，比如地热系统、分布式的能源系统。

图2
家庭消费模式对区域
发展的影响

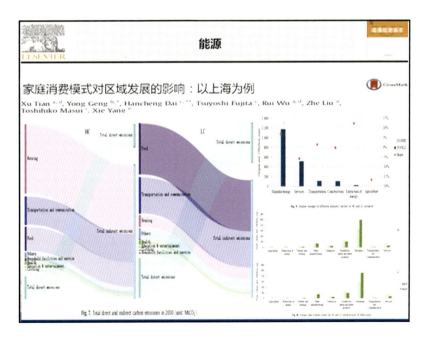

在沈阳案例中，我们希望能够量化应用地源热泵的效果（图3）。这是一种热能应用。由于所处地带气候原因，沈阳每年有五个月的供暖需求，市政府决定使用地源热泵这种技术。但是他们不知道二氧化碳排放减少的数量。因此，我们对地源热泵的效果进行了一些计算。根据计算，采用这种技术帮助整个城市减少了250万吨二氧化碳的排放，成果非常显著，大约占整个城市碳排放的4%。这一结果使沈阳市市长更加有信心，也更愿意支持这种技术的应用。这也解释了我为什么想要帮助推广这些创新技术。

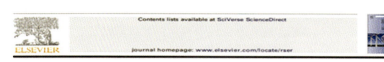

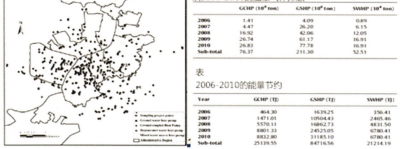

图3
中国地源热泵的区域性应用

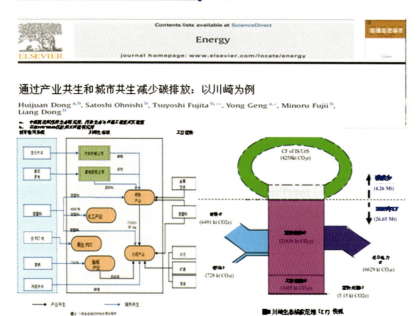

图4
通过工业和城市共生减少碳排放

再来讨论工业二氧化碳的排放。中国的城市和西方的城市不一样，中国城市有很多产业园区，这些都是碳排放的主要来源。但关键在于如何去评价这种产业园区的减排效果。所以这项研究中我们使用了一种混合模型，这是日本川崎的一个案例（图4），我们把寿命周期和评价分析综合起来，这样碳排放的完整结果就可以呈现给工业园区的管理者。最后研究产业和城市的共生如何降低整个城市的碳排放。研究结果表明，整个产业园区的碳排放减少了15%，这一量化的评估会使决策者更有信心，也能让他们坚信这是正确的选择。

城市的转型

梅柏杰
世界银行社会、城市、农村和灾害风险管理
全球实践发展局首席城市专家

1. 城市转型的趋势及影响

本报告主要关注目前出现的一些大趋势，比如从生产型经济转向服务型经济的趋势，这意味着对土地和人的需求有很大的不同。我们有机会涉足金融、研发、设计、创新等服务业，但这就要求我们掌握不同的技能。如果从制造业转变成服务业，其所需的人员水平也要相应地调整，需要从普通劳动力转变为高技术人员。这同时也对经济发展驱动力提出了不同的要求。

在人口这一问题上，我们会提及"银色海啸"。随着年龄增长，我们要更加关注"银色海啸"这一现象。人口老龄化速度加快，而且适龄的劳动力规模在缩小。与此同时在城市中也有很多年纪较轻的人，这样人口出现了两个极端，既有年龄比较长的，也有比较年轻的。他们部分需求相同，部分需求不同。例如年轻人喜欢自由，愿意在不同的岗位尝试，他们经常会跳槽，而且对于职场的态度和老一代的人不同。除此之外还有一些移民，他们进入城市生活，却享受和本地居民不一样的城市服务。

上述这些因素就导致了城市土地的使用问题。经过深入研究后，我们发现城市的人口密度越来越小，因为城市居民往四周扩散，"他们像煎饼一样往外扩散开来，而不是像结婚蛋糕一样一层层聚集"。当他们回过头来看，会发现大面积的土地被滥用，这使得可扩展的绿地面积越来越少。

这些趋势对互联互通的工作场所需求越来越高。如果是知识经济，就会寻找互联互通的工作场所，而不是大型工业区或工业园。土地规划方面，我们需要更灵活地使用土地，这意味着不能像过去把土地用于工业经济那样，固定土地的使用时间。转型之后，土地要满足不同的需求。这也影响人们对公共交通的需求。因为现在的年轻人阵脚不稳，他们买车也没有我们这一代人买得多。对他们来说，有车但没有停车位是一个负担。这样年轻人和中老年人会有不同的需求，因此社会融合以及对基础服务的平等使用显得十分必要。很多国家都在不停地强调这个问题。

2. 城市规划的包容性

我们也能从纽约市的发展中总结一些经验（图1），它进行的是包容性的而非排斥性的城市规划。旧产业关闭时，纽约努力创造新的就业机会，或吸引新的就业机会。哥本哈根市也做了类似的规划。

图1
纽约的"硅巷"和创新走廊

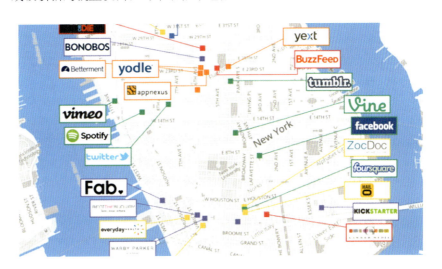

另外，我们也从老龄友好型城市学到一些经验（图2）。通常我们认为老龄友好型城市是针对年纪较大的人，但实际上它也面向年轻人。随着社会经济更加趋向于知识经济，城市对待年轻人也要友好。这就意味着城市设计要与以往不同。

图2
老龄友好城市

我们反复强调，未来的城市是那种不畏惧密度规划并将之结合的城市。我们把密度与以公交系统为导向的开发模式结合起来，如果各种公共交通系统和工作地点，以及岗位和车站密度增加，生活质量也会提高。因此，要允许土地使用的灵活性以及多用途性，因为这对老年人以及年轻人都是有好处的。另外比较重要的一点，现在人们，尤其是年轻人中存在的现实是他们可能不想买房，因为他们不知道下一份工作会在何处。他们更愿意去租房，所以租赁房的供应与灵活的分区规划一样重要。同时，提高城市对所有人（包括不同年龄、不同背景、不同性别的人）的包容性也十分重要。

实际上我们在世界银行一直重复强调的话题就是建立人与商业间的联系，规划宜居、可持续和包容性城市的重要性。我们不能只通过城市规划来解决这个问题，我们要把握宏观背景，做好城市规划。

图 3
可持续发展的城市

专家点评

蔡永立（华东师范大学地理科学院教授）：首先我对前面四个报告做一个简单的点评，然后再谈谈个人的观点。四位教授从不同的角度，对城市发展四个方面的问题做了深入精彩的报告。第一位诸教授关注目前的城市评价方法，特别是指数的问题，对此做了深入研究，也提出了一个很好的指数改进方案，而且被联合国采纳。第二位，阿里扎·弗莱舍教授，主要关注城郊农业旅游的问题，特别是在农业旅游的定量分析方面做了深入的研究。第三位是耿教授，耿教授对中国城市温室气体的排放及来源做了深入的分析，并在此基础上提出了很多有建设性的对策和建议。第四位教授提出了一个很有意思的话题，对城市有一个很好的展望。

下面是我个人的看法。我也在做生态城市的研究，去了中国几个典型的生态城市，专门做了一些调研，结合前面几位教授说的生态城市，我有几个看法。其一，我觉得中国生态城市走入了两个误区。第一个误区，我们真的不清楚生态城市到底是什么。因为国外说的生态城市和我们说的生态城市，有很大的不同。通过梳理国外案例，发现国外的生态城市主要强调两个方面，一个是关注能源的使用，另一个是碳排放的问题。但是中国的生态城市，实际上关心的内容比较多，既有城市生态建设，包括绿地建设、生活环境的改善；又面临着碳排放的压力。所以中国的生态城市面临的问题和国外的生态城市面临的问题不同，我们的生态城市建设压力更大。因此国外的一些方法和评价体系很难在中国使用。第二个误区有几个典型，崇明东滩最早提出的生态城市建设，到现在还没有建；天津生态城，这个生态城我去调研了，初具规模，但是问题也很多；另一个叫得比较响的是唐山的曹妃甸生态城，那个地方已经亏欠了很多资金，基本上是一片荒废的状态。通过宣传较多的生态城市，可以看出中国的新生态城市建设状态。

现在还有一个问题，对各个地方的老城市做生态城市评价时，生态城市已经是一个目标，还是仍然处于发展的过程中？对此还不是很明确。我们进行评价时，一百个城市可能就有一百个模式和标准，每个城市都不同。具体内涵我不太清楚，因为国外好像没有生态城市评价。还有一个最主要的问题是，生态城市的标准不一样，现在生态环境比较好的城市，如果经济比较差的话，是否还能够归入生态城市范围。所以就涉及权重问题。我觉得建设生态城市，不同的城市处在不同的阶段，具有不同的目标，具有不同的标准，所以现在如果对它进行统一化、标准化的评价，就面临很大的问题。

然后是区域合作和生态补偿问题。我在做长三角方面的研究，我有一个与诸教授有争议的地方，就是像上海这么大型的城市，生态平衡靠上海自身是无法实现的，必须把它放在区域的大生态环境背景里面。难点有几个方面：第一，大气污染是流动的，上海做得再好，而周边的大气环境不好的话，也达不了标，因为上海没法把大气隔开。第二，上海是在长江流域的下游，水的问题受到上游的影响。我们把苏州河和黄浦江水治理得再干净，上游浙江排放死猪，江苏太湖排放污染，马上会降低上海的水质。如果你把这两个指标作为标准，上海花再大的精力也很难达到生态城市的标准。所以我们必须把城市看作是区域的一个组成部分，生态城市建设才可能有希望。如果单打独斗地建设生态城市，很难建成真正的生态城市。除非有一天全中国的生态环境都变好了才有可能。

关于生态补偿问题，我专门去黄山——中国第一个做生态补偿的地方做了调查，但是遇到了问题。上海市和处于下游地区的浙江省对上游地区进行了一定的补偿，但黄山市认为对它的经济发展来说，补偿五个亿太少了，所以它宁愿发展也不愿意补偿。但是国家强制要求它达到水质标准。这里就涉及英国教授讲的城市不平等、区域发展不平等的问题。因为我们这样控制以后，就是限制了上游地区——黄山市的发展。黄山市还对哪方面比较有意见呢？它控制污染排放，但是在下游地区，杭州市却在发展一些污染产业，比如围网养殖，它不允许黄山市围网养殖，但是自己却在围网养殖，因为它在下游。这些问题都特别需要我们在区域合作上建立公平合理的机制。我觉得中国只是刚刚在区域城市合作方面起步，还有很多问题。

互动对话

提问者： 我对蔡教授说的区域合作和生态补偿有同感。我曾经做过苏州河水资源和太湖水资源的研究。当时我有一个想法，就是探索实施跨区域生态补偿和区域共治。希望通过中央的协调，上海、江苏实施区域共治，把环境治理好，确保上海饮用水安全。未来这种生态补偿能不能考虑区域合作？

高柏林： 当然，我们需要这样的协调。在中国，很多生态补偿是由政府驱动的。而世界上其他地方的生态补偿是市场机制，不是由政府驱动的。在纽约市，要用清洁的水源，就要向水务公司付钱；在中国，这样的情况可能会是政府的一个项目，然后再通过补贴项目给参与者。比如，清洁能源项目，那些使用清洁能源的人并没有因为使用清洁能源而付费。从长远来讲这是不可持续的，政府不应该做这种补贴。习主席也说到，要让市场发挥决定性作用。过去这种项目机制正在慢慢发生改变，至少让用户承担部分成本，否则这种生态补偿完全是政府的负担。现在中国有60多个生态补偿项目，如果都是由政府支出，将会是很大的负担。

提问者： 我想问一下诸教授，在改革之前中国绝大多数城市都是第一象限的状态，没有办法走直线到第二象限。现在这种状态是斜上去的。大量的西部城市目前可能还处在第一象限。我本人做了一些西部城市的规划，接触下来感觉到有一些担忧，就是国家的政策在倾斜，绿色产业在过去，但是事实上他们本地的发展与他们的认识，还有经济因素，实际上还是在重复走东部的老路。我想听听您的见解，从政府层面来讲，有什么好的办法能够避免西部生态的恶化？

诸大建： 这个问题问得很好。一个是应该怎么样，一个是实际上怎么样。中国实际上应该是我们经常讲的，不走西方国家先污染后治理的老路。但是这个声音的响亮程度和现在时间成反比，现在越来越不敢讲了。实际上包括东部、西部都在走从第一象限到上面第三象限的道路。但是，西部还是有机会的。另外补充一点，非常遗憾的是，从我们四年多的研究结果来看，只有一两年在第二象限出现了一个城市，即厦门。但是它没有保持在第二象限，又跑到第三象限去了。这很难调控。

Not By City Planning Alone

Garo Batmanian

Lead Environment Specialist and Agriculture/Environment/

Forestry Sector Coordinator for World Bank

Although our city planner is going to comment on my presentation, my presentation is not restricted to the city planning. The reason why I want to make this presentation is that public goods cannot be fully managed beyond city capacity. That is a typical problem for air quality and water quality here in China. You cannot manage air and water issues just by the internal city planning. So my presentation today is about why this is happening and what governance issues are related to that.

1. Difficulties and countermeasures of air quality controlling

In 2015, there are piles of big clouds. It is because of PM 2.5 that can travel as long as 500 km or more. Though Beijing is moving companies and polluting factories to Hebei, actually it doesn't help. As it is upwind, the clouds can still travel and continue to bring the smog back to Beijing.

This is the big event in December, 2015 that Shanghai and Hebei reached the similar level of smog. This is the air quality identified by different pollutants (Fig.1), including sulfur dioxide, black carbon, and PM 2.5. Most people don't know that half of the PM 2.5 is resulted from these chemicals, and the secondary compound of these chemicals constitute PM 2.5. China has not paid attention to some chemicals for agricultural uses until 2015, including ammonium fertilizer. China uses 30% more fertilizer than what is really needed. These fertilizers together with other chemicals become the major source of PM 2.5. The message here is that you cannot fix the problem by one city.

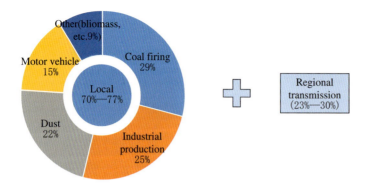

Fig.1
Air quality
by different
pollutants

This creates a concept called airshed. Airshed is the same notion as watershed. For example, Singapore is part of the Indonesian air shed. If Singapore gets polluted, Indonesia would be affected. That's the most striking example I can give in Asia. This is Shijiazhuang in Hebei province. Shijiazhuang is not known to be a green city. He's trying to be but he's not a green city. But as the capital city in Hebei, it still has 23% to 30% pollution from the outside. So even if they cut the pollution within by half, they still have 30% coming from the outside. So the solution is simple. Cities in Asia should develop a joint plan to prevent the air pollution so as to increase the effectiveness and decrease the relevant costs at the city level. From this perspective, we should also take agriculture into consideration and do overall control over what's happening up airshed. China has created 3 regional plans, one for Yangtze River Delta region, one for Zhujiang River Delta region, and one for Beijing-Tianjin-Hebei region. These plans have to be considered when you make the city planning because otherwise you are putting more burden on one city than another. The distribution need to keep a balance when considering how many factories are going to be closed down. Chances are that companies in Hebei don't produce energy but those in Mongolia still do. It's still going to cause air pollution.

2. Difficulties and countermeasures of water resource management

Let's go to water resources. China's water availability per capita is only 25% of the water availability in the world. China have very limited amount of water, 65% and 70% of which is used for agriculture. That's because there are a lot of rice and other crops need to irrigate. This was not a problem before. But now with urbanization, the demand for water supply is increasing greatly. It doesn't matter how efficient you are when planning the city in water recycle and utilization. The point is you still don't have enough water. That's the first problem.

The second one is what comes from my country Brazil and other countries. You may get water but they are already polluted. For instance, you live near the river bank in Shanghai, so what you get is the water with the pollutants. You have to spend a large amount of money to clean the water before you make it available for use. Therefore, we cannot just fix the water issue and meet the needs of citizens by optimizing city planning inside.

The cities are growing. Not all the cities are like Shanghai. Beijing and other cities are not in the course or near a large river like here. I want to give you more examples. The most famous one is in New York and it is famous for environmental services. So those who provide indirect environmental services get paid from doing this and those who benefit from environmental services pay for the services. So if you apply that mechanism to Beijing, you should find a way to pay people upstream so that they protect water quality. That works well and the logic is simple. The people upstream will use the land and get the benefits.

Apart from the given case, we have several other cases from Brazil. I'm going to show you one of them (Fig.2). It shows the southern part of the country. This is a small river not necessarily the size of New York. The city is like the

Fig.2
Water resources
program in Brazil

size of Beidaihe and the sort of place you have in China, with a population of 150 000. The town has a water company and a water source but not big. They have a lot of pig farms upstream and the water is more or less polluted. So the staff went to this area and offered the farmers solution. The solution is to set a new watershed water for 8 million dollars, with its operation fees of 125 million dollars per hectare per year.

3. Providing urban public goods needs coordinative governance

My final remark is that sometimes cities cannot manage public goods, especially water, air, because they are far beyond city limits. Therefore, cities in the same airshed and watershed should develop joint plan and divide responsibilities proportionally. That's the key because otherwise there would be imbalanced workload among cities. It can help us increase effectiveness and decrease costs. Also, we need a mix of governments and markets to implement the action. If you have a regional plan to manage the water or air pollution, then you can have city level measures to change the fuel of vehicles. But do mind that these city level measures are only part of the big strategy. That's why by city planning alone is not to be effective and is going to be more costly. But here in China, like in my country Brazil, we should start with government regulation and collaborate government supervision with market mechanism to practice a system, like Proposes of Environmental Services in Brazil.

Energy Concepts along the Life-cycle of Sustainable Cities

Gunnar Gruen

Professor, Deputy Director of Fraunhofer Institute in Germany

It's obvious that our cities need energy and the need also changes along the life time. As we can see (Fig. 1), we expect that in 2050 we will have 50% of population living in our cities, while we already have almost half of the population living in the city at present. The topic of urbanization is now becoming increasingly important in Europe and Asia. Although the speed of urbanization is not as fast in Europe as in Asia, we still have to meet the challenge.

Fig.1
Growth of urban
population

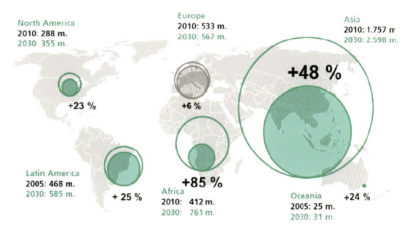

1. The energy optimization in city systems

When we look into city systems, there are several favorable factors which can be made use of to better develop our cities. The first one is to build a green attractive city environment to attract talents and form emotional bondage with our city. And also, we have to build green industry parts so that they can create values for those in need.

If we look at the energy supplies, we can see much energy comes from new energy. On city scale, we have different levels. First we have cross-energy management. Secondly, on district level, especially when we come to heating and cooling. We are also considering whether we can save energy in heating and cooling system and use it at different time. On building level, it is known to all that we can produce electricity by heat energy. So what we want to do is to optimize renewable resources and obtain more heating. Now we can have a look at how to reconstruct energy at a community level. As we have a big energy demand, we need to improve our energy use efficiency and manage renewable resources in heating and cooling systems at the community level. That's the thing we do a lot in Germany. If you look at the energy optimization, you have also to look at the different needs. So you have different times of use, different types of energy, and different forms of heating and cooling at different times. For example, the supermarket we offer heating loads because we have demands of heating for cooling food.

2. The energy management in city operation

We also have a heating demand in building, so the question is how to make use of this energy to be available for other sources. The same applies to our ice rink where they have huge demand for cooling and heating. So what we do in Germany is to look at how to supply energy from renewable sources and how to use energy efficiently. One example I want to show you is a city in the southern part of the country with a very intense automobile industry. In this case, we can see how to increase energy efficiency at a city level through energy supply companies and the participation of authorities and public. First, it is necessary to engage in a public organization and promote energy saving programs in schools. And then education is an important step. The concept of energy saving is also included in curriculum so that people from the very beginning can have the awareness of energy efficiency. Additionally, we also give training to employees in companies. Second is to improve supply energy efficiency. We have met the demand of heating through renovation of energy supply system on district level.

We also use intelligence measuring system to improve the way we use energy. As for renewable energy, our city has already installed PV but not all the roofs are suitable for that. We also built straw fired power plant outside the city and developed a concept to publicize energy conservation in our city. We have to get some indicators and measures to prove whether these ways are effective. In Germany, we always talk about primary energy use. When we talk about energy efficiency, how much primary energy we are using to supply energy? Our goal is to reduce the primary energy use. In April, 2000, we have launched a program to decrease the primary energy demand and finally achieved success. In 2020, we hope to see 20% less energy use at a very industrialized area than we had before and at the same time increase the demand in automobile industry. This is very important success we achieved.

The second example is in a northern city in Germany. The city is half way substituting all the energy it uses with renewable energy. They want to increase the energy use efficiency in the whole system and maximize the scale of renewable energy. Also, they would like to see the further apply of intelligent technology in production, distribution, and enlarge its participation. Otherwise, it's difficult to manage the whole system. Now look at the CO_2 emission (Fig. 2). We developed several strategies to reduce the CO_2 emission compared with the situation in 1990s, and we achieved a great success by 2020. And then it goes more challenging to bring down the emission. We should not only focus on the building level, but also on the district and city level of our energy system. So we work together with other colleagues in the International Energy Agency to develop a tool called "Energy Concept Adviser" when you look at district level.

Fig.2
Development
of the primary
energy use

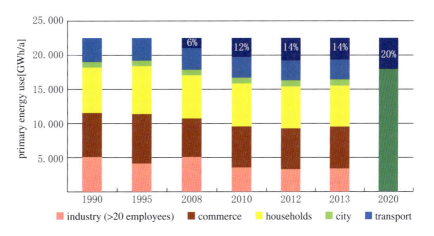

The target is to include those who build the building into the group of decision makers in administration and local policy making. Thus, the tool is very easy to use with detailed instruction. Even a layman can know the energy potential with this tool.

3. The energy management in city renovation

Here is another example from another southern German city. It's a city which needs to be renovated. And we've also renovated its district heating by resources and techniques, like housing, industry, supermarket, hospitals, etc. You can connect it with different energy supply systems so that you can know how much energy you use before and how much you use after that. You can have the information before project and after project to see how much energy or primary energy you use. We manage this by energy contact systems. This is what the energy adviser gives us as advice which shows a very rough idea predicting the effect before and after the renovation and whether we would have a very successful energy system or not. From this fossil distribution system, we can see that the primary energy use is decreased by 25% after our program.

In conclusion, we need to pay attention to energy efficiency because we have increasing energy demand and growing cities. Reducing energy must be altogether with energy efficiency. Renewable energy must be managed with our energy efficiency so that it can keep pace with our needs. Also, the integration of these systems is a prospect we embrace for our future.

Eco-city and Development Index of Urban Ecology

Che Shengquan

Professor, Vice-dean of Agricultural and Biology School
of Shanghai Jiao Tong University

The indicator system for eco-cities includes four aspects: the status of eco-city at present, the indicators for city ecology, the system of ecological indicators for Chinese cities, and the development index of city ecology. There are some representative eco-cities in America, in Europe, in Asia, and some other places. They develop quite well in the eco-system from different climate.

Table 1
The Representative eco-cities
around the world

Cities	countries	continents
Vancouver	Canada	North America
Berkeley	America	North America
Portland	America	North America
Phoenix	America	North America
Baltimore	America	North America
Curitiba	Brazil	South America
Copenhagen	Denmark	Europe
Erlangen	Germany	Europe
Freiburg	Germany	Europe
Malmo	Sweden	Europe
Stockholm	Sweden	Europe
Whyalla	Australian	Oceania
Adelaide	Australian	Oceania
Kitakyushu	Japan	Asia
Singapore	Singapore	Asia

Strategies	Vancouver	Berkeley	Portland	Phoenix	Baltimore	Curitiba	Copenhagen	Erlangen	Freiburg	Malmo	Stockholm	Whyalla	Adelaide
Land use and urban structure adjustment			✓	✓		✓	✓				✓		
Traffic optimization	✓	✓	✓	✓		✓	✓				✓		
Ecological protection and reconstruction	✓	✓		✓							✓	✓	
Urban green space and open space	✓		✓	✓			✓				✓		✓
Improving municipal facilities	✓	✓	✓	✓	✓	✓		✓	✓		✓		✓
Energy and resources	✓	✓	✓	✓	✓	✓	✓	✓	✓		✓		✓
Eco-economy	✓	✓											
Ecological city management institutions		✓	✓										
eco-culture		✓			✓	✓		✓			✓	✓	
Ecological legislation		✓									✓		
Ecological demonstration community												✓	

Table 2

Strategies of international eco-cities

1. The status of chinese eco-cities at present

We have a collected data for more than 300 cities (Table 3). In China, the eco-system develops from 1980s and now some Chinese ecological towns are still doing some attempts in this development. Here comes the index for our research so far. We have 45 first class indicators with conditions of green land, quality of water, utilization and consumption of energy, and also GDP energy consumption unit particularly, and also social cultural factors. We want to take a look at the eco-development here in cities in China. In terms of the green land in China, the regional indicator difference represents its green land development at different levels. For example, the area of those green lands is increasing in these big cities while declining in middle cities. Those are the features of the city.

Table 3
Demonstrations
of Eco-cities in
China

Cities	Sections	Provinces
Sino-Singapore Tianjin Eco-city	North	Tianjin
Caofeidian Area TangshanBay Eco-city	North	Hebei
Wuxi Low-carbon city	East	Jiangsu
Chongming Eco-city	East	Shanghai
Wuhan Eco-city	Mid	Hubei
ShenzhenEco-city	South	Guangdong

Table 4
Indicators and
current value of
urban ecosystem
in China

Indicators	Mean
Green space ratio in built areas（%）	33.3
Green coverage ratio in built areas（%）	37.5
Urban green area per capita（m^2）	31.3
Urban park area per capita（m^2）	13.76
More than 10 hectares Urban parks per million person	0.26
Protected area rate of administrative region（%）	10
Urban road greening penetration（%）	97.32
Urban road greening achieved rate（%）	77.5

Indicators	Mean
Ecological land rate of planning land（%）	40
Annual runoff control rate（%）	40
Groundwater overdraft rate（%）	1.07
Ratio of 500 m service radius coverage areas of public green space（%）	77.68
Integrity of the urban parks which bigger than 10 hectares	—
Urban green corridor density（1 km/km²）	—
The connection degree at least 2 belt park ratio	—
Wetland area loss rate of administrative region（%）	1.5
Local woody plant index	84.89
The ratio of wild animals in the built-up area to the city（%）	0.4
Natural water shoreline rate（%）	80.94
Comprehensive bio-diversity index（%）	0.4
Extent of biological invasion（%）	0.523
Old and Famous Treesprotective rate（%）	96.91
The proportion of Urban air quality better than the two class standard days（%）	82.96
Urban heat island effect（℃）	0.91
Water environmental quality compliance rate（%）	86.10
The proportion of water quality of drinking water source >= class III（%）	97.00
Unit GDP carbon emission intensity (t/y)	62.54
Environmental noise compliance area coverage（%）	90
Urban sewage treatment rate（%）	89.27
Living garbage harmless treatment rate（%）	96.40
Vehicle emission compliance rate（%）	80
Living garbage per capita（kg/d）	1.2
Damaged and disposal land restoration rate（%）	70.76

	2009	2010	2011	2012	2013	Mean of growth rate（%）
National average（%）	34.17	34.47	35.27	35.72	35.78	1.16
Growth rate（%）	—	0.88	2.32	1.28	0.17	
East region（%）	36.63	36.41	37.62	38.01	38.25	1.10
Mid region（%）	33.32	33.81	34.29	34.58	34.68	1.01
West region（%）	30.87	31.76	32.64	33.58	33.42	2.01
North east region（%）	31.59	33.15	33.97	34.02	33.65	1.62

Table 5
Annual variation of green space ratio between 2009—2013

In terms of international index system, UN, universities from EU and the UK have a different index system to measure the eco-development of a city. Those indexes can be divided into four categories: sustainable development, environmental management, ecological system, and human welfare. These indexes can be mainly summarized into political, practical and also theoretical ones. These categories come from different city orientations, such as sustainable city, comfortable city, green city, low carbon city and so on. Also, all these indexes can be classified into 15 main categories (Table 6). Policy management,

Table 6
Indicators and frequency

Indicators	Frequency	Indicators	Frequency
Policy management	17%	Water quality	15%
Quantity and scale	11%	Air quality	9%
Structure and layout	8%	Ecological service function	8%
Refuse disposal	7%	Institutional improvement	6%
Resources and energy consumption	6%	Public participation	3%
Biodiversity	3%	Application of new technology	3%
Abandoned land treatment	2%	Noise pollution	1%
Soil quality	1%		

water quality and air quality management are among most frequently used measurement of the eco-development.

2. The constitution of eco-cities indexes

In China, if we make a comparison between the present and the past eco-system, we need to supplement related indexes. These indexes can be divided into natural, social, and ecological ones. Cities could have an integrated organic system in which ecological burden should not go beyond.

This is the indicator structure (Fig.1). Concerning the protection and construction of eco-system, we have divided them into primary indicators and secondary indicators. For example, we have the structure of ecological space. We focus on the green land and the green area rate. And we also look for environmental indicator, like water, air, and soil.

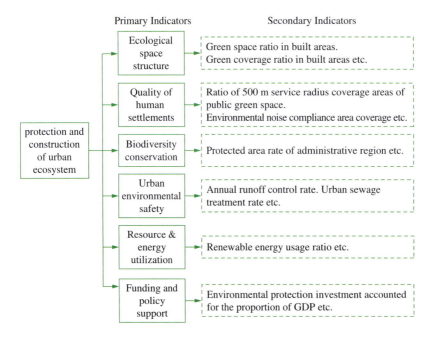

Fig.1
Indicator structure

The third one is bio-diversity which is closely related to preservation of lands. We are also interested in ecological space. From energy and resource efficiency, we have different indicators to define it. In China, we have indicators for eco-development for eco-garden city and eco-city. We do hope the indicators can help to assist the government.

3. The future of eco-cities indexes

Those indicators are what we need in the process of eco-development. We also want to have a development index to show the eco-development of city and predict the objective for city development. We divided the index into four parts: natural resources, eco-environment, eco-policy, and eco-behavior. So there is a pressure caused by human behavior. In this case, human beings have to be cautious of their behavior and it is also a very important dimension of eco-system.

In terms of natural resources, we have green land ratio, protection ratio, eco-resources. In terms of eco-environment, we want to focus on water quality, air quality, and also impaired land. We actually have a lot eco-behavior, such as GDP's ecological behavior. When we refer to green garbage and low carbon traffic, it is hoped that some indicators can be evaluated and guide the development of our eco-city.

Examining Sustainable Cities Frameworks: the Impact of Different Relationships between Public Policies and the Provision of Public Goods

Shailaja Fennell

Professor of Centre of Development studies in University of Cambridge

1. The challenge to urban public policy

I'd like to talk about different frameworks for our public policies. In particular, I am also going to emphasize public private partnership (PPP). Apart from water and air, I would like to say some soft structure, like health and education. Cities like Shanghai have 25 million population and have to accommodate 5 million migrants. We hope to find some solutions to deal with theses challenges and learn some lessons from other countries in the developing world. Cities and sustainability is not the topic I need to emphasize in this city forums, but I'd like to identify other relevant sustainable objectives. In the academic world, we need a partner to cooperate with the governments and other corporate, so as to make cities more inclusive. It's a challenge for everybody. It's a data challenge, research challenge, as well as policy challenge.

2.The inequality in cities

Cities are powerful places, but powerful places are also unequal places. It increases the inequality between the haves and the have-nots. I want to show you some graphs (Fig.1, Fig.2). If the world continues to grow, the challenges for China, India, and Brazil, also the smaller countries, Mexico, Pakistan, Bangladesh will be how to get these large numbers of new city dwellers accommodated. And among them, many are young, particularly if I take a look at southeast Asia and Africa. A challenge for young people is to have skills if they will move to a city. So the international survey is telling us that from rural to urban means a challenge for jobs. China ranks the first in giving laborers education. But even within Shanghai, there are great contrasts between the top schools and bottom schools for education. We need to pay attention to the idea of cities and inclusion to challenge and try to reverse the inequality we see in Asia. Asia is growing, and especially China and India, have grown hugely. But inequality has also grown.

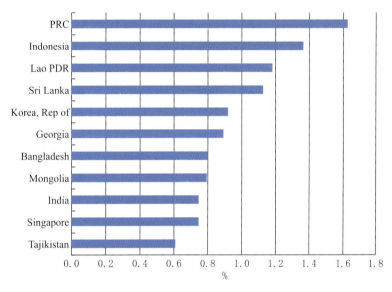

Fig.1
Annual growth of Gini coefficients, 1990s—2000s
Source: Asian Development Bank (2012).

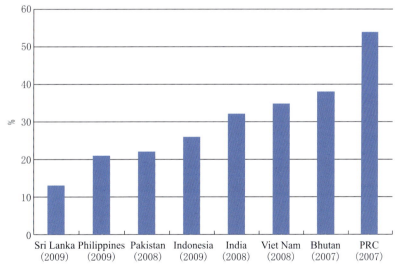

Fig.2
Contribution of spatial inequality to overall inequality
Source: Asian Development Bank Institute(2014).

We can see inequality primarily from the top and bottom 1% in the graph. It is an opportunity to use education to reduce stratification. It's difficult to achieve equality outcomes, but at least we could create opportunities to be treated equally.

Everybody should have access to health and education. And if we look at the top 1/5 and the bottom 1/5, just during these past 2 decades of development, many Asian countries, including the PRC, have witnessed sharp increase in these two parts. Thus, the gap between the rural and urban area is very clear.

3. The innovative measures to provide public goods

Urban areas have most social services, but they also have more poverty. Poor people move to this place to get these services. Therefore, cities are more unequal than the country where they are located. Now let's look at the provision of public goods (Fig.3). Public goods are important because they are for the public, but they also have externalities, just like water and air for the families and their health. The challenge is that quality and quantity, complements as they are, don't always work together. Indeed, the governments are able to provide public sanitation and public education, but in many countries, the question is whether public sectors could continue to produce quality services considering various income level habitants. Think about rural migrant workers who move to the city in China. Their poor education levels have resulted in low incomes. And if looking at public and private expense sector of the same period (Fig.4), Southeast Asia, East Asia, South Asia, all of them have seen a greater rise in the expenses of private sectors over this period, while the expenses of public sector in all these areas held the line.

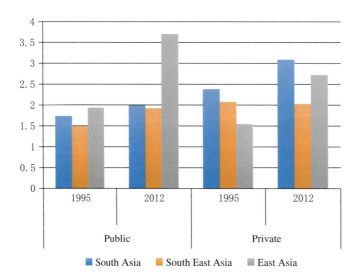

Fig.3
Public and private sector expense percentage in GDP (1995 vs. 2012)

Fig.4
Public and private
expense sector of
the same period

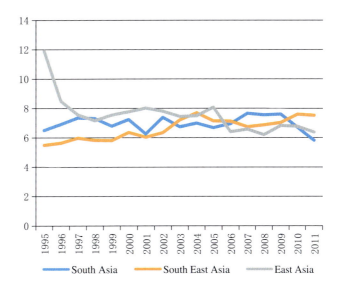

Actually, both education and sanitation need to introduce new partners. So what is PPP? We have a specific example on transport by contracting between the public and the private sector. That is actually what happens between the Europe and the UK. Besides that, governments can sell products and services to the markets. Hence, we could develop new methods and use the current PPP thinking to better our education and sanitation. PPP at the current stage asks for not only profits, but also new appeals for people.

In my opinion, institutional learning does not be the fortress of a country. As we can see in television, more and more non-government organizations are providing diagnoses in rural area. Thus, we need to look for local success within the big city in Shanghai. We had a heart charity foundation getting elderly care in China, but today more people need that care. And so PPP in Asia needs to think much more comprehensively and look into local examples to provide necessary health care and education to make cities truly inclusive.

Remark

Li Bingdi (Senior Planner): Mr. Garo Batmanian raises the idea of cross-domain and emphasizes the compensation mechanism for environment. Mr. Gunnar Gruen puts forward a concept of synergetic development from building level to city level and gives examples of energy management in community. He also stresses efficiency and the idea to substitute primary energy with renewable energy. Mr. Che Shengquan talks about eco-city and eco-development index after his research of 350 cities in China in a macro scope. Last but not least, Mrs. Shailaja Fennell analyzes PPP cooperation and the integral development among different classes. In conclusion, they all inspire us in three aspects.

Firstly, the concept to construct eco-cities in China is already included in the sustainable development concept in the context of global ecology.

Secondly, when it comes to ecology, we must use the most basic idea, like synergism, co-existence, co-sharing, co-management, and co-governance. We have to pay attention to these ideologies when different industries are dealing with different energy, different atmosphere, different water sources. And our objective is to realize co-governance through the same objective, the same index, and the same action. Mrs. Shailaja Fennell also tells us to give our concern to our citizens.

Thirdly, as a metropolitan city of great influence, Shanghai has to shoulder more responsibilities in constructing eco-city and promoting more international cooperation to bring in advanced ideals in China. At the same time, we also need the cooperative action of government, market, and citizens. Therefore, the construction of eco-city is the common pursuit of us all.

Dialogue

Audience: Prof. Che, can you tell us how you concluded the 5 indicators?

Che Shengquan: The eco-development of a city can be divided into 3 aspects: the first one is to reduce the source of pollution from the very beginning; the second one is to control the process; the third one is to repair the damage. These aspects all include natural ecology, social ecology, economic ecology, and cultural ecology. Therefore, firstly, we have to maintain the balance so that cities could have an integrated organic system in which ecological burden should not go beyond.

Secondly, it is about the environment. Thirdly, we have to emphasize the management, including policy, mechanism, and encouragement measures. The fourth one is ecological behavior which is beyond my research focus. The indicator is different from normal city ecology and ecological evaluation indicator. We hope to reduce it and make it a response to city management or city development. We are still on that part.

Audience: Mr. Garo, I wonder how we can clearly define the boundary of the wind?

Garo Batmanian: There is prevailing wind and an average speed which depends on the size of cloud. It may change but it won't move from Beijing to Guangxi. So it's not easy to draw on a map geographically because we have water and mountains. However, if you want to do it, you can find a center. For example, you can start at Beijing and get to know the prevailing wind around it and its speed. The same goes for Shanghai. So the boundaries between airsheds are fixed and clear. But we need to take the center into concern. If the wind centers at Shijiazhuang, about 250 km west from Beijing, it goes all the way to Shanxi. But if it centers at Beijing, it probably stops at the mountain area that separate Shanxi from Shaanxi. In this case, we can see that when doing a planning, we should consider the political borders. Sometimes the distribution of watersheds has nothing to do with political units, so we need to have the whole picture of political border in mind. So there are two factors we have to bear in mind, prevailing wind and political units.

Audience: I have a question. To introduce PPP into our educational system is a good advice, but compared to infrastructural investment, it's difficult to have output. So if we adopt the last mode of PPP in education, like charity, how do we measure its output?

Shailaja Fennell: There are always methods that we can evaluate outputs for education, for example, how many years you get education for the income change. In the early 1950s and 1960s, the assumption was if you could complete secondary school when you were 18, your income would increase. In the last 20 years, that asked for college education. So another 20 years later, it might ask for master's degree. Hence, there is a relationship between the numbers of the years of education and the return for your payment, which depends on the payment of education for the public. That's actually a benefit for both sides. For example, everyone benefits from good roads because there are fewer accidents and you pay for good roads because you can go faster. Similarly, for education, if you improve the quality of the provider, you may have to study less hours. In return, it will benefit both you and the society. In the past, we only have one provider and it is public organization. But now you have different providers for different skills. So it is very possible to look at the output from different providers. As a result, we just need different indicators from academics, city governance, and civil society and we should consider what indicators we want. It is also true for health care.

Performance Evaluation and Classification of Sustainable City
—from Weak Sustainability to Strong Sustainability

Zhu Dajian

Professor of School of Economics & Management of Tongji University

My topic today is an often-heard one, but few people really paid close attention to it. We often talk about the sustainable development level of certain cities. And we can also see rankings of sustainable cities in China or abroad. Should we believe in these rankings or not? Recently, an European company as famous as McKinsey made an international ranking of sustainable cities in which Shanghai and Beijing ranked first and second respectively. According to this ranking, there are three subsystems in the sustainable development, namely: economic system, social system, and environmental system. And the economic system of Shanghai ranked top of the list. However, in case of environment system, Shanghai ranked bottom. But in the overall rankings of sustainable development, Shanghai is still number one. So, do you believe in this so called sustainable ranking? Therefore we need a theory to illustrate why these rankings won't work. I call this weak sustainable development, and I'll share my view of what is strong sustainable development with you.

1. The insufficiency of traditional indexes and ranking

If we want to make clear what are the index of sustainable development, let's start with this picture (Fig.1). As we can see, here are economic, social and environmental systems. A basic technique of making index is that we disassemble sustainable development into three objectives, an economic objective, a social objective and an environmental objective. And then we can disintegrate the economic sub-objective into several aspects. We can gradually make the dimensionalizable economic indexes dimensionless. As to the social indexes, we can also make non dimensionalize the social indexes like gap of wealth and social inequity dimensionless. So do the environmental indexes, such as energy costs, land costs, etc. By doing so, we will have a clear overview of the economy, society and environment. The only difference is the weight of certain indexes. But the technique I'm going to share with you today will prove that no matter how skillful you are, the results will be unbelievable. There is a theory in the ranking list I mentioned before, that is, a weak environment index can be hedged by a strong economic index. And hedging here means to substitute. So this is a theory dilemma of economics, what is the ceiling of the substitution? If there is no upper limit, even if your environment rating is zero, that's alright as long as you have high marks on economy and society. As an analogy, we have two methods of PhD. candidate admission, the first one is to count the total points. But if he/she performs too bad on English and only got 20 points, will you still enroll him? Therefore, another way is to set a threshold which determines the admission. Thus, the problem of that ranking list is that they are lack of in-depth thoughts about those theories.

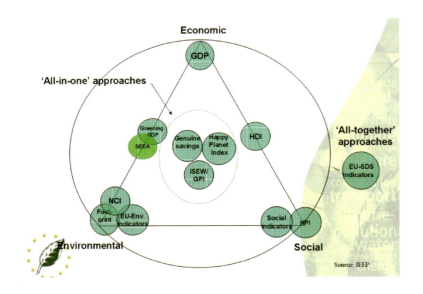

Fig.1
Categorization
of sustainable
development
indicators

2. Indexes system of strong sustainable development

So what is sustainable development? It's very easy to understand but we often get entangled in its literal meanings. Sustainable development means we should set certain threshold for resources and environment, and we cannot break it. And we must set two thresholds if we want to use two indexes. This picture is often used by European experts, in ideal situations, social and economic indexes increase gradually while the environment index decreases (Fig.2), an index is disconnected. Just like the analogy I made before, which kind of method we should use to decide the admission? According to the overall score or the score of single subject? We should make decision according to the comprehensive development. Back to our topic, we have been doing studies of sustainable development for nearly twenty years, but we still have some problems in this theory.

Fig.2
Framework of
sustainable
development
indicators

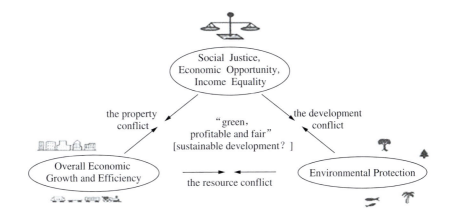

I'm fortunate to make an index which is certificated by UNDP to be sustainable. Every well-developed city have two hemispheres (Fig.3), the hemisphere above including per capita GDP, HDRA and GNH, and they are all in a growing trend. And the hemisphere below is called Ecological Environment, the few it was depleted the better. Two dimension should be treated separately. I have a sample image here, we can see indexes like education, life, per capita GDP, and each has its own upper limit. For example, 80% is acceptable now. Likewise, I can also make an index of ecological costs, and that's the lower hemisphere which includes a per-capita usage of resources. Which quadrant shows the quality of a sustainable city (Fig.4) ? It should be the second one. Beijing and Shanghai belong to the third quadrant, but they are not sustainable due to high costs of resources and environment. If we substitute the poor environment performance with high economic growth, and get a good evaluation which indicates they are sustainable, it would be absurd. On the other side, we can't call the western part of China "sustainable", even if these regions are famous for their ecological civilization and green development, they are not well-developed economically and socially. So when we are talking about green development, we should make it clear whether we are talking it in single dimension or two dimension of sustainable development.

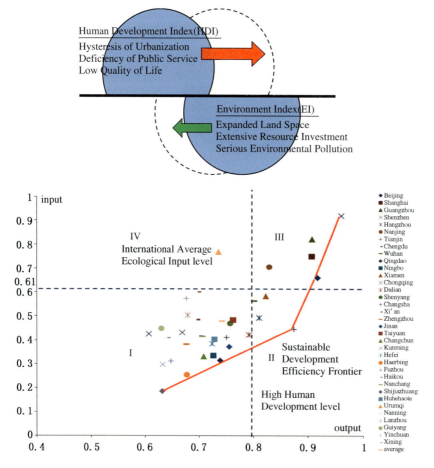

We made a chart of Chinese cities, and you can easily find that it's of 0.8 HDI, which is pretty high (Fig.4). So we are successful in development. And this is ecological footprint index above which an unsustainable development is confirmed. This is another threshold. So with a directed line added, it looked like this. Ideally, the environmental curve should be in growing trend. We can see from the picture that the development in this region is not positive, while Shanghai and Bejing is performing well with a high ecological rating. Therefore, we should focus on this region, and we can use plenty of methods to solve that. So it's not enough to apply formula mechanically in our research, especially in quantitative analysis, because thoughts are far more important than formulas.

3. The practical path for sustainable development

Lastly, we draw a conclusion as each city has it own sustainable development path according to its own situation (Fig.5). These are the directed lines of goals, this one represents development only, it has nothing to do with ecology. And this one represents ecology only, and this represents both of them. So we can call this mode "Mode B", this is the mode of developing countries. And China does not have to follow this pattern, we can try to achieve leaping-over development, let's call it "Mode C", we don't have to move downwards and then go up. Normally, we go from A to B, and drop to C. Of course, we should study sustainable development from two aspects, but for quantitative expression, it would be three. I will give you an example which is applicable for Beijing, Shanghai as well as Guangzhou. The city development is just like human growth. We should grow up healthily without being corpulent. We should be aware of weight before we get fat. Each human has two phases in life, when we're young, we should focus on growing up. But in middle age, we should lose weight for maintaining good health. So sustainable development is just like playing mahjong, you touch 13 cards, that's increments. But if you touch more than 13 cards, then you break the rule, this is what we call "stock", or in other words, the red line. Now we have to figure out how can we develop under the pressure of China's red line. Now the 13 cards remain unchanged, you take one out and you put one in, there are still 13 cards, but you win with a pure one suit.

Fig.5
Different
development
paths of different
cities

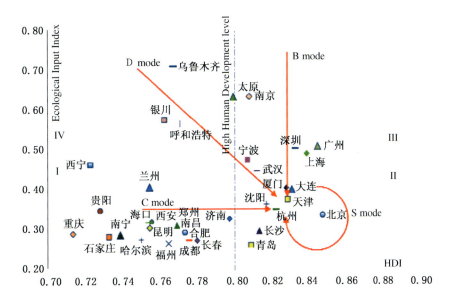

Agritourism in Peri-urban and Rural Regions
—Integrating Economic and Environmental Issues

Aliza Fleischer

Professor of Hebrew University of Jerusalem

1. Characteristics of agritourism

I will take you out to the outskirts of urban area, to the peri-urban area and may be rural areas. we'll discuss today's agritourism enterprises in peri-urban areas and also rural areas. Developing agritourism is actually beneficial to the urban and to the rural area. A little bit of the background, the definition of agritourism attractions include pick-your-own harvest festivals, farm tour, the visitor center, hospitality services, and outdoor recreations. Little farms and little rural enterprise are actually starting to get involved in tourism. Some of them base their tourism activities on the active farm, and some of them base it on the rural area, on the green world environment.

What are the attributes of agritourism? It's located in peri-urban and rural areas, it can be outskirts of the urban areas, or far away in the rural areas. It serves visitors from urban areas, if visitors don't have enough green space in urban centers, peri-urban areas become the playground of urban citizens. Agritourism benefits urban citizens as much as it benefits peri-urban and rural citizens. It is based on the rural environment, farm and community and on the traditional culture. It's open space, contact with nature, heritage, and "traditional" societies. It's not just based on the green world spaces. It is also based on the traditional society and local culture. It can provide personal contact, you actually get in touch and get to know the person. It's small-scale and high percentage of revenues are going to stay in the region and don't flow outside.

2. The economic process and influence of agritourism

The objective of my talk today is to describe what is the economic process leading to the development of agritourism. Because you see it in many countries and regions, and it's sort of natural economic development that happens a lot. Actually, yesterday, I visited the agritourism attractions center here, in Shanghai outskirt. It describes the role of agritourism in peri-urban and what is its role in rural development. And I will give you a case study in which we analyze the agritourism in Israel.

Why do we see agritourism in so many places of the world and why is it happening? Because of the rapid urbanization, people leave from rural areas to urban areas, it's happening in Europe, it's happening in North America, it's happening in India and China and other parts of the world. And farmers who stayed in peri-urban and rural areas are searching for additional income, except the income they made from agriculture. What they are looking for is an alternative, and agritourism become an alternative, it's a good alternative because it's based on what they have on the farm and environment, and it has a lot of demands from urban citizen and people who live nearby. So in some cases we see bottom-up development, the initiatives start from local area, from farmers themselves, and in some cases the governments of some countries actually initiated it and gave a lot of subsidies and support for it.

Why agritourism is good and how much it can achieve to help rural development and peri-urban development? It benefits the rural and the urban communities; it provides additional income to rural unemployment, to the rural communities; it provide closely located recreation opportunity to the urban citizens or people who live nearby. If the citizen of Shanghai are sick or tired of the cement, of the air pollution, they can drive for an hour or an hour and half to these green open spaces. It's based on existing local production factors, rural amenities and communities, they don't have to build huge infrastructure, and there is synergy with agriculture and nature, and on top of all it helps conserve the environment, and local heritage and cultural resources. It helps sustain and create local employment and income. It's basically good for the local rural area and the local rural development. It's also good for urban area which is nearby. Therefore, it's a win-win situation.

Why a lot of rural tourism and agritourism enterprise are receiving a lot of subsidies? For example, the EU allocated 60 billon Euros to support tourism and agritourism between 2007 and 2013. It's part of their help for rural development, they do it to support agritourism. There are lot of market failures that call for subsidies. Agritourism achieved national goals, for example, less people moving from rural to urban areas. There are also externalities and public goods. All these open spaces, beautiful landscapes are preserved by farmers and they don't get paid, so they need subsidies for these externalities. And there is a significant information that few farmers ever go to banks, banks don't know anything about them, so the banks won't give the farmers any loans although they might be very viable business. Thus, there are different types of support and a lot of money is being paid in Europe, Israel, and Japan. Also a little bit here in China as I heard yesterday .

3. An analysis of israel 's agritourism market

Now, I'll show you a case study where we analyze the agritourism market in Israel. Our objective was to analyze and simulate the agritourism attraction market, which is like pick-your-own, farm tours, all those little things the farmers started to move into tourism. And we were interested to know the answers to these questions. We wanted to see the answers in Israel but you can apply the same model in other places. Hopefully we can do it in Shanghai and answer different questions that people are interested to know about here.

What we wanted to know in Israel is what are the links of the attractions to agriculture? Is it important to base it on the active farm? Or is it better to base it on just the nature open space? We also wanted to know what type of support scheme is better, or efficient support schemes, direct or indirect, which one works better?

And we used all these measurement, the measurement for the economic welfare. We were able to estimate the profits and consumer. And we were be able to compare and simulate different scenarios. Israel is a small country with eight million people, it is not that much. We have about 200 growth communities and they include different types of attractions. And all attractions actually enjoyed support from the Ministry of Agriculture, and they all receive some kind of support and subsidies.

In order to simulate the whole market, we developed a theoretical model and empirical model and then we estimated the parameter, and we had a tool to work with. For the agritourism market, we look it as a oligopolistic differentiated goods market. It's not homogeneous goods, each one is different. One of them is an visitor center, the other one is a pick-your-own strawberries, etc. In order to modally and empirically estimate it, we cannot use regular perfect competition market. Different attractions are described by the attributes.

So with the model, in terms of consumer we have the utility. And each consumer maximizes the utility by choosing different agritourism attractions. The attributes can be the price or anything, and one of the attributes here we see is the price, they describe the attraction. Then we look at the producer itself, the producer maximize the profit, it's also part of the attribute.

The utility the ith consumer derives from firm j

$$u_{ij} = x_j\beta - \alpha p_j + \zeta_j + \xi_{ir} + (1 - \sigma)\,\varepsilon_{ij},$$

x_j: vector of the firms attributes;

p_j: price;

$\zeta_j + \xi_{ir} + (1 - \sigma)\,\varepsilon_{ij}$: unobserved utility component attached to the unobserved firm's attributes;

ζ: Firm specific;

ξ: Specific to the consumer and the region;

σ: the nested-logit parameter;

ε_{ij}: $i.i.d.$ E $(\varepsilon_{ij}) = 0$, specific to the firm and the consumer.

Consumer i will choose the firm j if and only if:

$$u_{ij}^* \geqslant u_{ik}\ \forall\, k \neq j.$$

The oligopolistic profit function

$$\max_{p_j} \pi_j = p_j q_j\,(p_1,\ \cdots,\ p_L) - c\,(z_j,\ q_j)$$

z_j-vector of firm's attributes

F.O.C

$$q_j + \left(p_j - \frac{dc\,(z,\ q_j)}{dq_j}\right)\frac{dq_j}{dp_j} = 0$$

And then we have an empirical function of the demand and the pricing. We estimate all the parameters, the beta (β), the sigma (σ) and the alpha (α). And now we have all models on the computer to play with. And we can see one of the attribute is if the enterprise or the tourism attraction is based on active farm or is based on nature, which one is better? And we can see if it's based on the active farm, it has a disadvantage in terms of demand, supply and pricing in the marginal cost.

Aggregated demand for firm j:

$$\text{in}\left(\frac{p_j q_j}{\beta - \sum_{i=1}^{j} q_j p_j}\right) = x_j \beta - \alpha \text{in} \, p_j + \sigma \text{in}\left(\frac{p_j q_j}{\sum_{jctig} p_j q_j}\right) + \xi_j$$

Firm j pricing equation:

$$\text{in}\,(p_j) = W_j \gamma - \text{in}\left(\frac{\alpha\,[1 - \sigma S_{j/g} - (1 - \sigma)\,S_j]}{\alpha[1 - \sigma S_{j/g} - (1 - \sigma)\,S_j] + 1 - \sigma}\right) + \omega_j$$

The solution of the system of equations yields price and market share for each firm, profits, consumer surplus and total welfare.

Table 1
GMM estimation of the market model

	Coef.	Std. Err.	Elasticity
Demand (market share)			
Constant	−8.719 4***	1.577 3	
Rural based activities	2.825 1***	0.659 5	0.54
Visitors' center	0.706 1***	0.236 6	0.57
Agri-produce sale	0.963 4***	0.368 6	0.97
Food sales	1.168 2***	0.261 4	1.18
Guided act	−0.563 4**	0.247 2	−0.47
Investment scaled	0.000 3	0.000 7	0.03
Access	0.631 7***	0.217 2	3.58
Upper Galilee	0.657 4***	0.263 4	0.23
Pricing (marginal cost)			
Constant	3.581 0***	0.518 1	
Rural based activities	1.295 6***	0.180 3	0.001
Visitors' center	0.327 2***	0.117 2	0.01
Agri-produce sale	0.475 3***	0.143 2	0.01
Food sales	0.348 0***	0.129 2	0.004
Guided act	0.064 2	0.127 4	0.000 6
Investment scaled	−0.000 5*	0.000 3	−0.001 6
Access	−0.027 0	0.136 0	−0.003
Activity size scaled	−0.016 1***	0.005 6	−0.000 2
Alpha	0.837 3**	0.374 8	2.21
Sigma	0.351 3***	0.129 7	

Note: Asterisks (*, **, ***) indicate that the coefficient is significantly different from zero at the 10%, 5%, and 1% levels, respectively.

If we cannot get the answer just from the parameters, we have to simulate all the scenarios. That's what we did, we basically simulated two scenarios, one scenario we based the attractions on active farms. Unlike the present scenario that some of them are based on nature, that was the first simulation.

The second simulation, we compared two types of support schemes, and these are the results. This is the current situations of welfare, and this simulation shows us what happens if we changed the situation now, if we base all the agritourism attractions on active farms, what will happen? We can see we will lose 58% of the welfare, that means, in the case of Israel, agritourism attraction are better off basing their activities on the rural amenities and nature more than on the active farm because they add the demand and cause here.

And in terms of supports, one investing in infrastructure, and the other giving capital and, directly to farmers. We find the better one in terms of welfare is the indirect supporting of the infrastructure. In other cases we can choose different attributes and check questions whatever each country or each region is interested to check. In the case of Shanghai, we can check if you belong to a kind of agritourism organization. Does it benefit you, or how does it benefit the welfare?

These are my conclusions: (1) Basing agritourism attractions on the active farm is more cost efficient; (2) Visitors have a strong preference to visitors' centers or rural/nature based activities; (3) In the simulation where in all the attractions are based on the active farm a decline in welfare is demonstrated; (4) Direct support is preferable to indirect support.

Table 2
The simulation of different conditions

Average price(USD)	Current state	All attractions are based on the active farm%	Improving infrastructure — regional level %	Capital support —individual level %
Total visitors	2 344 350	−22.71	3.48	2.12
Consumer surplus (million USD)	35.5	−60.17	2.70	1.55
Producer surplus (million USD)	17.2	−54.96	3.32	1.40
Welfare (million USD)	52.7	−58.47	2.90	1.50

Studies of Urban Carbon Emission

Geng Yong

Dean of School of Environmental Science and Engineering of
Shanghai Jiao Tong University

It's my great pleasure to be here. I deal with GHG emissions at the city level. I myself have served as the lead officer of a certain group in 2010. And my role in this activity is trying to evaluate how the innovative efforts like eco-industrial park can really help to reduce the overall gas emission. And based upon that experience, I also conducted several studies related to green house gas emissions at management level of cities.

1. Current and future urbanization trends

By year 2050, the global population in the urban area is expected to increase by between 2.5 to 3 billion, corresponding to 64% to 69% of the world population. And also due to intensive economic activities, urban areas can present much higher GDP. But of course, with the intensity of economic activities, urban areas will become a key source of greenhouse gas emissions. Currently the urban areas account for between 71% and 76% of carbon dioxide emissions from global final energy use and between 67%—76% of global energy use. However, urbanization shouldn't equal to emissions growth, which means that we have to adopt innovative approach to try to induce innovative activities so that we can really reduce the urban carbon dioxide emission.

2. Measurement and influencing factors of urban GHG emissions

In terms of how to count urban GHG emissions, there are three major methods. The first one is very much similar to the tier 1 approach. So it really focuses on the direct information of territorial or production-based emissions accounting. And the second method is that territorial plus supply chain accounting approaches, inter-relative, mainly related to the purchase power plus the gas emissions. And the third method is more important, that's consumption-based accounting approaches - the Users Pay Principle. Because we have to understand those important emissions. If we really want to reduce the carbon dioxide emissions, we have to allocate the responsibilities to the final users. And then in order to prepare for problem-mitigating policies, we have to uncover the key drivers that induce the urban GHG emissions. The current studies have been conducted and found that people's income, population dynamics, urban form, locational factors and economic structure are the key factors really induce the urban GHG emissions. And it's also very interesting in terms of per capital energy use and GHG emissions. In developed countries, the per capital green house gas emission of cities is lower than national averages. However, in developing countries, per capital carbon dioxide emission of the cities is higher than national averages. That is mainly due to the gap between urban and rural areas, due to different incomes and different economic status.

The above-mentioned factors present the key drivers which really induce carbon dioxide emissions. However, the impact is quite different. So here if we look at the impact of GHG emissions, it's much higher for economic geography, income, urban infrastructure, but here it's lower. However, if you want to prepare policies, it's much easier for you to focus on the lower level factors. So that's a conflict which means different stakeholders have to have a dialogue to make sure that all the concerns can be addressed before you can really find mitigation policies. And then another key area should really be focused is infrastructure. Because when you measure a city, infrastructure often induces a lot of carbon dioxide emissions. And then there are key driver of emissions, for example the construction, the use or operation and end-of-life of the infrastructure. These are key areas that induce carbon dioxide emissions. Average per capital carbon dioxide emissions embodied in the infrastructure of industrialized countries is five times larger than those in developing countries. Because mainly if you go to cities in developing world, they do not have mature infrastructure, sometimes it lacks basic infrastructure, for example they cannot find or provide adequate water to their residents. And often we see a lock-in effect of energy and emissions pathways, lifestyle and consumption patterns. So those factors also should be addressed by the policy makers.

As for urban form in different countries. They have different perceptions to design their cities. Then we have to think about those factors such as density, land use mix, connectivity and accessibility. These features further present if you have different urban forms, you may have different carbon dioxide emissions. Let's take an example. Maybe you all know the city of Atlanta in the United States. That city almost has the same population as the city of Barcelona in Spain. But in terms of urban area, Atlanta is around thirty two times larger than Barcelona. So this kind of reality actually means that in the city of Atlanta, most people live in independent houses and they have to drive to their workplace to enjoy a better life. That will induce higher emissions. While you think of the city of Barcelona, it's denser. People actually live in apartment buildings. So they have the ability to access this distribution system. Then of course, since the city size is smaller, it's much easier for them to transfer from one place to another.

Then we often think about climate mitigations. In the mature or established cities, they will have to think about those factors. But in less developed countries, we have to consider how to shape urbanization infrastructure environment towards sustainable and low carbon pathways. And then those key factors often need to be considered like institutional arrangements, multi-level governance context, spatial planning and sufficient financial flows and incentives. For example in China, we will have the National Carbon Trademark. For that one we provide adequate financial drivers to really reduce not only anti-practice but also the personnel to consider how you can change our behavior, how you can change our production models that can really reduce carbon dioxide emissions. And then, we also need to think about co-benefits. Co-benefit is a new concept, which means if you have low carbon policies, probably you can also reduce the overall air pollutants. And vice versa, if you have really mature air pollutants reduction policies that can also induce the overall carbon dioxide emission reductions.

3. Some case studies of urbam GHG emissions

Here I want to share some of my research outcomes. This is a study on the Chinese mega cities (Fig.1). They are all province-level cities. But with different functions, they have entirely different carbon dioxide emission profiles. For Beijing and Shanghai, they are the so-called supercities, which means politically, they are higher than most other mega cities. Tianjin and Chongqing are traditional industrial cities, which means they mainly develop different businesses. Then here the red parts represent the purchased power, for Beijing and Shanghai, since they can really enjoy much better policies. Beijing hosted the 2008 Olympics and Shanghai hosted 2010 World Expo. So the central government allows them to purchase power so that they can shut down their own coal-burning power plants. But the thing is different for Tianjin and Chongqing, they are the traditional industrial cities, they cannot simply rely on the purchased power. So they have to rely on their own coal-burning power plants and they have very limited purchase power. And then the carbon dioxide emission for industrial centers is still increasing, but both Beijing and Shanghai reduce their overall carbon dioxide emissions. Another fact is quite interesting, that's the brown part here that represents the carbon dioxide emission from the transportation sector. As you all know many Chinese families become richer,

Fig.1
Features, trajectories and driving forces for energy-related GHG emission from Chinese mega cities

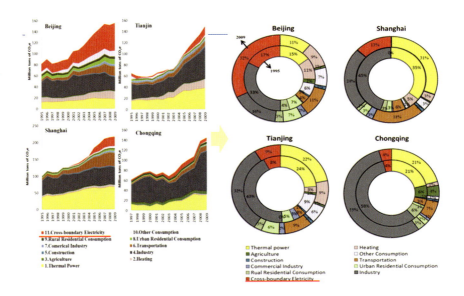

they have purchased vehicles, which really induce carbon dioxide emission from transportation sector. And then of course, it's not enough. We also need to know what are the key drivers to really reduce carbon dioxide emissions for mega cities. We actually employed approach called in-depth content analysis. We also found that increasing economic scale is the key driver to induce carbon dioxide emissions. You all know that many people move to big cities. They want to get jobs. The city government also wants to induce economic development. There are a lot of newly established industrial parks in the mega cities. So that one is the key driver to really induce higher carbon dioxide emissions. But of course, technology improvement is always functional and can offset carbon dioxide emissions, however, it is not enough. So in China the reality is that how we can improve the overall situation, not simply just reduce the emission intensity. That's not enough because the economic development is so fast.

Another key area is how we can account the complete picture of carbon dioxide emission at city level. In the case study of Shenyang which is located in north-eastern China. Within one city, there are a lot of movable sources like train, airplane and vehicles. It's very difficult . For example, I can drive a car from Suzhou to Shanghai. But actually I fueled my car in Suzhou, maybe I will fuel in Shanghai. So how you can count my carbon dioxide emission? From the direct information, that one should be accounted in Suzhou, not in Shanghai. So this kind of thing actually induces a lot of uncertainties. Therefore, in this paper (Fig.2), we present the rules how we can count those uncertain areas so that the complete carbon dioxide emissions can be presented to the decision makers. And similarly, people's behavior is also quite crucial. So we have to study the

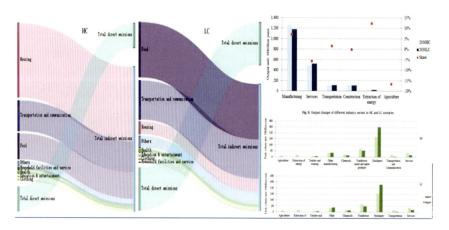

Fig.2
The effects
of household
consumption
pattern on
regional
development

effects of household consumption pattern. So in this paper we employed the GHG model. We tried to quantify the impact of human behaviors. As you all know in Chinese we will say, for all the daily life, it's "Yi Shi Zhu Xing", that means you need food, clothes, transportation and you also need to get really suitable housing. That's the key areas for people's daily life. However, you have to understand which sector is the key so that you can put more resources on that area. In this paper, we actually present that the carbon dioxide emission from human's transportation and housing are higher sectors. Therefore, we have to put more efforts to try to improve green transportation structures, to encourage people to use public transit system, rather than ask everyone to drive. And also in terms of housing, we have to consider the application of green buildings because that's very important so that we can drive some really efficient and mature technologies like green source heat pumps distribution system.

Table 1
Regional
application of
ground source
heat pump in
China

GHG emission reduction from GSHP application from 2006 to 2010		
Year	GCHP (10^4 ton)	GSHP (10^4 ton)	SWHP (10^4 ton)
2006	1.41	4.09	0.89
2007	4.47	26.20	6.15
2008	16.92	42.06	12.05
2009	26.74	61.17	16.91
2010	26.83	77.78	16.91
Sub-total	76.37	211.30	52.51
Energy savings from GSHP projects during 2006—2010		
Year	GCHP (TJ)	GSHP (TJ)	SWHP (TJ)
2006	464.30	1 639.25	356.41
2007	1 471.01	10 504.43	2 465.46
2008	5 570.11	16 862.73	4 831.50
2009	8 801.33	24 525.05	6 780.41
2010	8 832.80	31 185.10	6 780.41
Sub-total	25 139.55	84 716.56	21 214.19

So in this case of Shenyang, we try to quantify the impact of the application of the ground source heat pump in China (Table 1). That's a geothermal application. There is a five-month heating demand every year due to their climate zone. So the city government decided to employ the technologies of ground source heat pump. But they don't know how much carbon dioxide have been mitigated. We actually counted the contribution of the application ground source heat pump. From our calculation result, it's very clear, the application of this technology helped the whole city reduced 2.5 million carbon dioxide. That's a great achievement. It's almost 4% of the overall city carbon dioxide emissions. By presenting this kind of result, the mayor becomes more confident and supports application of those kind of technologies. And this explains why I need to really help and promote the application of those innovative efforts.

Here I just want to talk about the industrial carbon dioxide emissions. We all know that Chinese cities are a little different from western cities. We have a lot of industrial parks. They are the key source to generate carbon dioxide emissions. But the key is that how you can count the impact of the depreciation and also the achievement. So in this paper we present a hyper model, this is the case of Kawasaki (Fig.3). We combine life cycle assessment into our analysis. And the complete picture of carbon dioxide emissions can be presented to industrial park managers. And finally we also count how the innovative efforts of industrial & urban symbiosis can further reduce carbon emissions for the whole city. From our result, it's very clear, 15% of industrial emissions can be reduced for this whole industrial park. This kind of result can really provide a lot of confidence to the decision makers. And they will believe it is the right thing for them to do.

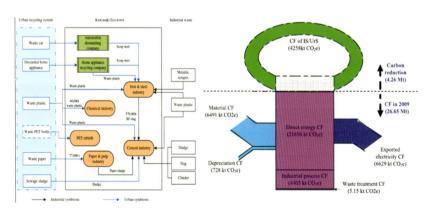

Fig.3
Achieving carbon emission reduction through industrial & urban symbiosis

Urban Transformation

Barjor Mehta

Lead Urban Specialist of Social, Rural, Urban &
Resilience Global Practice of World Bank

1. The trend and impact of urban transformation

I'm the last speaker of the day. My topic is mainly focused on the fact of some major trends that are going on in the economy. That is moving from a manufacturing-based to a service economy. That means a huge amount of demand difference on land and on people. There are opportunities to gain ground in services like finance, R&D, design, innovations, etc. And this requires very different skills. If you are actually a manufacturing economy and you move into a service economy, your skills have to change. So you move from an unskilled labor to skilled people, to very different type of jobs, and that changes the economy forces in different demand.

On the demography, we basically have "silver tsunami". As we grew older, I believe that we should pay more attention to the "silver tsunami". We have a rapidly aging population, a smaller workforce; we also have very young people in the economy. So in the cities you have relatively older and younger people at the same time. We basically have the two ends of the demographic side coming together. And their demands are different in some ways, but not different in others. The youngsters are far more footloose. They prefer to move from job to job. Their attitudes towards job are very different from those of the older people. Then we have the floating population of migrants who came in with unequal access to the urban services.

And all of these get into the urban land use. After an in-depth study of these cities, we realize that cities are becoming less dense, because the citizens are spread out, "they become pancakes other than wedding cakes". When they look back, what really happens is the sprawled land use. It decreases the overall density. Therefore, there is less available greenfield land for expansion.

These trends essentially lead toward higher demands of integrated and connected work spaces. So when you have a knowledge-based economy, you are basically looking at connected work spaces rather than large industrial areas and states, etc. On the land use planning side, that means putting demands on flexible land use. So you cannot fix the land use for too long as used to be in an industrial economy which uses it for many years. In the new economy, we basically need a land use which can change with the different demands. This affects the access to public transport, because you have footloose young people who are moving from place to place. And they are not buying as many cars as my generation used to buy. It's a burden for them to have a car with no parking-lot, etc. You basically have the two ends more or less demands together, thus you have the need for social integration and the equal access to basic services. This is becoming an issue repeated again and again in many different parts of the world.

2. The inclusiveness of urban planning

The global lesson from New York City is that instead of exclusionary zoning, we have the inclusionary zoning. The New York City wanted to build

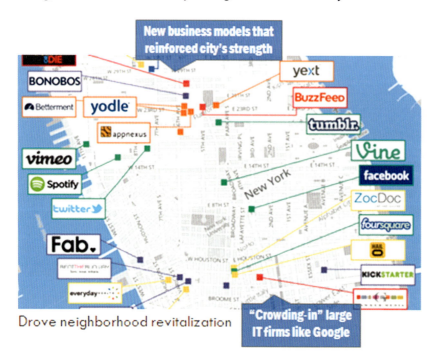

Fig.1
The innovation allies and corridors in New York City

large numbers of new jobs and attract new jobs at the time when their old industries were closing, and these are the innovation allies and corridors (Fig.1). It's similarly in Copenhagen.

We can also learn the global lessons from age-friendly cities (Fig.2). Generally, when we talk about age—friendly, people think about the older people. But age-friendly is also about the younger people. As your economy becomes more dependent on the knowledge economy, it has to become friendly to the younger people as well. That means it needs a different kind of urban design.

So cities of the future, we have been trying to say it again and again, will not be scared of design density and work with the design density. We align density with transit-oriented development wherever we use a special design. If transit and locations of jobs, density of jobs and stations increase, we will have much better quality of life. Therefore, you must allow flexibility in land use and incorporate mixed land use. That is to say, it's not necessary any more to have just one type of industrial use. Having a mixed land use is friendly to both the younger and older people. Actually, a very important thing is that you have this reality in the population, the younger people don't want to buy or own houses because they don't know where their next job will be. They want rental housing and the supply of rental housing is actually as important as it is to have flexible zoning and to promote inclusive urbanization to all, including age, background and gender.

Essentially, this is a theme we have repeated at the World Bank that it is very important to connect people and business, plan for livable, sustainable and inclusive city (Fig.3). However, my colleague is worried and saying earlier the day that we can't solve the problems by urban planning. I agree with him. All I would say is that once you have taken care of the larger picture, urban planning also matters equally.

Fig.3
Sustainable
Developed Cities

Remark

Cai Yongli (School of Geographical Science of East China Normal University): First, I will give a review on the reports made by the four speakers, and then I will give my personal comments. The four professors have presented us wonderful reports on the problems of urban development from four different angles. Professor Zhu focused on the methods, especially the indicators of evaluating the city development, and he has done a profound study on this aspect. He also put forward a proposal to improve the indicators, which has been adopted by the UN. I'm going to show my own view on this topic later on. The second speaker professor Aliza Fleischer mainly looked into agri-tourism in suburbs and has done a quantitative study on tourism in rural areas. Since Professor Che has done a lot of work on rural tourism, his feedback on this topic will be more persuasive. As for the third speaker Professor Geng, I do admire him because his English is better than my Chinese. He conducted a profound analysis on the emission and sources of greenhouse gases in China's major cities, on basis of which he has proposed many constructive solutions. The fourth professor put forward a very interesting topic, cities in the future. That is to have good expectations toward cities in the future. That is my review on what the four professors reported.

Now I'm going to show you my personal views. I'm working on the eco-city construction as well. I have gone to several typical cities in China and done some researches, so I have several viewpoints on this topic. My first view is that China is walking into two mistaken zones in developing eco-city. One is that we are not clear of what an eco-city actually is. The eco-city concept we stated is quite different from that stated in foreign countries, which puts emphasis on two aspects, energy exploitation and carbon emission. This is what we have concluded according to foreign cases we searched. However, the eco-city development involves too many aspects in China, including eco-city construction, living standards improvement and what Professor Geng mentioned, the pressure on carbon emission. That is to say, the problems faced by China are different from those faced by foreign countries in this perspective. China has more pressure in constructing eco-city. So the methods used by foreign countries in building or evaluating the eco-city are difficult to be applied in China.

What is another mistaken zone about? As we all know, there are several typical cities involved in eco-city building in China. The first is Dongtan, in Chongming Island, Shanghai. The area was the first to propose building itself into an ecological town, but it hasn't started yet. The second is Tianjing Eco-city. I have gone there and done some research, finding that it did achieve some results, but there are still many problems to be solved. The third is Cao Feidian Eco-city in Tangshan, Hebei Province. It has many debts and is now basically in failure. Therefore, we can see that China's eco-city construction is not successful.

Now there is another problem. When making evaluations on old cities in terms of their eco-city construction, we are not sure whether we should take eco-city as a goal or a goal to be attained. If there are a hundred cities, then there may be a hundred evaluation criteria. I am not very clear about that, because there is no such evaluation in foreign countries. Still another problem is that our standard on eco-city is different from that of foreign countries. If a city enjoys a good environment, but presents poor economic growth, should it be labeled as an eco-city? This problem often occurs, and it involves what Professor Zhu has mentioned how to weigh different indicators. I think different cities in different stages should have different goals and different criteria. Thus, if we use one standard to evaluate the eco-city development, we will face serious problems. This is one of my views on eco-city construction.

Then, I want to talk about regional cooperation and ecological compensation, which have been previously mentioned by the first speaker, Professor Garo Batmanian. I am working on the eco-city development of the

Yangtze River Delta area, and my viewpoint may contradict to that of Professor Zhu. That is, it is difficult for mega cities like Shanghai to achieve ecological balance simply by itself, and we must put it in the large context. And this involves several difficulties. The first is the flowing air pollution. That means if you take quality of air as the indicator, Shanghai cannot meet the standard no matter how good a work it does in protecting the environment, because you just cannot separate the air in one area from that in other areas. The second is that the water quality of Shanghai, in the lower reaches of Yangtze River, can be affected by that in the upper reaches. So, our water quality can be lowed immediately, no matter how wonderful a work we have done in treating the Suzhou River and Huangpu River, if Zhejiang discards dead pigs and Jiangsu emits pollutants into the river. Therefore, if you take the two indicators as the standard, no matter how hard we work, we cannot meet the standard of an eco-city. We must put the city in a broader context. If we try to build an eco-city independently, it is very difficult to build an eco-city in the real sense, unless there is a day to come when cities all over China enjoy good environment.

Here comes the problem of ecological compensation. I have come to Huangshan, the first place in China involved in the course, and problems emerged in the compensation process. Shanghai and Zhejiang, in the lower reaches, have given some compensation about five million RMB, to Huangshan which is located in the upper and middle reaches. But the Municipal Government of Huangshan thought it is too little, thus it prefers promoting economic growth rather than accepting the compensation. The problem is that it is mandatory for them to meet the standard on water quality. Then inequality exists in the development of different cities and different regions, which has been mentioned by a British professor, because we have restricted the development of Huangshan by forcing such a requirement on the city. What other aspects did Huangshan complain of? It thinks that it has been forced to control discharges and emissions, but in the lower reaches, cities like Hangzhou are developing polluting industries which it does not allow Huangshan to do, such as fish breeding. All these problems require us to establish a fair and feasible mechanism for regional cooperation. I think that China has just started in regional cooperation, and there are still a lot of challenges and problems.

Dialogue

Audience: Hello, everyone, I share a common idea with Professor Cai on regional cooperation and ecological compensation. I did a lot of study on water resources in Suzhou Creek and Taihu Lake. At that time, I had an idea about cross-regional ecological compensation and co-governance. So in the future, with the coordination of the central government, are Shanghai and Jiangsu able to improve the environment and their economy through regional ecological compensation as well as joint efforts on governance of economy, environment and water safety? If this goal can be achieved, Shanghai can gain a safe water source from Taihu Lake.

Garo Batmanian: Of course, we need such coordination. But in China, the problem is that our ecological compensation is more driven by the government, while in the rest of the world, it is a mechanism more driven by the market than by the government. In New York City, if people want to use clean water, they have to pay for the water company. But in China, the government gets involved in the project and gives subsidies to the participants. So we can say from this perspective that those who use clean energy do not pay for the clean energy they use. Instead, the government is assuming the burden. This is not sustainable in the long run, and the government should not give the subsidies. President Xi also emphasized that the market should play a more important role. Now the mechanism is gradually changing. Users of clean energy should at least bear part of the cost, otherwise such ecological compensation is entirely a burden for the government. There are more than 60 ecological compensation projects in our country. If all is paid by the government, it will be a great burden.

Audience: I would like to ask Professor Zhu Dajian a question. It can be said that the vast majority of cities in China were in the state of the first quadrant before the implementation of the reform policy. They could not go in a straight line to the second quadrant. At present, this state is developing ramped up as a whole, and a large number of cities in the west may still be in the first quadrant. But after having done some planning on some western cities, I feel somewhat worried. Although the national policy is inclined toward the west and green industries are moving into the region, the cities in the west are actually repeating the old road of the east, considering their local development and their understanding of economic development. I would like to listen to your views. Is there a good solution to avoid the deterioration of the west of China?

Zhu Dajian: This is a very good question, which involves how cities should be and how they actually are. Actually, China should not go the old road of outweighing development over environment which was adopted by the Western countries. This is what we often say. However, with the passing of the time, we become more and more afraid to talk about this topic. In fact, the east and west are taking the road from the first quadrant to the third quadrant. But the west still have a chance. I would like to say just a little more. I feel sorry that we have done the research on some indicators for four years, but only one city was found in the second quadrant, that is Xiamen. But it did not remain in the second quadrant, but somewhat went to the third quadrant. This policy is really difficult to control.

FORUM V

分论坛五

Protection and Inheritance of Urban Culture
城市文化传承与保护

主持人 · HOST
陆邵明 · Lu Shaoming
上海交通大学城市空间文化与科学研究中心教授
Professor of the Institute of Urban Spatial Culture and Science of
Shanghai Jiao Tong University

孙一民 · Sun Yimin
华南理工大学建筑学院常务副院长
Executive Vice Dean of School of Architecture of
South China University of Technology

城市文化保护与传承分论坛现场嘉宾聆听演讲

Guests at the Protection and Inheritance of Urban Culture Parallel
Forum are listening to the speeches attentively

上海交通大学城市空间文化与科学研究中心教授陆邵明主持平行分论坛五并作专题演讲

Lu Shaoming, Professor of the Institute of Urban Spatial Culture and Science of
Shanghai Jiao Tong University, hosts the Parallel Forum V，and delivers a speech

华南理工大学建筑学院常务副院长孙一民主持平行分论坛五

Sun Yimin, Executive Vice Dean of School of Architecture of South China
University of Technology, hosts the Parallel Forum V

英国利物浦大学建筑中心主任和视觉艺术创始主任理查德·科克在平行分论坛五上作专题演讲

Richard Koeck, Founder and Director of Visual Arts and Director of Architecture
Center of University of Liverpool, delivers a speech at the Parallel Forum V

南京艺术学院教授李立新在平行分论坛五上作专题演讲

Li Lixin, Professor of Nanjing University of the Arts, delivers a speech at the Parallel Forum V

上海交通大学船舶海洋与建筑工程学院教授王林在平行分论坛五上作专题演讲

Wang Lin, Professor of School of Naval Architecture, Ocean and Civil Engineering of Shanghai Jiao Tong University, delivers a speech at the Parallel Forum V

上海交通大学人文学院院长刘恩芳教授在平行分论坛五上作点评

Liu Enfang, Professor and Dean of School of Humanities of Shanghai Jiao Tong University, comments on the Parallel Forum V

北京大学建筑与景观设计学院教授汪芳在平行分论坛五上作专题演讲

Wang Fang, Professor of School of Architecture and Landscape Architecture of Peking University, delivers a speech at the Parallel Forum V

上海档案馆编研部主任总编曹胜梅在平行分论坛五上作专题演讲

Cao Shengmei, Chief Editor of Compiling and Research Department
of Shanghai Archives, delivers a speech at the Parallel Forum V

南京艺术学院教授李立新在平行分论坛五上作点评

Li Lixin, Professor of Nanjing Arts College, comments on the Parallel Forum V

城市可视性：城市遗产保护背景下的意象策略

理查德·科克

英国利物浦大学建筑中心主任和视觉艺术创始主任

今天上午肖林教授提到的修订后的经济战略很好，他特别提到要重视城市文化和遗产的保护。我想补充一点，就是共享空间也很重要。肖林教授在他的演讲中也提到了共享空间是软环境。与历史遗产联系在一起的共享空间，对于世界范围内全球城市的发展具有重要意义。

1. 软性城市及其重要性

上世纪70年代，有位作家乔纳森·雷班撰写了一本书，书名叫《软性城市》。软性城市这个概念也是我今天演讲当中要格外强调的。软性城市就是我们记忆中的城市，是我们大脑想象的城市。硬性城市就是现实中的城市，是由钢筋水泥构建的城市。雷班认为，软性城市可以和硬性城市一样真实。我认为，软性城市在社会、文化、建筑、经济、旅游等方面都具有重要意义，有利于提升城市吸引力，即城市吸引投资、吸引知识、吸引人才的能力。同时，软性城市在依托共享空间来分享城市特质也起着至关重要的作用。由于软性城市是通过城市叙事在我们的记忆和头脑中形成与构建，因此如何保护、塑造城市叙事就显得特别重要。城市叙事不仅是基于我们的概念，也是基于对地点的感知——由都市环境和嵌入整个城市框架形象塑造而共同形成。接下来，我将以"城市可视性：城市遗产保护背景下的意象策略"为题，结合城市意象所涉及的实体形象、空间以及人等三方面，通过案例对人们如何把历史性时刻、历史档案，以及其他流动的或静止的形象融入城市景观和风貌当中等进行介绍。也将把人们关于如何使用城市形象构建空间、塑造叙事与软性城市等方面的使用策略一并分享给大家。

2. 城市可视性创新的案例

城市意象涉及三个方面，一是我们的实体形象，如建筑功能空间等；另外是空间，还有就是在我看来最重要的人。这三个形象，人、物和空间结合在一起，不管是在现实领域还是在数字领域，都是我的研究对象。首先，我讲一个大家比较熟悉的内容。这个策略是充分利用城市的历史形象，并与公众分享。在下一个案例中我们可以看到把博物馆和美术馆作为可控的环境给人们展示城市的过去。我们在利物浦博物馆中制作了一个互动装置，其展现的是我对利物浦这座城市里拍摄的最古老的电影文化研究，可追溯到 1897 年。人们不仅可以进入互动装置，置身于呈现的历史图像中；还可以在利物浦博物馆的屏幕上看到穿过整个城市的行程，以坐在火车里的视角观看车窗外原始的景观。通过档案影像，人们就可以追寻 100 年前火车上电影拍摄者的脚步，游览整个城市。在很多美术馆、博物馆当中也都有类似的演示方法。

我在研究中探讨的另外一个概念，就是把城市作为一种有形的互动界面。这是我几年前的一个想法。制作这些装置，把历史档案连接起来变成动画在屏幕上演示，已经很棒了。但我的想法则不同，我想做的是用脚步丈量城市，去亲自体会这个城市的遗产，所以就有了发展便携城市历史这个想法。英国在这方面已经有几个项目。其中一个是比较有名的伦敦博物馆项目，他们开发了一款手机应用，可以让人们在漫游伦敦时，一边在街上走，一边去了解城市。如果游客到达某一个特定地点，他们可以举起手机，并看到过去发生在该地点上的档案照片浮在空中。通过手机摄像头，图像和地点相互衔接，显现在手机画面上。柏林也有一个项目，就是柏林墙附近场景的项目，这个项目很漂亮。因为大部分柏林墙已经消失，所以这一历史的建筑遗产已经被城市拆除。柏林利用手机应用把档案资料叠加在建筑的表面，人们可以直接播放历史影像。也就是说，该手机应用依托城市留存的实物或遗迹，与原来的档案资料相重叠，让人们可以通过手机观看和体验。伦敦巴特西区也研发了一款手机应用。在过去一百年有很多电影在巴特西区拍摄，该区也曾经拥有超过 25 家电影院。通过手机应用，在街上漫游的游客一旦走到曾经影院的地点，手机就会提醒。此时，人们可以举起手机，观察曾经电影院的外观以及在该影院拍摄的电影片断。我将这种通过手机重现的历史，称为便携数字历史。

这里我再简单提及另外一个概念，就是把城市作为一个有形的界面，通过这种形式希望能够保存城市的一些表面或者形象。大家可以在欧洲到处看到，在中国也能够看到。比如说某栋历史建筑需要翻新或者历史街区需要重建时，保护城市形象、保留历史风貌日益重要。比如，布拉格向建筑者施压，希望建筑者制作一些材料置于重建或翻新建筑物的表面，以保留城市的形象，保留城市的历史遗产，维持其作为历史建筑的感觉。同时，类似"翻新"措施也可以有效隐藏不宜展示的城市形象。比如，当时我们要在利物浦举办一次文化遗产活动，城市管理者认为部分建筑物不适合展示给游客。所以他们给这些建筑物外面挂上在文化活动中适宜展示的图像，让这些不宜展示的建筑物"消失"。

我们还有一个想法，就是把在柏林推出的意象称为城市的历史记忆。柏林很重要的一个地方——莱比锡广场需要重建，但柏林市没有寻找到重建莱比锡广场的投资。为了再现广场过去的形象，他们制作了一个全尺寸的模型，让人们假想历史上的莱比锡广场仍存在的实际效果，有效展示了柏林市为重建中心空间的努力程度。此外，柏林还为人们提供了通向过去的门或窗户，即当人们走在路上，可以发现一些相关的档案或早期的元素。接下来要讲的是中国的案例，南京的老门东，它是历史韵味非常浓厚的地方，整条街道的台阶都刻画着 100 年前的街景图。当人们触摸了这些图画，他们将有强烈的愿望去与图画沟通，抑或穿梭时空，回到一百年前这些图画所展示的时代。

3. 混合现实的时代正向我们走来

过去一百年，人和屏幕是分离的，我们已经习惯了看向屏幕。未来，这将会发生反转。这是基于两个事实而得出的结论：一是越来越多的屏幕，尤其是屏幕背后的网络希望能够回过来看我们，比如说广告；二是我们已经进入了一个混合现实、超越屏幕的时代，人们和屏幕之间的有形边界会逐步消失。如果大型软件公司可以实现愿景，在未来我们将会看到一个混合现实，通过佩戴设备，就能够把图片、3D 动画、活动图像、电影加在日常生活场景中，如一面墙、一张桌子、一座城市、一个长凳，如此人类就能够走入屏幕，以前所未有的方式体验这种场景。

六朝烟水与造物记忆

李立新

南京艺术学院教授

六朝是中国历史上最辉煌、最有创造力的一个时代，也是最被低估、最被忽略的一个时代。今天我以"六朝烟水与造物记忆"为题，通过六朝时期的造物和城市文化对这个时代进行重新评估。

1. 六朝选择在南京建都的原因

在公元 3 世纪到 6 世纪末，中国历史上的三国东吴，之后的东晋，南朝的宋、齐、梁、陈皆建都在建康（即今南京）。中国古代非常重视都城的选择。春秋时期管仲就说凡立国都要么是在大山之下，要么是在大平原上。我曾去过管仲所在齐国的都城，即现在的山东临淄，发现齐国国都就是在大平原上。中国古代选择都城的条件主要是三点：经济、军事、地理。当时，六朝的第一个朝代是东吴，有三个地方可以选择：第一个是春秋时期吴国的首都，即现在的苏州，但是那里远离长江，不利于扩张；第二个是京口，即现在的镇江，但是在镇江的对面，吴王夫差开凿了一条邗江，通过这条江，北方的军队可以直接冲击镇江，所以它不安全；第三个是武昌，武昌是个军事重镇，守住武昌，整个江南就安全了，但因为武昌地处长江上游，江南一带的物资运输需要逆流而上，所以不能在武昌建都。当时有一句民谣"宁饮建业水，不食武昌鱼"，因此最终选择了建康，即现在的南京。南京的地理位置十分特殊，其西边是长江，北边是玄武湖，东边是钟山，南边是秦淮河，构成了一个天然的防御屏障。

2. 六朝时期的建筑记忆

我们现在对六朝的记忆，大多是借用后来诗人的一些诗句。比如，"无情最是台城柳"，实际上这个台城和六朝的台城相去甚远。又如，古诗《乌衣巷》中所说，乌衣巷里面有王谢两大家族，王导是帮助东晋南渡立下大功的宰相，王导的侄子就是王羲之，这个家族的贡献显著；谢安是淝水之战的指挥官，他以8万晋军打败了北方来犯的80万大军，同时谢家还出了大诗人谢灵运。但是现在乌衣巷、朱雀桥早已不是当时的样式，现在六朝时期的唯一遗址是最近南京城发掘出来的御道。我们说石头城代表南京，但是考古学家认为石头城是明代所建，并不是六朝时期的（图1）。

图1
石头城

再如，《资治通鉴》里曾提及建康的宫殿，其外廓是一个巨大的竹篱。建康城有三层，最中间是用砖砌起来的，非常华丽、豪华；外面一层都城是用泥土建造起来的；最外的城隔是一种竹篱的样式。西晋的左思在《吴都赋》描述的东吴都城工程非常华丽和真实。现在东吴建筑的唯一遗存就是人面瓦当（图2）。考古学家认为人面瓦当有它的谜，只是东吴有，东吴结束后，人面瓦当就不存在了。到了东晋，就出现了兽面瓦当（图2），不知其从何而来，于是也成为了一个谜。但是图3左边的人面瓦当在西汉山东的东平陵曾经出土过，右边的人面瓦当是湖北鄂州早期的吴王城井里面出土的。从东平陵到鄂州城再到建业城形成了传播学上的一个链接，也就是说东吴的建筑样式必然是来自北方，而不是凭空形成的。

图 2
人面瓦当与兽面瓦当

人面瓦当　　　　　　　　兽面瓦当

图 3
西汉与东吴时期人面
瓦当的比较

东平陵西汉　　　　　　　鄂州吴王城-东吴早期

所谓后来的兽面瓦当，是人面瓦当逐渐演变形成的。东吴晚期的人面瓦当，脸上有很多线纹，到了东晋早期线纹越来越明显，人的脸逐渐变成了动物的脸。到了东晋的中期和南朝就形成了兽面纹，图像学上是一个演变的过程。从人脸到兽面的变化，实际上是造型上的规律。东吴时期选择人面，是因为"天生神物，以应王者"，为东吴建国提供一种合法性。到了东晋以后，不存在合法性。此时面对北方的大军压境，出现了一种"避兵除凶"的心理，所以兽面在那时候逐渐兴盛起来。这可以看出六朝时期的造物并不是一成不变的。

另外，建康园林强调和自然的融合（图4）。诗句中南朝有四百八十寺，其实寺庙大概有七百多所。六朝定都建康有四方面的意义：第一，政治中心与军事中心分离，并开创了政治中心与经济中心结合的先例；第

图 4
建康园林

二，政治经济中心南移，从东晋开始移到了南方，同时推进了城市经济和文化的全面繁荣；第三，高度集权的统一王朝消失，从动乱分裂走向再度统一；第四，文化上汉代经学消退，玄学、佛学、道学兴起，形成了三位一体的局面。

3. 六朝时期的器物记忆

描写六朝时期画面的诗句，总是比较华丽，正所谓"江南佳丽地，金陵帝王州"。但是对六朝城市文化新格局的理解，不能仅仅从诗歌、宗教、政治、思想等方面来解释，而应结合"物"的世界来把握。那时，贵族的服装和出行工具都不同于汉代。

佛教进入中国以后，象征着佛教的莲花开始在瓷器等生活器物上大量出现。中国的瓷器从西周的原始瓷开始到六朝时技术已经成熟，达到高峰；甚至普通的锄头上也有莲花的样式，装饰非常华丽；当时煮茶喝茶的风气开始盛行，一些煮茶相关的用具上也出现了莲花图案。其中很多器物并不是中国自己生产的，而是来自西亚，这表明东西方交流频繁。六朝时期的权贵就以此来炫耀财富。与此相反，六朝时期的文人，如竹林七贤，他们蔑视这种权贵。例如，嵇康的《广陵散》并不是存在意义上的音乐，而是内含批判现实的思想。另外，平民的器物也十分丰富，如漆器、挖耳勺、棒槌、剪刀。这不同于汉代传统的城市文化新格局，是在遗传和变异中间形成的，这就是六朝文化的基因——在普通器物中的体现。

六朝的城市生活并不平静，经常出现战乱，就像杜牧的诗里面讲到"商女不知亡国恨"，最终都亡国了。被李约瑟称为改变了世界历史进程的马镫是中国人发明的，马镫最早是在西晋发明的，但是西晋的马镫是木头做的，外面包了镏金的铜皮。真正用于战争的马镫是在东晋，东晋时期为了对抗北方的侵犯出现了铁马镫，对付骑兵的铁蒺藜、平头短刀等。

4. 六朝时期的文化记忆

侯景之乱使得梁朝灭亡，也宣告了六朝城市文化的终结，陈朝只是落日余晖。现在散落在南京周边的这些巨大设施，虽然被风化，变得残缺，成为失落的坐标，但它依然威严雄伟，向我们展示了一个辉煌的时代。六朝城市文化的特征包容、吸收、共存，这有利于形成开放交流的城市文机制。这三大特征形成的主要原因包括：一是对人和生命价值的重视和表现；二是对自然美的发现，王羲之的书法、顾恺之的绘画，都是对自然美的发现、欣赏；三是佛道思想的影响和体现，深刻地影响了六朝的城市观念和人们的精神价值取向，比如竹林七贤这样的人物。通过中外交流、南北相荣、佛道互补、相互叠合，促成了中国历史上第一次大规模和外部世界的交流，也深刻影响了中国文化的历史发展。包容、吸收和共存，直到现在还是南京的城市特征。因此，当我们说到六朝，只说它政治上是分裂的，甚至是偏安的、短促的，轻视其地位和实际贡献是片面的。六朝的城市文化既创造了六朝人的生活价值，同时也创造了六朝人生命的价值，体现出了中古时期中国文化的智慧，应该是世界文明史的一个典范。

城市保护与有机更新
——上海实践与创新思维

王 林

上海交通大学船舶海洋与建筑工程学院教授

在城市发展过程中，历史保护一直是上海在过去十年中坚守的一个底线，但是面临的问题和困难非常大。因为我们是在一个发展的城市中做历史遗产保护工作，所以这种协同发展、共享利益和在坚持底线基础上的创新思维，是我们在城市未来发展、历史遗产保护和城市有机更新中应当坚持的理念。

《上海城市总体规划（2016—2040）》在提出"卓越的全球城市"目标时所放的一张图片，是在上海石库门里弄拍的一个儿童。这代表城市的记忆，要永远留在这个世界，在人的一生中传承。城市记忆不仅仅是老人的记忆，而应该是整个全人类的宝贵财富，也应该从年轻人开始。15 分钟社区生活圈是对上海未来规划的一个理念想法，但也应该在 15 分钟内找到上海的历史或者上海的历史记忆。

1. 上海历史保护面临的困难和挑战

一是快速增加的人口对历史保护造成压力。上海处于快速发展时期，在过去的 10—15 年中，人口每年以 50—100 万的速度增加。在这样巨大的压力下，历史保护工作面临新的挑战。二是原来的历史遗产地尤其是历史街区城市密度非常低，其面临着高容积率和城市发展利益的挑战。如何在城市发展过程中，既保持城市的多元性，传承城市的历史，又完成城市的有机更新和有机发展，是我们必须解决的一个问题。

在上一轮《上海市城市总体规划（1999—2020）》编制过程中，我们提出三个"三分之一"：三分之一的土地用于城市建设，三分之一的土地用于生态建设，三分之一的用于农田。但是目前上海约二分之一的土地已经被城市建设所占用，所以在新一轮的城市总体规划中提出 2040 规划的建设用地就是 2020 年的规划指标，2030、2040、2050 年不再有增量，面临这样的情况，我们需要进行重新思考。比如，上海源头包括了外滩和陆家嘴地区，但不同地区的尺度是完全不同的。城市仍然存在许多空间可发展，不需要通过摧毁历史遗产保护的建筑来兴建城市，这些城市肌理、城市空间，甚至一百米宽的大道，是否存在合理性，毕竟并非一定要宏大的建筑、宏大叙事的风格，而是需要适合我们的城市生活。随着城市社会发展，在新的基础上我们有无可能重新思考。其实上海在历史街区的尺度里，跟西方很多国家的核心区相同，是否有可能在新的规划、新的城市建设包括建筑，或者原有建设里，进行适当修复？这也是历史文化传承中非常重要的问题。

2. 上海城市遗产保护的规划和案例

2005 年，上海划定了一百处历史保护建筑。虽然当时交通问题非常严重，并且只有两条轨道交通，但是我们认为上海不能再拓宽城市道路，而应该发展大规模轨道交通。为此，划定了 144 条风貌保护道路，其中 64 条永远不拓宽。比如复兴东路现在宽是 18.3 米而当时规划的是 32 米。又如，老厂房似乎是破败了，没有意义了，功能也已经消失了，但是很多地方街道工厂搬走以后，被改造成小剧院、小咖啡厅和联合设计室。在静安区如此核心的地方，老厂房的肌理也被留下来了，保留了城市记忆。再如，上海的龙华机场。当时那里的建筑即将被拆除，而我们认为里面可以举行大型的城市活动，应该被保留。这条马路本是龙华街道原来的机场跑道，通过改建成跑步道，形成了跑步公园。记忆保留对城市而言非常重要，当然可以采取多元化的传承手法，通过景观、建筑、结构，甚至再利用，而不仅仅是博物馆式保护。

第一个案例是关于外滩的历史遗产保护和城市更新。这个案例是在政府的牵头下由开发商共同完成。外滩地区是上海的第一块租界，是上海城市的源头。经过多年的城市发展以及我们的努力，保留了所有的历史建筑，也赋予了它新的功能。但是吴淞路闸桥、友谊商店以及很多原来政府六层楼的办公楼都被拆了，所有的新建都是在老建筑的后面。城市在生长，我们不能拒绝城市的生长，但是我们要保护好历史。历史保护很重要的一点是恢复城市的公共空间，外滩原来是对老百姓开放的。在 2008 年、

2010 年之前，所有人要穿过十个车道，才能进入外滩的空间，现在把六个车道放到地下，保持了城市历史街区和滨江空间的可达性，人们可以走路到达，体现了以人为本的理念。

第二个案例是关于田子坊。它是由百姓和艺术家提出，政府在协调了开发商的各方利益之后达成了由下至上的历史保护。田子坊的空间是多元复合的。2003 年，这块土地已经被批租了。经过研究以后，提出历史遗产保护、公共空间维护、创意产业园区开发等三个理由，而且最重要的是这个开发商同时拥有南边和这边两块土地，所以我建议把所有的容积率转移到南边的地块，把这块地留下来，才有了现在的田子坊。

第三个是历史街区的规划和设计。通过规划和设计，在城区中促成城市的有效保护和有机更新。在城市治理过程中，我们要坚持协同治理。有时候政府不要做全部的事情，要充分发挥民间的力量，但是政府需完成维护公共利益的部分。这种协同的关系会促进城市更加多元、更加有机，以及更多的共享发展。

最后一个是新场。它是通过一个实践活动来促进城市的发展。新场是江南的古镇，但是知名度不高。因此我们邀请顶尖的设计师和媒体，要求所有的设计师在当地做设计，贯穿人们的日常生活。这些专门为新场而做的设计，受到了百姓的欢迎。所以，规划设计需要植根于土地，植根于历史文化，也要符合当代的需要。

此外，治理和多元性都非常重要，不是只有非常辉煌的建筑才可以保留。像建于 1991 年的华东电力大楼这样的建筑，也要保留下来。为了更好地理解城市空间的意象，我们通过规划把上海所有历史街区现有的建筑做了一个地毯式的普查，把每一个建筑做了一个定义，这种定义可能随着社会发展还会有所调整。我们认为老建筑都是要贴着道路红线建的，所有的绿化率、建筑退建、城市肌理、空间要求都要尊重这个地区文化和肌理。

最后，规划是城市治理的源头，城市设计是政策的工具。我们要利用城市规划的公共政策，以城市设计来协调和平衡各方的利益，用城市规划的方法来协调各方的关系。这是城市治理里面授之以理、动之以情、诱之以利、绳之以法的方法。当然，城市的保护和更新都要有利于传承，有利于经济环境和政治等综合发展。希望文化历史传承不仅在城市中植根，而且在方方面面都能够植根。

专家点评

刘恩芳（上海交通大学人文学院院长、教授）：刚才五位嘉宾给了我们特别精彩、特别丰富的演讲，我从中得到了很多的启发。联合国当时设立"世界城市日"，旨在要让更多的人、更多的国家来关注城市可持续发展，让更多的人来关注和发现在城市化过程中，全球所面临的问题，而且更进一步发现如何应对这些问题。

今天三位嘉宾从不同的视角、不同的切入点，给我们展现了在现代城市发展过程中解决问题的方式，每个地区可能面对的问题不一样，解决方法也会多样。这些解决问题的途径和方法十分丰富，也给我们带来了深刻的思考。今天这个"记忆"的主题特别强调了在城市发展当中，全球都可能会面临的问题。我们身在上海，或是身在世界其他城市，都能感觉到城市文化的传承以及记忆在城市文化传承当中的作用，我自己也感同身受。刚才理查德·科克教授给我们展现了一个全新的视角，他把历史遗产和当代生活相结合，比如用互联网手段——手机上的应用软件，让人们身临其境地感受到每个街区不同历史的场景呈现，这是非常有价值的。既是教授又曾是城市管理者的王林则从城市管理的角度进行了探讨。其他教授和嘉宾也是从不同的角度，比如从历史等方面探讨了城市文化。各位专家的演讲都给我们带来了深刻的启发。

北京城市记忆：历史建筑与历史街区

汪 芳

北京大学建筑与景观设计学院教授

2007 年，我投标参加北京宣武区的项目，获得了第一名。当时做城市记忆研究的时候，还是属于档案馆类，或者是博物馆类的。2009、2010 年我又接连申请北京市自然基金和国家自然基金，都是以城市记忆为主题，在这个过程中，城市记忆反而变成了自己的主要研究内容。当时我做宣武区的城市记忆规划时，还是从比较传统的规划学的视角，从碎片的信息、空间载体的信息以及如何把它进行重现的思路在做。在研究过程中，"主体、客体、时间"三个词慢慢凸显出来，除开比较熟知的客体规划之外，城市记忆应该与主体的认知以及时间序列的梳理是相关的，除了时间轴，还有一些典型的时间剖面，以及重要的相关事件。我们常说要做一个街区更新的时候，到底应该选择哪个时间段作为它的主导记忆呈现，这常常是我们工作中遇到的一个问题。现在城市记忆已经纳入我自身的研究视野。

1. 城市记忆研究框架

在学科构建方面，我认为城市记忆应该还是属于传承地方的特色、对城市文化进行丰富和发展的重要途径。它和传统的规划学科所关注的静态元素相比，加入了动态的元素。为此，在研究期间我构建了一个城市记忆的理论，包括构建一个客体主体时间自主研发记忆因子正交分解技术、空间互相关分析技术，获得软件著作权。从内外两种作用力、城乡两类人群的视角、点线面三种空间尺度构建模型。

关于内外作用力，城市记忆一直是属于动态、变化的过程。从它的内在来说，像老城区由于旧城改造，原有的居民搬出去了，外地的打工人群住进来，当主体发生变化的时候，记忆会发生断崖式的变化。还有原来是用作居住的，结果在功能转化中变成了会馆，或者是变成了茶馆、餐厅的，就像原来的名人故居，这种空间转化的过程中也会有记忆，因为使用方式发生变化了。从外作用力来说，社会本身发展的状态，例如现在的关键词就是快速城镇化，城镇化导致外来人口大量涌入，使得原来那些在老北京城里面放鸽子、溜蝈蝈的老北京人搬到五环以外，住在老社区里面的人来自河南、安徽，各地来打工的集聚成群的新移民，这些人群的涌入，毕竟跟政策是直接相关的，有时候这种记忆的发展是缓慢的，这种变化是不知不觉的，但有时候在一个比较强大的外界作用力的情况下，很有可能今年和前五年、前十年相比就发生了相当大的变化。

针对城乡这两种人群，我曾在出版的书中以北京旧城的历史建筑中轴线承沿历史阶段为对象进行居民认知的调查，然后对北京内城的 345 处历史建筑进行研究，发现在这个过程中，不同居民的认知差别非常大。我们刚刚对北京前门进行了调查，住在前门街区和住在二环以内的人和像我这种虽是北京户口但其实是读书以后留在北京工作，且住在五环以外的人，对前门的认知差别非常之大。虽然都是对北京的认知，但是人的主体身份不同，对记忆认知的结果就存在差异。我们还做了关于人的乡村记忆的研究。北京有很多的农村改造，随着城市的蔓延和扩张，农民搬进了新的城市社区，他们因为对传统的乡村生活情感上难以割舍，会对城市社区进行自发性的改变，因此我们就从他的改变动机、态度以及空间改造类型上进行了研究。

2. 城市记忆研究案例

三种尺度上，在点状尺度上我选了两类，一种是名人故居，一种是旧城大杂院。名人是属于有身份的人，可能他原来在政治、经济、文化上具有影响，他们搬出之后，原来居住的故居在记忆主体变迁之后发生变化。大杂院居住的是普通的市民，记忆在大杂院几次的变迁中逐渐变化，我们以解放 60 年来的变化，对其进行了自发性空间演变模态的研究。在线状空间方面，我是在做中轴线研究时，发现了城市记忆研究的空间尺度问题，包括适应范围和边界。尽管这个确定起来有点模糊，类似于像北京很出名的东西南北两条轴线，但是在认知上东西南北各自的终点差别很大，所以关于记忆，它的空间对应尺度的关系，也是我们比较关注的问题。在面状空间方面，我们选择两个案例跟大家分享，一个是关于人的情感认知。北京奥运会的时候，有一些胡同人家的项目，即胡同人家接待外宾，在这个过程中会出现情感幕布的问题，像原来我住在这里，可能早上就喝豆汁、吃油条，外国人过来感觉不太适应豆汁的味道，就改良为豆浆，这个过程有点改变我自己的生活方式来适应新的需求，但这个中间必定会有空间防线和情感防线。那么，我们正在研究这个防线处于什么位置，保存下来才能对大杂院和胡同的记忆保存有利。另外一种类型，是选取了鸽哨景观。在曹禺的著作《老北京人》里面，第一章有六个地方提到了钟鼓楼放鸽哨的场景，这个场景五年前还比较能见到，现在比较少。这也是因为居民的变迁之后，人不同了，他们的生活方式也发生了转变，因此我们这个叙事框架能不能记忆主体诉求，大家愿不愿意记忆，以及目前的时代背景和环境下让不让记忆，这几个环节进行鸽哨景观的研究。

最后，我认为，在城市记忆发展历程中，有些记忆本身是经过遴选的，有时候你非要刻意把它保持下来，就像城市布景，更像一个游戏的空间、体验的空间，并不是我们真实的空间，所以记忆的保存选取什么样的断面留下来，会不会在未来重新适合的土壤中，自己再萌芽出来。是不是有永远消失的记忆，有一种能保存下来的记忆，还有也许有一段中断、但是又可以在新的土壤当中萌芽的记忆，因此记忆本身是割舍不掉的，有时候必须放弃，有时候必须维系它。

留住城市的"乡愁"
——从上海市档案文献遗产评选谈起

曹胜梅

上海档案馆编研部主任、总编

乡愁肯定不独是对乡村的一种情感，从希腊的词源上来考证，语义宽泛得多，泛指对故土的眷恋，我们每个人都有对故土的眷恋，当然有城市也有乡村。

上海市档案馆保存着自上海 1843 年开埠前后，一直到上世纪八九十年代重要的官方记录，馆藏量已经超过 360 万卷件了。因为上海历史上也曾经有一段时间是有租界的，租界的历史差不多有 100 年，包括法租界、公共租界当局的城市管理档案也都在上海市档案馆收藏着。研究上海历史的中外学者中有相当一部分都会到上海市档案馆查阅档案。

1. 城市记忆及其困境

今天分论坛的主题是记忆。记忆有个体的记忆，也有城市的记忆。记忆是需要被唤醒的，通过文字、图象、影像就可以使记忆再现。说到上海的城市记忆，一座城市的历史记忆和文化个性不仅是生活在其间人们的乡愁之源，也是城市居民文化认同的精神纽带。在我们档案馆当中有各个时期有关外滩的照片，这里我们可以看到 1890 年和 1925 年两张外滩的景象（图 1），图片非常直观，就能够看到整个外滩区域的变化。这也是从上海市档案馆看到的外滩的全景。

记忆跟遗忘是一对矛盾，所以我们需要用种种的方式去唤醒记忆。关于记忆的毁灭，有各种因素，比如贫穷、灾害、战火、无知等等。关于记忆的缺失包含两个方面，一种是有意的缺失，一种是无意的缺失。有意的缺失从城市方面来说，肯定也有一部分的弱者，可能他的记忆在里面没有得到充分的体现。

图 1
1890 年（上）1925
年（下）外滩全景

2. 城市记忆的收集

　　城市记忆的保护和传承，需要全社会机构的力量、需要民间的力量。尔冬强是位摄影师，在上世纪 80 年代立志于记录上海的城市变迁。他原来有两个野心，一个是记录正在消逝的上海，还有一个是记录日新月异的上海。正在消逝的上海是因为上世纪八九十年代上海的城市改造速度相当快，如果他没有及时地用照相机记录下来，很多景观就再也看不到了。另外上海新的东西不断地被引进来。有一次电视台采访他的时候，他感觉无法完成这两方面的工作，他只能两者选其一。现在可能也很难，因为他已经去做"一带一路"丝绸之路的摄影记录了。

　　上海档案馆的官方记录是比较完整的，缺的是来自民间的记忆。如果记忆只是官方冷冰冰的统计数据，而没有民间个体的感受，这个记忆还是有缺陷的。有这样一个例子，有一个市民非常有心，也很勤俭，几十年把每天到菜市场买菜这些都记录下来，几十年之后他把这些都捐赠给档案馆。档案馆有官方的统计数据，也有他个体的这些记录，研究者把这两方面的材料两相印证对城市历史的研究。对记忆的留存，将是更加全面的，也更加有情感的温度。

　　上海记忆不仅仅在上海，历史上上海有很多外来的移民、侨民，他们可能现在已经不在上海了，但是他们的记忆当中也有关于上海的。最近几年在全球征集"上海记忆"，有一个西班牙著名的画家，他的祖上曾经生活在上海，他在 2015 年把他祖上拍摄的有关上海的老照片捐赠给我们上海市档案馆，丰富我们的城市记忆。

另外，我们面向全球启动了一项跟世界记忆工程有关的，叫上海市档案文献遗产名录的评选，凡是跟上海的城市记忆有关的珍贵档案文献都可以进行申报评选。其目的主要是保护珍惜档案、深入解读和延伸发掘蕴藏的上海城市记忆。2011年首届启动，2014年第二次启动，通过媒体的宣传报道，有很多包括民间的藏家一起来申报。第二批的入选是2015年6月9日向社会公布的，共有八项，其中有非常著名的盛宣怀档案，差不多有十五六万卷；也包括辛亥革命日记、近现代中国婚书这样的，完全来自民间收藏的入选了上海市的档案文献遗产。

这是有关上海犹太难民的生活档案（图2），也是入选了我们第二批的上海市档案文献遗产。当时有两三万犹太人在上海生活，是非常珍贵的记录。

图2
20世纪三四十年代犹太难民上海生活档案

签证　　护照　　船票　　抵达上海后用餐

3. 城市记忆的传播

上海档案馆外滩馆的一楼和二楼有一个免费开放的永久陈列叫上海近现代历史发展陈列，其中陈列了开埠到现在的主要历史发展变化。我们也有上海档案信息网，网上关于上海城市记忆方面的展览有25个，也有100集追忆档案里的故事，有关上海历史、上海城市规划、城市建筑方面的故事。每年我们也会出版杂志和出版物，很多都是跟上海记忆有关。

上海记忆也要向全球传播，所以我们到南非开普敦、智利圣地亚哥去办"印象上海"的展览。最新拍摄了一个八集的微纪录片《上海记忆——

他们在这里改变中国》，是关于上海的红色记忆的。这部片子最重要的一点是把中共党史和城市史交织在一起，把历史事件从城市地理格局的视野上来考量。我们请了几个英国 BBC 的资深记者，由《毛泽东传》的作者也是历史学者来担任全篇的历史叙述人，面向全球受众进行全英文讲述。接下来，还要拍的一部是金融方面的，主题是金融与国运，因为上海在上世纪二三十年代也是亚洲的金融枢纽。之后，我们可能会拍关于上海文化方面的纪录片。这都是关于上海记忆的内容，目的是向全球推广上海的城市形象。

国际城市滨水廊道开发
实践及其启示

陆邵明

上海交通大学城市空间文化与科学研究中心教授

1. 城市记忆研究的两个热点

通过对城市记忆近十年的文献综述，我们最终发现有两个热点。热点之一就是保护名单外的记忆场所（图1），我们每天生活、生产的空间也有记忆，但这种记忆不明显。现在主要做的遗产保护就是官方认定的记忆遗产，所谓的遗产名单。上海与伦敦保护记忆方面的工作差距在于官方界定遗产之外的语境里。我们对保护名单外的记忆场所不太重视，而欧洲目前比较关注这个部分。

图1
城市记忆遗产

日常生活中的小桥流水以及很多街道，可能无法列入 UNESCO 的记忆遗产当中，但它们是有意义的。2012 年我在人民日报发表了《拯救记忆场所，建构文化认同》，提出这种记忆场所最大的特点是不再有个体，它可能是有一群，或者是不同大小的在不同的点上出现。举个例子，像黄浦江沿岸的很多工业遗产、工业的厂房，是不同时间段建成的，这样形成了一群而不是一个点。这也被称为遗产廊道，是拥有特殊文化资源集合，具有突出的、普遍性价值的线性景观，特点是多样性以及综合性保护。这是值得关注的点，也是目前的热点。

2. 廊道规划

到 2025 年，世界人口的 60%—70% 生活在沿海地区，使得海岸线面临很大的压力。回顾一个城市的发展也可以看到，城市的起源就是一条河，城市中心、城市郊区、城市工业区等都是沿着水去发展的，这是个规律——水孕育了城市。无论是伊斯坦布尔还是东方的城市，都是滨水开发、利用和保护的，这是世界性的文化现象。那么，城市滨水廊道开发的驱动力是什么？第一个是经济，经济的驱动使其成为世界性的文化现象；第二个是社会的需求；第三个是环境，环境提供了可能性，文化蕴含着有故事有积淀的历史场景，再有就是政策干预。

泰晤士廊道的规划（图 2），起源是伦敦转型。原来的规划聚集于大伦敦，但是这片区域不足以支撑城市的发展了，而且中心区和郊区发展不平衡。为了保持继续增长，维持平衡、共享、可持续，于是提出了泰晤士廊道的开发。这一开发的目标明确，除了吸引居民、住房、就业，最重要的是人文和自然资源的利用。开发涉及棕地、农田、湿地三个区域，还有城镇在廊道的这个区域，政府对其做了不同的解释和不一样的做法。

对于泰晤士廊道的遗产保护，有三点值得肯定。一是历史性。它把沿岸从头到尾做了一个综述，名列了包括国家、地区、社区等不同级别的遗产，并且利用不同的诠释途径，沿着整个河道用照片、活动、叙事等途径呈现这种历史。它的历史一方面是再利用，利用既有的历史，例如老厂房；一方面是保护有价值的、可以更待开发的东西。

图 2
伦敦泰晤士滨水廊道
规划

二是地域特色有效传承。开发是必然的，但怎样在开发过程中传承地域特色。一种是利用老的厂房改造成可居住的住宅，一种是将地方特色在新的建筑中传承；有的是在住宅上，有的在宫殿上。地域传承并不全部是高强度的现代化的开发。此外，地域特色还可以进行创新，即界面是一个传统建筑的形象，但整个形象完全是创新的。三是可达性。无论是通过快速轨道交通，还是公路交通、步行交通等方式，把这些点沿水和纵向串连起来，让老百姓在日常生活当中感受到亲近感（图3）。

图3
伦敦滨水廊道的可达性

3. 廊道发展的几点经验启示

一是构建周密新颖的城市规划设计。为保护文化、复兴文化，伦敦通过规划体系，以法律强令的方式对开发强度做了限定条件，规定每个地方结合历史文化保护点，或者是社区记忆，都有相应的开发强度控制。

二是重视管理，保持滨水的特色和吸引力。不是孤立的为保护而保护，而是结合公共空间，将公共设施、住宅、就业岗位结合起来保护开发。此外，这些遗产在吸引就业、吸引新居民方面产生的影响都有统计。住宅也是多样化的，有经济适用房，投资性用房，这些都是利用文化遗产改造的。

三是健全运作机制，完善开发秩序。伦敦在开发过程中的公私合作也经历了周折，从自由主义经济到国家干预，最后还是发展到了公私合作。教训是过度的开发，商业化、绅士化。

最后，滨水廊道对于一个城市尤其像上海这样的国际性城市具有重要的意义，我们要重新认知滨水廊道，将其中包含的历史性资源和生态资源通过专项规划做好保护。同时，我们不能孤立地进行保护，而是需要跟其他的产业、就业、住房、社会、健康等方面整合起来，这可能是未来保护的发展方向。

专家点评

李立新（南京艺术学院教授）：三位专家围绕城市记忆阐述了各自的理解，也带来了不同的经验。城市记忆和人文地理密切相关，一座城市的个性必定与这个城市的人和环境所形成的人文现象有关，由于各个城市在历史上的活动和地理环境所形成的空间分布，以及变迁的不同而形成城市之间的差异。但是，这种差异正在逐渐缩小。当代的城市文化现象是历史时期人文经济地理现象的延续和发展，不了解这个历史人文地理无疑会阻碍真正了解当代的城市文化。如果将人文地理视为一个城市在时间维度上的回溯，那么人文地理的发展现状就是衡量这个城市发展的标尺。所以，人文地理和城市文化是两个密切相连的学科领域，今天讨论的价值和意义就在于此。

汪芳教授谈到了北京城市的记忆，非常重要的是她利用了定量测量，寻找它的主因。形成一个现象的因素很多，以前的研究大部分是用个案的方式去寻找主因，但那是单个的经验；量化以后会形成普遍的意义，这是它的重要价值。另外，她还强调了人在城市记忆中的主动性、能动性，谈到了情感的幕布，还有鸽哨的景观，鸽哨很可能就是北京城市文化的一种基因，也是值得我们去学习的。

上海档案馆曹胜梅主任讲的是留住城市的乡愁，她通过档案文献谈到了记忆的困境，一方面是容易遗忘，有的是毁灭了，有些是缺失了，这种缺失有些是有意的，有些是无意的。也谈到了民间真正的记忆，举了很多例子。我们讲一个城市最基本的基因可能就是在民间，民间的记忆非常重要。记忆的传播也很重要，因为传播能够使得文化活化，能够唤醒文化。

陆邵明教授谈到了滨水廊道里的自然资源和地域人文资源，世界各个城市特别重视和强调人文和自然的融合；讲到了历史性，怎么去保护它、活化它；同时存在着地域性、生态性和可达性。这些都是重要的经验，尤其他建议定位黄浦江两岸在上海都市格局中间的地位，这就是滨水廊道的设计。

三位在探求城市记忆的时候，看到了历史、地理、人文因素所具有的独特作用，这是非常重要的。自觉地关注城市研究和未来城市格局的前景，这无疑是为城市发展提供了一个重要的途径。现在看来无论是在历史地理还是城市文化的旗帜下，对城市记忆的研究都是可行的、必要的。这不仅仅在西方是一个热点，也应该成为中国城市，包括中国的中小城市研究的路径。关键就是要坚持自然景观与历史人文两大主干，不仅要用自然来解释自然的现象，用历史解释历史现象，还要用自然来解释人文的现象，用人文来解释自然的现象，我想这些都将有利于当代城市的建设。

Urban Imageability: Image Tactics in the Context of the Preservation of Urban Heritage

Richard Koch

Founder and Director of Visual Arts and Director of Architecture Center,
University of Liverpool, UK

It's very interesting what Director General Dr.Xiao Lin said earlier today around the revised economic strategy that particular in regards to livable cities and he made direct reference to the importance and great focus of protection of culture and heritage, and I would like to add the importance of what I would call a shared space. A shared space, that he also mentioned in his presentation, is one that has soft qualities. And such a sense of a shared space that related to the past heritage is the one that I think will be of great importance for the urban development of globalized cities around the world.

1. Soft city and its importance

There is a writer called Jonathan Raban who wrote in the 1970s a book called *Soft City*, and it's exactly the soft cities concept which is what I would like to probably highlight in my talk today. The soft city is the city in our minds. It's the city as we imagined. Raban says that soft city can be as real as the hard city. The hard city in this instance translated as physical city as we know made of brick and water. So the notion of the soft city which I think is of great, not only social, cultural, architectural, but also economical importance. Particularly in regard to things, such as tourism. The attraction of investment to the city, of attracting knowledge and talents to the city, to make cities attractive, to have shared space and to share that qualities is also of great importance. Soft cities are shaped and constructed in our memory and mind through urban narratives. Thus, how do we protect and shape urban narratives, is of great importance.

And they are of course, shaped by our concept and perception of place. And that perception of place, of course is shaped by urban environment, but it is also increasingly shaped by images that are embedded in the urban fabric. So my talk today is called Urban Imagineability: Image Strategies in the context of preservation of urban heritage, it's going to be a short journey of simple observations on how people have inserted heritage moments, archival materials and other moving images and still images in urban landscape. And I also would like to share with you a few observations about the strategies that people have used, and how they use images in cities to create a sense of space, to shape those narratives, and to shape the notion of the soft city.

2. Innovative cases of urban imageability

This is to me, obviously a professional subject centered around three areas. On the one hand, we are dealing with artifacts, with architectural buildings, with operation space, building themselves, then we are dealing with space, and in my mind most importantly, we are dealing with people. And it's the interception of all three areas in the physical but also digital realm that the research I do is concerned about.

So, as a warming up, I'm going to tell you what you are probably most familiar with. This is a strategy of how they are using images, historic images of the city and share with the wide public. Inside, in the next case, of course, you can find in a controlled space of environment of that coincidence of the museum and gallery. I had worked on a piece of installation for the National Museum of Liverpool. It is a culture whereby I researched on the oldest films that were ever shot in the city. The films could be dated back to the year 1897, and they created a physical installation and the interactive installation by which people can seat themselves within these historic images and for that matter, we created a series of things like that. For example: there is one panel in the museum of Liverpool, you could see that, in this instance, a journey through the city. You sit inside of a train. On the outside of the window, you see the original archive footage. Literally, it's sort of digital collective notion of how it might have been if you would have traveled as the filmmaker did 100 years ago on that train. This is the one probably you're most familiar with when you go to galleries and museums.

Now I'm moving on to another concept that I explored in my work. And that is the notion of using the city as a physical interface. And it's something, a few years ago, I had the idea. It's already nice to create these installations, to stitch archival materials into formal radio animations and radioactive panels. But actually, it's not the same. Because what I really want to do is to explore the city ideally by foot and then get a sense of the city's heritage. So the development of this idea of portable city histories came into my mind. A number of projects has run up in the United Kingdom. A quite famous one by the London Museum is that they used their mobile phone application that allows you to walk through London. And when you are in a particular spot or a particular location where an old archived image has been taken, you can hold up your mobile phone and you see that image actually floating in the street. So when you look through the camera of the mobile phone, you see the image literally stitched into the position that stays in the middle of intersection. There is another project from Berlin which I find is particularly beautiful. This is around the Berlin Wall. If you've ever been to Berlin, you'll probably know that much of the Berlin Wall has disappeared from the landscape. So the architectural physical heritage has been removed by the city. So they are using this application to overlay archive materials onto the facades of these buildings. And what's beautiful is, you see the little narrative being played directly where it displays. So the idea here is to use the artifacts in the city, the remains of the city, and then overlay them with the original archive material. This can all be experienced by you looking through your mobile phone. I have my own project in London in Battersea, we also made a working application. There is a research on a Borough in London where a lot of film making activities took place for the last 100 years. We did research around what sort of films have been shot there and what we found out is that this part of London once had over 25 cinemas, and they all have been disappearing. So we are using this application that you have in your pocket to allow visitors to stroll down the street. And once you walk in an area where there has been an coincidence of a cinema in the past, your mobile phone would alert you. You can hold it up, and you can see how the old cinema looks like and you can see some of the films and film clips that are very short and shot in the cinema. So this is what I called portable digital histories.

There is another concept that I touched upon, it's the notion of using the city as physical interface again, but in this case, to preserve city images or city surfaces. It's something that you see all over Europe, I'm sure you see here in China as well. It is around a piece of architecture, a building, or a historical environment which is being reconstructed and renovated. For example, in Prague, they could put a little pressure on builders to print a fabric and to layer it in front of the façade, to maintain the image of the city, to maintain the heritage, the image and the sense that it is a historic building. There is another strategy that shows you how much effort goes into this notion of preserving the image or images in the city. When we have a cultural heritage event in Liverpool, the city leaders thought that there were some buildings in the city that they did not want to show to visitors. So the strategy they used is to hang images over those buildings that were deemed undesirable, and it's sort of an idea to make a building disappear by using images that the city council decided would be appropriate to be showing instead.

Now here is another idea that you can see for instance in Berlin again. The station of images of the past, I could call it urban sinography. A particular important section in Berlin-Leipziger Platzhad to be recreated, but the city could not actually find the investors to build the Plaza as it was in the past. So they decided to do something quite interesting, a full scale model which is a simulation of how the city would look like if the buildings would be there. So this is the extent to which the city authorities go to recreate a centered space. Lately, I discovered these earlier images where you passed by street, and suddenly you see, a piece of archive footage in the underground of Berlin. I call these portals or windows to the past. The next case is here from China. Laomendong in Nanjing whereby in an area that has very strong cultural heritage. The entire street steps are covered with the images of how old street would look like in this area 100 years ago. And what I find fascinating by this is the amount of the desire that people have to connect to these images. There is a haptic element in these. People touch the surface, they are stopped obviously by the screen because they cannot penetrate the screen. But there is a very strong desire to travel through time in the age the images that are used.

3. An era of mixed reality is coming

What I would like to tell you is that for the past 100 years, there has been a divide between we as people and the screen. We're used to watching the system by which we as human look towards the screen. This notion is going to be reversed because we have seen two things. First, more and more screens will have the desire to look back to us, not the screens themselves, but the network behind the screen. Think about the advertising for instance. Secondly, I think the physical boundary between us and the screen will be dissolved and we are entering an age of a mixed reality, a reality that goes beyond the screen. And if the visions of some very strong and large software company become true, then we will in the future see a blended reality. We will be wearing a device, and we will be able to overlay images, 3D animation, moving images, film, over everyday environments, a wall, a table, a city, a bench, suddenly we will be able to step inside the screen and experience that environment in presently unprecedented ways.

Urban Culture and Handcraft Memory in the Six Dynasties

Li Lixin

Professor of Nanjing University of the Arts

The Six Dynasties is the most brilliant and most creative era, as well as the most undervalued and the most neglected era in China's history. Today, the title of my speech is Urban Culture and Handcraft Memory in the Six Dynasties. I will reevaluate this era through the goods production and urban culture in Six Dynasties.

1. The reason of choosing Nanjing as the capital in the Six Dynasties

From the third to the end of the sixth century AD, in China's history, one of the Three Kingdoms, the Kingdom of East Wu (229—280), the following Eastern Jin Dynasty (317—420), the Southern Dynasty, including Song, Qi, Liang and Chen, their capitals were all built in Jiankang (now Nanjing). The ancient Chinese attached great importance to the choice of the capital city. During the Spring and Autumn Period, Guan Zhong (famous political thinker, 723—645 BC) said that the founding of the country are either under the mountains, or in the great plains. I have been to the capital city of the Kingdom Of Qi, which is Guan Zhong's mother country, is now Linzi in Shandong province. The capital city of Qi is in the Great Plains. In ancient China, the selection of the capital city are mainly referring to the following three aspects: economy, military and geography. The first dynasty of the Six Dynasties is the Kingdom of East Wu. There are three places to choose as capital, one is the capital of the Kingdom of Wu in the Spring and Autumn Period, that is now

Suzhou, but it is far away from the Yangtze River, which is not conducive to expansion. The other is Jingkou (today's Zhenjiang), but Fu Chai, emperor of Kingdom of Wu opens a Kan River in the opposite of Zhenjiang, so that North army can directly attack Zhenjiang, so it is not safe. The third is Wuchang, which is an important military town. If Wuchang is hold, the entire south area along the Yangtze River will be safe. But because Wuchang is close to the upper reaches of the Yangtze River, goods transported from south area along the Yangtze River ride upstream. Therefore, Wuchang cannot be the capital city. The final choice goes to Jiankang, today's Nanjing. Nanjing's geographical location constitutes a natural defense barrier, as its west is the Yangtze River, north the Xuanwu Lake, east the Zhongshan Mountain, and the south is the Qinhuai River.

2. The memory of architectures in the Six Dynasties

Our present memory of the Six Dynasties is mostly through borrowing some poems of later poets. But the Taicheng (where the central government and imperial palace are located) we see through the poem " willow trees in Taicheng are the most ruthless", is totally different from the actual Taicheng in the Six Dynasties. In the poem referring to Celebrity Lane. There are two families, Wang and Xie, living in the Celebrity Lane. The Wang Family is the prime minister who helps the Eastern Jin Dynasty move to the south and makes meritorious achievement. Wang Xizhi is the nephew of Wang Dao, this family has made great contribution to the Country. Xie An is the commander of the Battle of Fei River. He led 80 000 Jin army to beat the 800 000 northern troops. The great poet Xie Lingyun also comes from Xie family. But now, Celebrity Lane and Zhu Que Bridge are not the previous style. The only relics we see now in the Six Dynasties is the recently unearthed Imperial Road in Nanjing City. We always say the stone city is the representative of Nanjing, but archaeologists believe that the stone city is built by the Ming Dynasty, not the Six Dynasties period (Fig.1).

In addition, Zi Zhi Tong Jian (a history book written by Sima Guang), describes the palace in Jiankang, whose outermost city is a huge bamboo fence. The Jiankang city has three layers. The middle building is built with the brick,

Fig.1
Stone city in
Nanjing

which is very gorgeous and luxurious. The outer layer of the city is built with mud. The outermost city is a kind of bamboo fence style. Zuo Si of Western Jin wrote Rhapsody to the Capital City of Kingdom of East Wu. The capital city he described boasts gorgeous yet real works. Now the only of existence of Eastern Wu building we can see is the human-faced eaves tile (Fig.2), which is considered as a mystery by the archaeologist and exclusive to Eastern Wu. After the end of East Wu, the human-faced eaves tile ceases to exist. Then in the Eastern Jin Dynasty, there are animal-faced eaves tile (Fig.2), and its source is also a mystery. But in this picture (Fig.3), the human-faced eaves tile on the

Fig.2
Human-faced eaves
tile & animal-
faced eaves tile

Human-faced eaves tile   Animal-faced eaves tile

Fig.3
The Comparison
between Human-
face Eaves Tiles
in Western Han and
Eastern Wu Dynasty

left side with such middle line has been unearthed in Dongping Mausoleum of Western Han Dynasty in Shandong. While the human-faced eaves tile on the right side was unearthed from the well in the city of early King Wu, Ezhou, Hubei province, it is the tile of Eastern Wu Dynasty. Thus, from Dongping Mausoleum to Ezhou City and then to Jianye City, we can see communication connection, which means that building styles of Eastern Wu must be from the north, and are not formed out of air.

The so-called animal-faced eaves tile is the gradual evolution of the human-face eaves tile. There are many lines in the face of the human-face eaves tile in the late Eastern Wu. To the early Jin Dynasty, the lines become more and more obvious, and the human face gradually turns into animal face. To the Middle Eastern Jin Dynasty and Southern Dynasty, beast face pattern comes into shape. Iconologically, it is a process of evolution. From the human face to the animal face, in fact, it is the rule of the shape, but it conforms to the fact that it is the human face in the Eastern Wu, because people believe that the heaven gives birth to fetish to respond to the king. The building of Eastern Wu requires legitimacy, so they choose human face. To the Eastern Jin Dynasty, there is no existence of legitimacy. At this time, facing the army of the North territory, they has a kind of mentality of avoiding war and eliminating non-auspicious activities, therefore animal face gradually flourishes at that time. This is an example of the fact that these goods of the Six Dynasties are not immutable.

Moreover, Jiankang gardens emphasize integration with the nature (Fig.4). There is a line in the poem, four hundred and eighty temples in the Southern Dynasties. Actually, the number of temples then was probably more than 700. The significance of the Six Dynasties set up capital city in Jiankang lies in the following aspects: First, political center is separated from the military center, creating the precedent of combining the political center with the economic center. Second, political and economic center moved to the south from the Eastern Jin Dynasty, promoting prosperity of the city's economy and culture. Third, the highly-centralized dynasty disappeared, and the whole country went from chaotic division to the reunification. Fourth, culturally, Confucian classics in the Han Dynasty declined, metaphysics, Buddhism and Taoism were on the rise, creating Trinity situation.

Fig.4
Jiankang garden
in Nanjing

3. The handcraft memory in the Six Dynasties

The poems depicting the Six Dynasties are always quite resplendent. As the line goes like "beauties live in the southern region of Yangtze River, while emperors live in Jinling (today's Nanjing) ", showing the gorgeous situation during the Six Dynasties. But the understanding of the new pattern of the Six Dynasties, cannot be explained just from poetry, religion, political thought, but should be explained through combining the objects. Clothes and travel vehicle of the aristocrats are different from the Han Dynasty.

After Buddhism entered China, lotus, as its symbol, began to appear in a large number of daily utensils, like porcelain. Chinese porcelain originated in the Western Zhou Dynasty, and had been mature and reaching its peak in the Six Dynasties. Even the ordinary hoe had lotus style and the decoration is also very luxurious. Meanwhile, cooking and drinking tea began to prevail. Thus, lotus pattern also appeared on the tea-related appliances. Most of these appliances were not China's own production, but from West Asia, indicating that there was frequent exchange between the East and the West. Bigwigs in the Six Dynasties took this to show off their wealth. On the contrary, the literati of the Six Dynasties, such as the Seven Sages of the Bamboo Grove, were contemptuous of such dignitaries. like "A Song of Guangling" by Ji Kang, doesn't stress the sense of music, but the thought of critical reality. Civilian daily objects are also rich in number. Such as: lacquer ware, digging ear spoon, wooden club and scissors, which are different from the traditional pattern of urban culture in the Han Dynasty, and are formed in the middle of inheritance and variation. These are some genes of the culture in the Six Dynasties. It is realized via ordinary objects.

Urban life in the Six Dynasties was not calm. There were wars often. Just as Du Mu's poem "the singsong girls did not know the hate of subjugation", and ultimately the country perished. We should note that stirrup that is viewed by Joseph Needham as changed the process of world history, is invented by the Chinese people. The stirrup was first invented in the Western Jin Dynasty, and was made of wood. The outside surface was covered with gold-plated copper sheet. Using stirrup for real intention of the war was in the Eastern Jin Dynasty. It was used against the invasion of the North. And in order to fight against the cavalry, tools like caltrop, flat-headed knife, etc., were invented.

4. The cultural memory of the Six Dynasties

Hou Jing Riot (548—552 BC) exterminated the Liang Dynasty, which also declared the end of urban culture of the Six Dynasties. The Chen Dynasty is only sunset afterglow. Now, these great facilities that are scattered around in Nanjing, although weathered, and incomplete, they are still majestic. They are coordinates of the lost grander, but they show us a glorious era. Therefore, the characteristics of urban culture in the Six Dynasties are inclusion, absorption and coexistence, which make such a mechanism of urban culture.There are three important joints in the formation of such features. First, it is the emphasis and expression of humans and value of life.Second, it is the discovery of natural beauty, like Wang Xizhi's calligraphy, Gu Kaizhi's painting, etc.. All of them represent the discovery and appreciation of natural beauty. Third, the influence and embodiment of Buddhism deeply influenced the urban concept and the orientation of people's spiritual values, such as the Seven Sages of the Bamboo Grove and so on.

Finally, the urban culture of the Six Dynasties created the life value of the Six Dynasties as well as the value of the lives of the Six Dynasties. So it reflects the wisdom of Chinese culture in medieval times, I think it should be a model of world civilization history.

Organic Growth of Urban Regeneration and Preservation: Rethinking Shanghai Practice

Wang Lin

Professor of School of Naval Architecture, Ocean and Civil Engineering,
Shanghai Jiao Tong University

In the process of urban development, historical protection has been a bottom line that Shanghai has maintained in the past decade, but it should be said that the problems and difficulties we face are very huge because we are doing heritage conservation in a developing city, so this collaborative development, shared interest and adherence to the bottom line based on the innovative thinking, are some of the ideas we stick to in our future development of the city, historical heritage conservation and organic renewal of the city. I would like to share some cases. The picture about the goal of "the pursuit of an excellent global city" of Shanghai by 2040 is a child taken in Shikumen Lane, Shanghai. It represents the city memory is to be forever inherited in this world and in one life. The city memory is not only the memory of the elderly, but should be the valuable wealth of all human beings, and should start from young people. The 15-minute social life circle is a conceptual idea for Shanghai's future planning, but we should be able to find the history of Shanghai or the historical memory of Shanghai within 15 minutes.

1. Shanghai faces great difficulties and challenges in historic protection

First, the rapid increase of population induces great pressure on historic protection. Shanghai is at the phase of fast development. In the past 10 to 15 years, the population of Shanghai increases by 50 to 100 million each year. Under such huge pressure, historic protection work is under a new challenge.

Second, the urban space density of original historical heritage place, especially the historical blocks, are very low. They face the challenge of huge volume fraction and urban development interests. How to maintain the city's diversity, inherit the history of the city, but also renew and develop the city? This is a problem that must be solved.

In last round of editing Overall Planning of Shanghai (1999 to 2020), we proposed three one-third. One-third of the land is for urban construction, one-third of the land is for ecological construction, and one-third is for farmland. Today's drawing is not the latest, but I would like to tell you that one-half of the land in Shanghai has been occupied by urban construction, so in the new round of urban planning, we propose that land for construction is only those allocated so far by 2020, and there will no incremental by 2030, 2040, 2050. The situation we face makes us rethink. The source of Shanghai includes the Bund and Lujiazui area, and the scale of different regions is completely different. The city still has much space for development. It is no need to destroy the construction of historical heritage protection to build the city. The existence of texture of these cities, urban space, or even a hundred meters wide road are reasonable or not. Not only grand buildings are suitable for city life. Along with the development of the city, on the new basis, can we have a rethinking? The scale of Shanghai's historical blocks are the same with the core areas in many Western countries. Will it be possible to do the repair in the new planning, new urban construction, or the inside of old building, which is very important in the historical and cultural heritage.

2. The planning and cases of urban heritage protection in Shanghai

100 historical protection buildings were designated by shanghai in 2005. Although the traffic problem in Shanghai was very serious and there were only two rail transits then. We put forward that Shanghai couldn't widen the city road, but should develop large-scale rail transit. So, 144 style protection roads were designated, and 64 roads would never be widened. East Fuxing Road now is 18.3 meters wide. At that time, the planned width was 32 meters.

The old plants seem to be dilapidated, meaningless and functionless. There were many places where after street factories were removed, now they are transformed into, small theater, small cafe, and a small joint designer office. In the core part of Jing'an District, its texture is preserved as well as the city's memory. Another example: Shanghai's Long Hua airport, at that time, the building there was to be removed, but we believe that it should be maintained, which may be used for holding big city activities. This road is the original airport runway of Longhua Airport. It has become a running park by turning into a running path. Memory maintenance matters a lot to a city. There are many ways of inheriting memory, like landscape, architecture, structure, and even re-use, not only museum-style protection.

The first case is about the historical heritage preservation and urban renewal of the Bund. This case is led by the government and jointly completed by developers. The second case is about Tianzifang, which is raised by the common people and artists. The government reached such a bottom up historical protection after coordinating with the interests of developers. The third is the planning and design of the historical block. The effective protection of the city and organic renewal in the downtown is promoted through planning and design. The last one is Xin Chang Ancient Town, which promotes the development of the city through practice.

Firstly, the Bund is Shanghai's first concession and the source of the Shanghai city. After many years of development and our efforts, all the historical buildings are retained and equipped with new function. However, the Gate Bridge on Wusong Road, the Friendship store as well as original six-storied government building are no longer to be seen. All the new construction is in the back of these old buildings. The city is growing, we cannot refuse it, but we have to protect history. One important point of historical protection is to restore the city's public space. The Bund was originally open to the public. Before 2008 and 2010, people need to pass through ten lanes into the Bund space. Now, the six lanes are put into the ground to maintain the city's historic district and the accessibility of Riverside space. People can walk to the bund, which reflects people first concept.

Secondly, the space of Tianzifang is of multi-composite. In 2003, the land had been approved to be leased. After research, three reasons were put forward: historical heritage protection, public space demand, and the development of creative industry park. Most importantly, the developer had both the southern and northern land at the same time. So I suggested that all the volume fraction were moved to the southern land and maintained this piece of land. That's how Tianzifang came into shape.

Thirdly, in the process of urban governance, we should adhere to collaborative governance. Sometimes, the government does not do all the things, but gives full play to the power of the people. The government should do its part of the public interest. This synergy will promote a more diverse, more organic and more shared development.

Fourthly, Xin Chang is an obscure ancient town along the southern Yangtze River. Therefore, we invited top designers and media and asked all the designers to do the design covering people's daily life at the local. These exclusive designs for Xin Chang are popular among the local citizens. So, planning should be rooted in the land, history and culture, but also meet the needs of the present.

Besides, governance and diversity are very important. Now, it is not true that only brilliant building can be retained. Buildings like East China Power Building, which was built in 1991, are kept too. In order to have a better understanding of the image of urban space, we have adopted the planning, made a carpet-style census of all the existing historical blocks in Shanghai, and given each building a definition, which may be adjusted as society develops.

We believe that the old buildings are to be built close to the red line of the road. All the greening rate, all the back construction, all the urban fabric, space requirements should respect culture and texture of this region.

To conclude, planning is the source of urban governance, and our urban design is a policy tool. We must use public policy of urban planning and urban design to coordinate and balance the interests of all parties, and employ the city planning to coordinate the relationship between the parties. In terms of city governance, we talk about that we should put forward sufficient reasons, persuade with emotions, lure with benefits, and bring illegal activities to justice. Surely, the city's protection and renewal should be conducive to inheritance, economic environment and politics, as well as comprehensive development. It is hoped that cultural and historical heritage should not only be rooted in city, but also in all the aspects.

Remark

Liu Enfang (Professor and Dean of School of Humanities of Shanghai Jiao Tong University): I believe we have the same feeling that the three guests have just given us excellent speeches which inspired us. In fact, the original intention that the United Nations set up the World Cities Day was to attract more people, more countries to pay attention to the significance of sustainable development of our city, to the problems we encounter in the process of urbanization, and further to find the ways of solving these problems in the process.

Today, our five guests have presented different ways of solving problems in the process of modern urban development from different perspectives and different entry points. Each region may face different problems, and the solutions may also be diverse. The methods the professors presented to solve the problems are splendid and diversified, bringing us deep thought. Today's theme of "memory" highlights the problems that we may face globally in urban development. Whether in Shanghai, or in any other cities in the rest of the world, we all can feel the city's cultural heritage, and the role of our memory in inheriting the city's cultural heritage. Professor Richard Koch has just shown us a new perspective, combining historical heritage and contemporary life, using applications to make people feel the different historical scenes of each block, which is of great valuable.

Wang Lin, as a professor and city manager, she illustrated her idea from the perspective of urban management. Several other professors and guests also discussed the urban culture from other perspectives, such as: history, etc.. All the speeches have given us enlightenment.

Beijing Urban Memory: Historic Buildings and Historic Areas

Wang Fang

Professor of School of Architecture and Landscape
Architecture of Peking University

In 2007, I bid for a project in Xuanwu District of Beijing and unexpectedly won the first place. So my team started the research. When we did the research on urban memory at that time, it still belonged to some old categories like archives. In 2009 and 2010, we applied for Beijing Natural Fund and National Natural Fund consecutively with urban memory as the subject of our research. In this process, urban memory became the main topic of my research. I originally studied Xuanwu from the perspective of ekistics but later three words—subject, object and timeframe became increasingly prominent. The study of the object is quite known to all, but subjective cognition and timeline are also highly relevant to the study of urban memory. Apart from timeline, there were also key timeslots and related events. In the regeneration of a block, which periods are those we should select and focus on the presentation of the memories is often a challenge of our study. Now urban memory is an essential part of my researches.

1. Framework of urban memory study

In terms of discipline construction, from my perspective, it should still belong to one of the important ways of inheriting local traditions and developing and enriching urban culture. Compared with traditional more static–focus planning discipline, it has more dynamic elements. So in my research, I established a new theory, including some analysis techniques which won soft copyright. Besides, we also constituted a model from the perspectives of both the internal and external forces, residents in the city and in the suburban areas, and the three dimensions.

As for the internal and external forces, urban memory is always changing. Internally, take some old districts as an example, the original residents moved out and some migrant workers moved in. The memory will be lost or change dramatically when the change of subject takes place. And some original residential buildings have given way to teahouses or restaurants in function. The change of spaces such as famous old residence of celebrities will have impacts on memory. And some external forces such as urbanization will have great impacts as well. Old Beijing residents used to go for a walk with a bird or cricket have moved out of the 5th Ring Road. As their replacement, people from Henan, Anhui moved in. This is directly connected to policies. These changes are unconscious but can be really huge in five or ten years' time.

I once analyzed the two types of residents in my book which highlighted a survey of the residents' cognition of the historical buildings in old Beijing. And then I selected one case, which is 345 historical sites in the inner city of Beijing. The result shows that people's views are sharply different. To cite Qian Men as an example, we just conducted a survey about Qian Men. It shows that people who live in that area have very different understanding from that of us who went to university in Beijing and stayed and worked here after graduation and still live outside of the 5th Ring Road, although we have Beijing Hukou. The identities of the subjects leads to the differences in their cognition. Another research of ours is about rural memory. There are a lot of rural villages under reformation in Beijing because of urbanization. Farmers moved to new city communities. But they still have strong attachments to their old rural or farming lifestyle so they will make some changes to their new communities autonomously. Therefore, we study their motives, attitudes and approaches of reformation.

2. Case study of urban memory research

In terms of the three dimensions, I chose two categories from one of them. One is former residences of celebrities and the other is tenements in old cities. The first one belongs to somebody, or someone used to be influential economically, politically or culturally. When they moved out, there would be changes. The second one is to study ordinary people who have undergone several changes with their tenements. We studied their changes during the past six decades since liberation.

In terms of linear space, we also carried out a study on the size of the space of the city by following the axis of the city and find that it is still a little bit vague to define its limits or borders. For example, people have very different cognitions of the ends of the famous east-west and north-south axis in Beijing. This is also a focus of the team.

As for planar space, we also selected two cases to share with everyone. One is emotion. I live in the Hutong of Beijing. When Beijing is throwing the 2008 Olympic Games, some residents in the Hutong need to host the foreign guests and there will be some emotional problems. To put it this way, we used to drink Douzhi with Youtiao for breakfast in the morning. But foreigners could not bear the taste of Douzhi so it was reformed into Doujiang. This change is something they need to change their own lifestyle to get used to. So there exists a line, a spatial or emotional line. We need to abide by this line so as to preserve the memory of our Hutong and tenements. This is also a small study I have done.

As for the other type, I chose the scene of Beijing Pigeon Whistles to study. In the book Old Peking Folk by Cao Yu, six scenes describe the pigeon whistle in the bell towers in the first chapter. This scene was very common five years ago but can be seldom seen today. Because of the relocation, people are different, so are their lifestyles. From this point of view, can we record the pursuit of the subjective? Do people have the intention to remember? Does the environment of the current era allow it? I started my study of pigeon whistle from this angle.

Finally, my attitude toward memory has never changed: during the process of development, memory itself is undergoing a sifter. It's like an artificial space, a game space, not the real space we live in. Which part of the memory will be preserved and will they reemerge again is a question. Memory itself cannot be left behind or given up. But sometimes it must be given up, sometimes it have to be held together. That's my basic points of view toward urban memory.

Retain the "Nostalgia" of Cities: to Start with the Appraisal and Selection of the Archival Documentary Heritage of Shanghai

Cao Shengmei

Chief Editor of Compiling and Research Department of Shanghai Archives

Nostalgiais by no means limited to the sentimental attachment to a countryside village. From Greek etymology, this word has very broad meaning. It can refer to the sentimental attachment to one's homeland generally. So cities should definitely be included.

Numerous important official records are kept in Shanghai Archives from around 1843, when Shanghai was open to the world in 1980s or 1990s. The total volume is over 3.6 million pieces. As Shanghai was a concession to some foreign government for a time lasts about 100 years, the archives during that period were also kept in our archives. The majority of, if not all, scholars studying the history of Shanghai have come to our Archives for materials.

1. City memory and its plight

Today the topic of the parallel forum is memory. Individual has memory and city has memory as well. It needs to be awakened and reproduced by text, image and video. As for the urban memory of Shanghai, the historical memory and cultural identity of a city not only are the origin of people's nostalgia but also serve as the spiritual bond for people living in the city. We have pictures of the Bund from different periods in our Archives. Here are two pictures of 1890 and 1925 (Fig.1). They show the changes of this area straightforward. And it was the panaroma of the Bund which could be seen from our archives during that time.

Memory and forgetting contradicts each other, so we need to use all kinds of methods to awake memory. There are a lot of factors, such as: poverty,

Fig.1
1890 (above),
1925 (below)
Panorama of the
Bund

disaster, war, ignorance etc., that cause the destruction of memory. As for the absence of memory, there are two kinds: one is intentional absence, and the other is unintentional absence. From the aspect of city, intentional absence could be weak which may not fully reflected in his memory.

2. The collection of memory

The preservation and inheritance of city memory needs the support from the society, organizations as well as the folks. Er Dongqiang is a photographer who determined to record the change of Shanghai in the 1980s. He had two ambitions, one is to record the vanishing places of Shanghai, another is to record the daily renewal of Shanghai. Recording the vanishing places of Shanghai is because the renovation process was really fast in 1980s, he was afraid that if he couldn't record it on time, most of the sites would never be seen. What's more, new things were introduced continuously to Shanghai. However, once in a TV interview, he mentioned that it was hard for him to achieve both goals, he might just choose one of them. Now, it seems even harder for him to finish one of the tasks for he is engaged in the photographing work of The Belt and Road.

The official records of our archives are relatively complete, what we are lack of is the records of folk memory. If there is only official statistics without any personal feelings, the memory is still flawed.Here is an example: there is a citizen who is very prudent and diligent, he recorded his daily life of going to the vegetable market for several decades. And afterwards he donated all his records to the archives. Now, with both the official statistics and the individual records kept in the archives, the researchers could make full use of both materials to prove their studies of urban history. Thus, the collection of memory will be more comprehensive and complete.

Shanghai memory is not just exists in Shanghai, historically, there are a lot of foreign immigrants who may not be in Shanghai any more, but in their memory there are something about Shanghai. Therefore, in recent years we are collecting "Shanghai memory" all over the world. In 2015, a famous Spanish artist, whose ancestors once lived in Shanghai, donated old photographs of Shanghai taken by his ancestors, to the Shanghai Archives. This enriched our city memory.

In addition, we launched an appraisal and selection for the world, which is related to the world memory project, called *the archival documentary heritage of Shanghai*. All the precious archival documents about Shanghai city memories can be declared and selected. Its main purpose is to protect in-depth interpretation of the precious archives and to explore the hidden Shanghai memory. The first round of the selection started in 2011 and the second round began in 2014, through the media's publicize and reports, many collectors including folk collectors have declared their collections. A total of eight items including a very well-known person -Sheng Xuanhuai's archive were released on June 9, 2015 in the second round of the selection. Almost 150,000 or 160,000 volumes, including the 1911 Revolution Diary and some folk collections like modern Chinese marriage certificates were also selected as *the archival documentary heritage of Shanghai*.

This is *the life archives of the Shanghai Jewish refugees* (Fig.2), and it was

Fig.2
The Life of
Shanghai Jewish
Refugees

Visa

passport

ship ticket

dinner after
arriving
Shanghai

also selected as *the archival documentary heritage of Shanghai* in the second round of the selection. There were two to three million Jewish living in Shanghai during that time and it was a very valuable record.

3. The dissemination of city memory

On the first and second floor of our Achives, there is a permanent display called the development of modern history of Shanghai, which is open to the public for free, shows the main historical development and change from port opening till now. We also have Shanghai Archives Information Network. There are about 25 exhibitions about Shanghai city memory and 100 episodes of stories from the remembrance archives, and they are about the history, city planning and urban architectures of Shanghai. Every year we also publish magazines and publications, many of which are related to Shanghai memory.

Shanghai memory also needs to be spread to the world, so we held Shanghai Image exhibitions in Cape Town (South Africa) and Santiago (Chili). Besides, an eight-episode micro-documentary called *Shanghai Memory—From Here China Was Changed* was lately shot. This is the first series and it is about Shanghai's revolutionary memory. The most important part of this documentary is the combination of the Communist Party of China with the history of the city, viewing the historical events from the perspective of urban geography. We have invited some senior journalists from BBC news and the author of *Mao Zedong Biography*, who is also a historian, as the narrator of the whole story. It was narrated in English for the global audience. The next series will be about finance and the theme will be *The Finance and National Destiny*, for Shanghai is Asia's financial hub in the twenties and thirties of last century. The following documentary after that might be about the culture of Shanghai. These are all about Shanghai memory and our purpose is to promote the global city image of Shanghai.

The Development of Waterway Corridors at International Cities

Lu Shaoming

Professor of the Institute of Urban Spatial Culture and
Science of Shanghai Jiao Tong University

1. Two research highlights of urban memory

We have done a literature review about urban memory covering nearly a decade, and ultimately we found that there are two research highlights. One of the highlights is to protect the places of memory other than listed places (Fig.1). The places where we live and work are also places of memory, but this memory is not obvious. What we mainly do about heritage protection at present is the protection of listed places identified by the authorities, the so-called heritage list. The gap between Shanghai and London of the urban memory protection lies outside the official heritage list. We do not pay much attention to the places of memory, while it receives more attention in Europe.

Fig.1
Urban Memory
Heritage

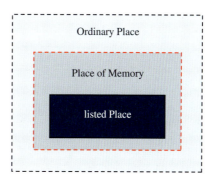

Many bridges, streams and streets, in our daily lives may not be included in UNESCO's memory heritage, but they are of great importance. In 2012, I had published an article named "Save Places of Memory , Build Cultural Identity" in *the People's Daily*. And I put forward the biggest feature of such places of memory is that they are no longer in individual, but rather in groups appearing at different places in different sizes. For example, our industrial heritage and industrial plants along the Huangpu River were set up in different time periods, thus forming a group rather than an individual. Such places are also known as heritage corridors, a collection of special cultural resources with linear landscape of prominent and universal value. Heritage corridors are characterized by diversity and comprehensive protection. This is a point worthy of attention and also a current hot issue.

2. The planning of the corridors

By 2025, 60% to 70% of the world's population will live along coastlines, and coastlines will be facing great pressure. Looking back on the development of a city, we can see that the city originates from a river, develops along the river, with the city center, suburbs and industrial areas spreading along the water. This is a rule that water gives birth to the city. Whether Istanbul or eastern cities, they all develop along the river, utilize the river and also protect it, presenting a worldwide cultural phenomenon. Then, what are the drivers of waterway development? The first is the economy, economic forces make it a worldwide cultural phenomenon, then there is social demands, the third is the environment, which provides the possibility. Culture is also important, of course, because there are historical scenes with accumulated events and stories. Finally, there is policy intervention.

The Thames Gateway (Fig.2) planning was initiated when London was in transformation. In the former planning, places were gathered in the Great London, and with the development, the Great London cannot provide enough spaces anymore, and the central area and suburbs developed out of balance. In order to maintain development and balance sustainable growth, the development of the Thames gateway was proposed. The goal of the development is clear, in addition to attracting residents, housing and employment, the most important aim is to make use of cultural and natural resources. The development involved three areas, including brown fields, farmlands, and wetlands. Besides, there were urban areas adjacent to the gateway. All these areas were treated differently.

As for its heritage protection, there are three points worthy of recognition. First, its historic significance. Thames and its coast was reviewed from its beginning to the end, each point was listed as national, regional or community heritage, and the history was presented by photos, activities and narratives. Its historical significance on the one hand lies in using existing history, such as old factories, on the other in protecting valuable and developable architectures.

Fig.2
Case study—
Thames Gateway

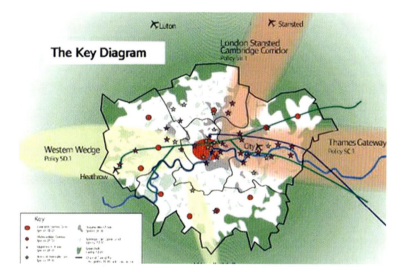

Second, its inheritance of regional characteristics. Since development is inevitable, but how to maintain regional characteristics in development? One way is to utilize old plants, transforming them into habitable residence. Another is to maintain local characteristics in the new buildings, including residences and palaces. Regional inheritance should not be all high-intensity modernization development. There can also be innovation of regional characteristics, with the overall scene as a traditional building, while the whole image is completely innovated. Besides, accessibility was also achieved, whether through rapid rail or highway and others, a series of lines of communication connected these points together, not only along the water, but also cross the river, so that people could feel the sense of intimacy in their daily lives (Fig.3).

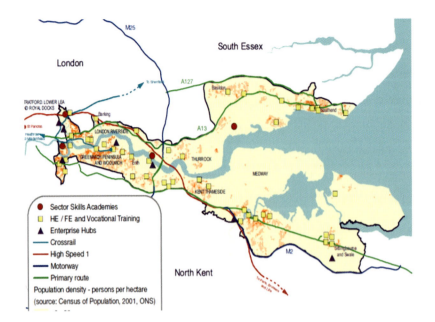

Fig.3
The accessibility
of Thames Gateway

3. The inspirations of waterfront corridor development

First, careful and innovative urban planning and design. They had a planning system for protecting and reviving culture, which is of legal validity, providing for the intensity of development of each place, which varies with historical and cultural protection area or community memory.

Second, emphasizing on management, maintaining the characteristics and attractiveness of the waterfront. The protection was not implemented alone, but in combination with public spaces, including public facilities, housing and jobs. In addition, they kept count of the impact of these heritage in attracting employment and new residents. Housing is also diversified, they have affordable housing as well as investment housing, all of which was the reformation of cultural heritage.

Third is to build a complete operation mechanism. With this regard, we arrived at the same end by different means. They had also experienced twists and turns in preliminary stage, developing through liberal economy to state intervention, and finally to the stage of public-private cooperation. There are also lessons to be learned, like excessive development, commercialization, gentrification.

Last, I would like to say that waterfront gateway is of great significance for a city, especially an international city like Shanghai. We need to re-recognize waterfront gateways, make special plans to protect its historial and ecological resources. And the protection should not be carried out in single item, but should be in combination with other industries, employment, housing and health, and that's may be the orientation of protection in the future.

Remark

Li Lixin (Professor of Nanjing University of the Arts): The above three experts stated their understanding about city memory, also showing us their different experience. City memory and human geography are closely related. A city's characteristic must be in close relation with its citizens and the humanistic phenomenon formed in that environment. The various historical events and geographical environment lead to the changes and differences between cities. And such difference is gradually narrowing. Contemporary urban cultural phenomenon is the continuation and development of the economic and geographical phenomenon in history.If one do not understand this human geography, he will never get a thorough understanding of contemporary urban culture. Taking human geography as a backtracking of a city in the time dimension, then the development of human geography is an important criterion for measuring the the city's development. Therefore, human geography and urban culture are two closely related disciplines, and that's where the value and significance of today's discussion lie.

Professor Wang Fang talked about the memory of Beijing city. There is an important point in her research, a quantitative measurement, namely, quantification. A phenomenon might be caused by many factors, and quantification is used to determine which is the main cause.Former researches mostly focus on one specific case, forming single experience, while quantification helps developing universal experience, that is very important. In addition, she also stressed people's initiative in urban memory, that's an essential point. She also talked about the emotion, as well as the view of the pigeon whistle which might be a gene of Beijing culture. And that is also worth learning.

Cao Shengmei, director of the Shanghai Archives, mainly mentioned retaining the nostalgia of the city. She talked about the plight of memory through archivals. On the one hand, the archival memory is easy to forget, some being destroyed, some were missing. Missing could be intentional or unintentional. She also talked about ordinary people's real memory with a lot of examples. The defining DNA of a city may reside among ordinary people, so ordinary people's memory is very important. The transmission of memory is also very important;transmission can help activate and awaken culture.

Professor Lu Shaoming talked about the natural resources and human resources in the waterfront gateway. Other big cities in the world also attach great importance to the integration of humanities and nature. He also talked about history, the way of protecting and activating it. Besides, Lu talked about its locality, as well as eco-friendliness and accessibility. These are all valuable experience. In particular, he made a proposal, positioning the Huangpu River in the middle of Shanghai, and that's the design of the waterfront gateway.

The three professors have taken into account the distinctive roles of history, geography and humanities in their exploration of urban memory; such attention is very important, because conscious concerning about urban research and the prospects of urban landscape is undoubtedly of great importance to urban development. Now it seems that whether in the context of historical geography or under the banner of urban culture, the researches on urban culture are both feasible and necessary. This is a hot spot in the West, and it should become a research highlight of China's cities, including China's small and medium-sized cities. The key is to adhere to the two backbones of natural landscape and historical humanities. We should not take nature and history separately, but rather consider them as interrelated subjects, that is, to explain historical phenomenon with nature, and to explain natural phenomenon with the humanities. These ideas, I believe, will be conducive to the construction of contemporary cities.

CLOSING SPEECH

闭幕演讲

上海市人大常委会副主任、上海交通大学党委书记姜斯宪
在全球城市论坛上作闭幕演讲

Jiang Sixian, Deputy Director of Standing Committee of Shanghai Municipal People's Congress and Secretary of the Party Committee of Shanghai Jiao Tong University, delivers a closing speech at the Closing Ceremony of the Global Cities Forum

实践、传承与升华

姜斯宪
上海人大常委会副主任、上海交通大学党委书记

今天大家围绕着城市"协同治理，共享发展"的主题，展开了热烈的讨论，取得了超出预期的良好效果。我们以这样一种方式来庆祝"世界城市日"，无疑是十分恰当的。

刚才各位分论坛的主持人与大家分享了主要观点，我很受启发，也十分认同。作为闭幕的演讲，我在这里简要地谈一点感悟和看法。

14 年前的 2002 年 8 月，我当选为上海市的副市长，成为市政府领导团队中的年轻人。一个月之后，我又获得了一项任命，担任中国政府特使，使命是争取国际展览局以及近 100 个成员国家支持中国上海申办 2010 年的世博会。事实上在那之前一年左右的时间里，我也深度参与了申办世博会的准备。其中一项任务，就是要提出上海世博会的主题。经过研究，我们先想好了主题的英文表述，可能各位都记得，就是"Better City，Better Life"。然后我们想，中文怎么表述？有一些争论，最后是集中到了"城市，让生活更美好"。2002 年底，上海成功获得了主办权，经过前后近 8 年的不懈努力，上海世博会闪亮登场，成为一届成功、精彩、难忘的盛会。有 7 300 多万人次前往参观，创造了难以打破的世界纪录。

2010 年 10 月 31 日，当世博会闭幕之际，发表了《上海宣言》。在《上海宣言》中提出，希望能够设立"世界城市日"。在此之后，在中国政府的积极推动下，联合国大会通过决议，设立了这样一个以城市为主题的纪念日。

2014 年 10 月 31 日，首个"世界城市日"纪念活动在上海拉开帷幕，其中活动之一就是"全球城市论坛"。此后，上海连续三年组织"世界城市日"相关活动。今年的全球城市论坛是第三届，已经形成了一定的影响力。

从 1994 年末到 2013 年末，我在上海市和海南省从政 19 年，对政府管理有些切身体会。从整体上看，中国有一个广义的强势政府。它在中国过去 30 多年的快速发展中，发挥了重要作用。同时，政府对城市发展的认知，乃至对自身的角色定位，也在逐步提升和改变。上世纪 90 年代，以上海市政府以及我当时当区政府的区长时的实践和理念为例，当时我们的主要注意力都集中在解决最急迫的危旧房的改造、产业职工转岗再就业上。取得了显著成绩，但也付出了不少代价。其中有些代价是必须付出的，也有些代价或许付多了。主要原因是当时的管理理念更新还不够迅速。比如我本人 90 年代末期出访巴黎，我在巴黎逗留期间，把几乎所有的时间放在了研究拉德芳斯的发展上，竟然没有抽出时间去看一看卢浮宫等文化殿堂，并不是说我挤不出时间，而是那个时候，我更关注的是上海是不是也能长得高、也能建成类似拉德芳斯这样一个新区。上海当时引以为豪的，不仅是上海长高了，变新了，还有上海的 GDP 保持两位数的增长。但对于城市的文化传承、环境友好，我们的关注还是偏弱。

我这样讲，并不是想苛求前人，包括我，现在对各位青年学子来讲，已经算前人了。但我想，我们应该努力增强自己的远见，从而更好地预知未来。我曾经参与了上海上一轮《城市总体规划》编制工作，包括向国务院常务会议汇报《城市总体规划》编制，那是在本世纪初。而今年以来，作为市人大副主任，我们审议新一轮的《城市总体规划》，也就是 2016—2040 年的全市总体规划时，我感慨万千。我深深地感受到，今天的规划理念，已经大幅度、全方位超越了当年。究其原因，新的城市建设、城市治理实践，以及国际交流的广泛深入，使得规划的编制者有了更为开阔的视野。同时，在这一轮规划编制过程中，更高的透明度和更广泛的社会参与，也使得我们在集中民智、形成共识上，更加游刃有余。

今天举行的全球城市论坛的主题是"协同治理，共享发展"。据我了解，这个主题是联合国人居署在与中国国家住建部深入讨论之后确定的。这个情况说明了什么？我认为至少说明了两点：

一是反映了中国关注人类命运共同体的发展，期待中国的发展成果能够为全球人民所共享，也愿意与世界各国人民分享中国发展的机会。

二是中国认同协同治理的重要性。虽然各国国情不同，发展道路和制度选择也必然各不相同，但是在城市治理方面，我们应当，而且也完全可能借鉴彼此的经验。一般而言，中国各级政府在城市管理方面能力比较突出，但我们也要防止把自己误认为是一个"万能政府"，防止政府超越了自己的能力，包揽全部的社会事务，防止我们忽略社会组织的力量，市场经济的力量以及广大民众的力量。城市治理也正由于这些忽视，难以进入更高境界。不仅如此，单方面由政府进行管理，或许还会失去城市发展的目标。即让城市更好地发展，让城市发展更好地为人民服务，要让发展的成果更多的为人民所共享。

善治下的人与城市，理应成为有机的和谐共生体。这个共生体，可以用一句话概括，那就是"我们的城市，共同的家园（Our City，Our Community）"。我们的城市，贯穿的是"以人为本"的治理理念，而"共同的家园"，则体现了"人人参与"的治理精神。

这其中，作为未来城市的主角，作为今日城市创新之源的青年人，你们的参与非常值得鼓励、引导。为了推动青年学子关注城市发展，探索城市治理之道，本次论坛组织方在昨天专门安排了大学生城市治理案例挑战赛展示。今天又向部分获奖团队及个人颁发了奖励。我希望这样一个活动，将有助于青年学生对城市治理的理念、方法和策略方面深入思考，提升解决实际问题的理论运用能力、树立更强的社会责任感。

今年的论坛是上海交通大学中国城市治理研究院的首次尝试。我们希望在论坛之后，认真地总结提炼各位专家学者以及与会朋友的真知灼见。我们会把你们所发表的高见整理出来，并且让它在更广泛的领域内产生积极作用。

与此同时，中国城市治理研究院将进一步与相关的组织、国内外的著名高校开展更深入的合作，将以开放的胸怀、机制，面向校内校外、国内国外，努力推动城市研究的多学科发展，充分发挥上海交通大学综合性大学的优势以及地处上海这个城市治理鲜活试验田的优势，鼓励理工科与人文社会科学等众多学科，就城市治理问题的研究进行有机的交融。希冀能为全球城市治理问题提供来自高等学校的智慧，并形成政、产、学、研、用紧密结合的城市治理创新平台。

Practice, Inheritance and Sublime

Jiang Sixian

Deputy Director of Standing Committee of Shanghai Municipal People's Congress and Party Secretary of Shanghai Jiao Tong University

Today we have had a heated discussion on "Collaborative Governance, Shared Development", and achieved even better results than expected. It is undoubtedly appropriate for us to celebrate the World Cities Day in such a manner.

The hosts of each forum have just shared their views and I was so inspired. As a closing speech, I would like to briefly share my inspirations and viewpoints.

Fourteen years ago, in August 2002, I was elected as the Vice Mayor of Shanghai and became a young leader in the Municipal Government's leadership team. One month later, I was assigned with a new mission as the special envoy of the Chinese government to get the support of the Bureau of International Exposition and nearly 100 member countries for Shanghai's bid for EXPO 2010. In fact, almost a year before that, I also closely participated in the preparation of the World Expo bid. One of the tasks was to propose a theme for Shanghai World Expo. After some study, we first came up with the theme in English expression—you may remember— "Better City, Better Life". Then we were thinking how to express it in Chinese? There were some controversies and finally we decided on the expression: Better City, Better Life. By the end of 2002, Shanghai successfully won the bid to host EXPO 2010, which became a successful, wonderful and unforgettable event that attracted over 7 300 million visitors after nearly eight years of unremitting efforts, setting a world record which is hard to break.

On October 31, 2010, by the end of the EXPO 2010, *The Shanghai*

Declaration was issued. In the Declaration, it is hoped that the World Cities Day could be established. Since then, with active impetus of Chinese government, the United Nations General Assembly finally passed a resolution to establish such a city-themed anniversary.

On October 31, 2014, the first "World Cities Day" commemorative event kicked off in Shanghai. One of the activities is the "Global Cities Forum". Since then, Shanghai have organized relevant activities of World Cities Day for three consecutive years. This year's forum is the third Global Cities Forum and it has formed a certain influence.

From the end of 1994 to the end of 2013, I worked for governments of Shanghai and Hainan Province for 19 years. Therefore, I have some personal experience of government management.

On the whole, China has a strong government which has played an important role in China's rapid development over the past 30 years. At the same time, the cognition of government to urban development, and even their own role, is gradually changing and upgrading.

In the 1990s, let's take my personal working experience in the Shanghai Municipal Government and the practices and ideas when I worked as District Mayor as an example. At that time, our main focuses were on problems like the renovation of most urgent, old and dilapidated houses and the re-employment of industrial workers. We have made remarkable achievements, but also paid a lot of price for it. Some of these costs must be paid, and some might be over paid. The main reason is that the management concept was not updated quickly enough. For example, I went to Paris in the late 1990s. During my stay in Paris, I almost spent all my time studying the development of La Défense and even didn't pay a visit to the Louvre and other cultural halls. It doesn't mean I don't have time, while I was more concerned about whether Shanghai can appear taller and build a new area like La Défense. At that time, it was not only the high-rise buildings and renewal of Shanghai, but also the persistent double-digit growth of Shanghai's GDP that we were proud of. However, our concern for the city's cultural heritage and eco-friendly environment was still not enough.

I am not being over critical about my predecessors. Actually I am also the predecessor for the young people here. But I think we should strive to broaden our vision so that we can better predict the future. In the beginning of this century, I have been involved in the compiling of Shanghai's last round of Urban Master Planning, including reporting the compiling of Urban Master Planning into the executive meetings of the State Council. This year, as deputy director of Municipal People's Congress, when we were deliberating on a new round of Urban Master Planning-the city's overall planning of 2016—2040, I was overwhelmed with emotions. I deeply feel that the planning concept this time has been substantially and all-roundly surpassed last time. The reason is that new urban construction, urban governance practice as well as extensive international exchanges broadened the horizon of the planning compilers. Meanwhile, in this round of planning and compiling, higher transparency and wider social participation have also helped us to pool the wisdom and achieve consensus.

The theme of this Global Cities forum is "Collaborative Governance, Shared Development". As far as I am concerned, the theme was decided after an in-depth discussion between the UN-Habitat and China National Ministry of Housing and Urban-rural Development. What does it mean? I think it at least reflects the following two perspectives:

First, it reflects China's concern for the development of the community and the shared future for mankind as a whole. We expect China's development achievements to be shared by people all over the world and we are also willing to share the opportunities of China's development with people around the world.

Second, China has recognized the importance of collaborative governance. Although national conditions are different which leads to the different development paths and systems, in terms of urban governance, we should definitely learn from each other's experience. In general, governments at all levels in China are excellent in the city management, but we have to prevent mistakenly regarding ourselves as an "omnipotent government", prevent the government from going beyond its power to handle all sort of social affairs, prevent us from neglecting the capability of social organizations, market economy as well as the public. Due to these neglects, it is difficult for urban governance to enter a higher level. What's worse, if we only rely on the unilateral government management, perhaps we could never achieve urban development goals. Therefore, if we want a better development of the city and let the city development serve the people better, we need to let the development achievements be shared by more and more people.

People and cities under good governance should become a harmonious community, this community can be summed up in one sentence, "Our city, our community." Our city runs through the "people-oriented" concept of governance, and our community reflects the spirit of governance-everyone is involved.

Among them, as the protagonist of the future city and the source of creativity, your participation is well worth encouraging and guiding. Yesterday, our forum organizer specially organized a demonstration of University Students Urban Governance Case Study Competition in order to encourage the youth to pay more attention to urban development and governance. Today, some teams and individuals have been awarded here. I hope that such activities will help young students to think deeply about the concepts, methods and strategies of urban governance, enhance the capability of solving practical problems by applying the theories and build a stronger sense of social responsibility.

This year, China Institute For Urban Governance of Shanghai Jiao Tong University functioned as the host of this forum for the first time. We hope to carefully summarize and refine the ideas and insights of experts, scholars as well as all friends present. After the forum we will publish and promote these ideas and enable them to play a positive role in a wider area.

At the same time, the China Institute For Urban Governance will further its cooperation with relevant organizations and prestigious universities both at home and abroad, open up to people inside and outside the university, to the universities and society at home and abroad and endeavor to promote the multidisciplinary development of urban research. Shanghai Jiao Tong University will give full play to its advantages as a comprehensive university and its location in Shanghai, the typical experimental field of urban governance, to encourage science and engineering, humanities and social sciences as well as many other disciplines to engage in the studies of urban governance problems so as to provide some wisdom of higher education for the resolution of the global urban governance problem and establish a platform for urban governance innovation with closely-knit integration of government, industry, academia, research and application.

APPENDIX

附 录

世界城市日简介

"世界城市日"（World Cities Day）是联合国认可的国际日，它来源于上海世博会的精神遗产，以上海世博会"城市，让生活更美好"（Better City，Better Life）作为总主题。"世界城市日"具有鲜明的时代特色，对人类社会的可持续发展具有重大意义。

1."世界城市日"的背景和意义

举世瞩目的中国 2010 年上海世界博览会于 2010 年 4 月 30 日在美丽的黄浦江畔隆重开幕。2010 年 10 月 31 日，在上海世博会闭幕当天举办的高峰论坛上，对整个上海世博会进行总结的《上海宣言》正式发布，宣言在结尾处发出倡议，建议将 10 月 31 日上海世博会闭幕之日定为"世界城市日"，让上海世博会的理念与实践得以永续，激励人类为城市创新与和谐发展而不懈追求与奋斗。

2012 年 4 月，中国政府正式启动"世界城市日"的申设工作。在中国政府和有关各方的共同努力与推动下，2013 年 12 月 28 日，第 68 届联合国大会最终通过决议，决定自 2014 年起，将每年的 10 月 31 日设立为"世界城市日"。设立"世界城市日"，汲取全球智慧，聚焦城市发展，有利于城市时代人类社会的共同进步与可持续发展，有利于提高各国城市建设和管理水平，有利于稳步推进健康可持续的城市化进程。每年一度的

"世界城市日"将呼唤各国城市关注城市化进程中的重大挑战，在全球范围内探讨和实践解决方案。这将为处于不同发展阶段的全球城市提供一个交流城市发展经验，共同解决城市问题的良机。

2. "世界城市日"主旨与年度主题

经过各方协商，明确了以上海世博会"更美的城市，更好的生活"（Better City，Better Life）为主旨，这一方案既揭示了"世界城市日"与上海世博会的紧密联系，同时也与联合国人居署历年所关注的城市可持续发展方向保持一致，更体现了举办"世界城市日"的终极目标和愿景。首个"世界城市日"的主题确定为"城市转型与发展"（Leading Urban Transformation）。第二届"世界城市日"的主题确定为"城市设计，共创宜居"（Designed to Live Together），这一主题既契合"城市，让生活更美好"的主旨，反映了国际社会对城市设计这一议题的高度关注，也体现了城市管理者、设计者和市民之间的互动关系，表现出了城市与居民共生的内在联系。第三届"世界城市日"的主题为"共建城市，共享发展"（Sharing Inclusive Cities），这一主题符合全球城市化发展趋势，体现了城市日对"人居三"这一重大历史事件的关切，同时也揭示了实现城市可持续发展的重要路径与终极目标；同时，也与"联合国住房与可持续发展大会"（简称"人居三"）公布的"新城市议程"中突出强调的"包容性城市"和"包容性目标"相一致，关注经济包容共享、社会保障融合，以及民众参与城市共治等核心内容。

3. 前三届"世界城市日"主要活动

3.1 第一届"世界城市日"主要活动

2014 年 10 月 31 日，首届"世界城市日"全球启动仪式在上海世博中心举行，来自 37 个国家的嘉宾出席，国务院总理李克强、联合国秘书长潘基文分别发来贺信和祝辞。当天，纽约联合国总部和全球 12 个国家也举办了数十场庆祝活动。上海举行了六场以城市发展为主题的高水平论坛。一是"上海 2040 高峰论坛"，与会嘉宾就面向未来 30 年的上海空间发展战略进行研讨，为上海新一轮城市总体规划编制提供经验借鉴。二是由上海市人民政府发展研究中心与世界银行共同主办、上海师范大学承办的"全球城市论坛"，邀请联合国经社部官员、世界银行专家、城市市长和国内外知名专家学者共同参与，探讨全球城市发展趋势，共同谋划上海美好蓝图。三是由中国市长协会和上海市健康产业发展促进协会共同主办的"2014 国际健康城市论坛"。四是"中国新型城镇化发展论坛"，邀请了多位院士大师、著名专家、企业家代表等参加。五是"第三届公共外交国际论坛"，围绕城市外交的实践与探索进行交流。六是"地下管线与城市安全学术论坛"，从地下管线规划、设计、建设和运营管理等各个方面进行讨论和交流。

3.2 第二届"世界城市日"主要活动

2015 年 10 月 31 日，第二届"世界城市日"纪念活动于意大利米兰举行，由联合国人居署、米兰市政府、上海市政府共同主办，国际展览局秘书长文森特·洛塞泰斯、米兰市长古里安诺·比萨比亚、上海市副市长蒋卓庆、中国贸促会副会长、2015 年米兰世博会中国馆政府总代表王锦珍、联合国人居署副主任埃莎·奇亚斯拉出席活动。

在国内，10 月 31 日住建部、上海市政府与联合国人居署在上海共同主办"2015 世界城市日论坛"，重点讨论城市规划设计、建设、管理等方面的议题，并探讨各国在城市可持续发展领域共同面临的问题，住房和城乡建设部部长陈政高、上海市市长杨雄、联合国人居署代表阿利乌尼·巴迪阿尼莅临致辞，世界各国的城市管理者、规划设计者、相关领域知名专家学者共 300 余位嘉宾出席论坛。同时，在上海、苏州等地举行了"全球城市论坛""上海建筑信息模型（BIM）国际论坛""城市更新与规划转型学术研讨会""城市外交的实践与创新研讨会"等多场世界城市日系列活动。其中，"全球城市论坛"由上海市人民政府发展研究中心、世界银行共同主办，中国社会科学院—上海市人民政府上海研究院、上海大学承办，来自世界银行、国务院发展研究中心和国内外学术界的著名学者和特邀嘉宾出席了论坛，与会嘉宾围绕未来 30 年上海迈向全球城市的诸多议题展开深入交流，产生了积极影响。

10 月 31 日至 11 月 2 日，作为世界城市日系列活动之一，中国建筑学会、上海世界城市日事务协调中心与联合国人居署在上海展览中心联合举办"2015 上海国际城市与建筑博览会"，展示国内外优秀的城市设计、城市规划和建筑创作作品以及重大基础设施工程经典案例，为参观者提供了近距离接触海绵城市、建筑工业化、低碳商务区、BIM 技术等未来城市发展理念与技术的机会。

3.3 第三届"世界城市日"主要活动

2016 年 10 月 31 日，上海市人民政府与联合国人居署及基多市政府在厄瓜多尔基多市举办了第三届"世界城市日"国际主场纪念活动，三方共同组织了高级别讨论会，并举办了城市日展览。联合国秘书长潘基文在活动开幕式视频讲话中指出，《新城市议程》是制定可持续城市发展全球标准的里程碑，激励我们重新思考如何进行城市规划和管理并在城市中生活。

10 月 31 日，联合国人居署、住房城乡建设部、福建省政府在厦门共同主办了"2016 世界城市日论坛"，论坛围绕"共建城市，共享发展"这一年度主题，重点研讨城市规划、建设、管理等方面的议题，深入探讨了中国与"一带一路"沿线及相关国家开展城市发展领域国家合作的途径。来自中国、美国、英国、德国等近 20 个国家、地区和国际组织的官员、市长、专家学者共 300 多人出席了论坛，重点研讨全球城市的可持续发展和宜居环境建设问题，并共同签署发表了《城市发展厦门倡议》。此外，联合国人居署、中国城市规划学会、上海世界城市日事务协调中心于 10 月 31 日至 11 月 2 日在厦门共同举办"世界城市日主题展"。同时，结合"世界城市日"活动，厦门市还举办了第 13 届中国厦门人居环境展示会暨中国（厦门）国际建筑节能博览会、厦门市绿色建筑与建筑节能高峰论坛等 4 个论坛和轨道交通研讨会等一系列宣传活动。

作为"世界城市日"的发起城市，上海继续举办了一系列主题活动，包括论坛、展览、国际大会等共计 10 余项。具体为："2016 全球城市论坛""2016 上海国际城市与建筑博览会""2016 世界城市日—上海论坛""古建修复保护与活化利用论坛""2016 健康城市论坛"以及首届"中国城市基础设施建设与管理国际大会"等。这些系列活动进一步提升了相关行业领域和社会公众对"世界城市日"的知晓度。其中，"2016 全球城市论坛"由上海市人民政府发展研究中心、上海市住房和城乡建设管理委员会、上海交通大学、联合国人居署、世界银行共同主办，上海交通大学中国城市治理研究院、上海交通大学国际和公共事务学院、上海世界城市日事务协调中心联合承办，邀请了国务院发展研究中心、联合国人居署、世界银行、美国哈佛大学和麻省理工学院、英国剑桥大学和伦敦大学学院、德国弗朗霍夫研究所、加拿大多伦多大学等国内外城市治理相关领域的著名专家学者，围绕"协同治理、共享发展"这一主题，聚焦未来 30 年上海建设卓越的全球城市的愿景目标，从城市政府管理、经济转型升级、交通规划管理、生态环境保护以及文化传承保护等五个领域，全方位、多角度探讨城市治理和发展面临的重大问题。

中国城市治理研究院简介

中国城市治理研究院是在上海市人民政府支持下，由上海交通大学和上海市人民政府发展研究中心合作建设，其目标是建成国际知名、具有中国特色的新型智库、优秀人才汇聚培养基地和高端国际交流合作平台。

联合国 2014 年《世界城市化前景报告》称，目前全球 70 亿人口中，有一半生活在城市地区。中国 80% 以上的经济总量产生于城市、50% 以上的人口生活在城市。但近年来，环境污染、交通拥堵、住房保障、医疗健康、公共安全、应急管理等问题日益成为城市治理中的焦点和难点。上海作为一个正在快速崛起的超大型城市，城市治理正在进入创新突破的关键阶段，必须从全局和战略高度深化对上海城市发展的认识，创新理念、把握规律、明确定位，加快构筑以人民为中心的城市治理新格局。在新的形势下，上海既需要学习借鉴先进国家和地区的经验，也需要不断总结自身已经取得的成功案例和经验，特别是把握网络时代特点，充分运用大数据、移动互联网、云计算等先进信息技术，加快推进上海城市治理体系和治理能力现代化，形成可复制、可推广的经验。

中国城市治理研究院按照上海作为"改革开放排头兵、创新发展先行者"的要求，紧紧围绕完善和发展中国特色社会主义制度、推进国家治理体系和治理能力现代化的全面深化改革总目标，围绕完善城市治理体系、提高城市治理能力开展工作。

中国城市治理研究院采取院务委员会领导下的院长负责制。院务委员会下设学术委员会。研究院作为面向海内外、校内外开放的研究平台，非常期待国内外城市治理与创新领域的研究者、实践者的共同参与、共同谋划、协同研究、合作共赢。

中国城市治理研究院将依托上海交通大学文理医工农多学科优势，整合校内城市治理相关学术领域，充分利用上海市与国内外各方面优势资源，创新组织形式，改革管理方式，着力构建强强联合、优势互补、深度融合、多学科交叉和协同创新的试验区与开放式平台，为党和政府科学决策提供高水平智力支持。

中国城市治理研究院将致力于利用"旋转门"机制汇聚城市治理的研究人才，以城市治理研究的具体内容为旋转枢纽，通过双聘机制使校内院际间、校际间、政府实践部门的人员、国际间以及其他高端智库的专家都可"旋转"到研究院，使国内外一流尖端人才汇聚在研究院，构建多个城市治理的核心研究团队。

中国城市治理研究院将致力于服务国家、上海市城市治理的战略需要，培养城市治理的高端、紧缺、复合型实践人才。研究院根据全国与上海市对现代化城市管理高端人才的紧迫需要，通过整合校内外不同学科以及政府、咨询公司的师资，充分发挥育人高地的优势，培养城市治理多层次的高端人才，面向城市治理实践部门工作人员提供岗前培训、职业进修等非学历教育培训。

中国城市治理研究院还将致力于打造国际交流合作平台，对外宣传中国城市发展道路、理念和实践，提升中国城市治理国际话语权，塑造中国城市治理的话语体系。动员上海乃至全国资源，总结中国特色的城市治理模式与理念，提出有中国特色的城市治理理论，实施中国城市治理研究"走出去"战略，加大国际学术交流，唱响中国声音，打造国际性的中国城市治理研究团队。对内引进国际城市治理的先进经验，破解城市发展的难题，搭建多种国际合作交流渠道，致力于吸引国际一流城市治理人才、机构和组织汇聚上海，贡献国际城市治理的先进经验，探讨上海与中国城市治理发展大计。

中国城市治理研究院虽然处于建设初期，但已取得初步成果：已经启动《城市治理研究》学术期刊建设、城市治理大数据研究中心等跨学科交叉平台建设；针对城市治理理论、城市公共安全、宜居与公共服务、智慧城市等四个领域，研究院已经整合资源，与联合国人居署、世界银行等国际组织和咨询机构积极合作；已通过上海市人民政府发展研究中心平台，于近期规划并发布了 2016 年度上海市人民政府决策咨询研究城市治理重点专项课题；研究院的多位教授也参与了《上海城市总体规划（2016—2040）》的研究和制定。

Introduction of World Cities Day

As an international day recognized by the United Nations, the World Cities Day is derived from the spiritual heritage of EXPO 2010 SHANGHAI CHINA and takes "Better City, Better Life", the theme of Shanghai World Expo, as its general theme. The World Cities Day bears distinct characteristics of the times and plays a significant role in the sustainable development of the human society.

1. Background and significance of the designation of the "World Cities Day"

The remarkable EXPO 2010 SHANGHAI CHINA was grandly opened on the bank of Huangpu River on April 30, 2010. On October 31, 2010, at the summit forum held on the closing day of Shanghai World Expo, *The Shanghai Declaration* which summarizes the whole EXPO 2010 SHANGHAI CHINA was formally released and became an important literature in the process of sustainable development of world cities. The ending of the Declaration proposed designating October 31 of every year when the curtain of EXPO 2010 SHANGHAI CHINA fell as the "World Cities Day", so as to permanently extend the ideas and practices of Shanghai World Expo and encourage human beings to make unremitting efforts for city innovation and harmonious development.

In April 2012, Chinese government officially started the work related to the application for the designation of the "World Cities Day". On December 28, 2013, under the joint efforts and driving of the Chinese Government and parties concerned, the 68th Session of the United Nations General Assembly finally passed a resolution on designating the October 31 of every year, beginning from 2014, as the "World Cities Day". Designating the "World Cities Day", drawing the wisdom of the world, and focusing on urban development are beneficial to the common progress and sustainable development of the human society in the urban age, the improvement in the urban construction and management level of all countries, as well as the steady advancement of the health and sustainable urbanization process. The annual World Cities Day will appeal to all countries to focus on major challenges in the urbanization process and discuss and practice related solutions around the globe. The World Cities Day will provide global cities which are in different development stages with golden opportunity to exchange urban development experience and commonly solve urban problems.

2. Permanent and annual theme of "World Cities Day"

Through discussions of parties involved, "Better City, Better Life" of EXPO 2010 SHANGHAI CHINA is set as the aim, which not only indicates the close association between World Cities Day and Shanghai Expo, but also accords with the UN-Habitat's focus on the sustainable development of cities over the past years, and more the ultimate target and vision of holding the "World Cites Day". After the discussion, the theme of the first World Cities Day was determined as "Leading Urban Transformation". In 2015, the theme of the second World Cities Day was set as "Designed to Live Together" which not only accorded with the spiritual connotation of "Better City, Better life" and but also reflected the interactions and internal relations between city administrators, city designers and city residents. In 2016, the theme of the third World Cities Day was set as "Sharing Inclusive Cities". Urbanization provides the potential for new forms of social inclusion, including greater equality, access to services and new opportunities, and engagement and mobilization that reflects the diversity of cities, countries and the globe. This year's theme is embraced by the action and implementation of the New Urban Agenda, which is putting the topic of inclusive cities as one of the main pillars of the urban shift.

3. Core activities of World Cities Day

3.1 Core activities of the First World Cities Day

On October 31, 2014, the launch ceremony of the first World Cities Day was held in the Shanghai Expo Center and honored guests from more than 37 counties had attended this grand meeting. Chinese prime minister Mr. Li Keqiang and United Nation Secretary-General Mr. Ban Ki-moon had sent their congratulations. New York, the headquarter of United Nations, had host a series of celebrations along with 12 countries worldwide. Shanghai held 6 high-end forums on the theme of urban development.

The First one was the "Shanghai 2040 Summit Forum". The attending guests discussed Shanghai's spatial development strategy in the future 30 years and provided experience references for the new round of urban overall planning of Shanghai. The second one was the "Global City Forum" cosponsored by the Development Research Center of Shanghai's Municipal People's Government and the World Bank and organized by Shanghai Normal University. The officials of the United Nations Department of Economic and Social Affairs, experts from the World Bank, city mayors and famous experts and scholars at home and abroad were invited to discuss the trend of global urban development and plan a beautiful blueprint for future Shanghai. The third one was the "2014 International Health City Forum" cosponsored by the China Association of Mayors and the Shanghai Health Industry Development & Promotion Association. The forth one was the "China New Urbanization Forum" which invited a host of academicians, experts and entrepreneurs. The fifth one was "The 3rd International Forum on Public Diplomacy" focused on the practice and exploration of city diplomacy. The sixth one was the "Underground Pipelines and City Security Academic Forum". This forum carried out in-depth discussions and communications concerning the planning, design, construction and technical measures of operations management.

3.2　Core activities of the 2nd World Cities Day

The memorial events of the 2nd World Cities Day was co-organized on October 31, 2015 by United Nations Human Settlements Programme, the Milan municipal government and Shanghai municipal government in Milan, Italy. Present at the events were Secretary General of the International Expositions Bureau Vicente Loscertales, Milanese mayor Giuliano Pisapia, Vice Mayor of Shanghai Jiang Zhuoqing, Vice President of China Council for the Promotion of International Trade and Chinese government's chief representative to China Pavilion in Milan Expo Wang Jinzhen, and Deputy Executive Director of the United Nations Human Settlements Programme Aisa Kirabo Kacyira.

Back at mainland China, Ministry of Housing and Urban-Rural

Development, Shanghai Municipal Government and the United Nations Human Settlements Programme co-organized 2015 Global City Forum in Shanghai at October 31 . The Key theme of this forum was design, construction and management issues of urban planning and sustainable challenges that various cities are facing now. Minister of Housing and Urban-Rural Development Chen Zhenggao, Shanghai mayor Yang Xiong, and representative of United Nations Human Settlements Programme Alioune Badiane gave the opening speech. City managers, planners and designers from around the globe, and renowned experts were present at the forum. Meanwhile, Global City Forum, Shanghai International Forum for Building Information Modeling, City Upgrade and Transform Seminar, Practice and Innovation in City Diplomacy Seminar and other serial activities of the World Cities Day were held in Shanghai and Suzhou. The Global City Forum was co-organized by Development Research Center of Shanghai's Municipal People's Government and World Bank, and was undertaken by the Shanghai Academy and Shanghai University. Renowned Experts and distinguished guests from around the world and officials of World Bank and the State Development Research Center attended this forum. Discussion was conducted on the issues of Shanghai's globalization course with positive influence.

Through 31st October to 2nd November, Architectural Society of China, Shanghai World Urban Day Coordination Center and the United Nations Human Settlements Programme co-organized one of the serial activities of the World Cities Day, the Shanghai International City and Architecture Expo. The Expo featured a wide range of outstanding examples for city design, city planning, architecture and major infrastructure engineering. All visitors were given the chance to further understanding the concepts and technologies of future city, such as sponge cities, architecture industrialization, low-carbon business zone and BIM technology and so on.

3.3　Core activities of the 3rd World Cities Day

The memorial events of the third World Cities Day were hosted in Quito, Ecuador, the international host city, by Shanghai Municipal Government together with United Nations Human Settlements Programme and Quito Government. The three parties organized the high-level symposium and the exhibition of World Cities Day. Ban Ki-moon, Secretary General of the United Nations, indicated in the video speech of opening ceremony that the New Urban Agenda was the milestone of formulating the global standard of sustainable cities' development and stimulated people to rethink how to conduct urban planning and management and live in the city.

United Nations Human Settlements Programme, Ministry of Housing and Urban-Rural Development and Fujian Provincial People's Government co-organized 2016 World Cities Day Forum in Xiamen on October 31. With the annual theme of "Inclusive Cities, Shared Development," the forum focused on the topics of urban planning, construction and management, and further discussed the approaches to the transnational cooperation between China and the related countries along the route of "the Belt and Road." More than 300 officials, mayors, experts and scholars from 20 countries including China, the United States, Great Britain and Germany attended the forum, mainly discussing the issues of sustainable development and favorable inhabiting environment of the cities all over the world, and jointly signing and issuing the Xiamen Initiative on Urban Development. In addition, United Nations Human Settlements Programme, Urban Planning Society of China and Shanghai World Cities Day Coordination Center co-organized World Cities Day Theme Exhibition in Xiamen from October 31 to November 2. Meanwhile, together with the events of World Cities Day, Xiamen hosted four forums such as 13th China (Xiamen) Residence & Environment Exhibition and China (Xiamen) International Energy Efficiency in Buildings Expo, the Summit Forum of Xiamen International Green Building and Energy Efficiency Exhibition, and a series of promoting events like railway seminars.

Shanghai, the initiator of World Cities Day, continued to host dozens of theme events including forum, exhibition and international meeting, namely 2016 Global Cities Forum, 2016 Shanghai International City and Architecture Expo, 2016 World Cities Day Shanghai Forum, Ancient Architecture Repair, Protection, Activation and Utilization Forum, 2016 Health Cities Forum and 1st China International Conference of Urban Infrastructure Construction and Management, which promoted the publicity of World Cities Day among the related fields and the public. 2016 Global Cities Forum was hosted by the Development Research Center of Shanghai Municipal Government, Shanghai Municipal Commission of Housing, Urban-Rural Development and Management, Shanghai Jiao Tong University, United Nations Human Settlements Programme and World Bank, and organized by China Institute for Urban Governance, School of International and Public Affairs of Shanghai Jiao Tong University, Shanghai World Cities Day Coordination Center. Many famous domestic and foreign experts and scholars in the field of urban governance from the Development Research Center of the State Council, United Nations Human Settlements Programme, World Bank and University of Toronto were invited to have comprehensive and multi-dimensional discussions on the major problems of urban governance and development from five perspective of urban governmental management, economic transformation and upgrading, transportation planning and management, ecological environment protection and cultural inheritance protection, with regard to the theme of "Collaborative Governance, Shared Development" and Shanghai's vision to build an excellent global city for next 30 years.

Introduction to China Institute for Urban Governance

With the support of the Shanghai Municipal Government, China Institute for Urban Governance was jointly run by Shanghai Jiao Tong University and the Development Research Center of Shanghai Municipal People's Government, with the goal of building a world-renowned think tank with Chinese characteristics, a talent pool and a high-level international platform for exchange and cooperation.

According to the UN's 2014 World Urbanization Prospects Report, half of the world's 7 billion people currently live in urban areas. More than 80 percent of China's total economic output is generated in cities, with more than 50 percent of the population living in cities. But in recent years, environmental pollution, traffic congestion, housing security, health care, public safety, emergency management and other issues have become increasingly the focus and challenge facing urban governance. As a large and fast-rising city, Shanghai is entering the critical stage of innovation breakthrough. It is necessary to deepen the understanding of Shanghai's urban development from the overall situation and strategy, innovative concepts, grasp the discipline, have a clear definition and speed up the construction of a new people-centered pattern of urban governance. In the new situation, Shanghai needs to learn from the experience of advanced countries and regions as well as its own successes and experiences. It is especially important to grasp the characteristics of the Internet era and make full use of advanced information technology such as big data, mobile Internet, cloud computing information technology to improve Shanghai urban governance system and the modernization of governance, forming experience that can be replicated and expanded.

In accordance with the requirements of Shanghai as "the vanguard of reform and opening-up and the pioneer of innovation and development",

China Institute for Urban Governance has been focusing on the overall goal of improving and developing the socialist system with Chinese characteristics, improving national governance system, the modernization of governance and perfecting urban governance system, and to improve urban governance capacity.

China Institute for Urban Governance adopted dean responsibility system under the leadership of the Governing Board. The Academic Committee is under the Governing Board. As a research platform, China Institute for Urban Governance looks forward to the participation of researchers and practitioners in the field of urban governance and innovation from both at home and abroad in collaborative research and institutional cooperation.

China Institute for Urban Governance takes a multidisciplinary approach in its study and research on urban governance by drawing on strengths of diverse fields such as electric engineering, environmental engineering, agriculture and medicine at Shanghai Jiao Tong University.

China Institute for Urban Governance will utilize the "revolving door" mechanism to gather research personnel of urban governance, with the specific content of urban governance research as a rotating bar. The dual-employment mechanism will channel experts from other universities, other colleges, government practice sectors, other countries and other high-end think tank to the institute, so that domestic and international first-class scholars can be gathered here and build a number of research teams on urban governance.

China Institute for Urban Governance will be committed to serving the strategic needs of the country, Shanghai urban governance, training high-end, compound and practical talents which are rare. Given the urgent needs of China and Shanghai on high-end modern city management talents, the institute integrates faculty inside and outside the school, from the government and consulting firms, gives full play to the advantages of training to cultivate high-end multi-level city governance talents and provide non-academic education and training to city governance department staff including pre-job training and vocational training, etc..

China Institute for Urban Governance will also be committed to international exchange and cooperation. It will utilize Shanghai and even national resources, sum up the model and ideas of urban governance with

Chinese characteristics, put forward urban governance theory with Chinese characteristics and build China's own internationalized urban governance research team. Domestically, it will introduce advanced international city governance experience to solve the problems of urban development, build a variety of international cooperation and exchange channels, attract world-class city management talents, institutions and organizations to Shanghai, contribute advanced experience of international urban governance and explore plans for China's urban governance.

Although China Institute for Urban Governance is still in the early stage of development, it has achieved certain results. It has started the preparation of an academic journal tentatively titled Journal of Urban Governance, a big data research center of urban governance and a case study center focusing on subjects such as urban governance theory, urban public security, habitability and public service as well as smart city. The institute has already started combining resources and actively cooperating with other international organizations and advisory bodies such as UN-HABITAT and the World Bank. The institute in collaboration with the Development and Research Center of Shanghai Municipal People's Government has recently announced the 2016 research grants.

POSTSCRIPT

后 记

　　世界城市日是联合国大会批准设立的国际日，它来源于上海世博会的精神遗产。作为"世界城市日"主题活动之一，2016全球城市论坛围绕"协同治理，共享发展"的年度主题，邀请了来自联合国人居署、世界银行、经济合作与发展组织、纽约大都会交通局、美国哈佛大学、美国麻省理工学院、英国剑桥大学、英国伦敦大学学院、加拿大多伦多大学、德国弗朗霍夫研究所、韩国高丽大学、日本广岛大学、新加坡运输学院、国务院发展研究中心、北京大学、上海交通大学、东南大学、同济大学、华东师范大学、华南理工大学、深圳大学、南京艺术学院、上海市住房和城乡建设管理委员会等机构的领导和专家，共同探讨全球城市治理的相关话题。中外嘉宾在开幕式、全体大会、平行论坛和闭幕式等环节，先后发表了致辞、主旨演讲、专题演讲、评议演讲和互动讨论。论坛形成了一系列富有启示性和前瞻性的观点和研究成果。为此我们特编辑此书，将本次论坛的宝贵观点和研究成果与读者分享。

　　本届全球城市论坛在上海交通大学徐汇校区举行，得到了上海交通大学党政办公室、宣传部、学生指导委员会、文科科研处、国际合作与交流处、发展联络处、保卫处、校医院、包兆龙图书馆、徐汇校区办公室、中国城市治理研究院、国际和公共事务学院、安泰经济与管理学院、船舶海洋与建筑工程学院、农业与生物学院、凯原法学院、城镇空间文化与科学研究中心等部门和单位领导的大力支持。

　　本书由上海市人民政府发展研究中心周国平副主任审订，改革研究处钱智处长、史晓琛副处长负责全书编辑工作。本书的出版得到了上海交通大学、世界银行、上海外国语大学和上海世纪出版集团格致出版社的大力支持。上海市人大常委会副主任、上海交通大学党委书记姜斯宪教授，上海交通大学原校长张杰院士，上海交通大学原党委常务副书记郭新立教授给予了亲切指导。上海交通大学国际和公共事务学院院长钟杨教授，常务副院长、校文科处处长吴建南教授，党委书记曹友谊，副院长李振全教授，校党政办副主任张丹丹，校党委宣传部副部长朱敏，校文科处副处长朱军文、谈毅，国际和公共事务学院院长助理张录法等，在论坛会议资料、现场录音、摄影图片收集和文字审校方面给予了鼎力帮助。上海外国语大学陆倩雨、迪丽呼玛等同志在文稿整理和翻译上做了大量的工作。上海市人民政府发展研究中心改革研究处、信息处、科研处和博士后工作站的同仁为本书的编辑付出了辛勤的劳动，在此一并表示感谢！

As an international day recognized by the United Nations, the World Cities Day is derived from the spiritual heritage of EXPO 2010 SHANGHAI CHINA. As one of the serial forums celebrating "World Cities Day", the 2016 Global City Forum themed on "Collabrative Goverance, Shared Development" carried out in-depth dissucssion on urban goverance by inviting leaders and experts from United Nations Human Settlements Programme, World Bank, Organization for Economic Co-operation and Development (OECD), New York Metropolitan Transportation Authority, Harvard University, MIT, Cambridge University, UCL, University of Toronto, Fraunhofer IZM, Korea University, Hiroshima University, Singapore Institute of Materials Management, Development Research Center of the State Council, Peking University, Shanghai Jiao Tong University, Southeast University, Tongji University, East China Normal University, South China University of Technology, Shenzhen University, Nanjing University of the Arts and Shanghai Municipal Commission of Housing, Urban-Rural Development and Management. The forum, consisted of opening ceremony, general session, sub-forums and closing ceremony, has achieved a series of enlightening and forward-looking viewpoints and research achievements.

This forum, held on Xuhui campus of Shanghai Jiao Tong University, was strongly supported by Shanghai Jiao Tong University's relevant departments including Office of Party and Government Affairs, propaganda department, student guiding committee, Social Science Research Department, International

Cooperation and Exchange Department, Liaison Office, campus hospital, Pao Sui-Loong Library of Shanghai Jiao Tong University, office of Xuhui campus, China Institute for Urban Governance, School of Public and International Affairs, Antai College of Economics and Management, School of Naval Architecture, Ocean and Civil Engineering, School of Agriculture and Biology, KoGuan Law School, Urban Space Research Center of Culture and Science.

This book is revised by Zhou Guoping, the deputy director general. Qian Zhi, chief of the Reform Research Division and Shi Xiaochen, vice chief of the division are responsible for the edition of the book. The publishing of the book has received great support from Shanghai Jiao Tong University, World Bank, Shanghai International Studies University and Truth & Wisdom Press of Shanghai Century Publishing House. Jiang Sixian, Deputy Director of Standing Committee of Shanghai Municipal People's Government and Secretary of the Party Committee of Shanghai Jiao Tong University, and Zhang Jie, then President of Shanghai Jiao Tong University, as well as Guo Xinli, then vice secretary of the Party Committee of Shanghai Jiao Tong University have given kind instruction. Zhong Yang, Dean and Professor of School of International and Public Affairs, Shanghai Jiao Tong University, and Wu Jiannan, executive vice dean China Academy of Urban Governance, head of the Division of Liberal Arts Advancement, Shanghai Jiao Tong University, and Cao Youyi, secretary of the Party committee, Professor Li Zhenquan, Party Committee Deputy Dean Zhang Dandan, Party Committee Propaganda Department vice minister Zhu Min and Zhu Junwen and Tan Yi from Social Science Research Department have given valuable assistance for collecting meeting material, records, photographs and text-proofing. Lu Qianyu and Dilihuma Yishake has made great contributions in text resorting and translating. Staff from Reform Research Division, Information Division, Scientific Research Division and Postdoctoral Programme Office of the Development Research Center of Shanghai Municipal People's Government has paid tremendous efforts on editing the book. We express our thanks to them all!

图书在版编目(CIP)数据

上海 2050.协同治理与共享发展:联合国第三届世界城市日全球城市论坛实录/周国平主编. —上海：格致出版社:上海人民出版社,2017.10
（面向未来 30 年的上海发展战略研究）
ISBN 978 - 7 - 5432 - 2479 - 7

Ⅰ.①上… Ⅱ.①周… Ⅲ.①区域经济发展-研究报告-上海 Ⅳ.①F127.51

中国版本图书馆 CIP 数据核字(2016)第 327014 号

责任编辑　忻雁翔
装帧设计　人马艺术设计・储平

上海 2050：协同治理与共享发展

——联合国第三届世界城市日全球城市论坛实录

周国平　主编

出　版	世纪出版股份有限公司　格致出版社	印　刷	上海中华商务联合印刷有限公司
	世纪出版集团　上海人民出版社	开　本	787×1092　1/16
	(200001 上海福建中路 193 号　www.ewen.co)	印　张	34.75
	编辑部热线　021-63914988	字　数	721,000
	市场部热线　021-63914081	版　次	2017 年 10 月第 1 版
	www.hibooks.cn	印　次	2017 年 10 月第 1 次印刷
发　行	上海世纪出版股份有限公司发行中心		

ISBN 978 - 7 - 5432 - 2479 - 7/F・1006　　　　　　　　　　　　　　　　定价：198.00 元